ESCAPE *from* "SPECIAL"

FANTAGRAPHICS BOOKS | 7563 LAKE CITY WAY NE | SEATTLE, WASHINGTON 98115

design by **ADAM GRANO** | *promotion by* **ERIC REYNOLDS**
published by **GARY GROTH AND KIM THOMPSON**

To receive a free full-color catalog of comics, graphic novels and other related material, call 1-800-657-1100, or visit www.fantagraphics.com. You may order books at our web site or by phone.

ISBN-10: 1-56097-804-X; ISBN-13: 978-1-56097-804-6
First printing, December 2006. Printed in Malaysia.

FOR JOHN TERHORST,
WHO'S HELPED ME
BEYOND REASON.

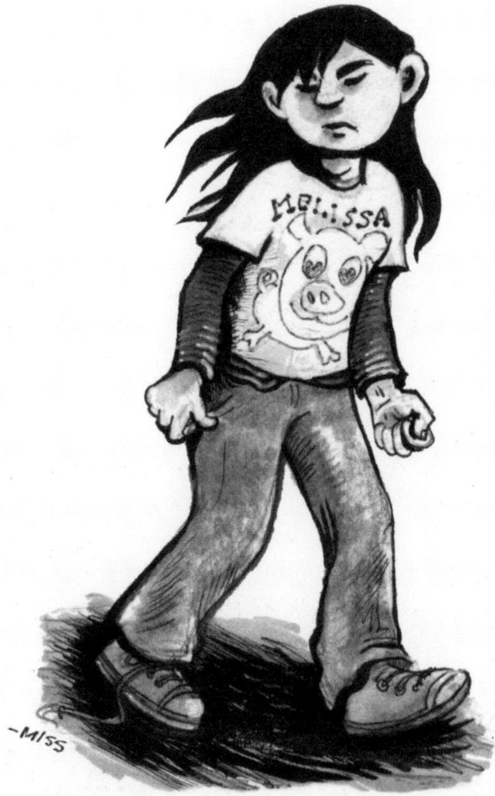
MELISSA
-MISS

ESCAPE *from* "SPEC

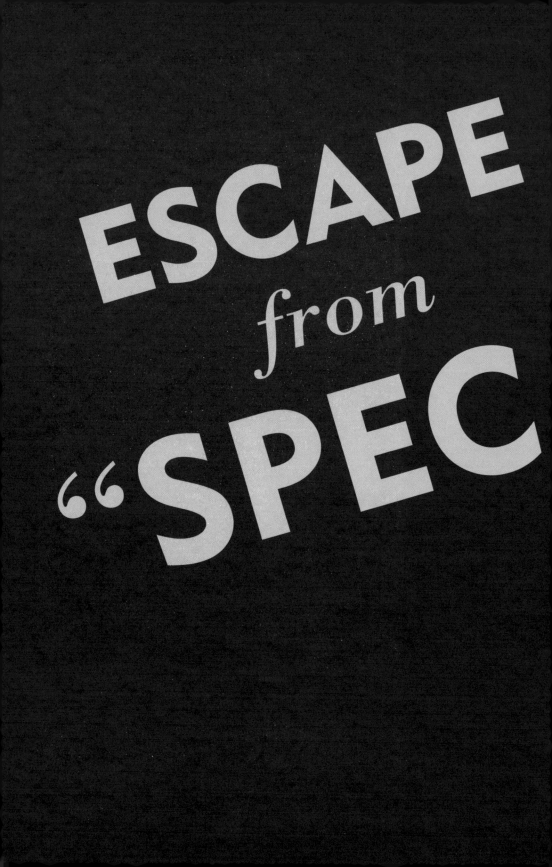

written & drawn by **MISS LASKO-GROSS**
published by **FANTAGRAPHICS BOOKS**

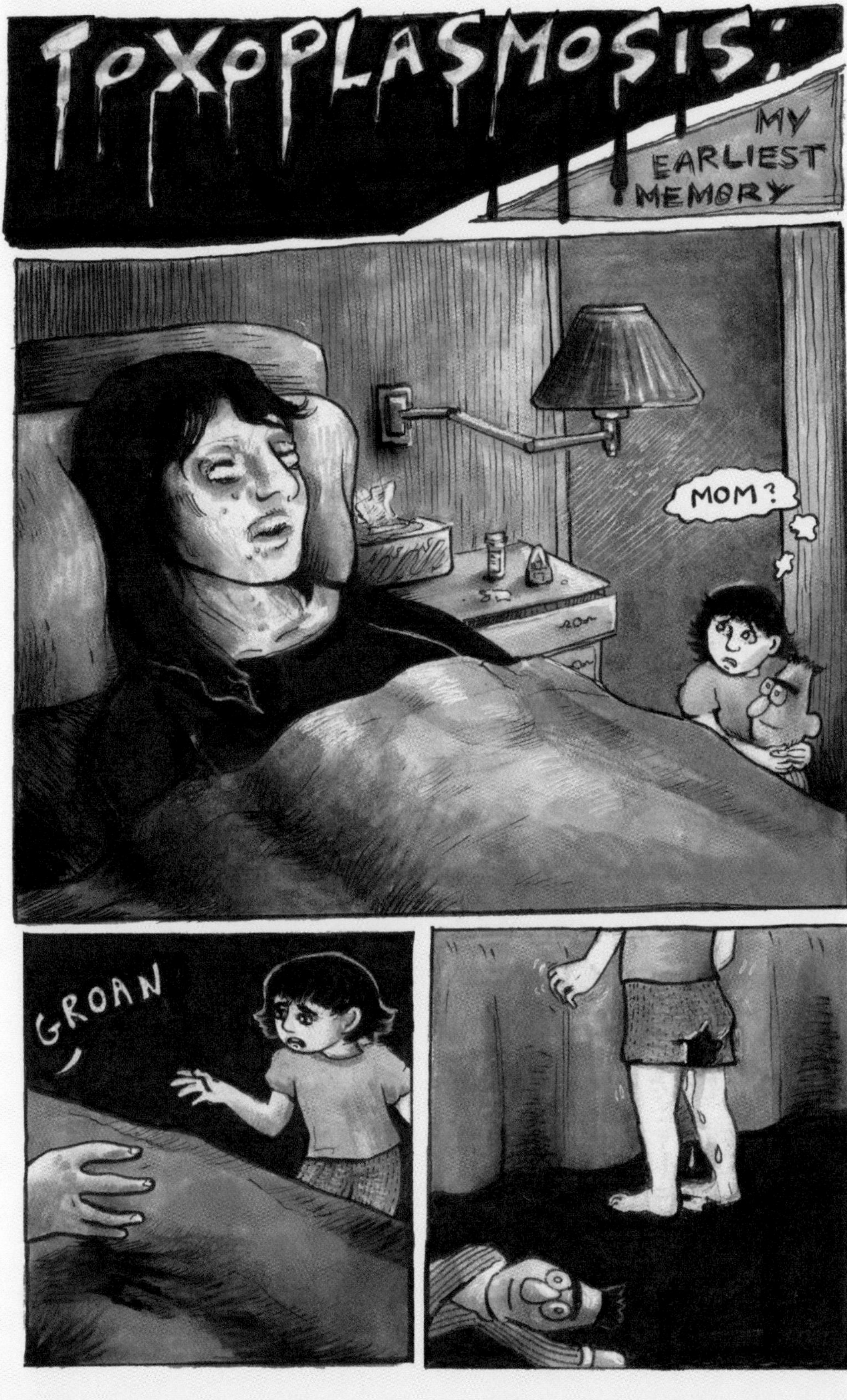
TOXOPLASMOSIS:
MY EARLIEST MEMORY
MOM?
GROAN

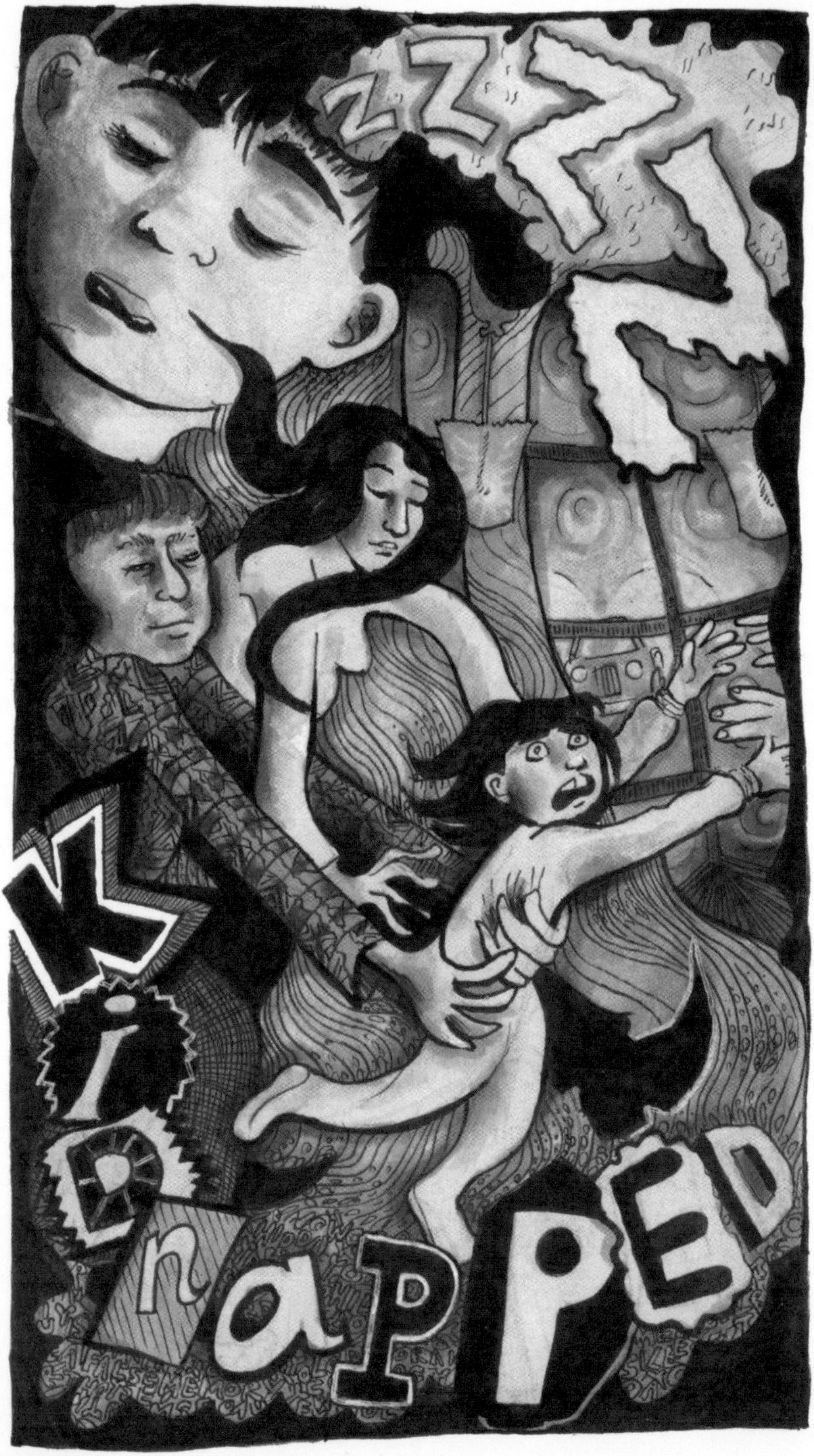
zzZZ
KiDnaPPED

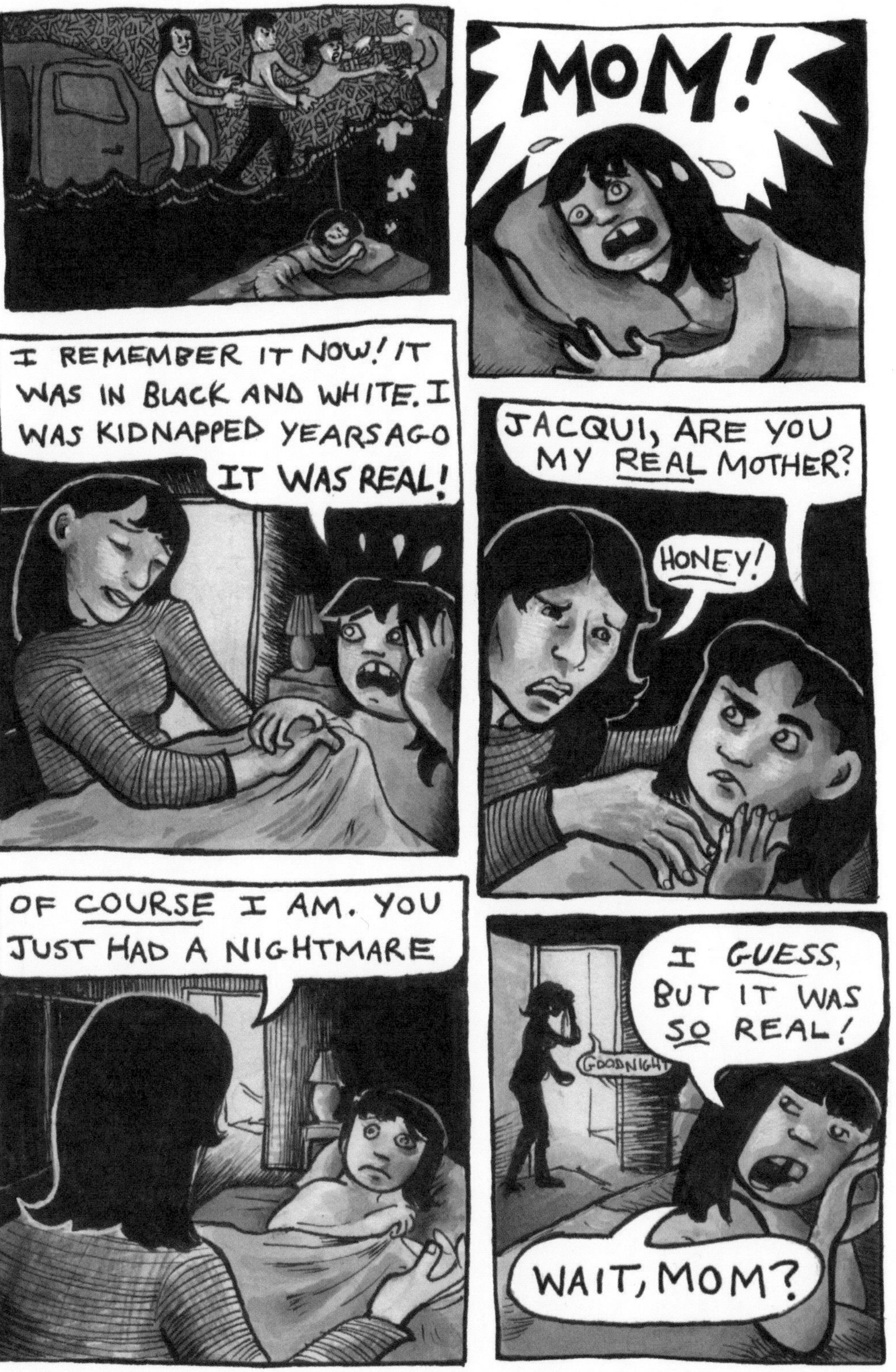
MOM!
I REMEMBER IT NOW! IT WAS IN BLACK AND WHITE. I WAS KIDNAPPED YEARS AGO IT WAS REAL!
JACQUI, ARE YOU MY REAL MOTHER?
HONEY!
OF COURSE I AM. YOU JUST HAD A NIGHTMARE
I GUESS, BUT IT WAS SO REAL!
GOODNIGHT
WAIT, MOM?

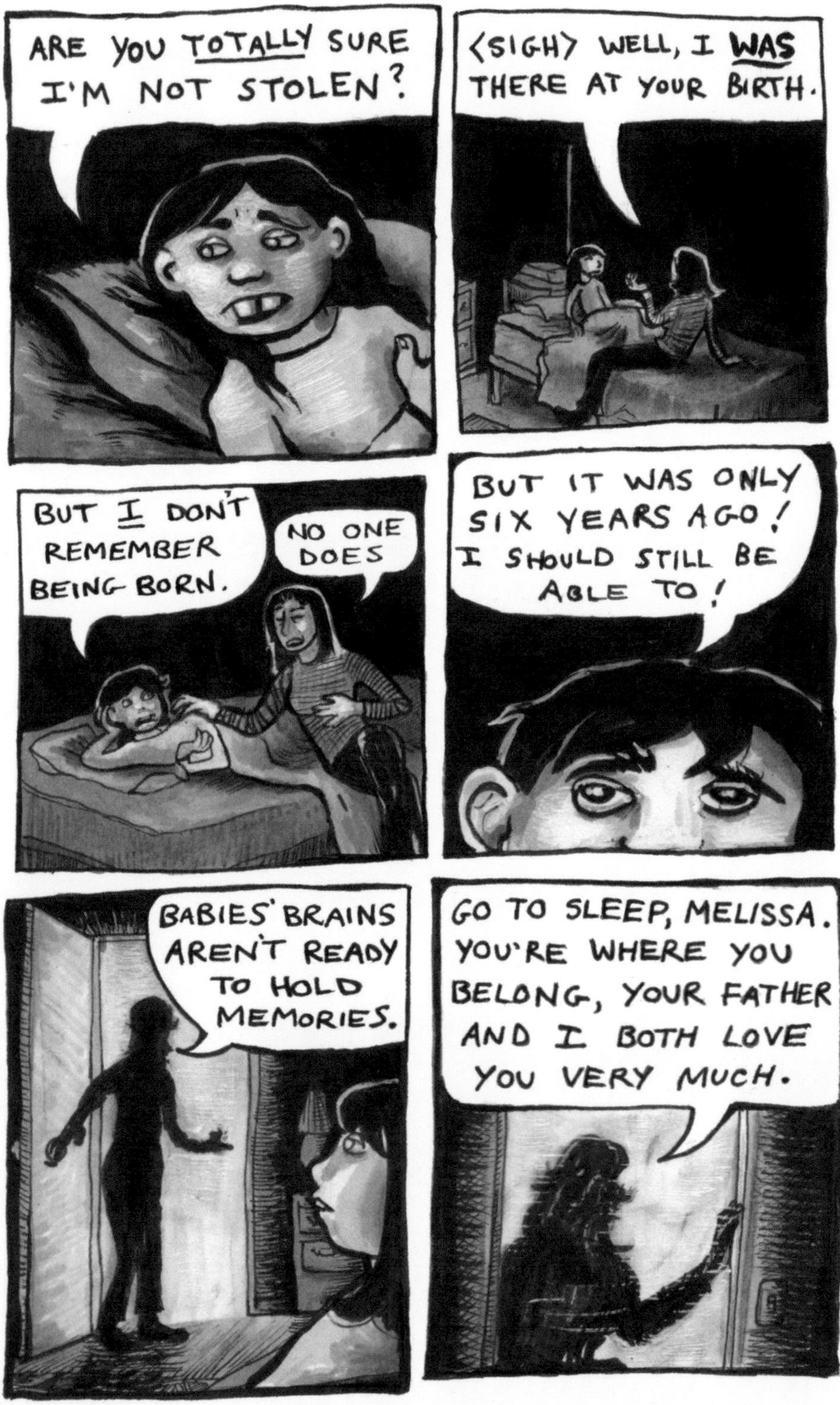
ARE YOU TOTALLY SURE I'M NOT STOLEN?
<SIGH> WELL, I WAS THERE AT YOUR BIRTH.
BUT I DON'T REMEMBER BEING BORN.
NO ONE DOES
BUT IT WAS ONLY SIX YEARS AGO! I SHOULD STILL BE ABLE TO!
BABIES' BRAINS AREN'T READY TO HOLD MEMORIES.
GO TO SLEEP, MELISSA. YOU'RE WHERE YOU BELONG, YOUR FATHER AND I BOTH LOVE YOU VERY MUCH.

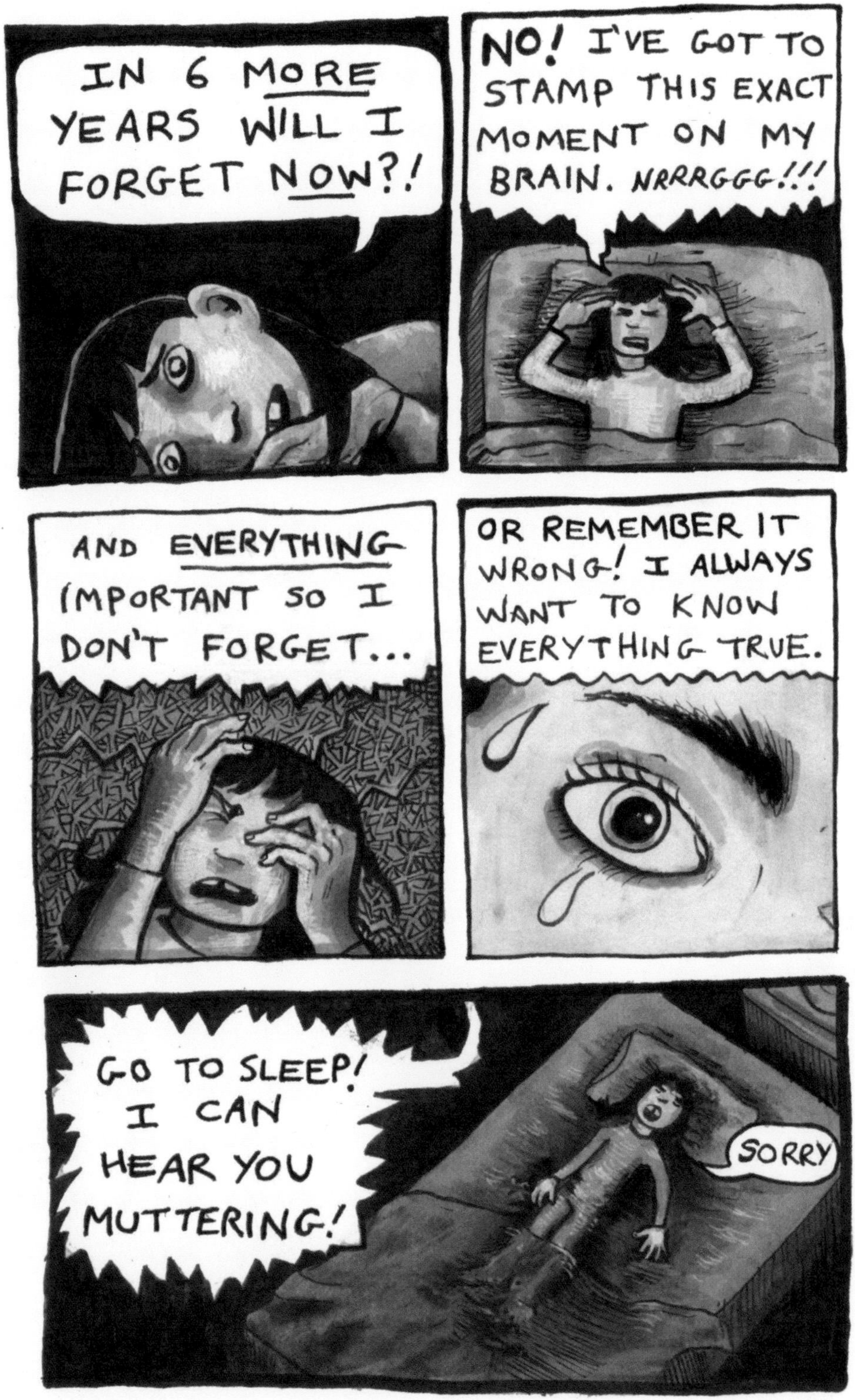
IN 6 MORE YEARS WILL I FORGET NOW?!
NO! I'VE GOT TO STAMP THIS EXACT MOMENT ON MY BRAIN. NRRRGGG!!!
AND EVERYTHING IMPORTANT SO I DON'T FORGET...
OR REMEMBER IT WRONG! I ALWAYS WANT TO KNOW EVERYTHING TRUE.
GO TO SLEEP! I CAN HEAR YOU MUTTERING!
SORRY

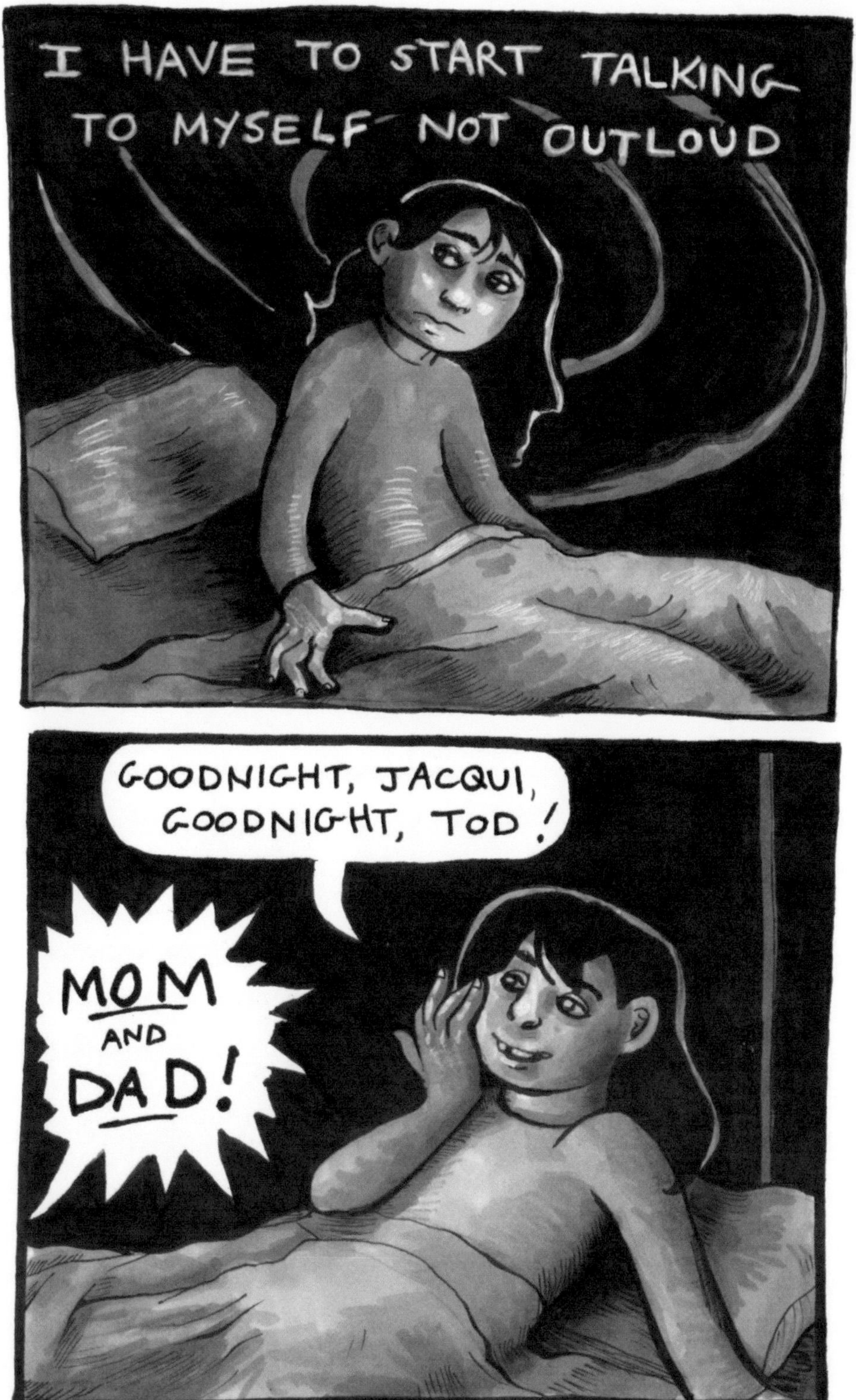
I HAVE TO START TALKING TO MYSELF NOT OUTLOUD
GOODNIGHT, JACQUI, GOODNIGHT, TOD!
MOM AND DAD!

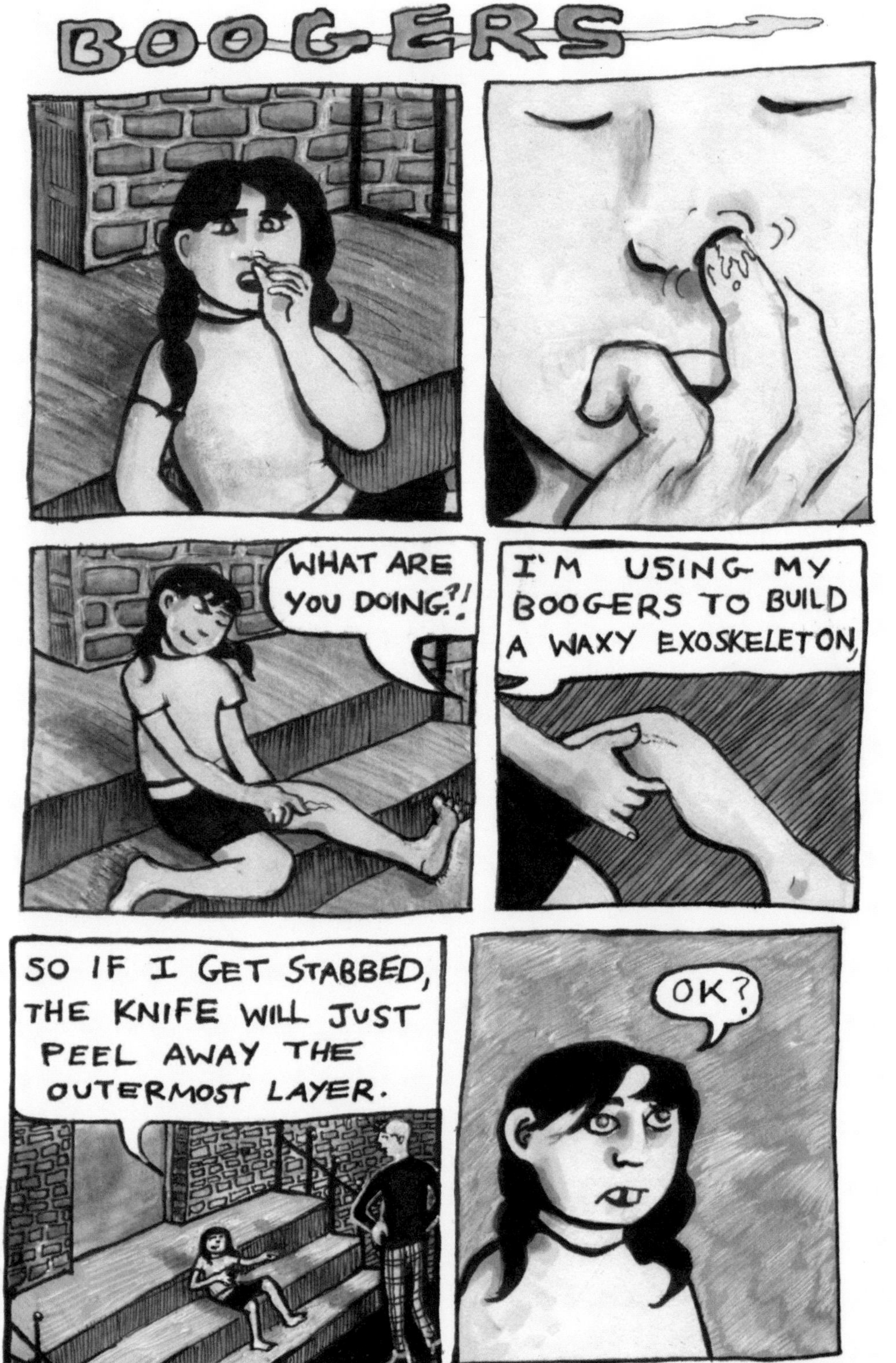
BOOGERS
WHAT ARE YOU DOING?!
I'M USING MY BOOGERS TO BUILD A WAXY EXOSKELETON,
SO IF I GET STABBED, THE KNIFE WILL JUST PEEL AWAY THE OUTERMOST LAYER.
OK?

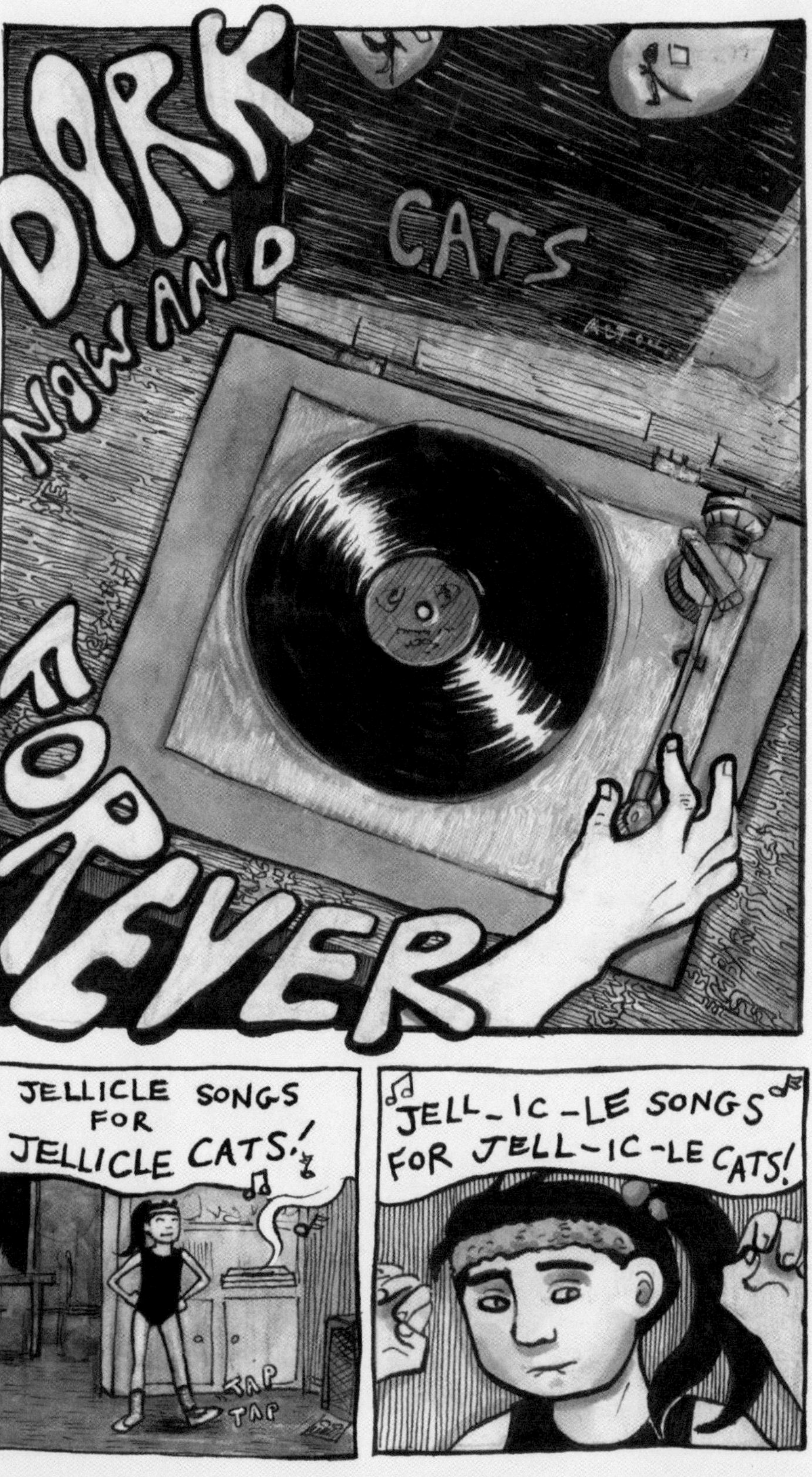
DARK
CATS
NOW AND
FOREVER
JELLICLE SONGS FOR JELLICLE CATS!
TAP TAP
JELL-IC-LE SONGS FOR JELL-IC-LE CATS!

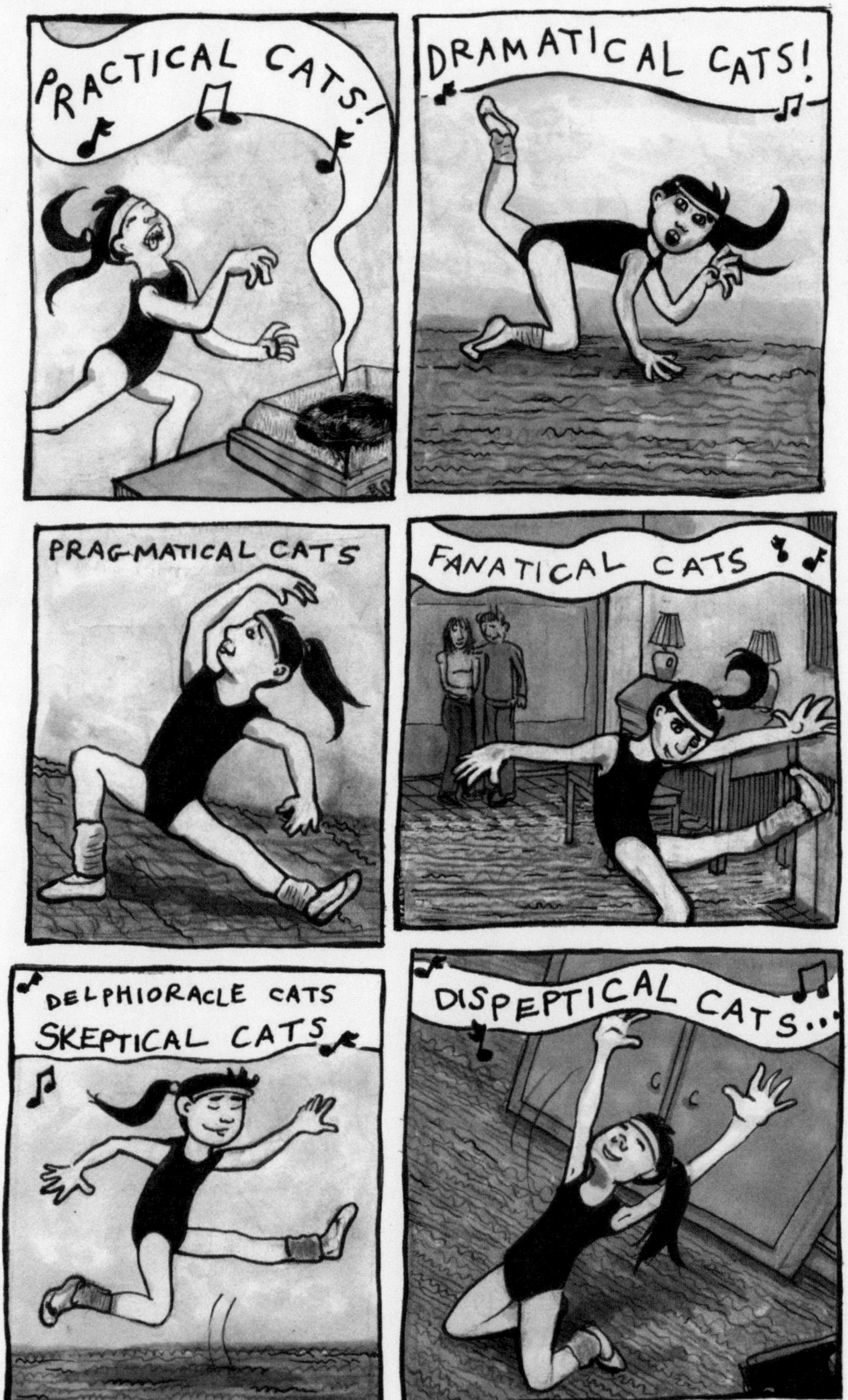
PRACTICAL CATS!
DRAMATICAL CATS!
PRAGMATICAL CATS
FANATICAL CATS
DELPHIORACLE CATS
SKEPTICAL CATS
DISPEPTICAL CATS...

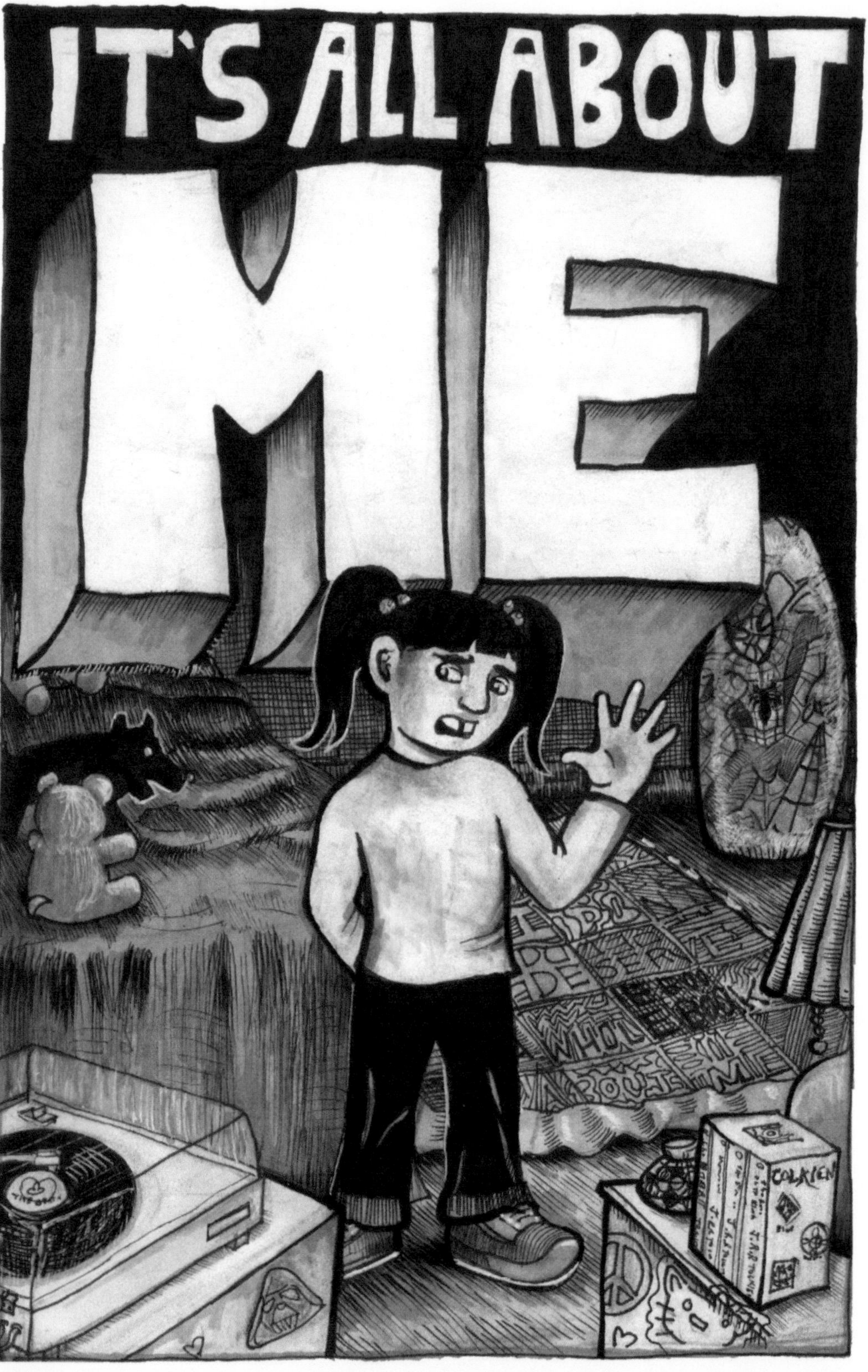
IT'S ALL ABOUT
ME

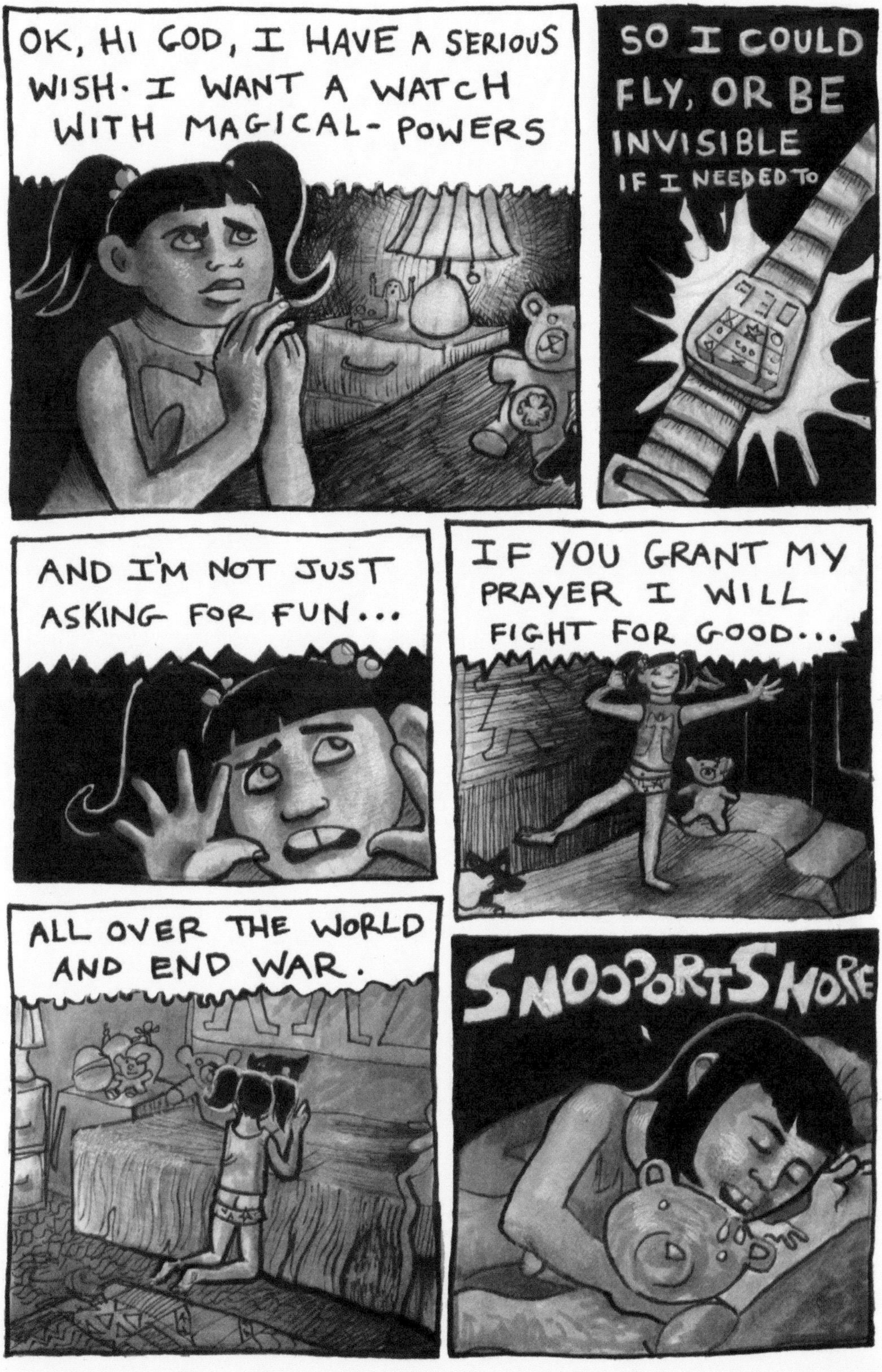
OK, HI GOD, I HAVE A SERIOUS WISH. I WANT A WATCH WITH MAGICAL-POWERS
SO I COULD FLY, OR BE INVISIBLE IF I NEEDED TO
AND I'M NOT JUST ASKING FOR FUN...
IF YOU GRANT MY PRAYER I WILL FIGHT FOR GOOD...
ALL OVER THE WORLD AND END WAR.
SNOOPORTSNORE

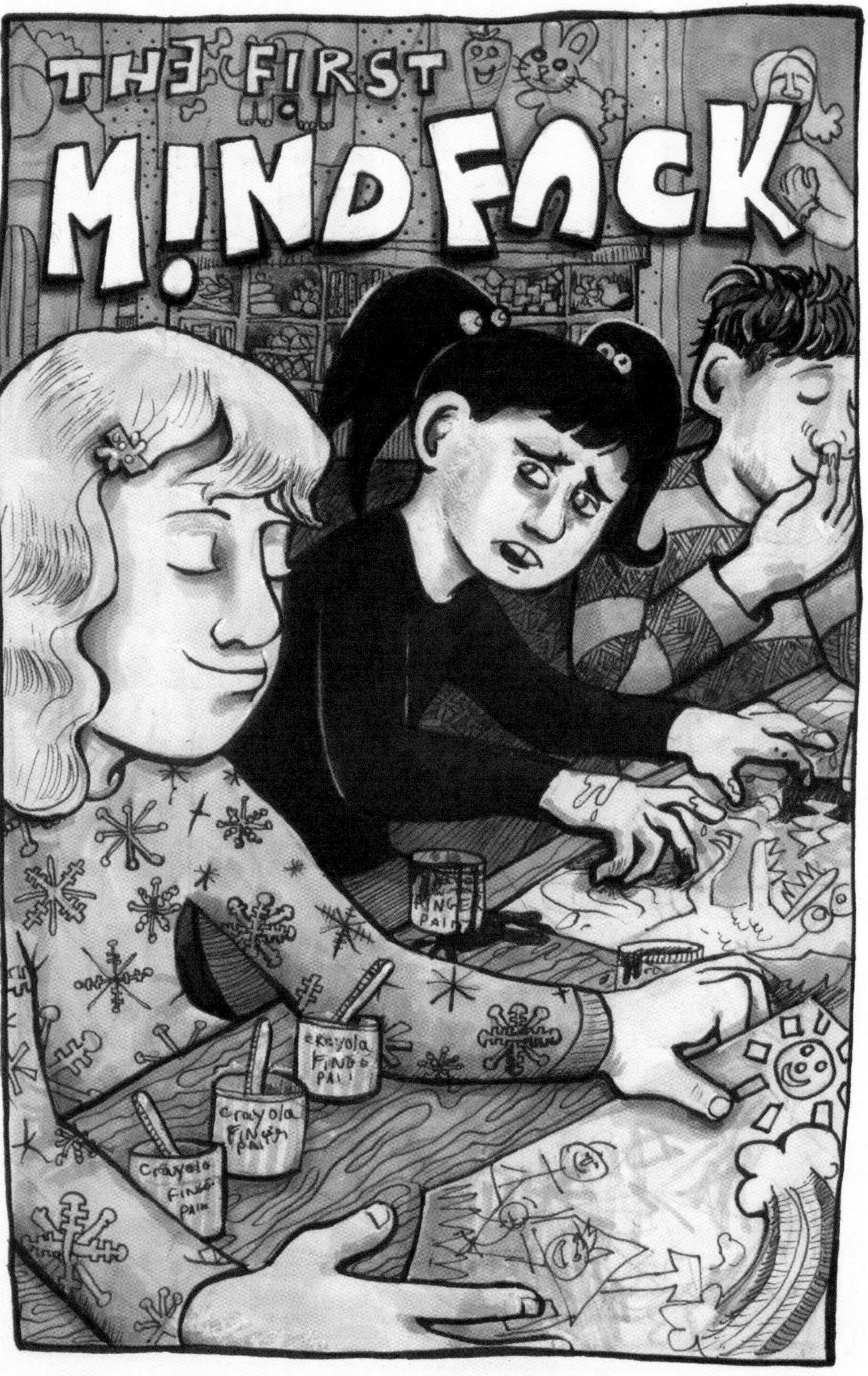
THE FIRST
MIND FACK
crayola FINGE PAIN
crayola FIN PAIN
crayola FINGE PAIN

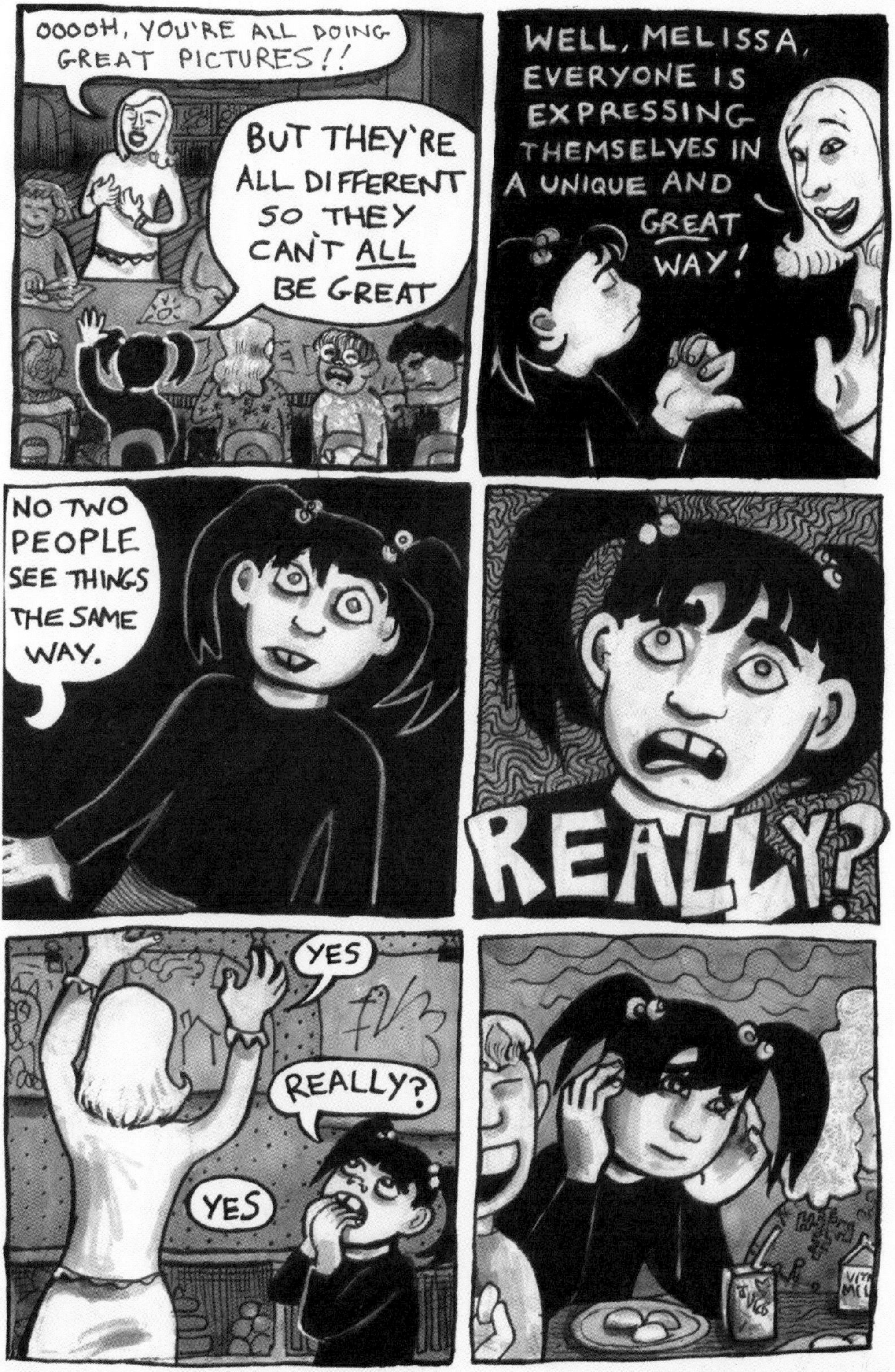
OOOOH, YOU'RE ALL DOING GREAT PICTURES!!
BUT THEY'RE ALL DIFFERENT SO THEY CAN'T ALL BE GREAT
WELL, MELISSA, EVERYONE IS EXPRESSING THEMSELVES IN A UNIQUE AND GREAT WAY!
NO TWO PEOPLE SEE THINGS THE SAME WAY.
REALLY?
YES
REALLY?
YES

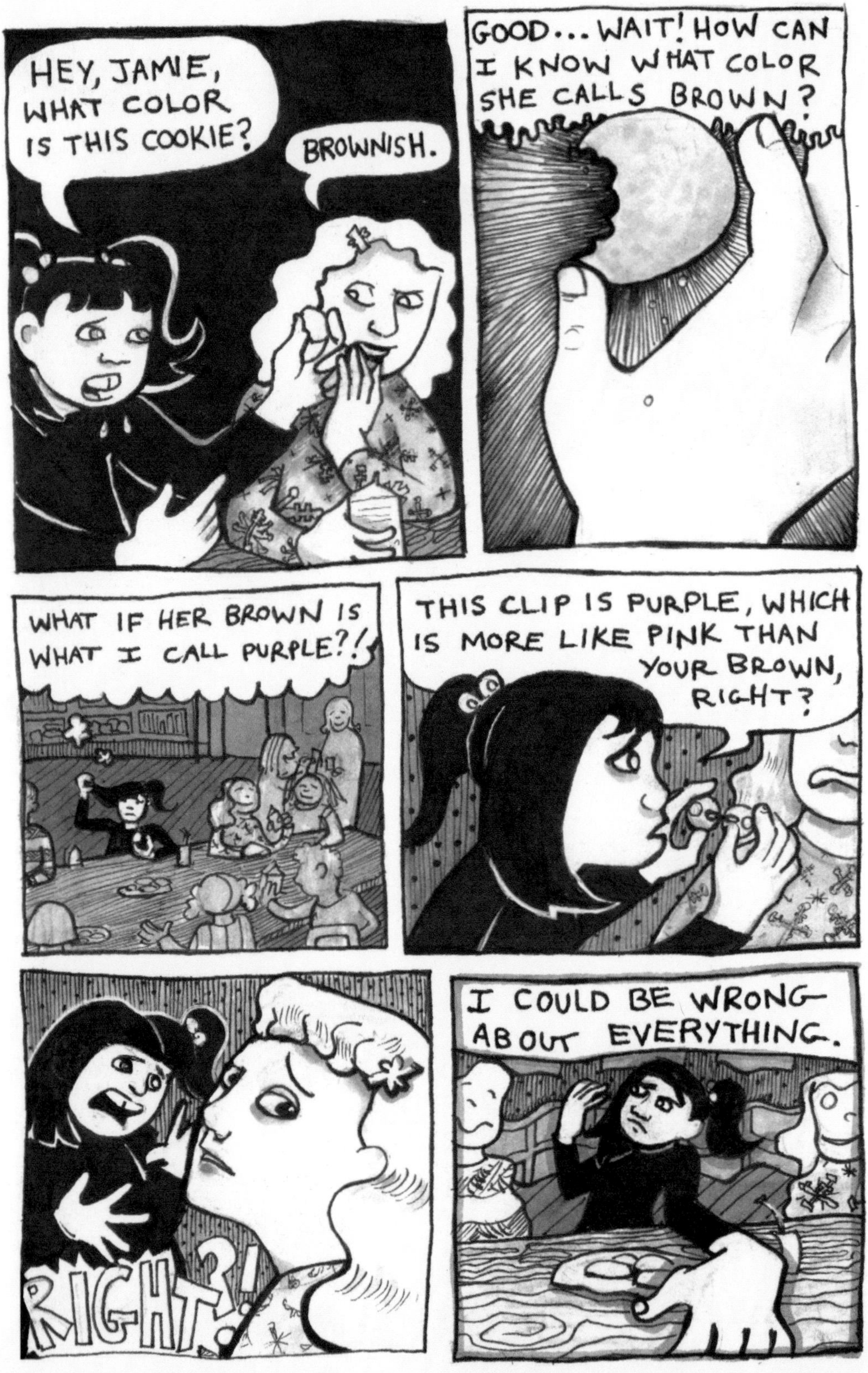
HEY, JAMIE, WHAT COLOR IS THIS COOKIE?
BROWNISH.
GOOD... WAIT! HOW CAN I KNOW WHAT COLOR SHE CALLS BROWN?
WHAT IF HER BROWN IS WHAT I CALL PURPLE?!
THIS CLIP IS PURPLE, WHICH IS MORE LIKE PINK THAN YOUR BROWN, RIGHT?
RIGHT?!
I COULD BE WRONG ABOUT EVERYTHING.

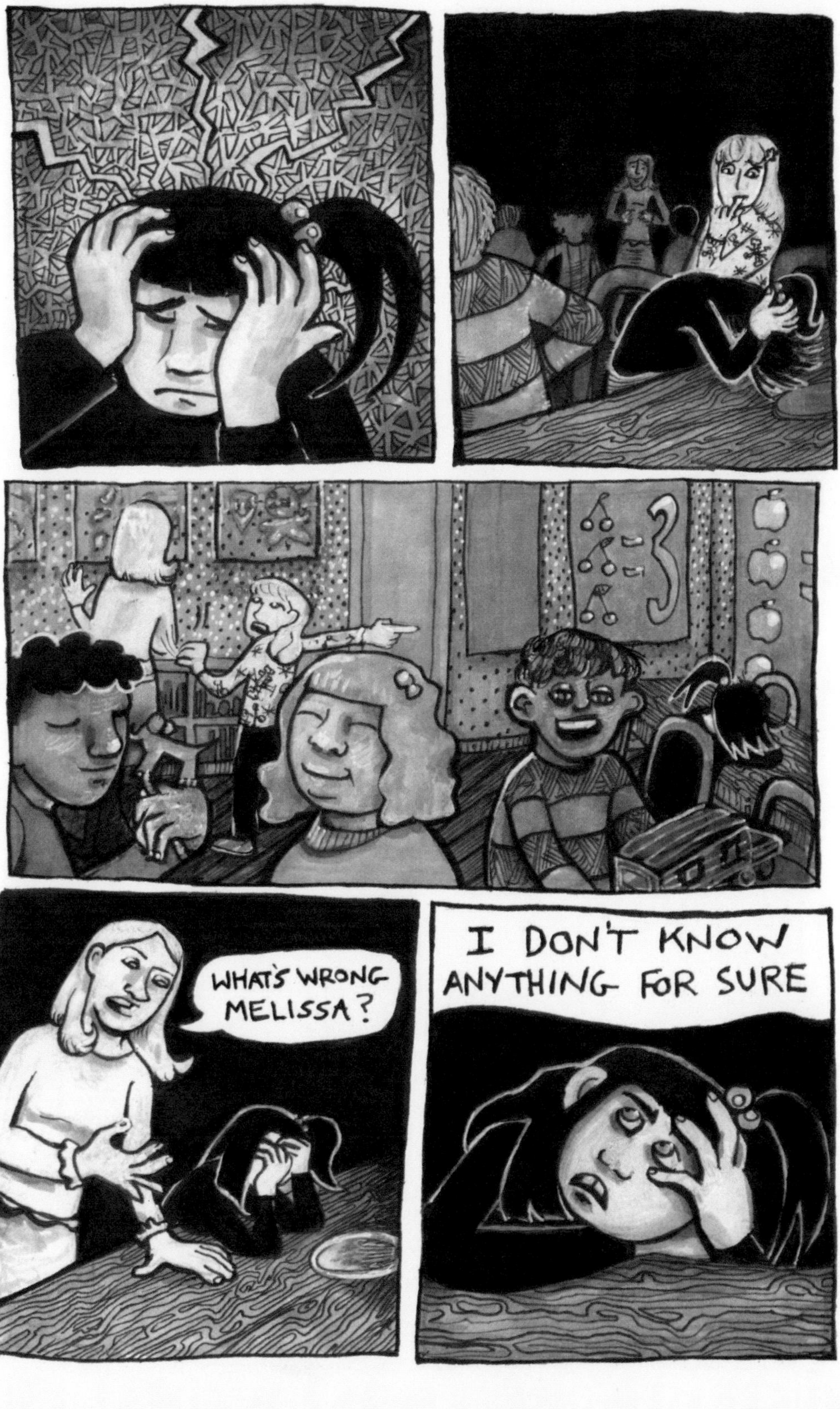
WHAT'S WRONG MELISSA?
I DON'T KNOW ANYTHING FOR SURE

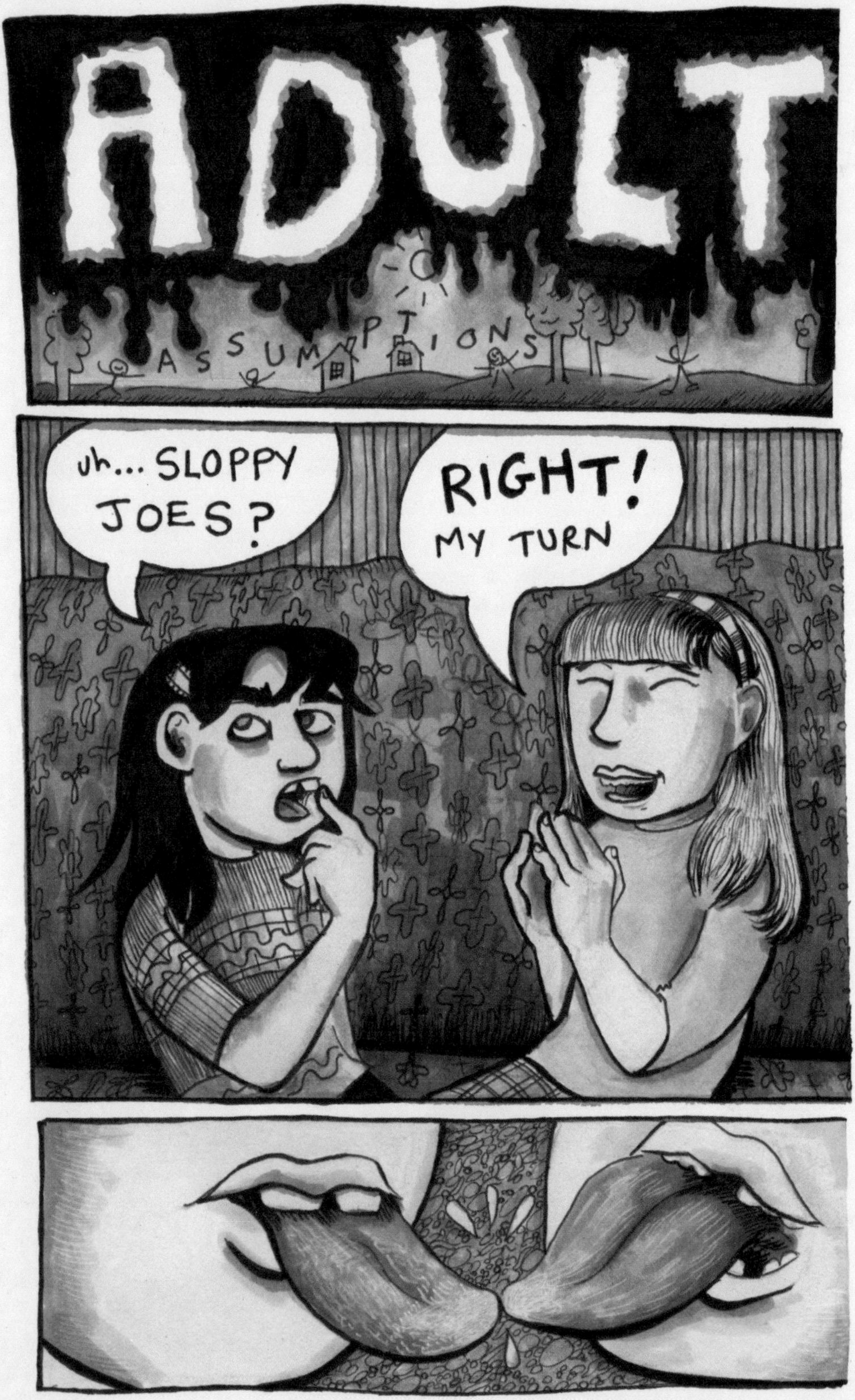
ADULT
ASSUMPTIONS
uh... SLOPPY JOES?
RIGHT! MY TURN

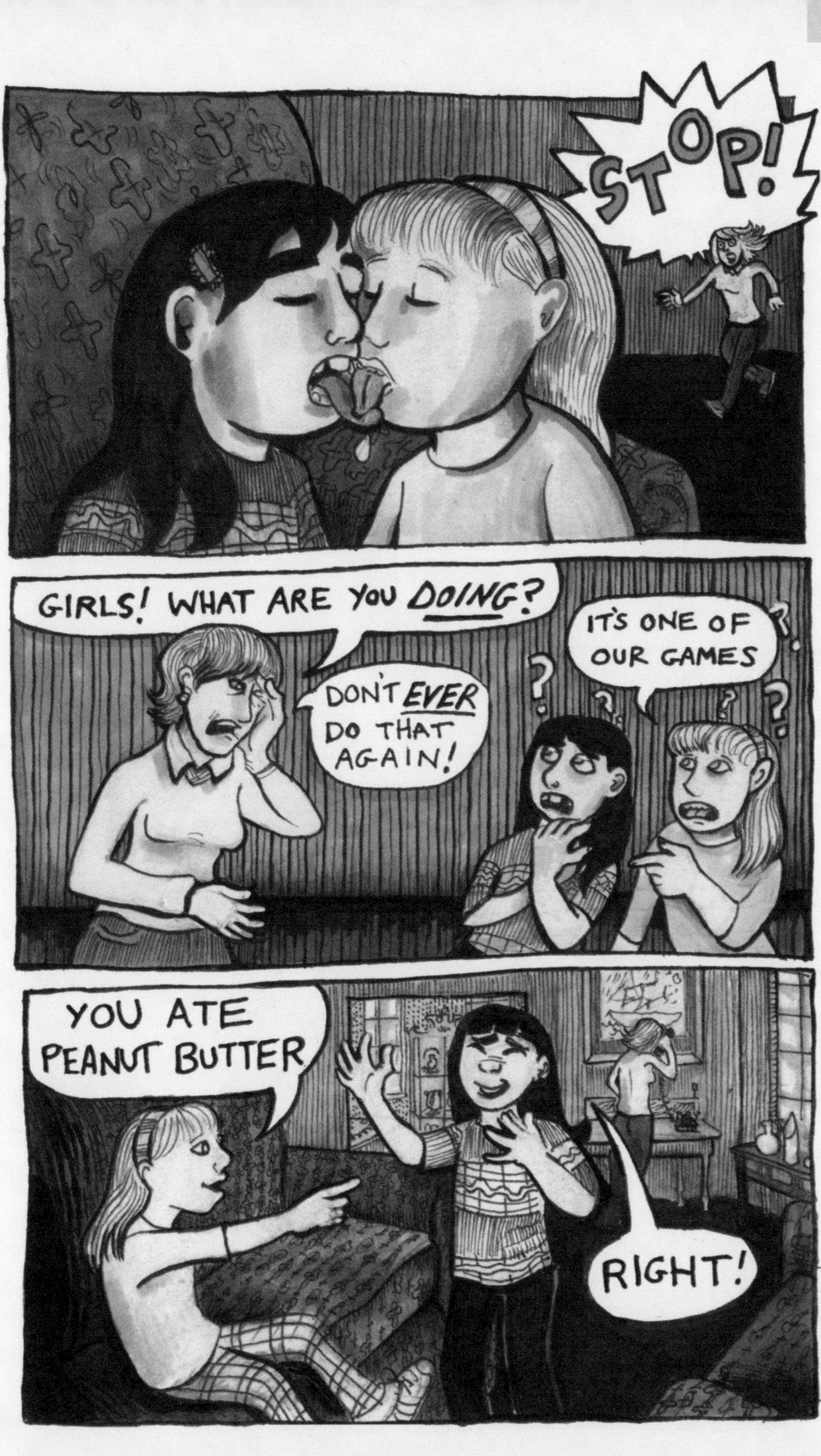
STOP!
GIRLS! WHAT ARE YOU DOING?
DON'T EVER DO THAT AGAIN!
IT'S ONE OF OUR GAMES
YOU ATE PEANUT BUTTER
RIGHT!

GAMES

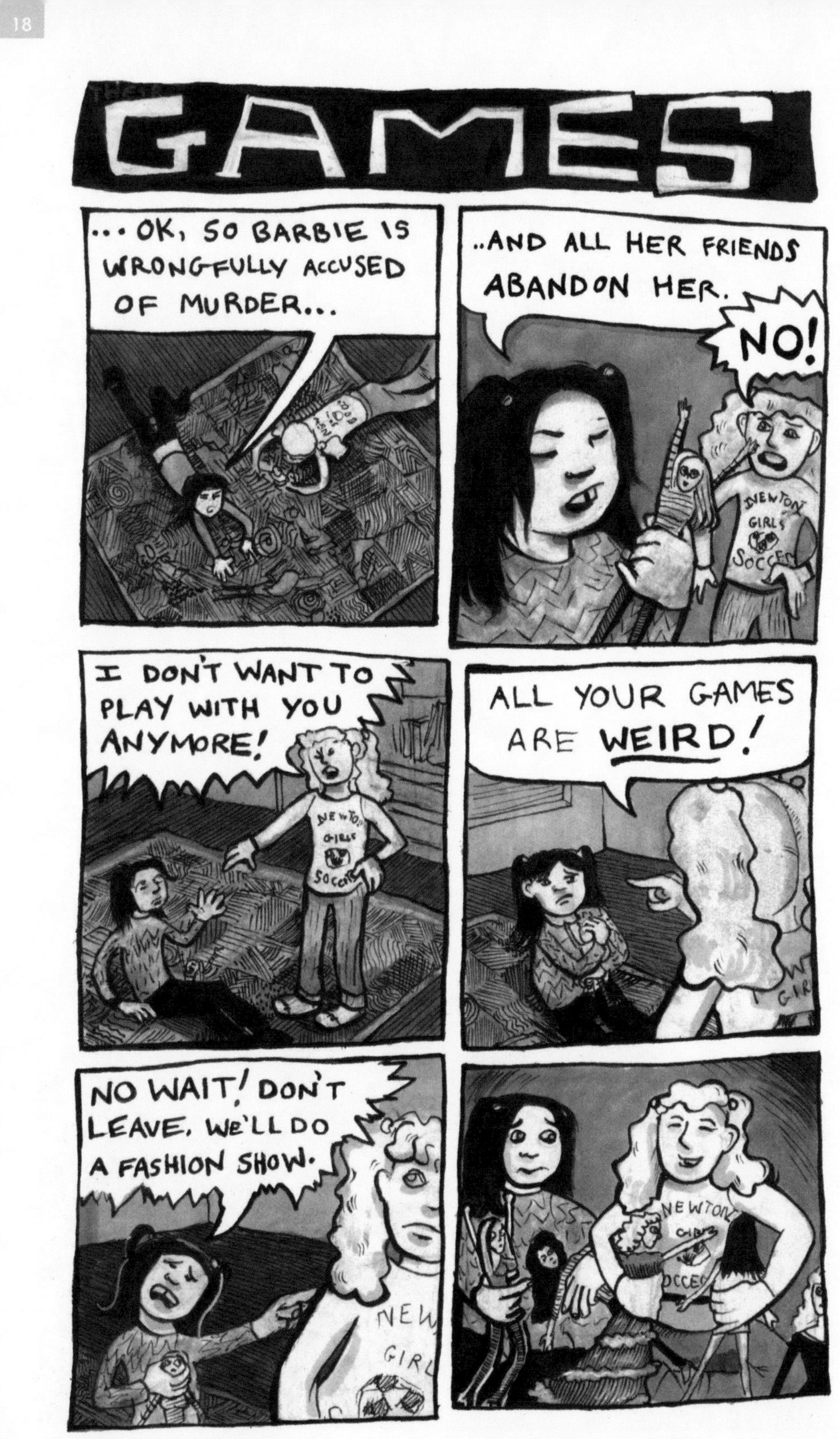
...OK, SO BARBIE IS WRONGFULLY ACCUSED OF MURDER...
..AND ALL HER FRIENDS ABANDON HER.
NO!
I DON'T WANT TO PLAY WITH YOU ANYMORE!
ALL YOUR GAMES ARE WEIRD!
NO WAIT! DON'T LEAVE. WE'LL DO A FASHION SHOW.

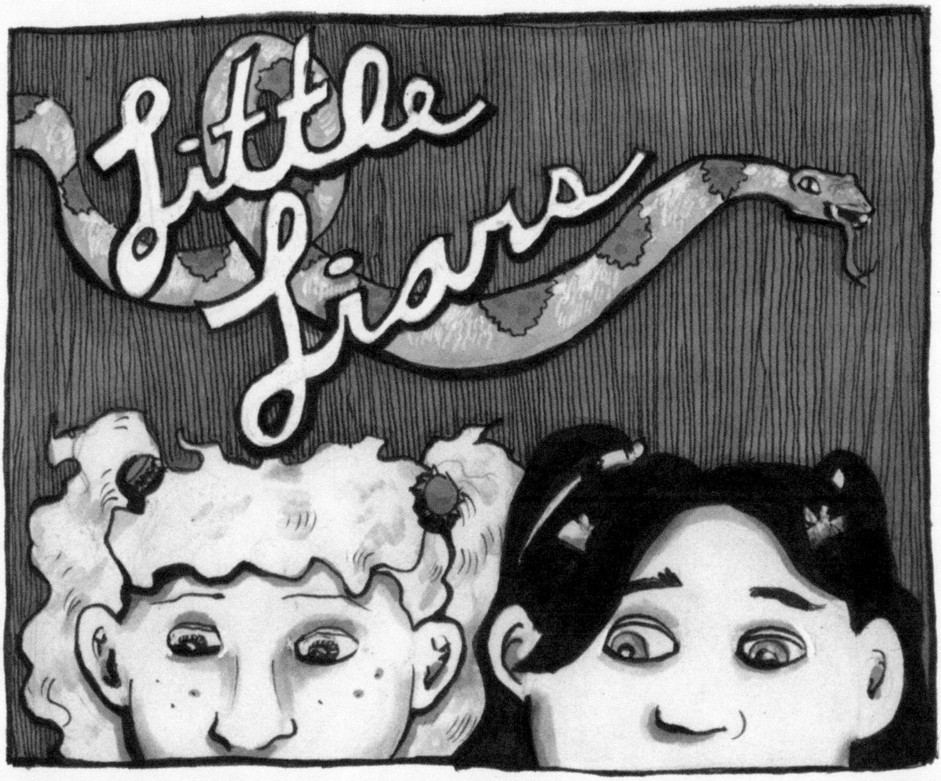
Little Liars

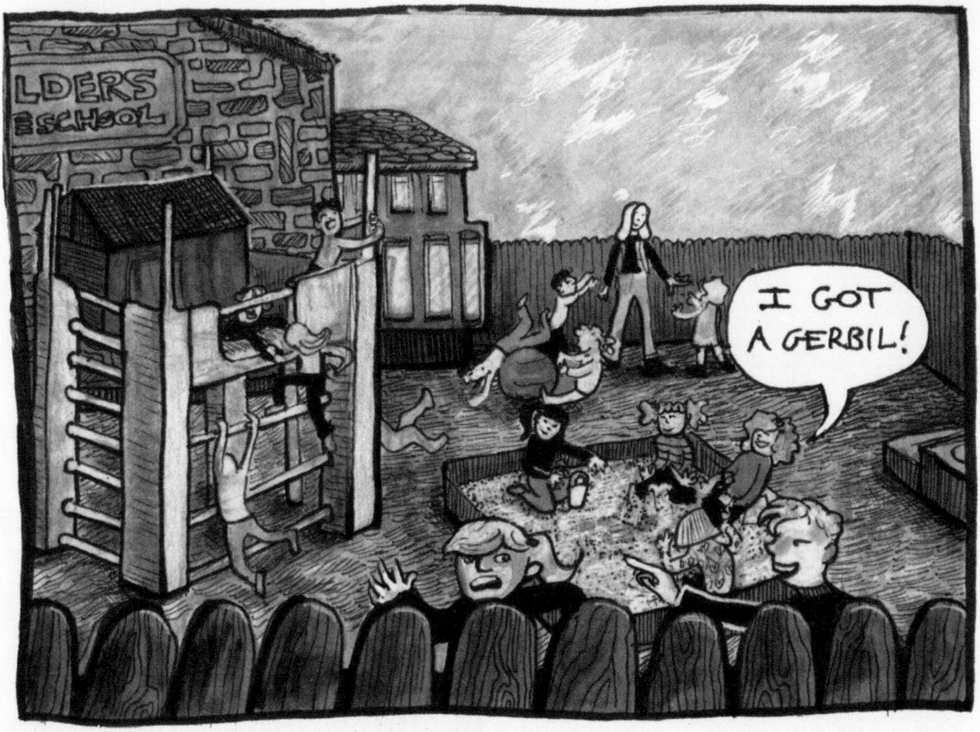
LDERS
SCHOOL
I GOT A GERBIL!

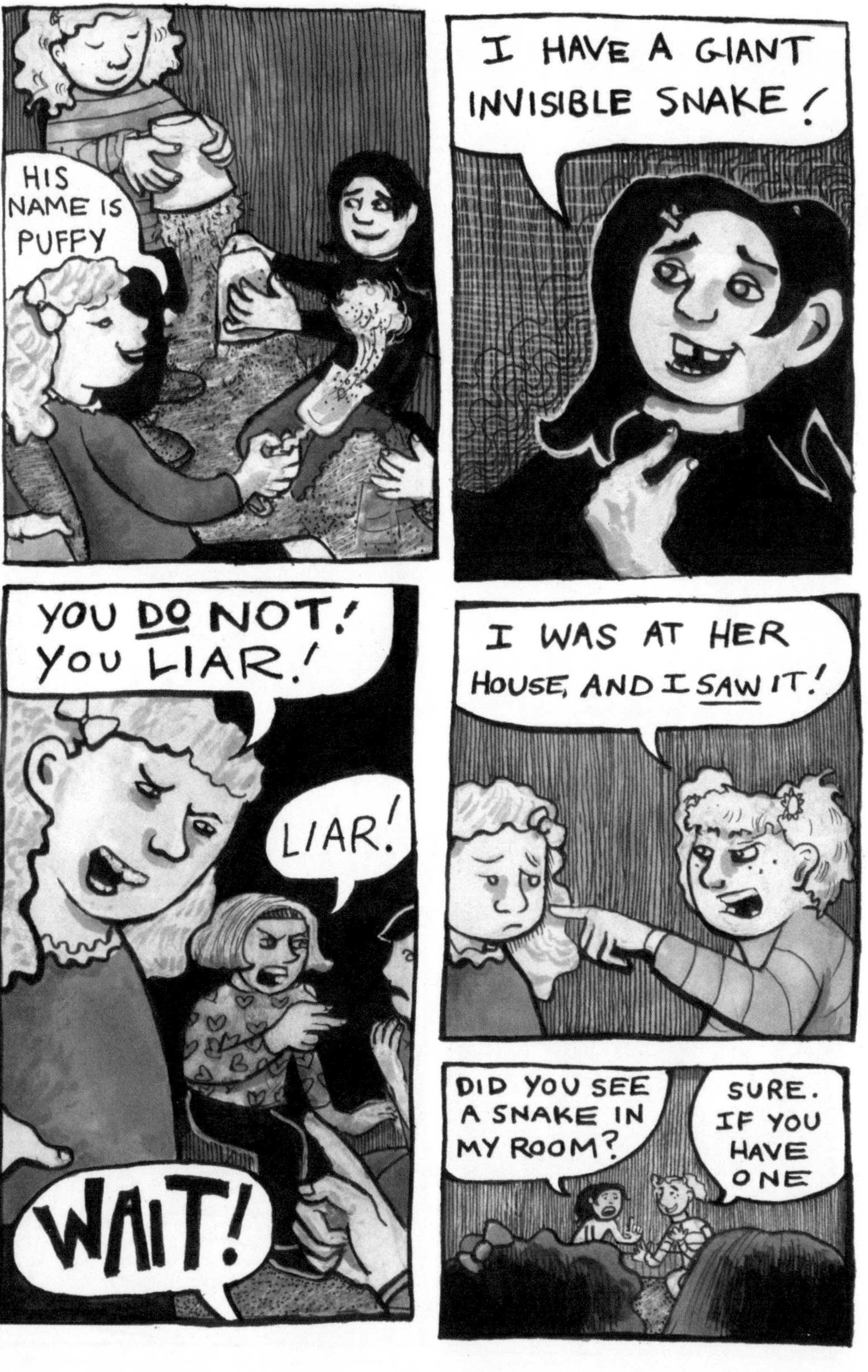
HIS NAME IS PUFFY
I HAVE A GIANT INVISIBLE SNAKE!
YOU DO NOT! YOU LIAR!
LIAR!
WAIT!
I WAS AT HER HOUSE, AND I SAW IT!
DID YOU SEE A SNAKE IN MY ROOM?
SURE. IF YOU HAVE ONE

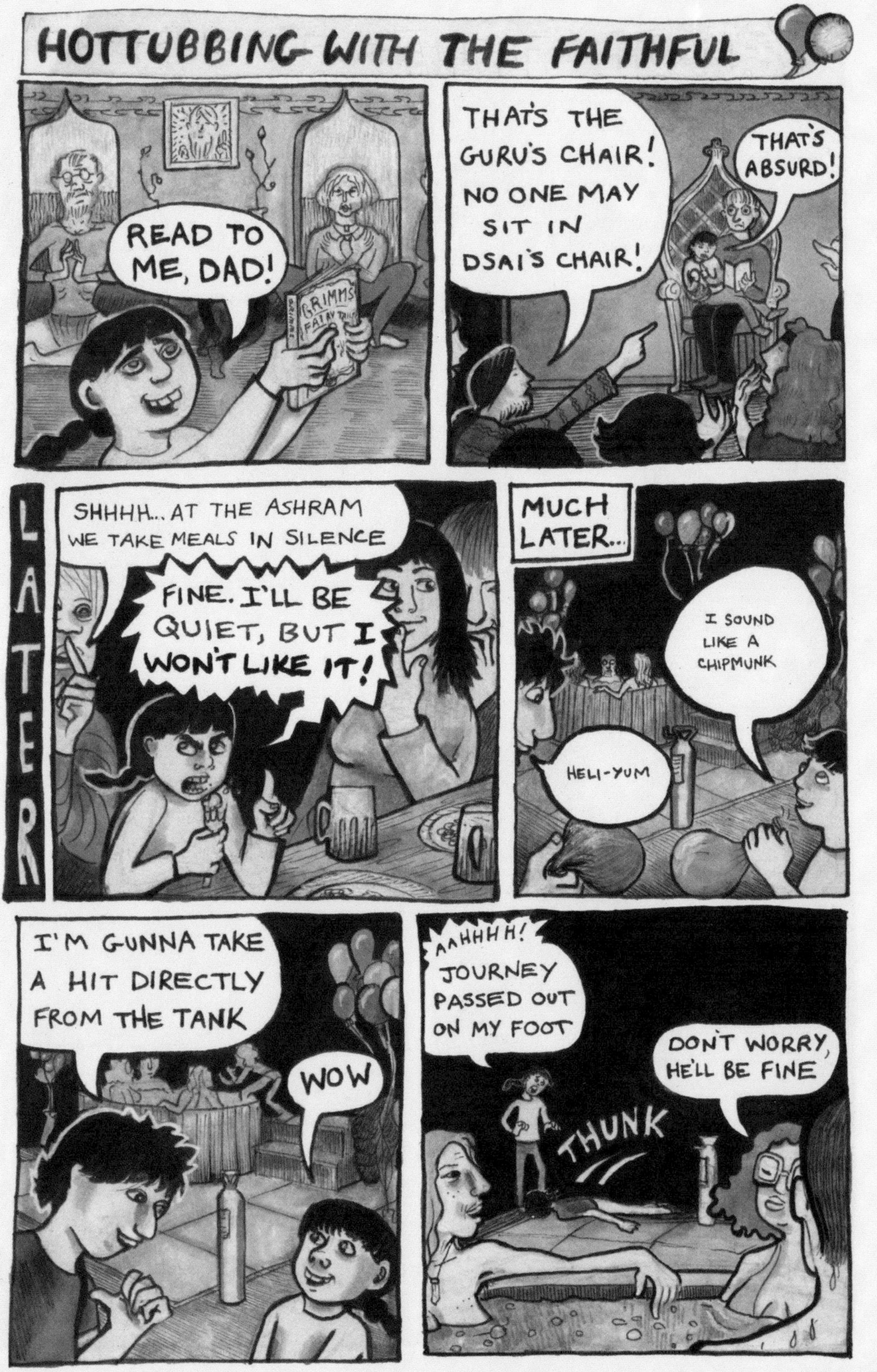
HOTTUBBING WITH THE FAITHFUL
READ TO ME, DAD!
GRIMMS FAIRY TALES
THAT'S THE GURU'S CHAIR! NO ONE MAY SIT IN DSAI'S CHAIR!
THAT'S ABSURD!
LATER
SHHHH... AT THE ASHRAM WE TAKE MEALS IN SILENCE
FINE. I'LL BE QUIET, BUT I WON'T LIKE IT!
MUCH LATER...
I SOUND LIKE A CHIPMUNK
HELI-YUM
I'M GUNNA TAKE A HIT DIRECTLY FROM THE TANK
WOW
AAHHHH! JOURNEY PASSED OUT ON MY FOOT
DON'T WORRY, HE'LL BE FINE
THUNK

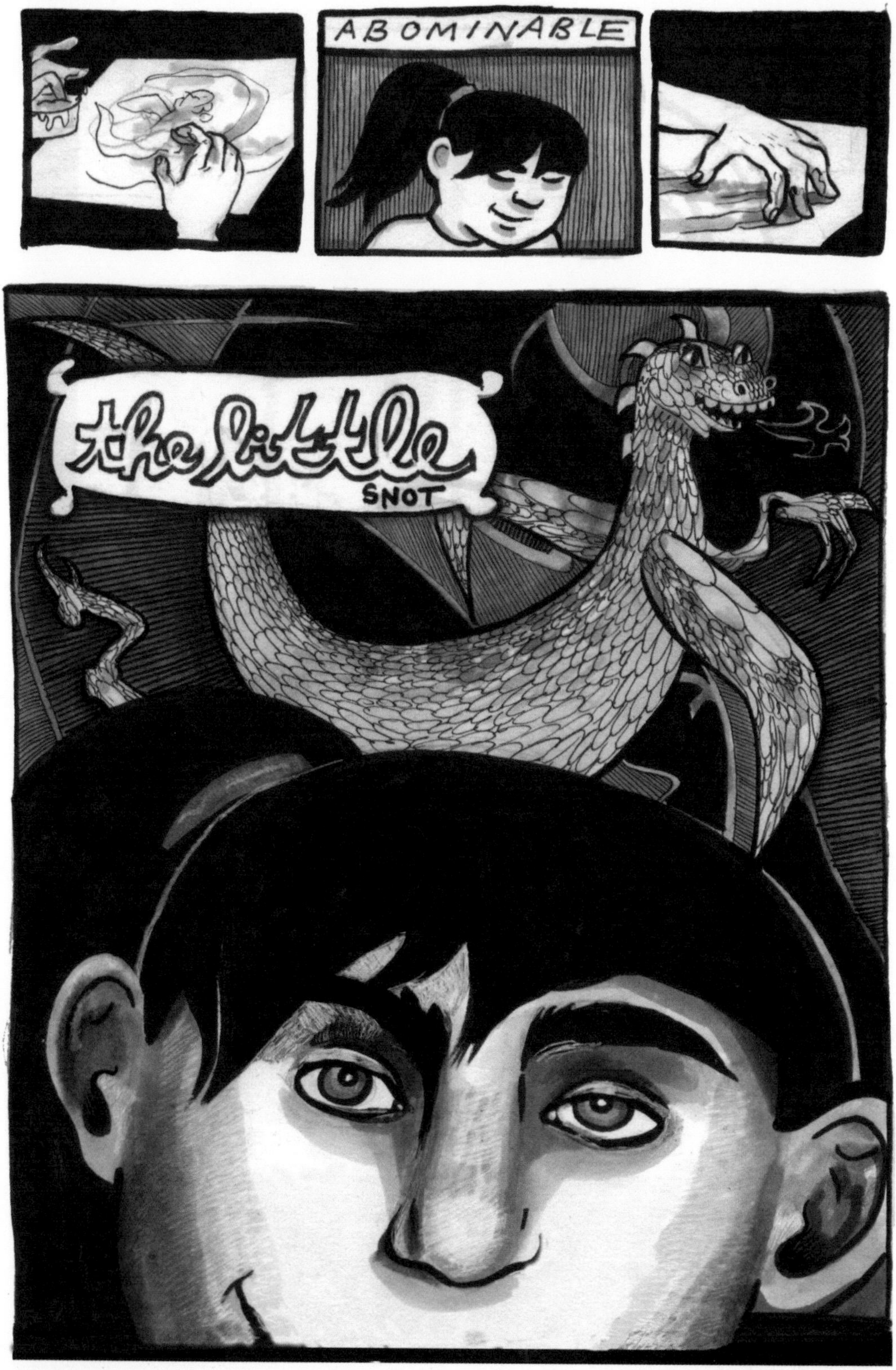
ABOMINABLE
the little
SNOT

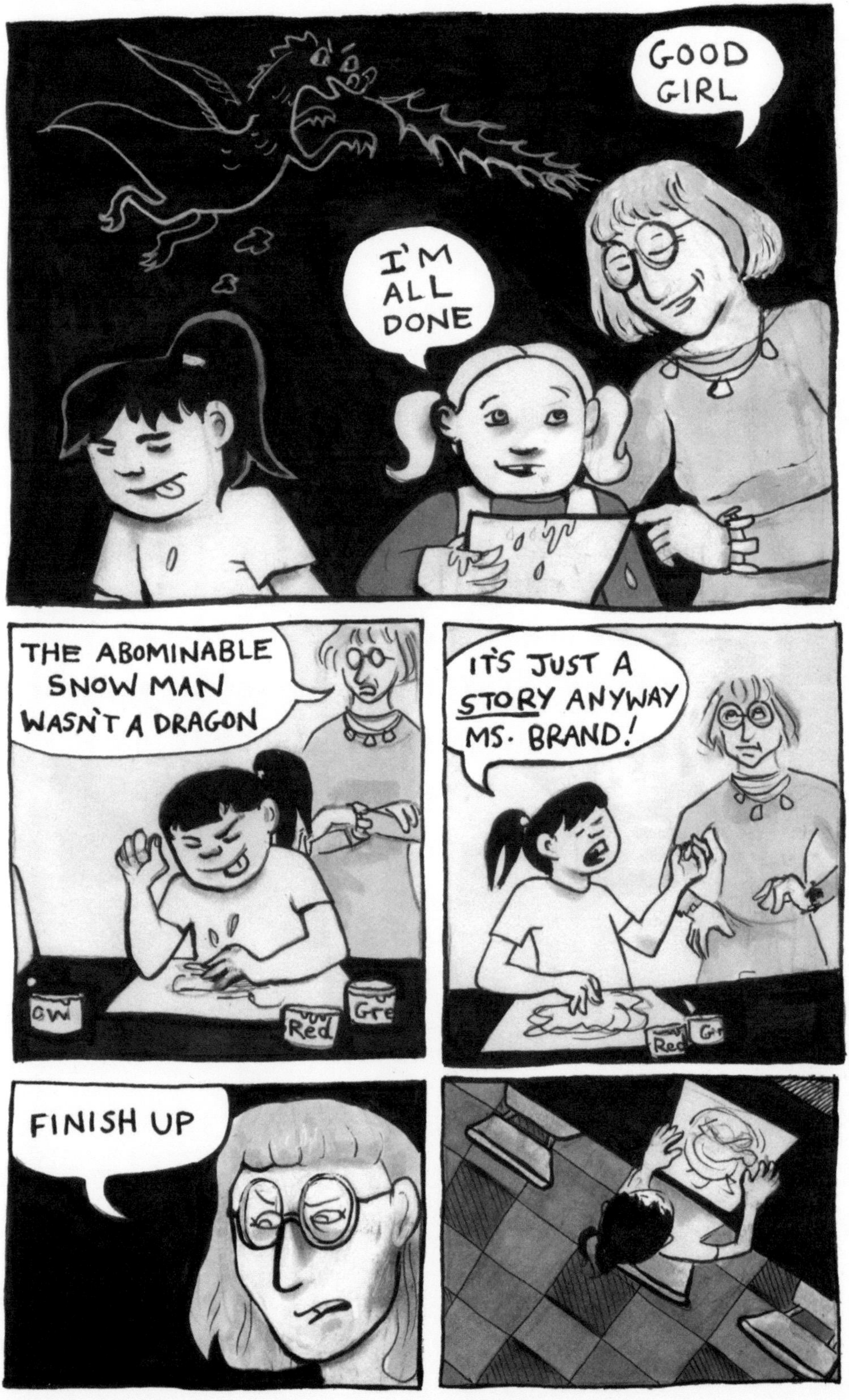
GOOD GIRL
I'M ALL DONE
THE ABOMINABLE SNOW MAN WASN'T A DRAGON
GW
Red
Gre
IT'S JUST A STORY ANYWAY MS. BRAND!
Red
Gr
FINISH UP

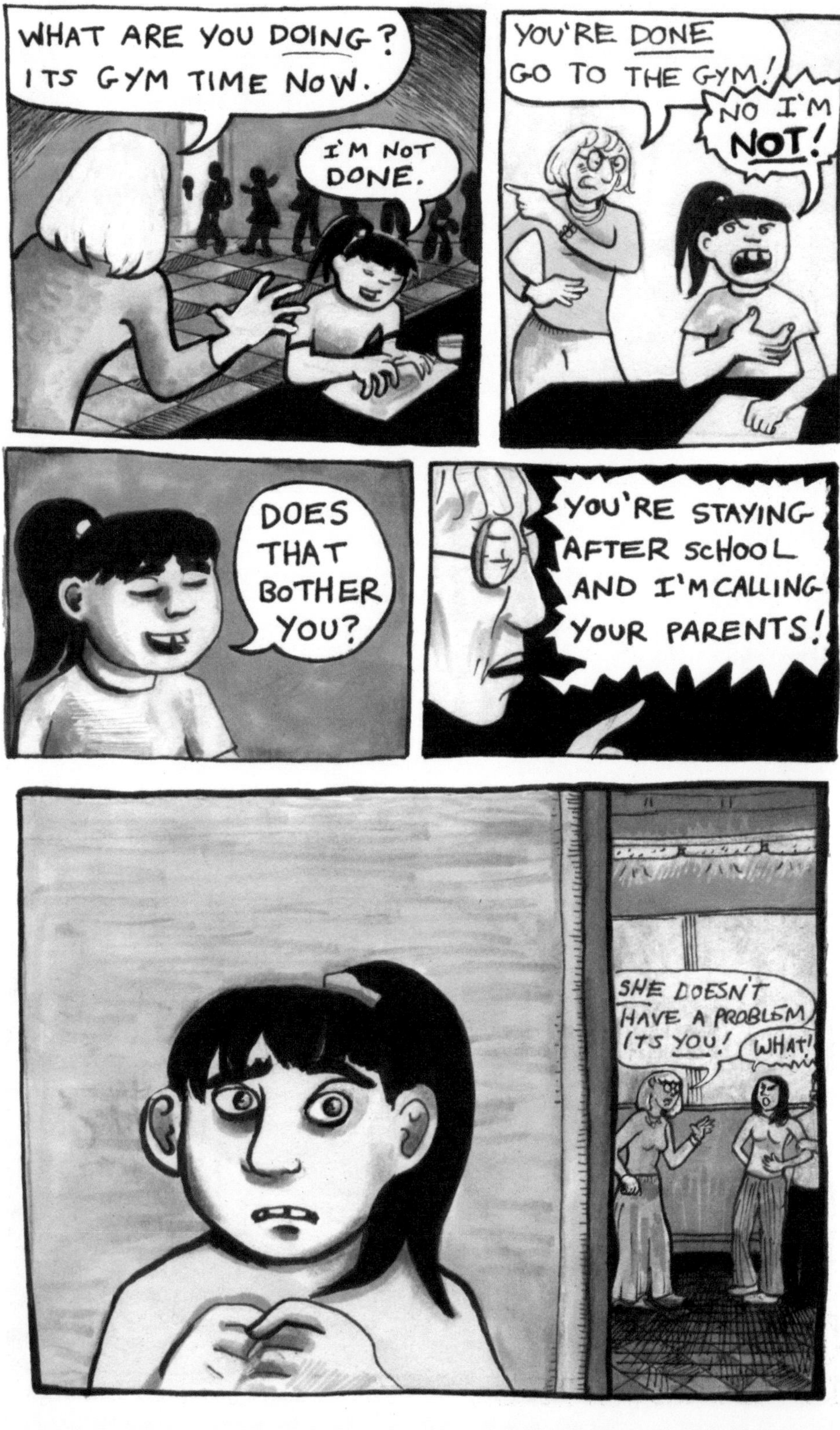
WHAT ARE YOU DOING? ITS GYM TIME NOW.
I'M NOT DONE.
YOU'RE DONE GO TO THE GYM!
NO I'M NOT!
DOES THAT BOTHER YOU?
YOU'RE STAYING AFTER SCHOOL AND I'M CALLING YOUR PARENTS!
SHE DOESN'T HAVE A PROBLEM ITS YOU!
WHAT!

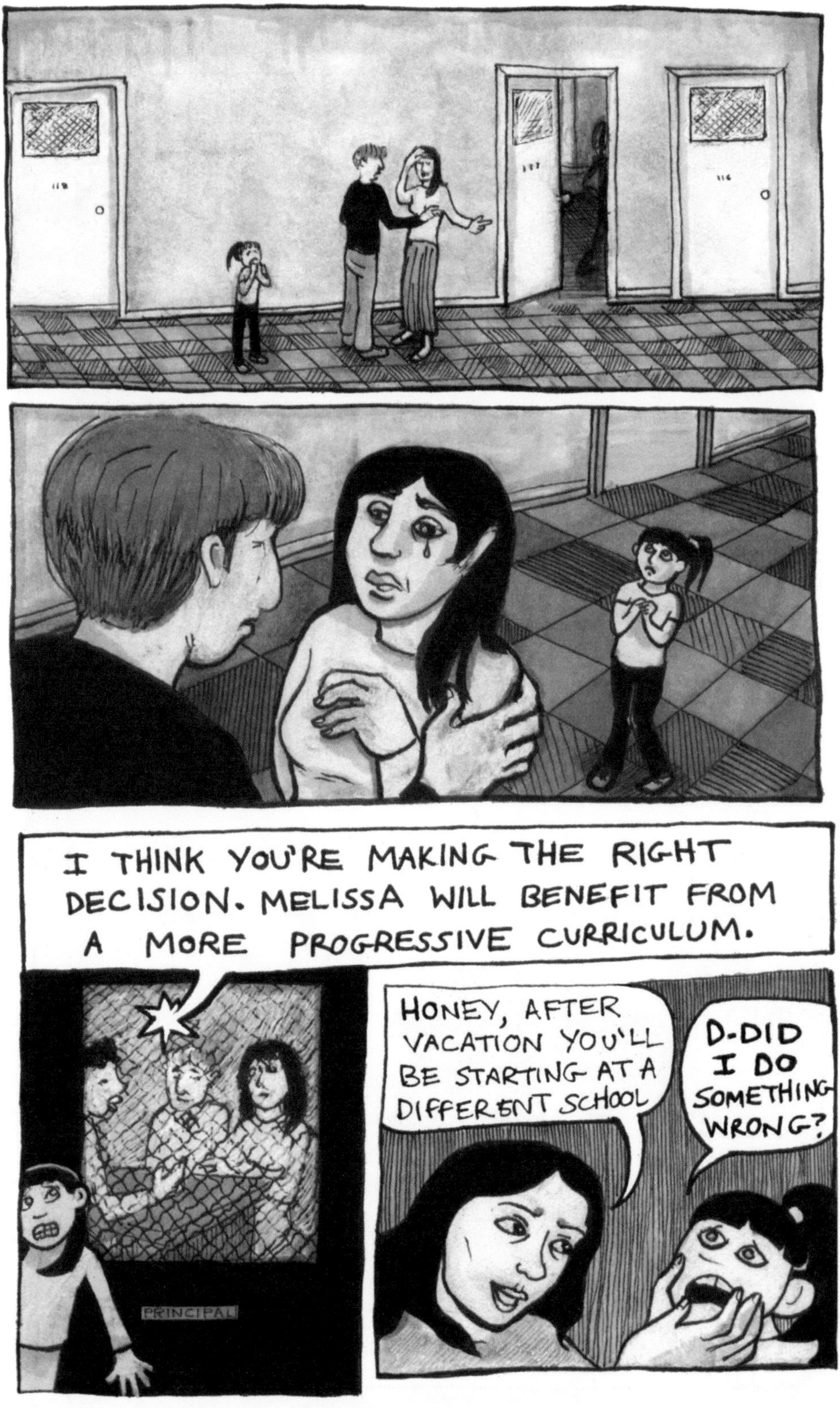
I THINK YOU'RE MAKING THE RIGHT DECISION. MELISSA WILL BENEFIT FROM A MORE PROGRESSIVE CURRICULUM.
PRINCIPAL
HONEY, AFTER VACATION YOU'LL BE STARTING AT A DIFFERENT SCHOOL
D-DID I DO SOMETHING WRONG?

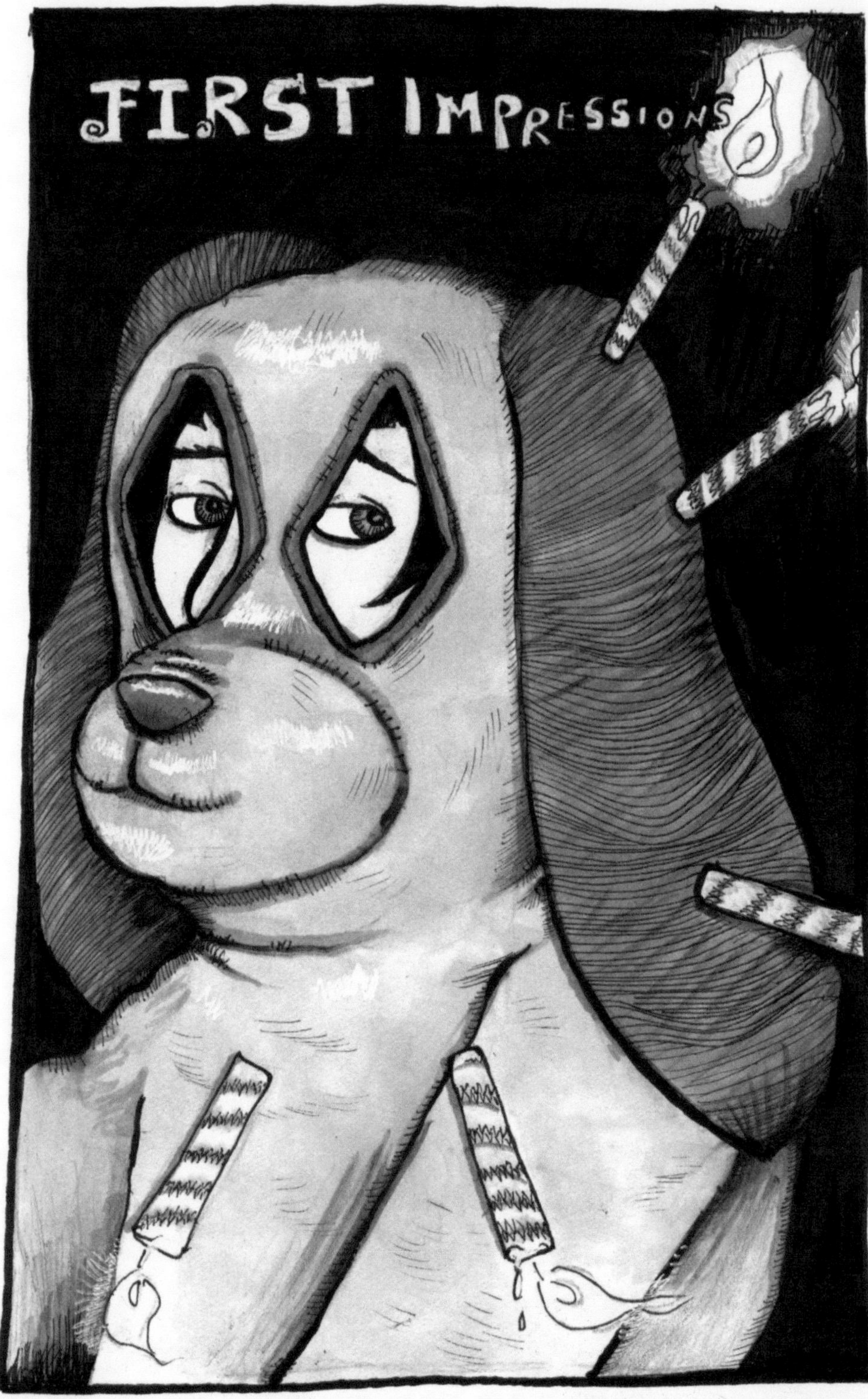
FIRST IMPRESSIONS

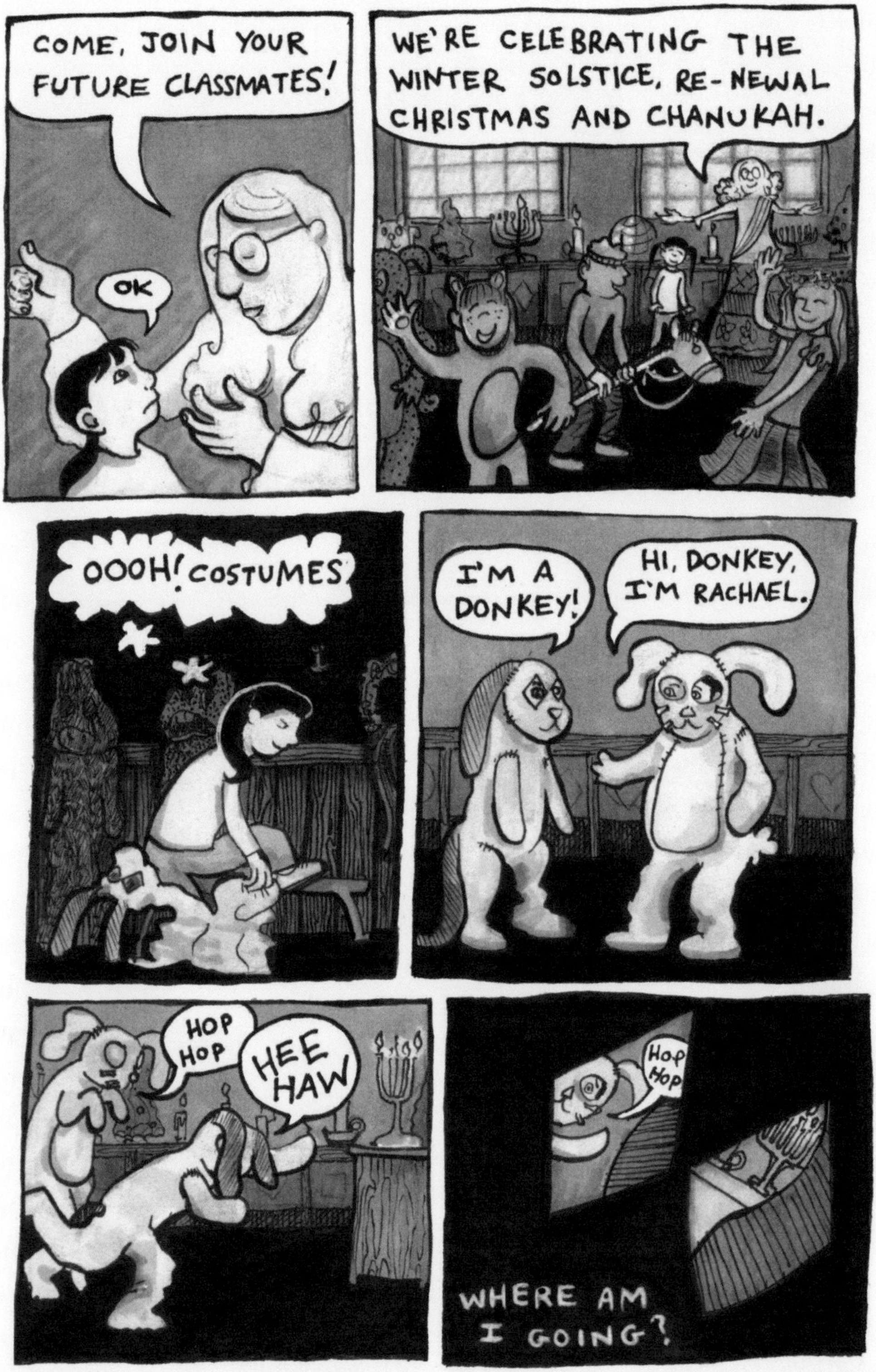
COME, JOIN YOUR FUTURE CLASSMATES!
OK
WE'RE CELEBRATING THE WINTER SOLSTICE, RE-NEWAL CHRISTMAS AND CHANUKAH.
OOOH! COSTUMES!
I'M A DONKEY!
HI, DONKEY, I'M RACHAEL.
HOP HOP
HEE HAW
Hop Hop
WHERE AM I GOING?

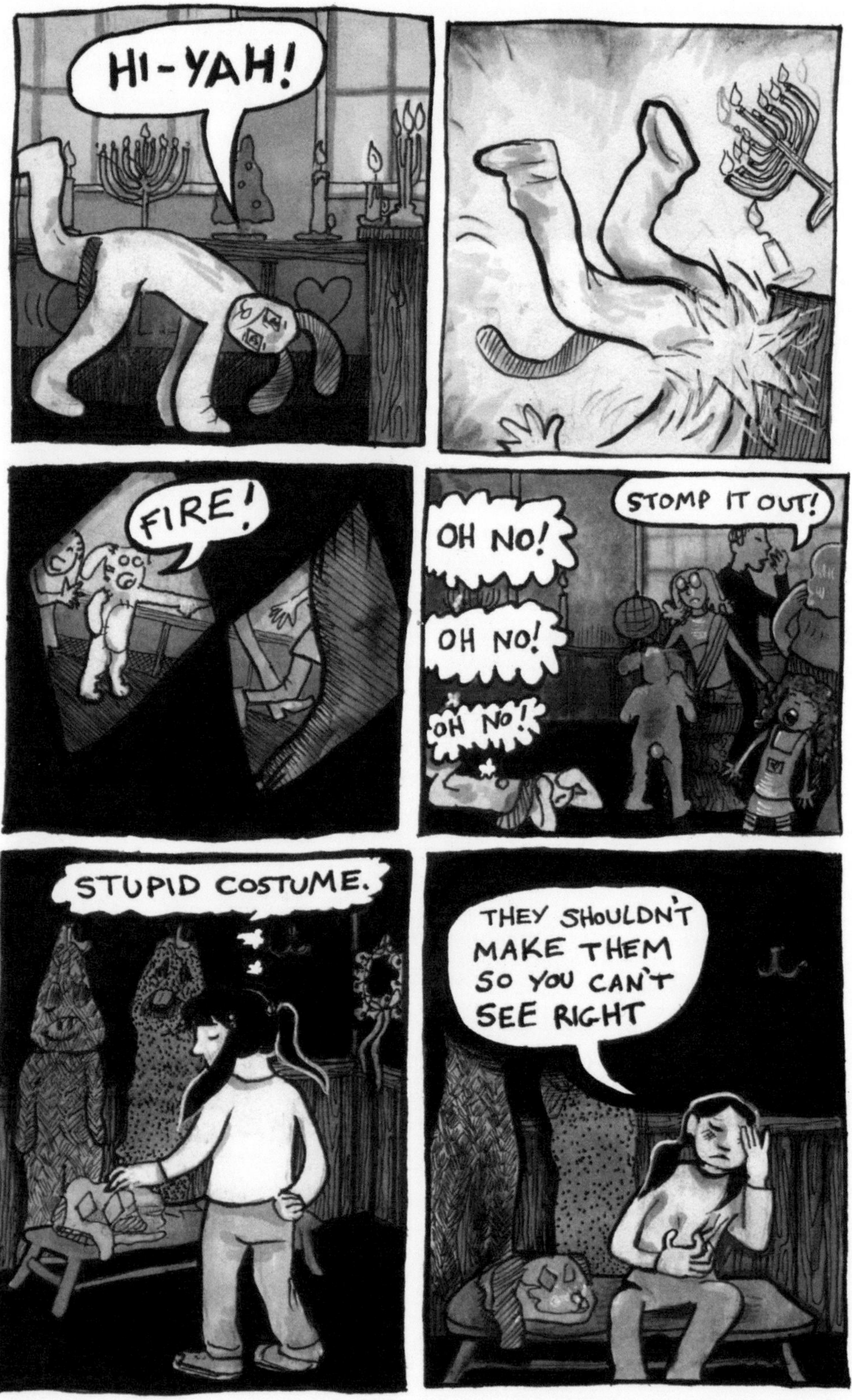
HI-YAH!
FIRE!
OH NO!
OH NO!
OH NO!
STOMP IT OUT!
STUPID COSTUME.
THEY SHOULDN'T MAKE THEM SO YOU CAN'T SEE RIGHT

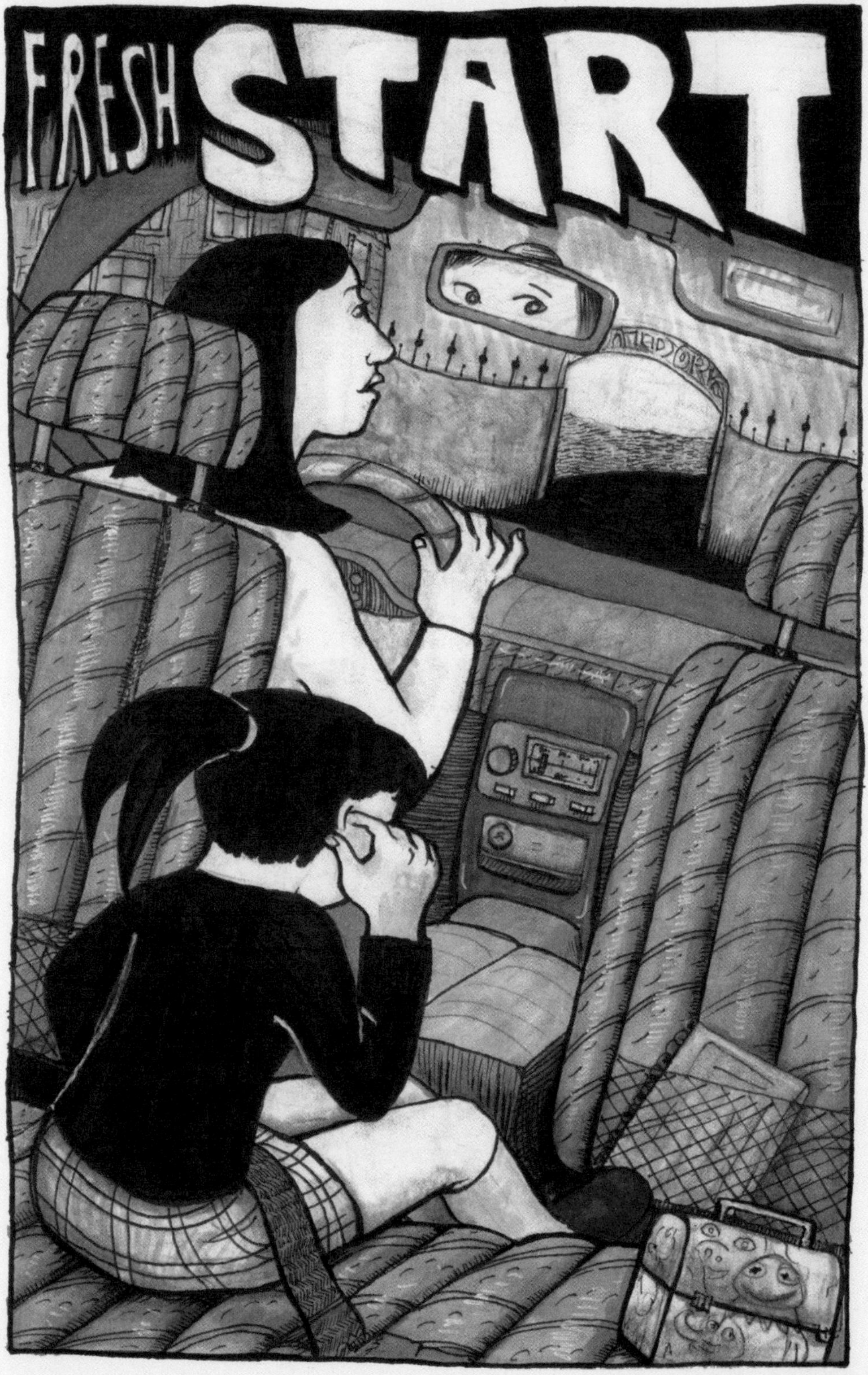
FRESH START

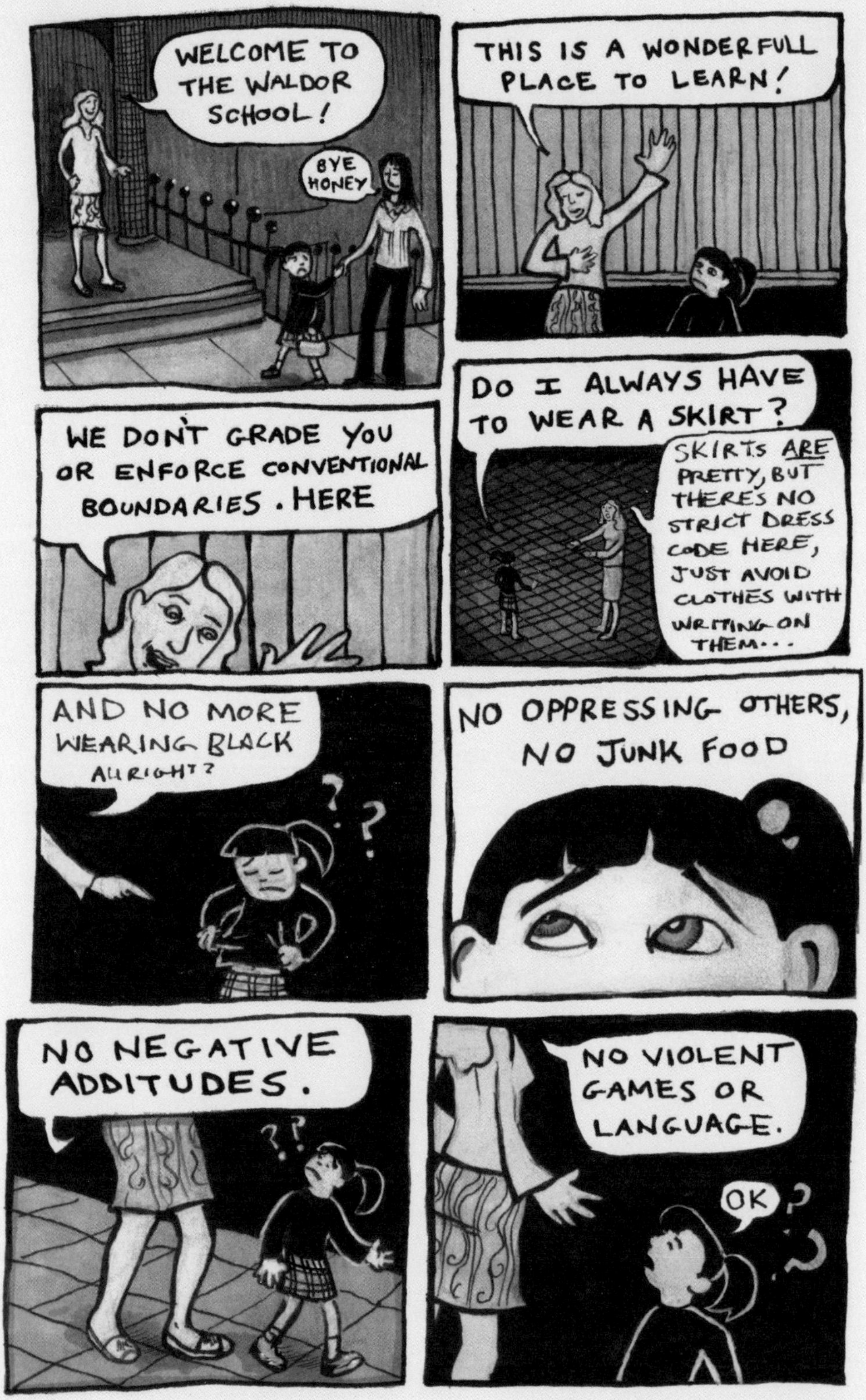
WELCOME TO THE WALDOR SCHOOL!
BYE HONEY
THIS IS A WONDERFULL PLACE TO LEARN!
WE DON'T GRADE YOU OR ENFORCE CONVENTIONAL BOUNDARIES. HERE
DO I ALWAYS HAVE TO WEAR A SKIRT?
SKIRTS ARE PRETTY, BUT THERE'S NO STRICT DRESS CODE HERE, JUST AVOID CLOTHES WITH WRITING ON THEM...
AND NO MORE WEARING BLACK ALLRIGHT?
??
NO OPPRESSING OTHERS, NO JUNK FOOD
NO NEGATIVE ADDITUDES.
??
NO VIOLENT GAMES OR LANGUAGE.
OK
??

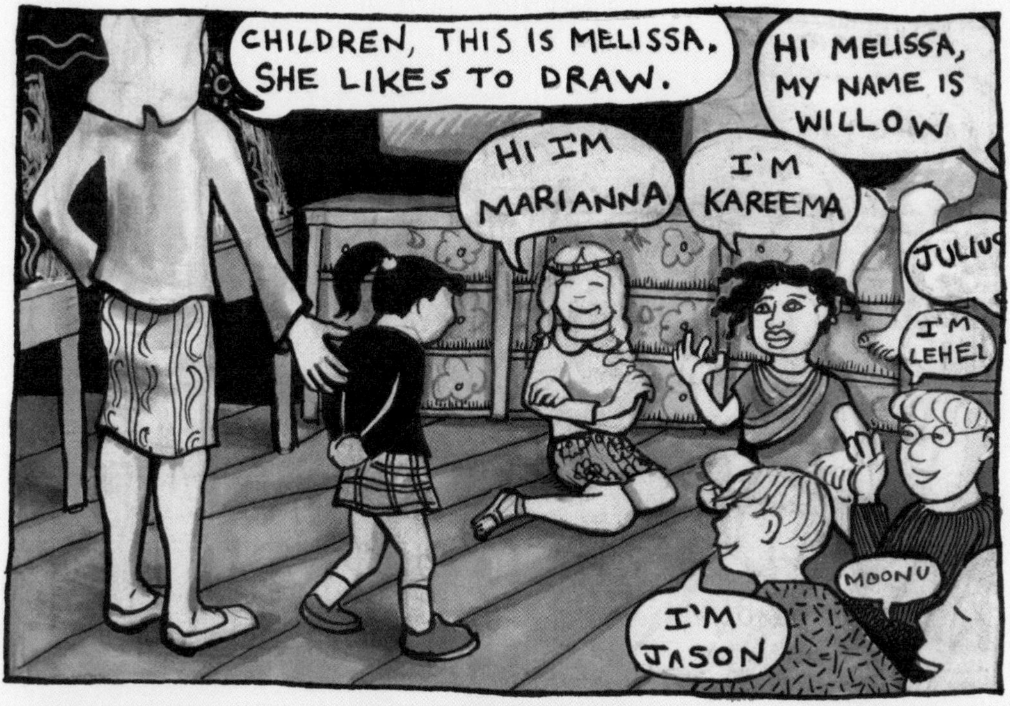
CHILDREN, THIS IS MELISSA. SHE LIKES TO DRAW.
HI MELISSA, MY NAME IS WILLOW
HI I'M MARIANNA
I'M KAREEMA
JULIUS
I'M LEHEL
MOONU
I'M JASON

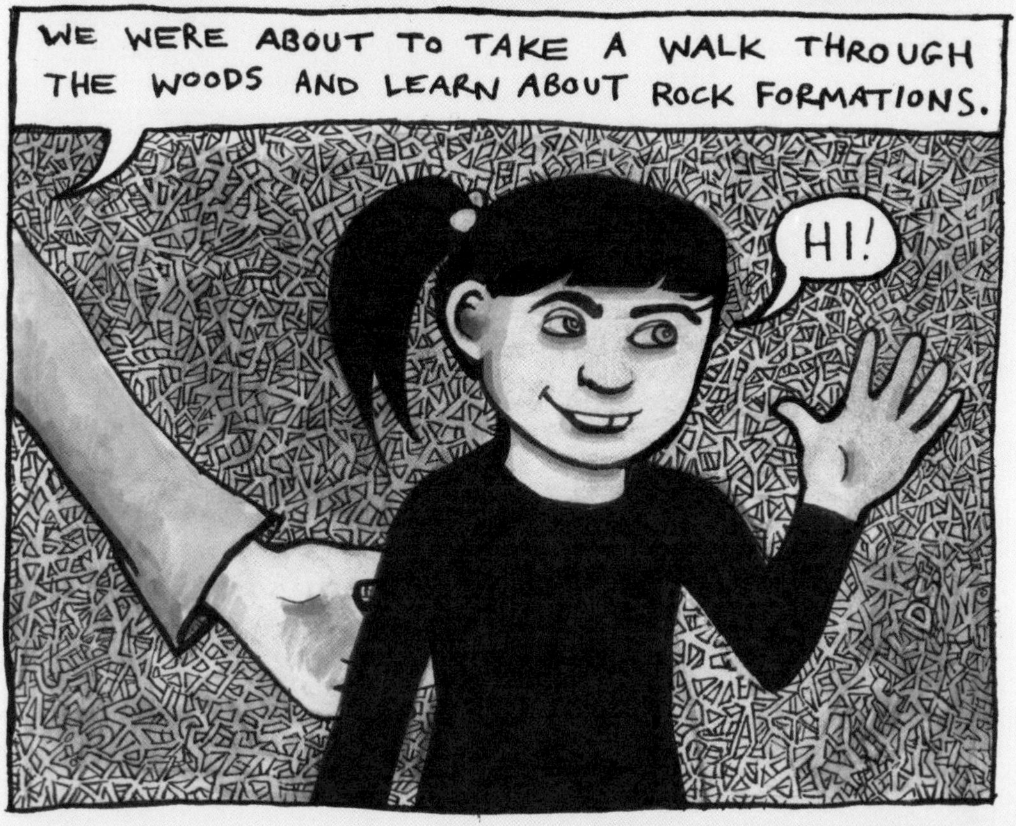
WE WERE ABOUT TO TAKE A WALK THROUGH THE WOODS AND LEARN ABOUT ROCK FORMATIONS.
HI!

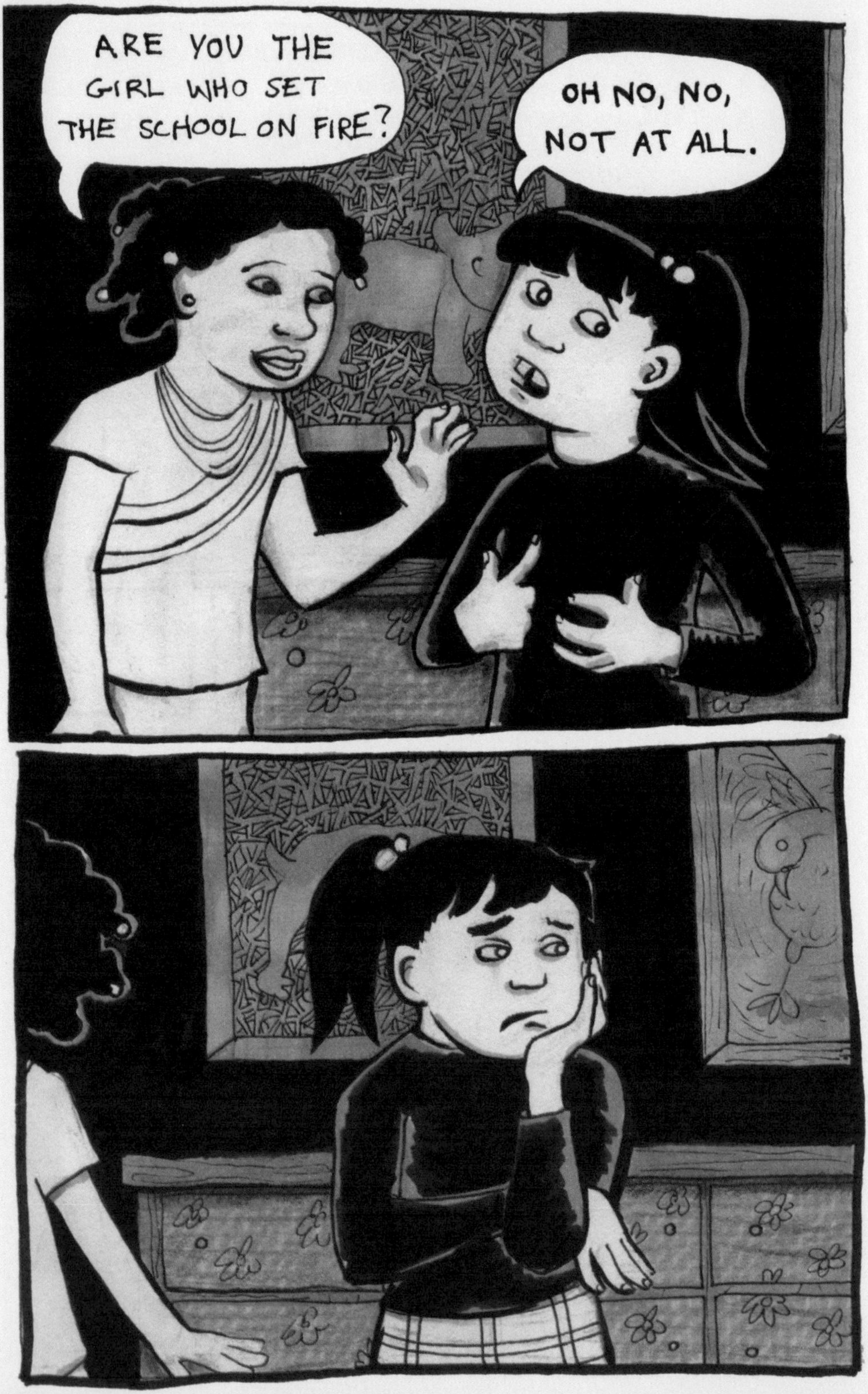
ARE YOU THE GIRL WHO SET THE SCHOOL ON FIRE?
OH NO, NO, NOT AT ALL.

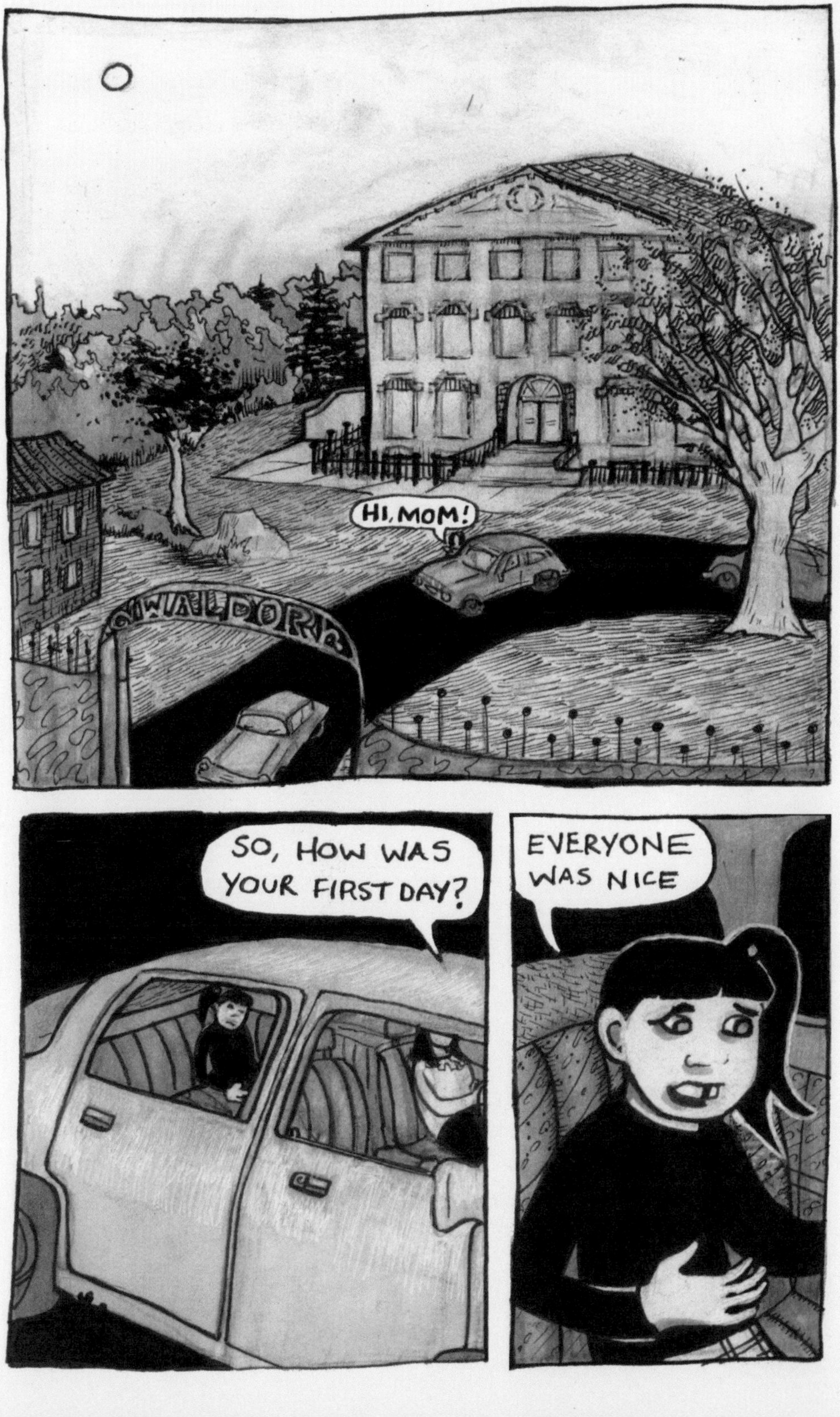
HI, MOM!
WALDORF
SO, HOW WAS YOUR FIRST DAY?
EVERYONE WAS NICE

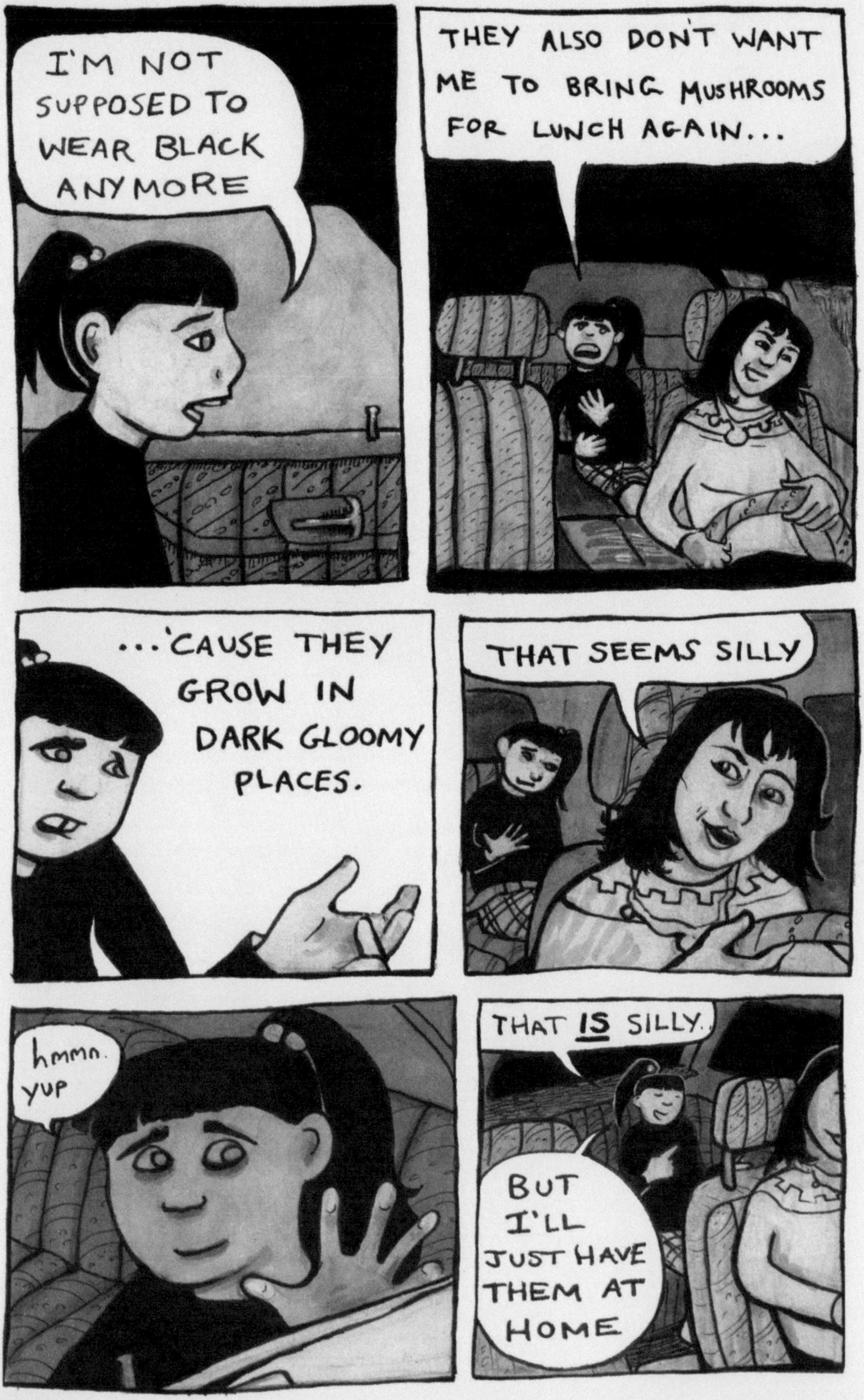
I'M NOT SUPPOSED TO WEAR BLACK ANYMORE
THEY ALSO DON'T WANT ME TO BRING MUSHROOMS FOR LUNCH AGAIN...
...'CAUSE THEY GROW IN DARK GLOOMY PLACES.
THAT SEEMS SILLY
hmmn. yup
THAT IS SILLY.
BUT I'LL JUST HAVE THEM AT HOME

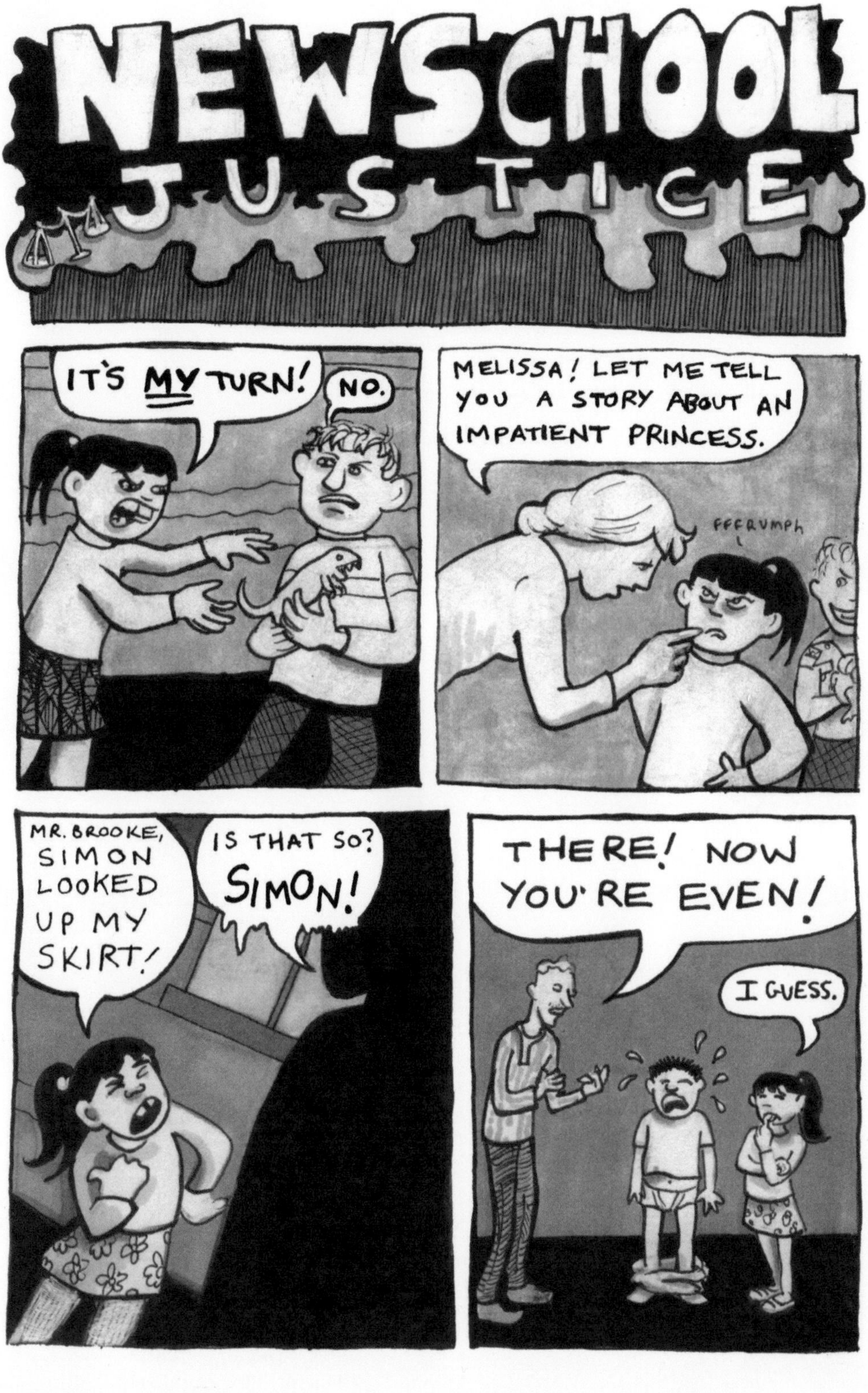
NEWSCHOOL JUSTICE
IT'S MY TURN!
NO.
MELISSA! LET ME TELL YOU A STORY ABOUT AN IMPATIENT PRINCESS.
FFFRUMPH
MR. BROOKE, SIMON LOOKED UP MY SKIRT!
IS THAT SO? SIMON!
THERE! NOW YOU'RE EVEN!
I GUESS.

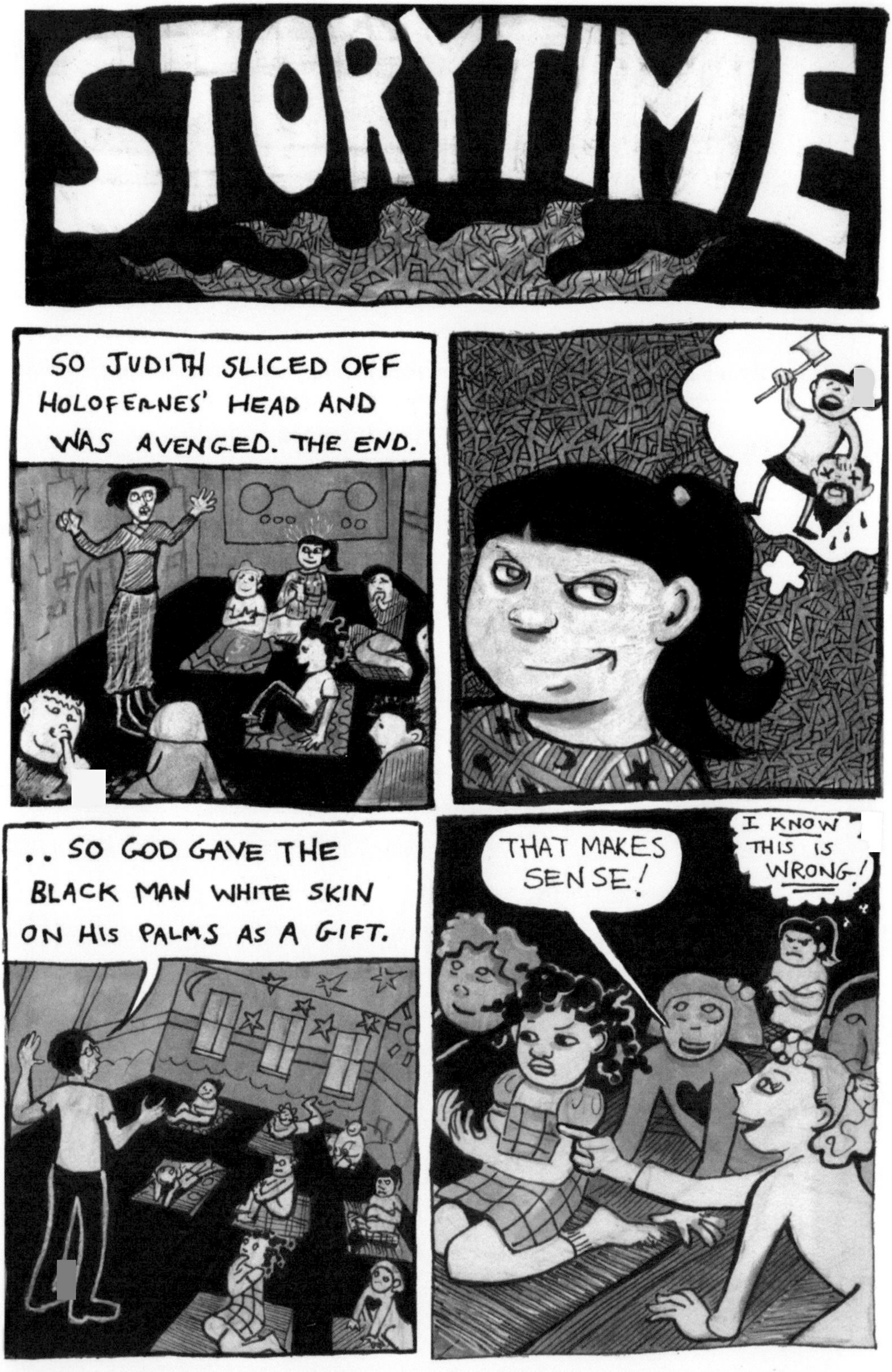
STORYTIME
SO JUDITH SLICED OFF HOLOFERNES' HEAD AND WAS AVENGED. THE END.
.. SO GOD GAVE THE BLACK MAN WHITE SKIN ON HIS PALMS AS A GIFT.
THAT MAKES SENSE!
I KNOW THIS IS WRONG!

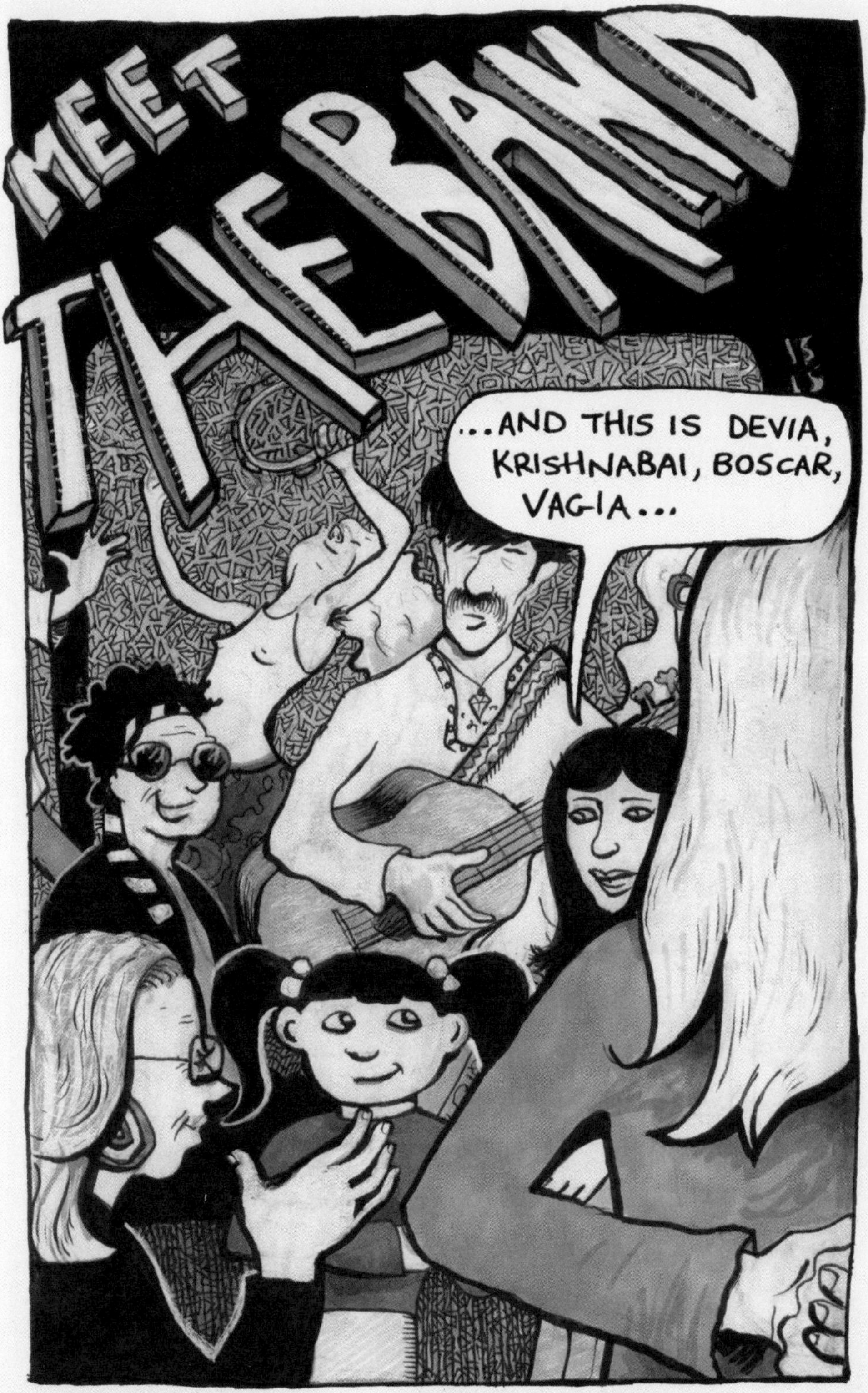
MEET THE BAND
...AND THIS IS DEVIA, KRISHNABAI, BOSCAR, VAGIA...

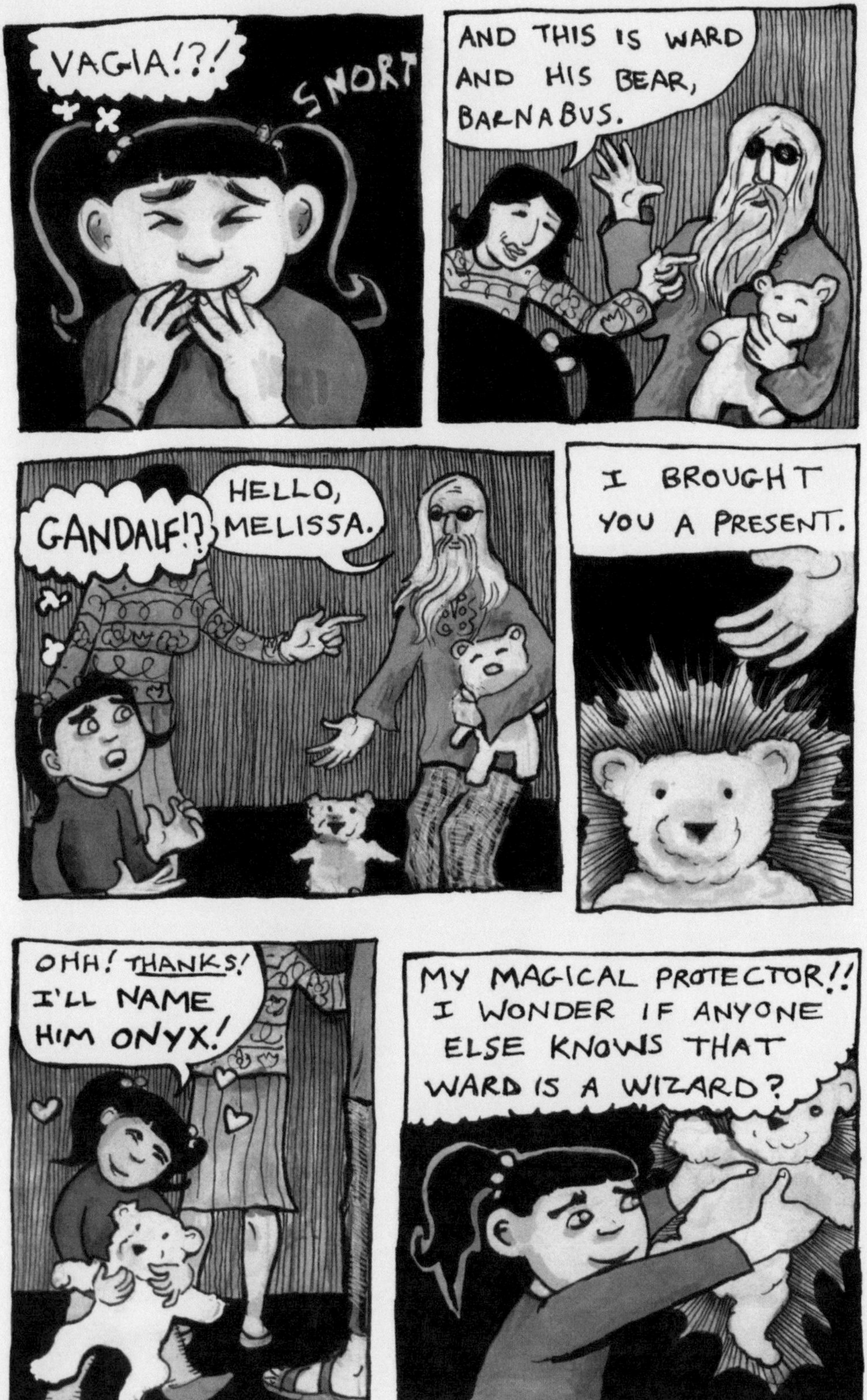
VAGIA!?!
SNORT
AND THIS IS WARD AND HIS BEAR, BARNABUS.
GANDALF!?
HELLO, MELISSA.
I BROUGHT YOU A PRESENT.
OHH! THANKS! I'LL NAME HIM ONYX!
MY MAGICAL PROTECTOR!! I WONDER IF ANYONE ELSE KNOWS THAT WARD IS A WIZARD?

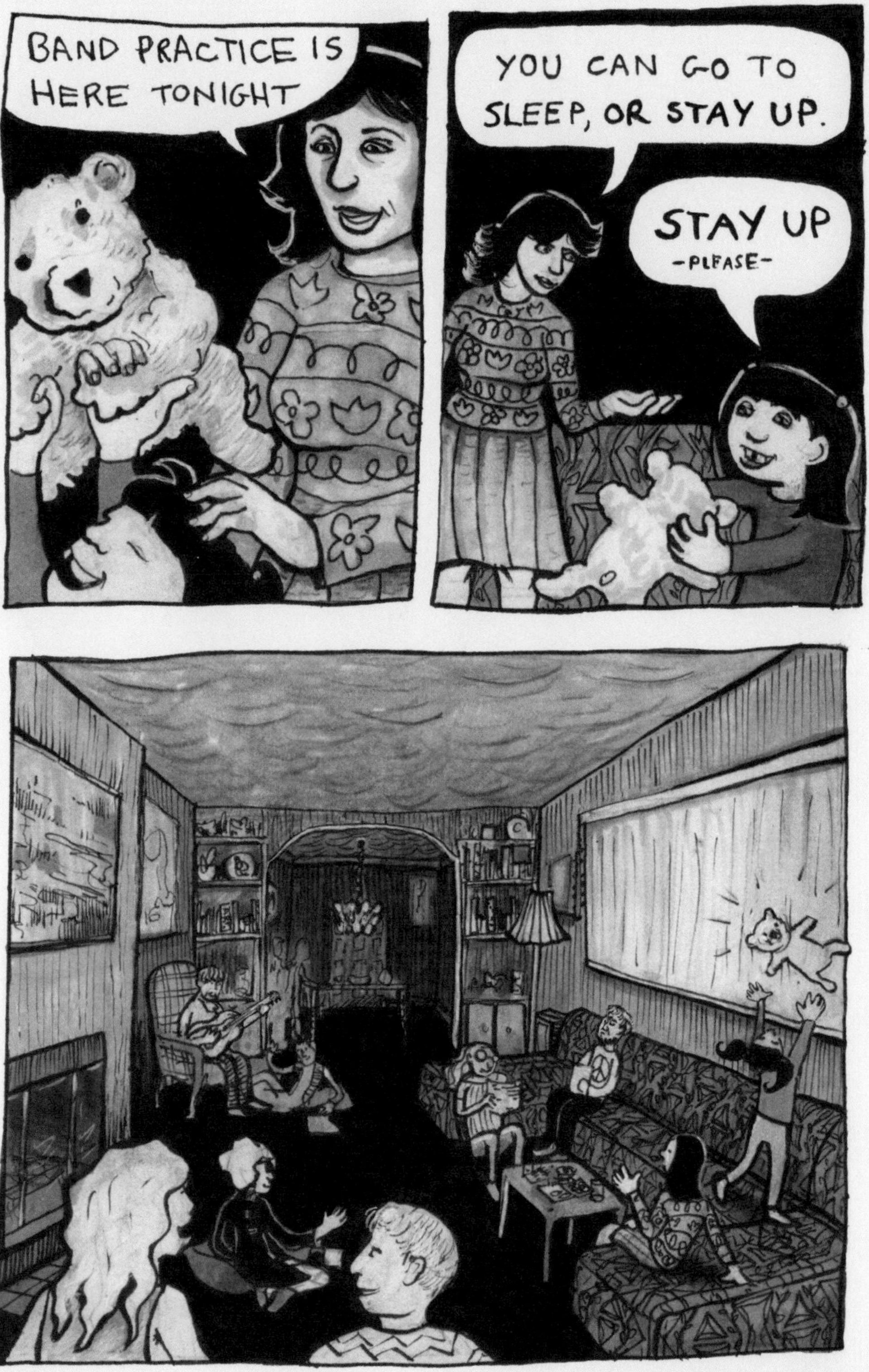
BAND PRACTICE IS HERE TONIGHT
YOU CAN GO TO SLEEP, OR STAY UP.
STAY UP
-PLEASE-

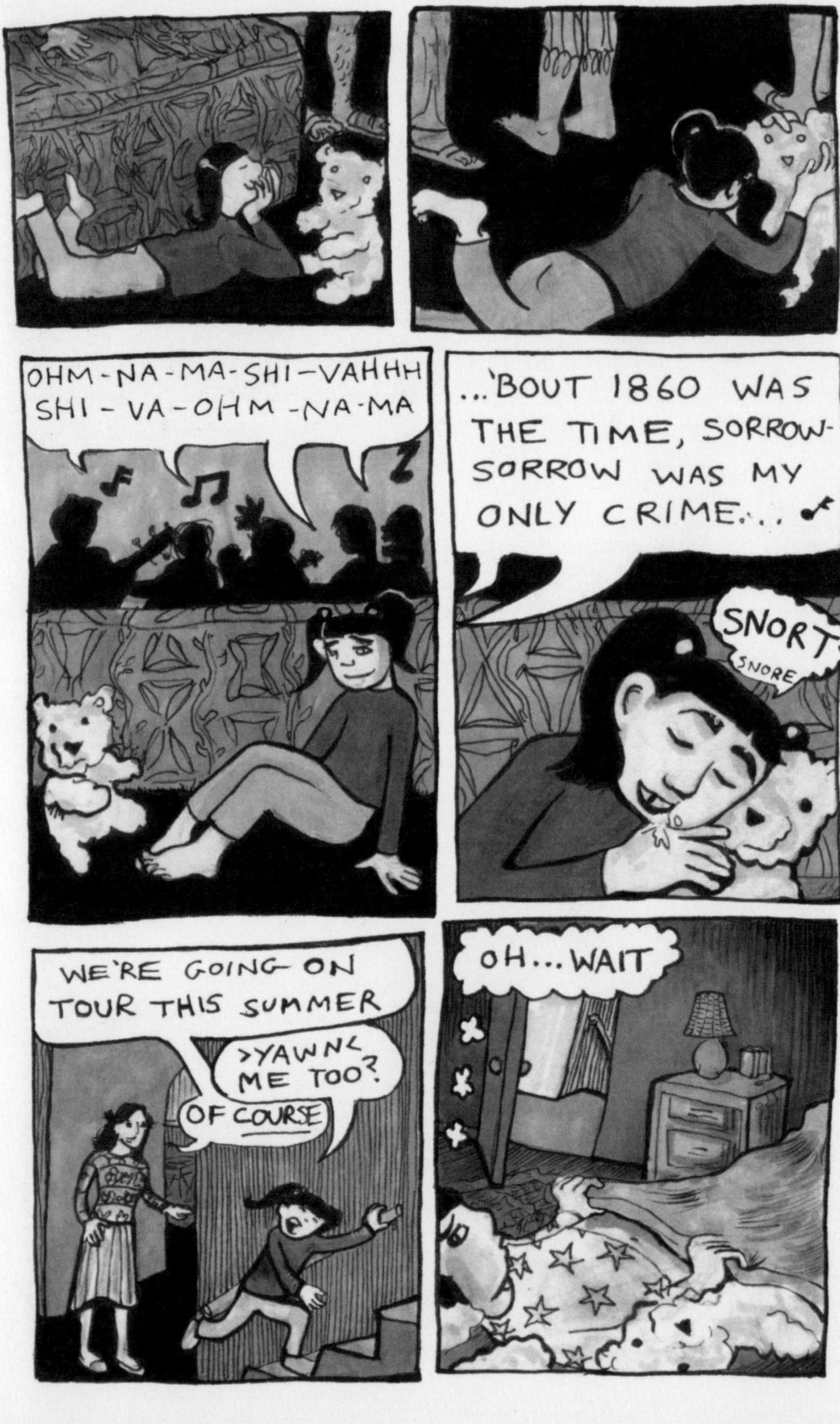
OHM-NA-MA-SHI-VAHHH
SHI-VA-OHM-NA-MA
...'BOUT 1860 WAS THE TIME, SORROW-SORROW WAS MY ONLY CRIME...
SNORT
SNORE
WE'RE GOING ON TOUR THIS SUMMER
>YAWN< ME TOO?
OF COURSE
OH... WAIT

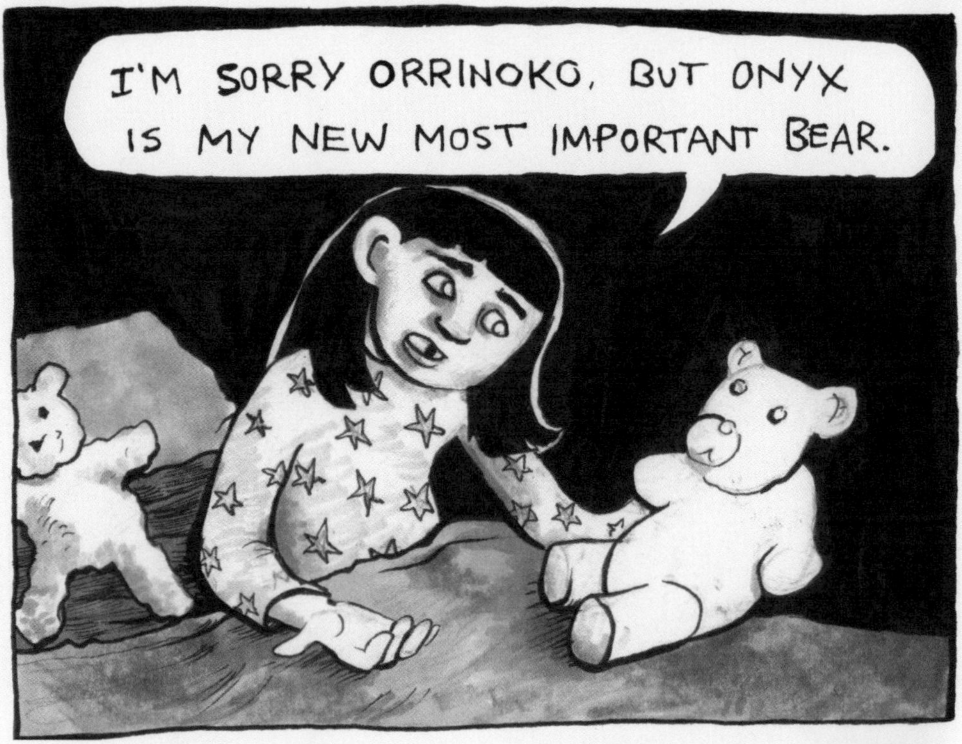
I'M SORRY ORRINOKO, BUT ONYX IS MY NEW MOST IMPORTANT BEAR.

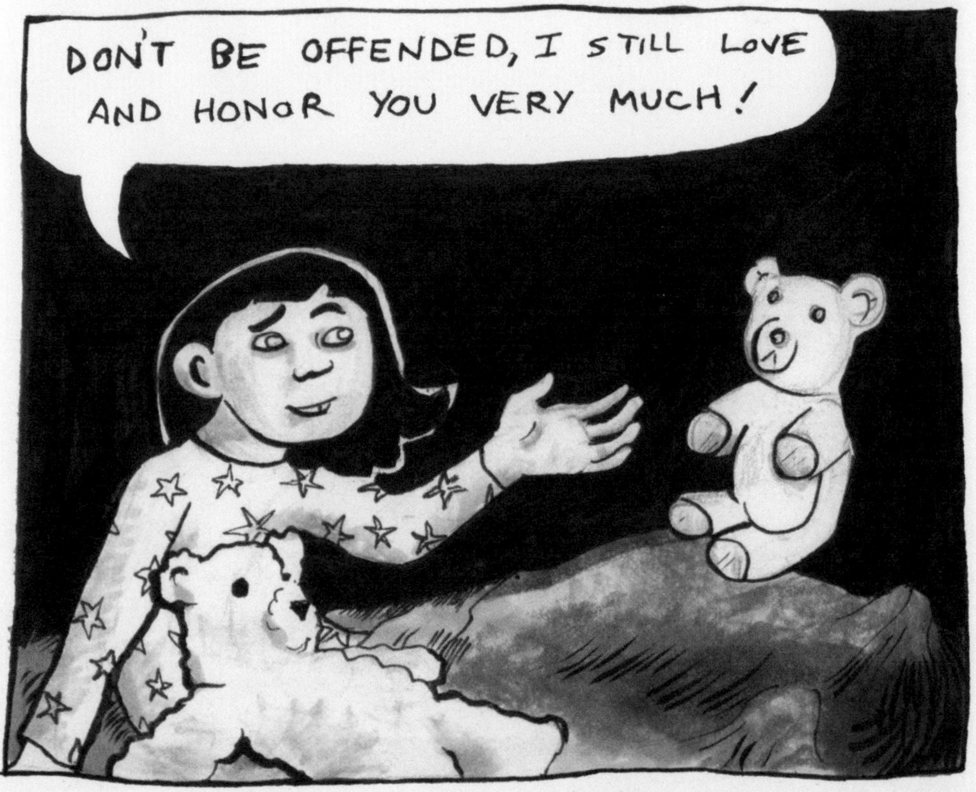
DON'T BE OFFENDED, I STILL LOVE AND HONOR YOU VERY MUCH!

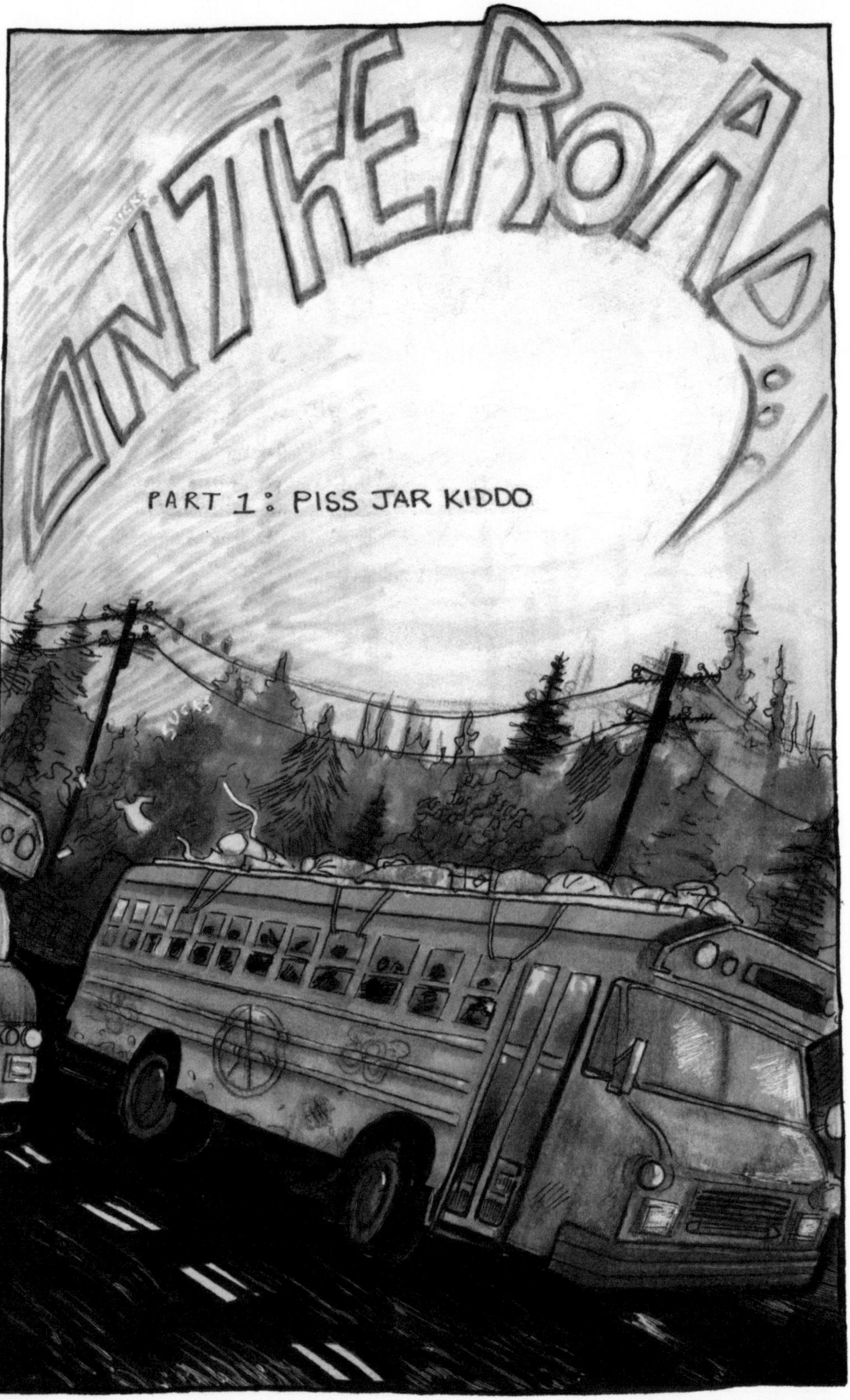
ON THE ROAD
PART 1: PISS JAR KIDDO

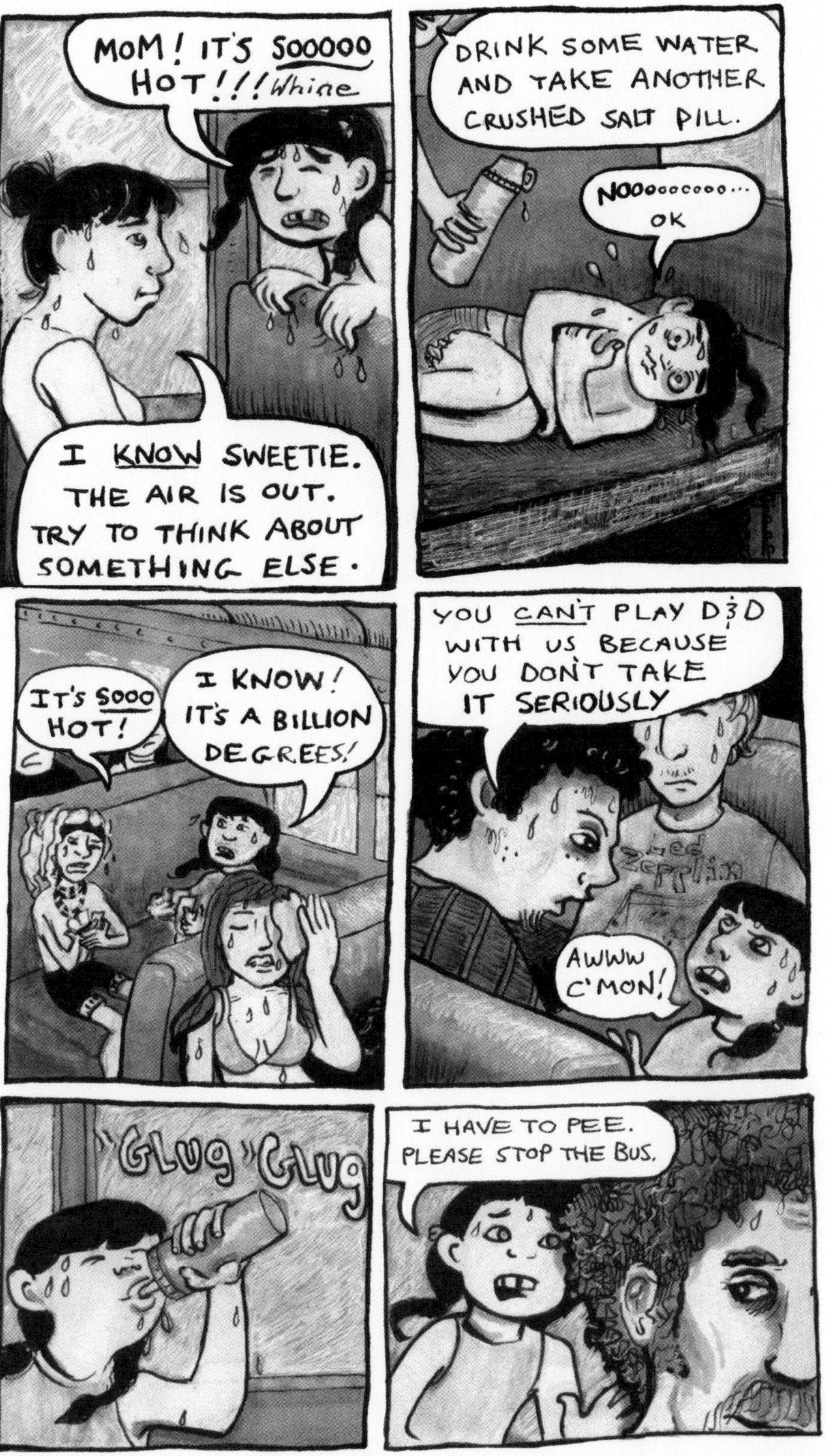
MOM! IT'S SOOOOO HOT!!! Whine
I KNOW SWEETIE. THE AIR IS OUT. TRY TO THINK ABOUT SOMETHING ELSE.
DRINK SOME WATER AND TAKE ANOTHER CRUSHED SALT PILL.
NOOooocooo... OK
IT'S SOOO HOT!
I KNOW! IT'S A BILLION DEGREES!
YOU CAN'T PLAY D&D WITH US BECAUSE YOU DON'T TAKE IT SERIOUSLY
Led Zepplin
AWWW C'MON!
Glug Glug
I HAVE TO PEE. PLEASE STOP THE BUS.

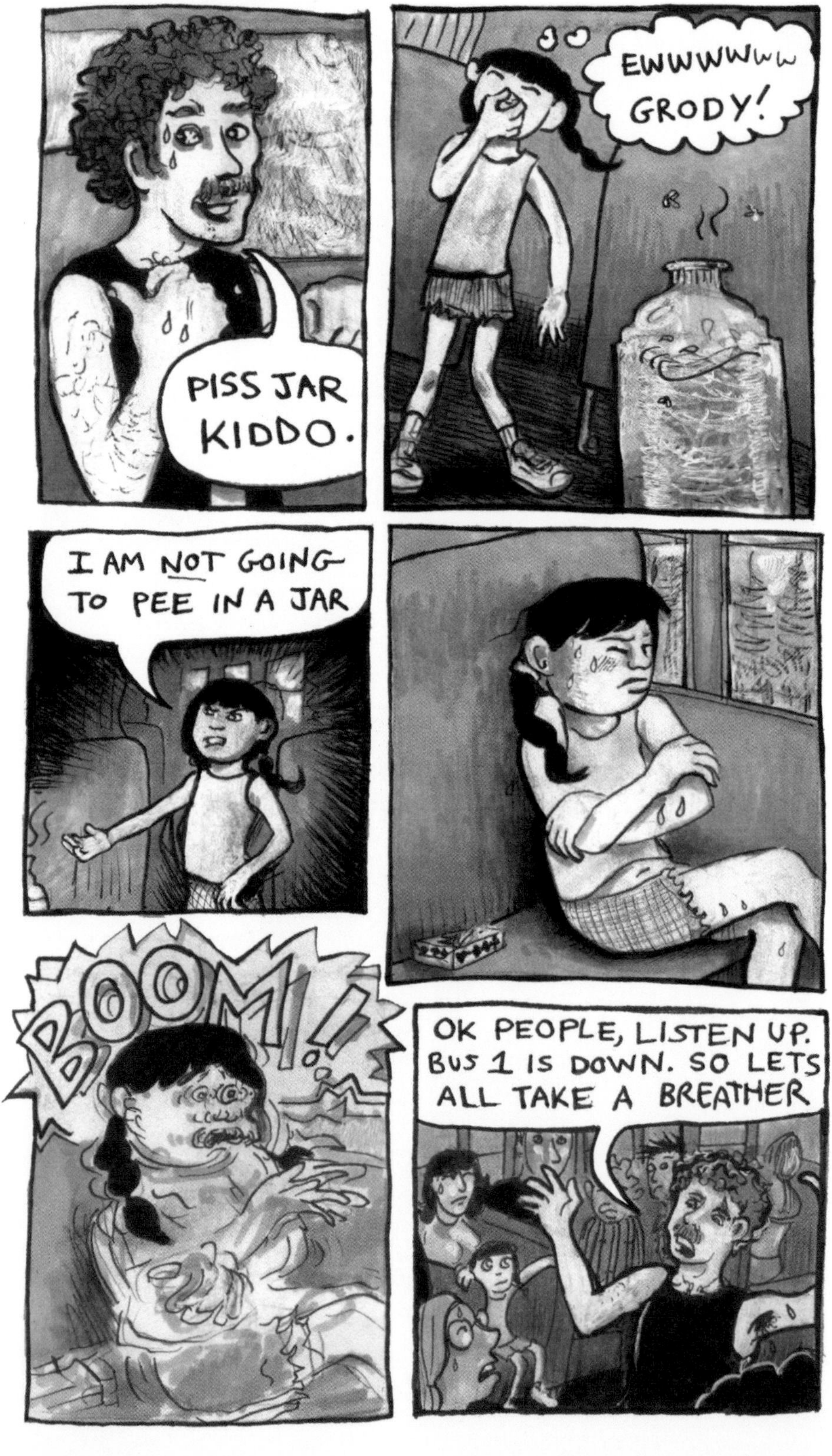
PISS JAR KIDDO.
EWWWWWW GRODY!
I AM NOT GOING TO PEE IN A JAR
BOOM!
OK PEOPLE, LISTEN UP. BUS 1 IS DOWN. SO LETS ALL TAKE A BREATHER

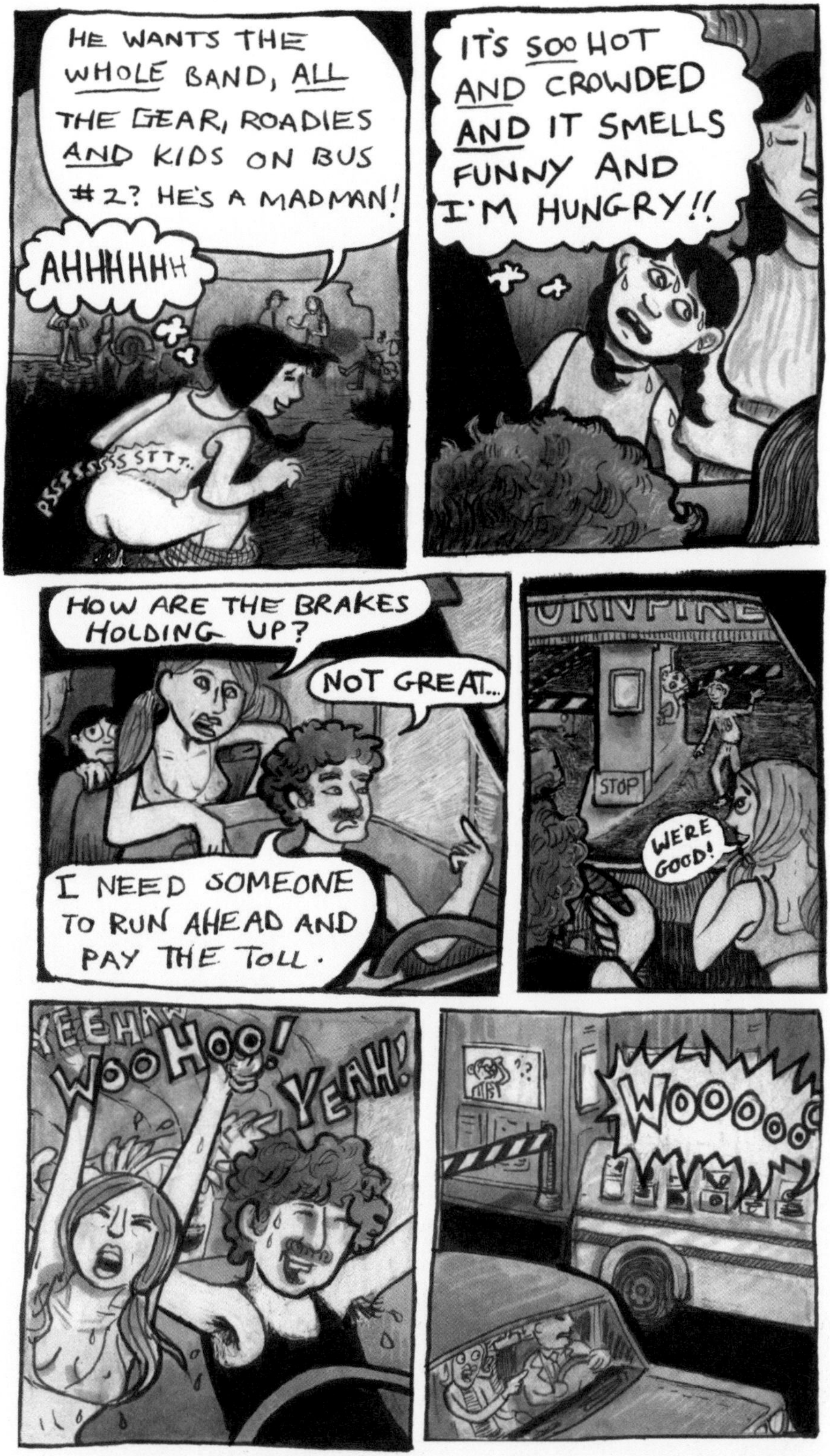
HE WANTS THE WHOLE BAND, ALL THE GEAR, ROADIES AND KIDS ON BUS #2? HE'S A MADMAN!
AHHHHHH
PSSSSSSSSSTTT..
IT'S SOO HOT AND CROWDED AND IT SMELLS FUNNY AND I'M HUNGRY!!
HOW ARE THE BRAKES HOLDING UP?
NOT GREAT...
I NEED SOMEONE TO RUN AHEAD AND PAY THE TOLL.
STOP
WE'RE GOOD!
YEEHAW
WOOHOO!
YEAH!
WOOOO..

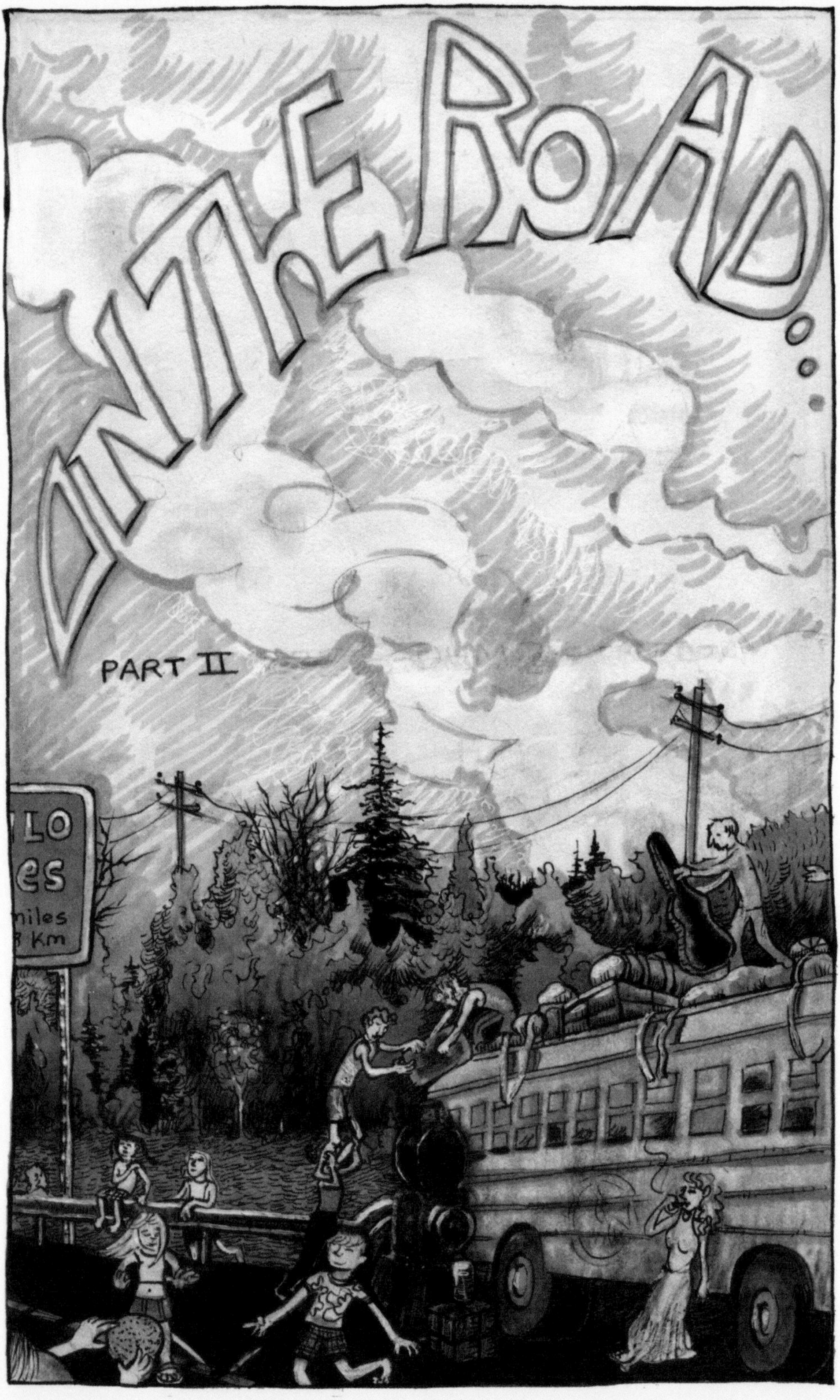
ON THE ROAD...
PART II
LO
es
miles
Km

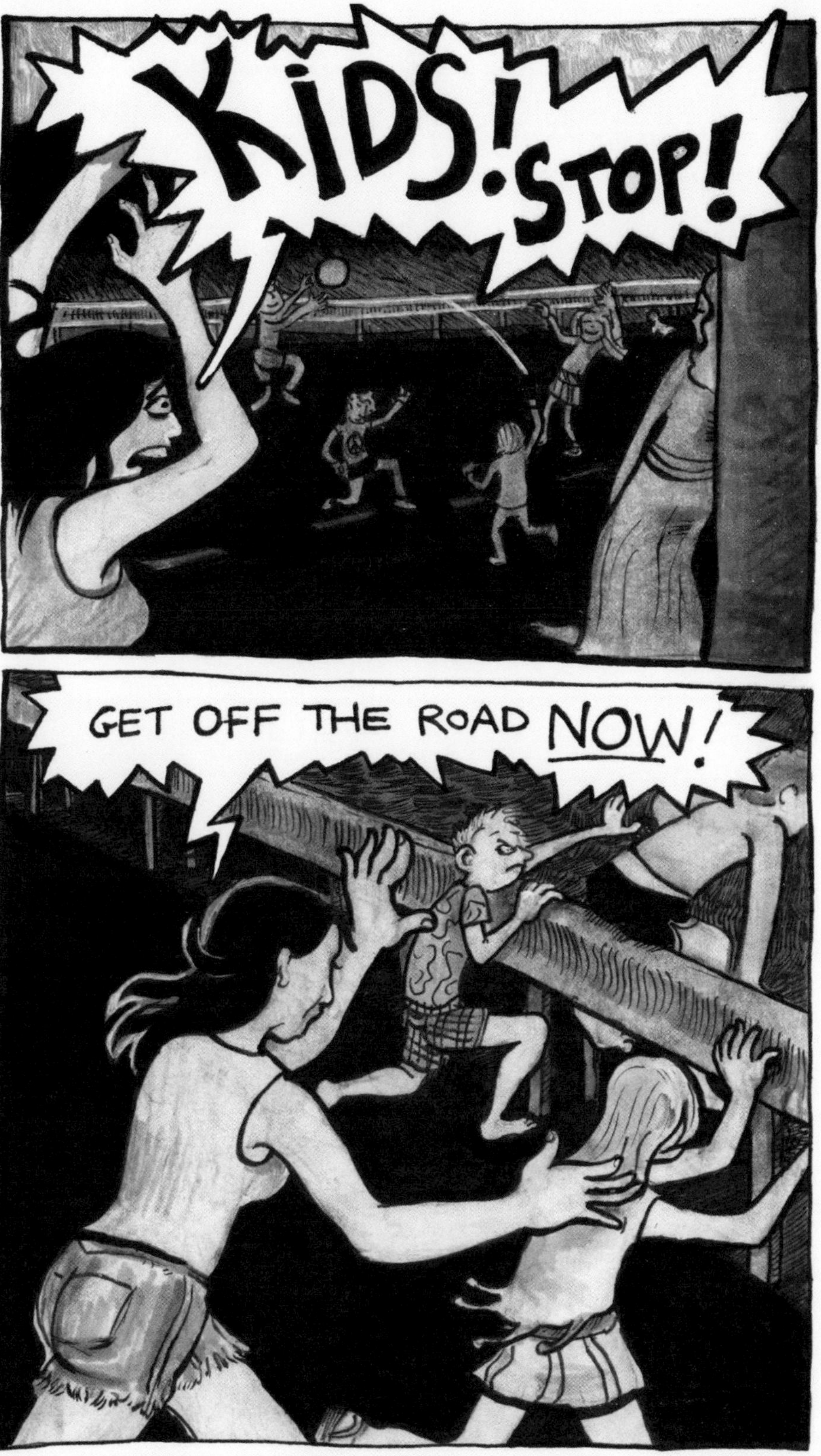
KIDS! STOP!
GET OFF THE ROAD NOW!

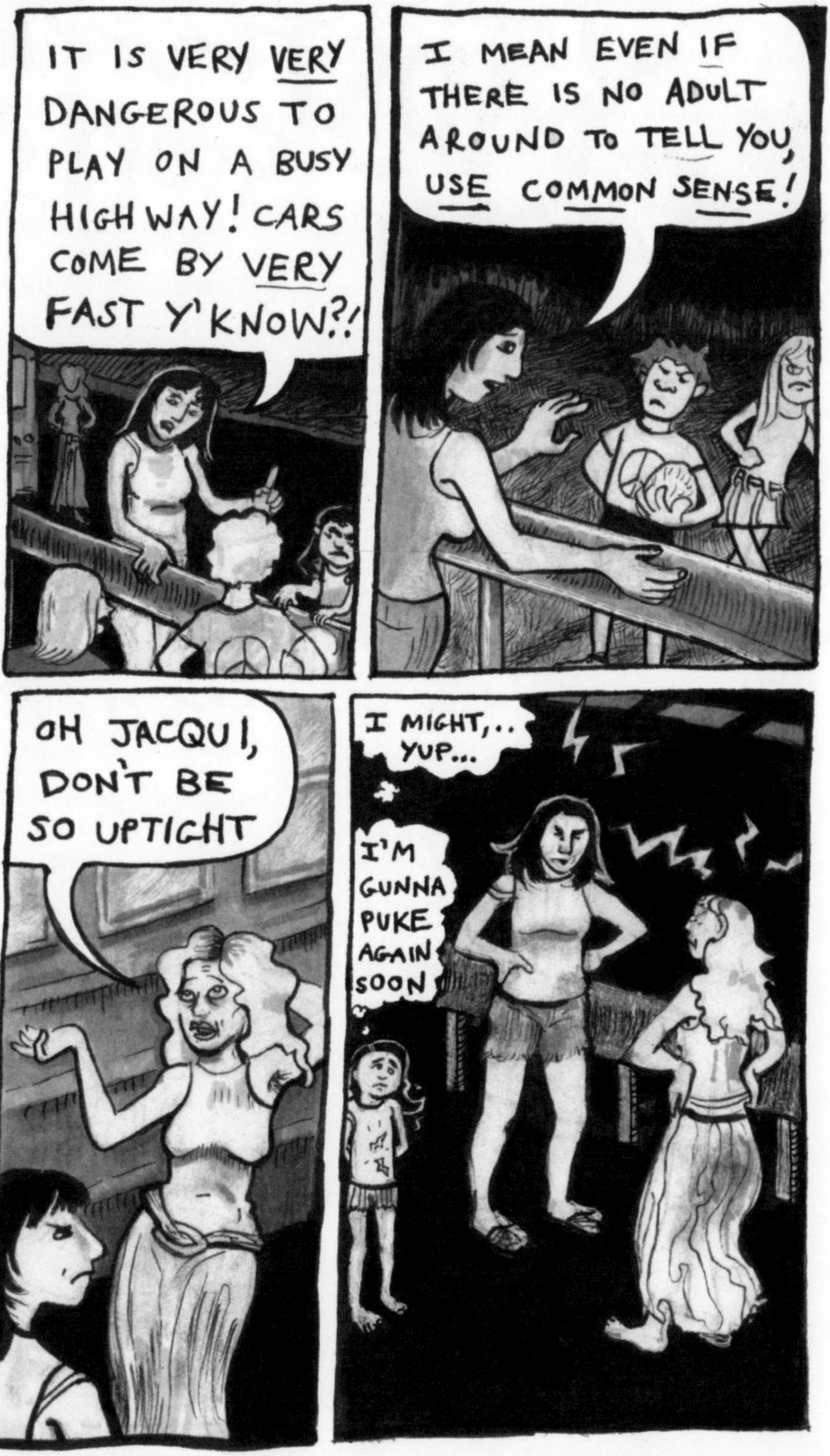
IT IS VERY VERY DANGEROUS TO PLAY ON A BUSY HIGHWAY! CARS COME BY VERY FAST Y'KNOW?!
I MEAN EVEN IF THERE IS NO ADULT AROUND TO TELL YOU, USE COMMON SENSE!
OH JACQUI, DON'T BE SO UPTIGHT
I MIGHT,.. YUP...
I'M GUNNA PUKE AGAIN SOON

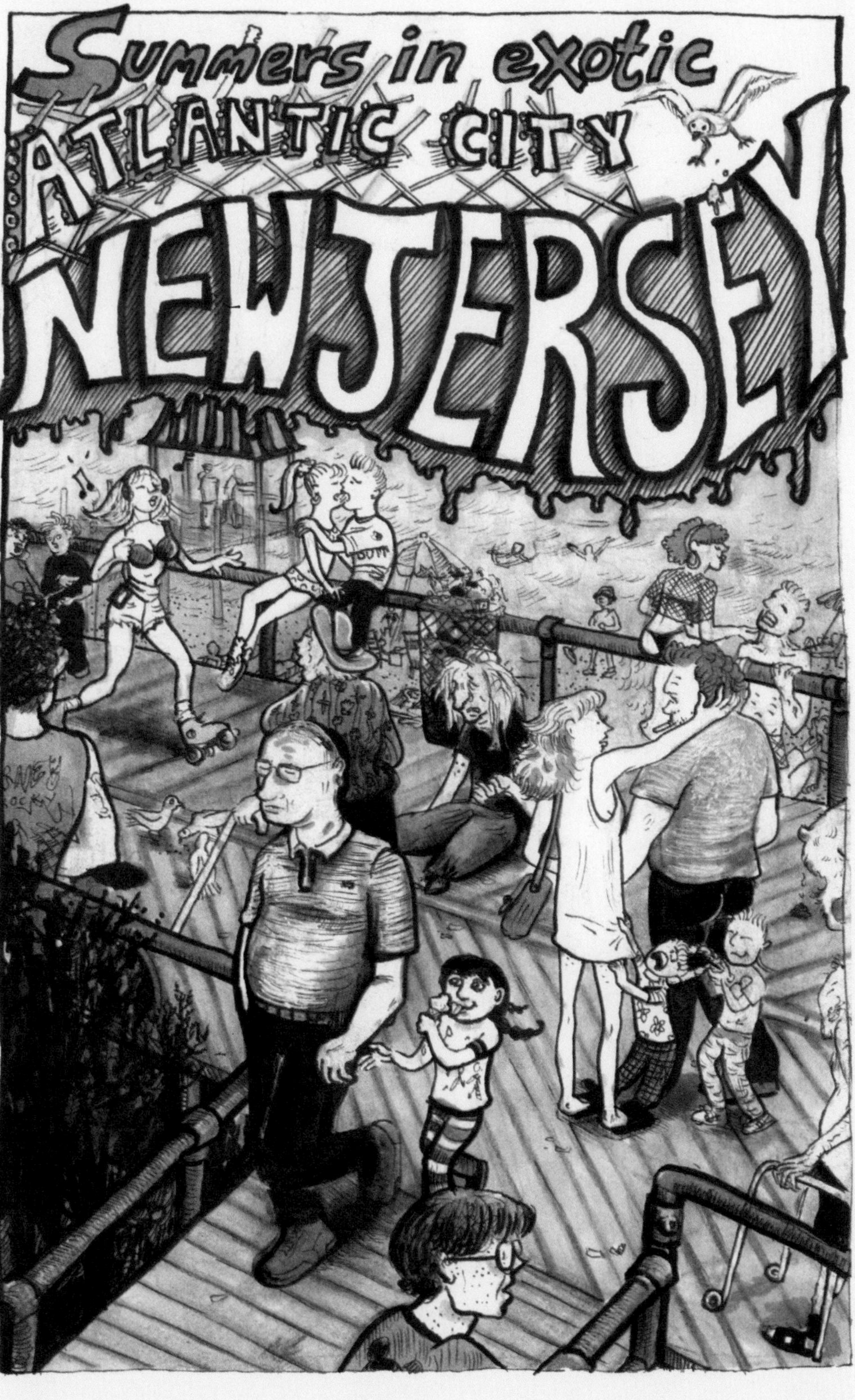
Summers in exotic
ATLANTIC CITY
NEW JERSEY

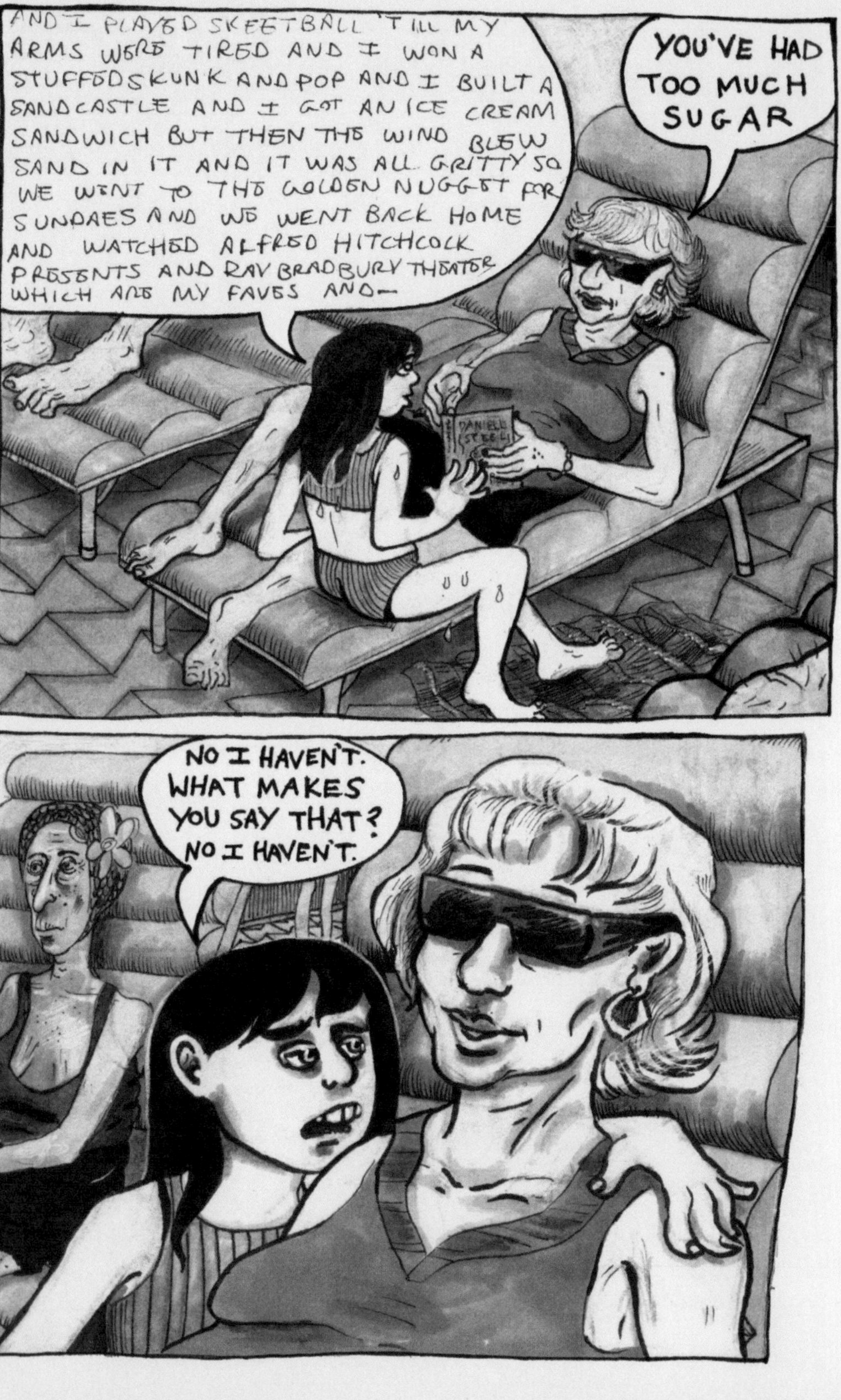
AND I PLAYED SKEETBALL 'TILL MY ARMS WERE TIRED AND I WON A STUFFED SKUNK AND POP AND I BUILT A SANDCASTLE AND I GOT AN ICE CREAM SANDWICH BUT THEN THE WIND BLEW SAND IN IT AND IT WAS ALL GRITTY SO WE WENT TO THE GOLDEN NUGGET FOR SUNDAES AND WE WENT BACK HOME AND WATCHED ALFRED HITCHCOCK PRESENTS AND RAY BRADBURY THEATER WHICH ARE MY FAVES AND—
YOU'VE HAD TOO MUCH SUGAR
DANIELLE STEEL
NO I HAVEN'T. WHAT MAKES YOU SAY THAT? NO I HAVEN'T.

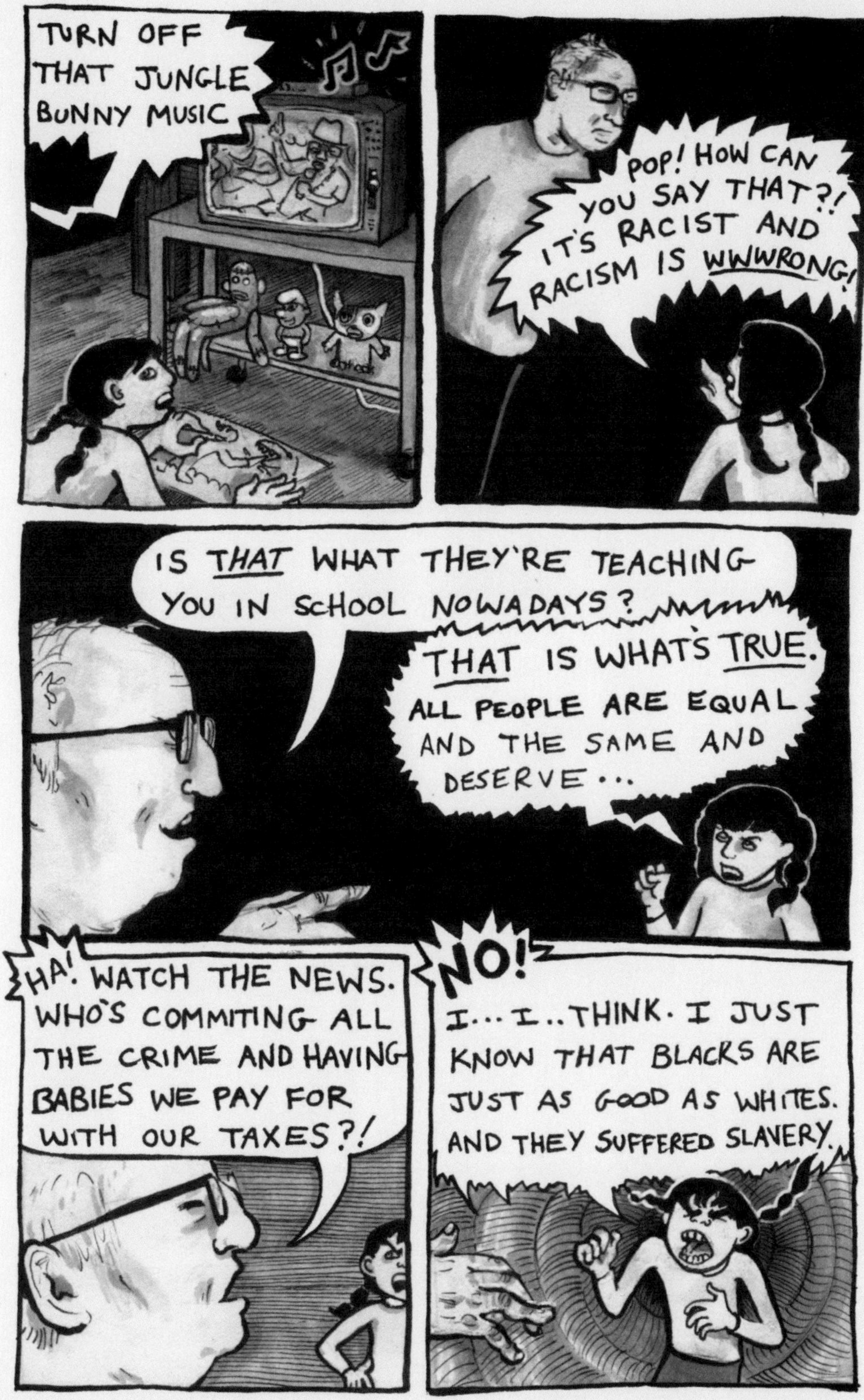
TURN OFF THAT JUNGLE BUNNY MUSIC
POP! HOW CAN YOU SAY THAT?! IT'S RACIST AND RACISM IS WWWRONG!
IS THAT WHAT THEY'RE TEACHING YOU IN SCHOOL NOWADAYS?
THAT IS WHAT'S TRUE. ALL PEOPLE ARE EQUAL AND THE SAME AND DESERVE...
HA! WATCH THE NEWS. WHO'S COMMITING ALL THE CRIME AND HAVING BABIES WE PAY FOR WITH OUR TAXES?!
NO!
I... I.. THINK. I JUST KNOW THAT BLACKS ARE JUST AS GOOD AS WHITES. AND THEY SUFFERED SLAVERY.

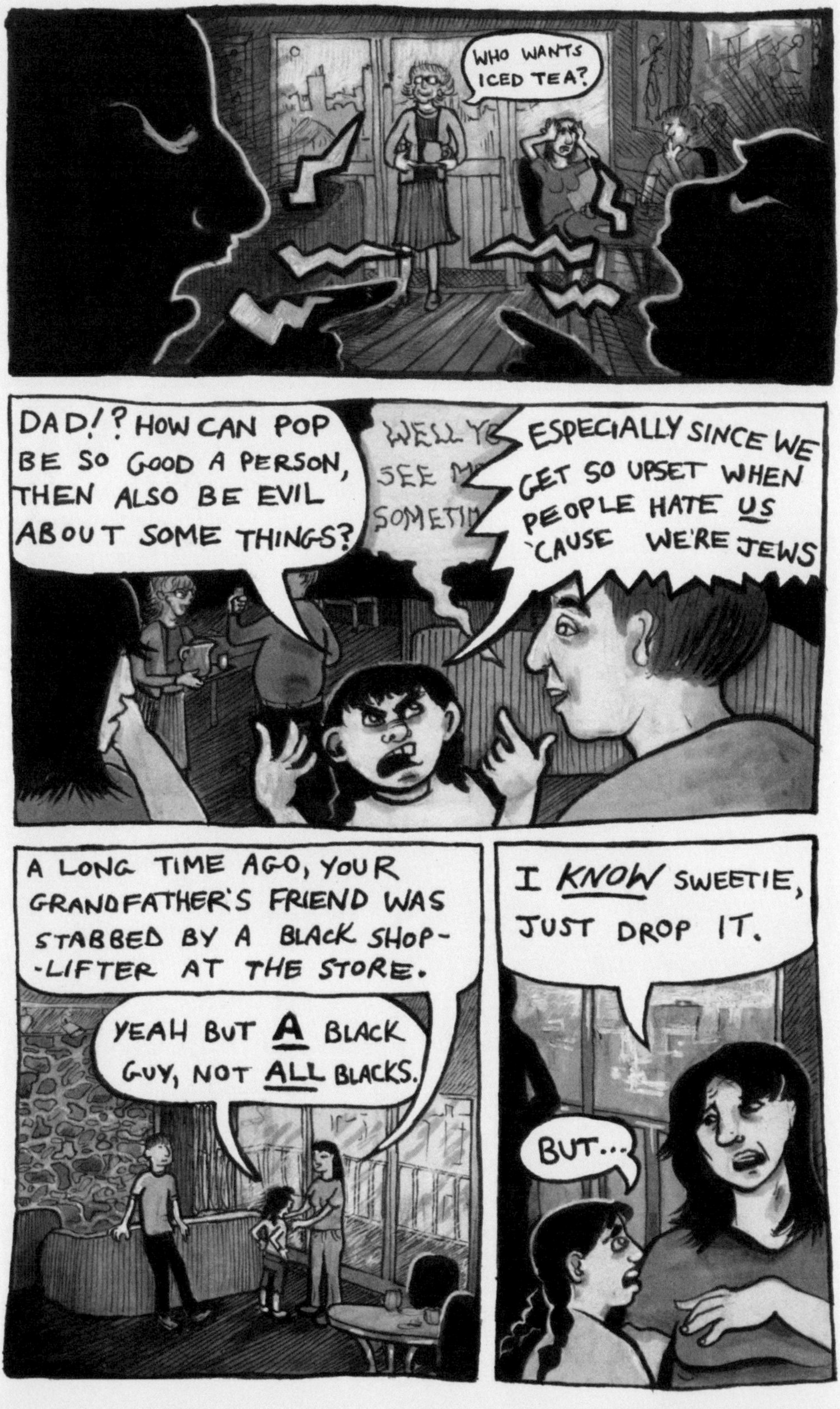
WHO WANTS ICED TEA?
DAD!? HOW CAN POP BE SO GOOD A PERSON, THEN ALSO BE EVIL ABOUT SOME THINGS?
ESPECIALLY SINCE WE GET SO UPSET WHEN PEOPLE HATE US 'CAUSE WE'RE JEWS
A LONG TIME AGO, YOUR GRANDFATHER'S FRIEND WAS STABBED BY A BLACK SHOP--LIFTER AT THE STORE.
YEAH BUT A BLACK GUY, NOT ALL BLACKS.
I KNOW SWEETIE, JUST DROP IT.
BUT...

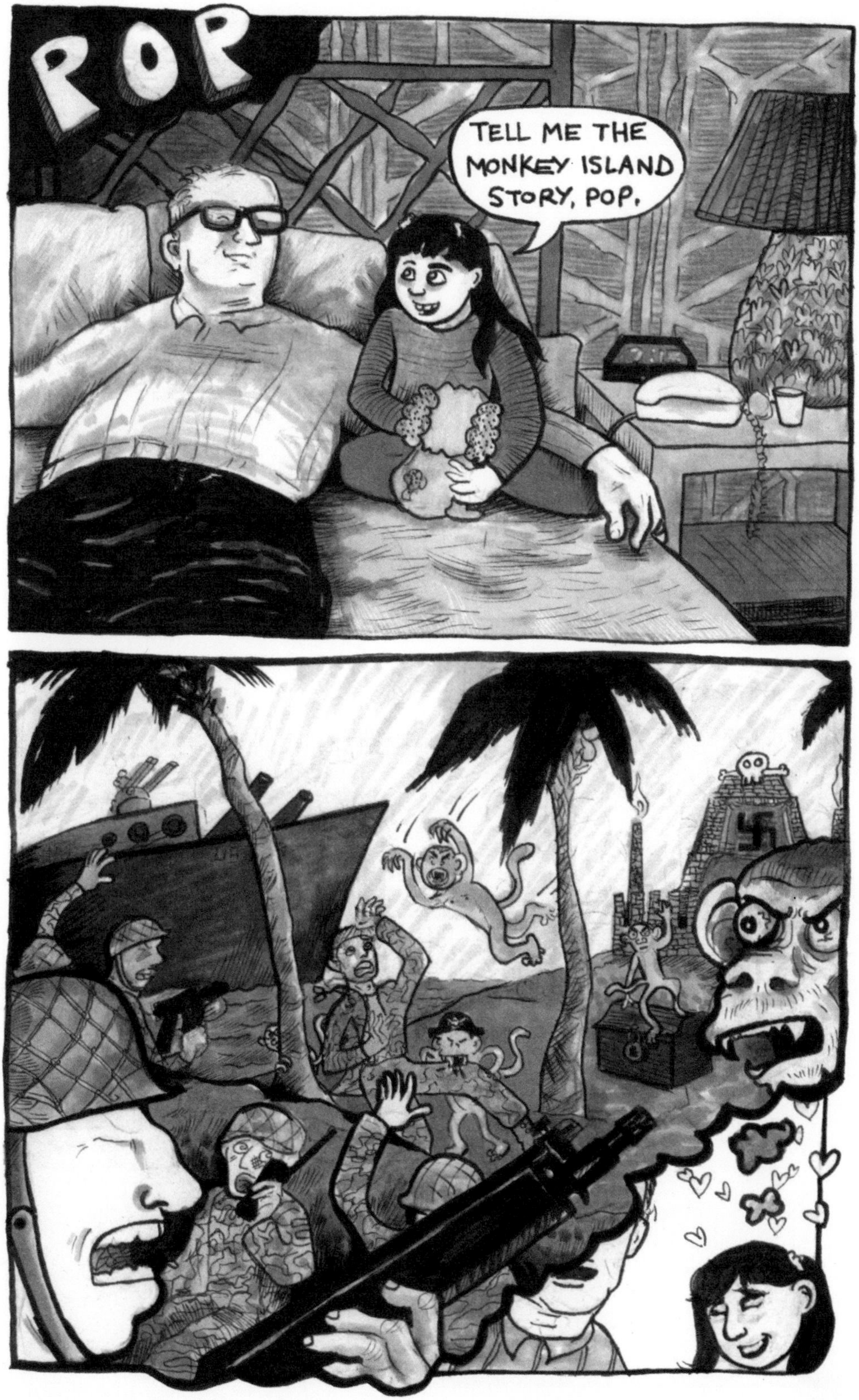
POP
TELL ME THE MONKEY ISLAND STORY, POP.

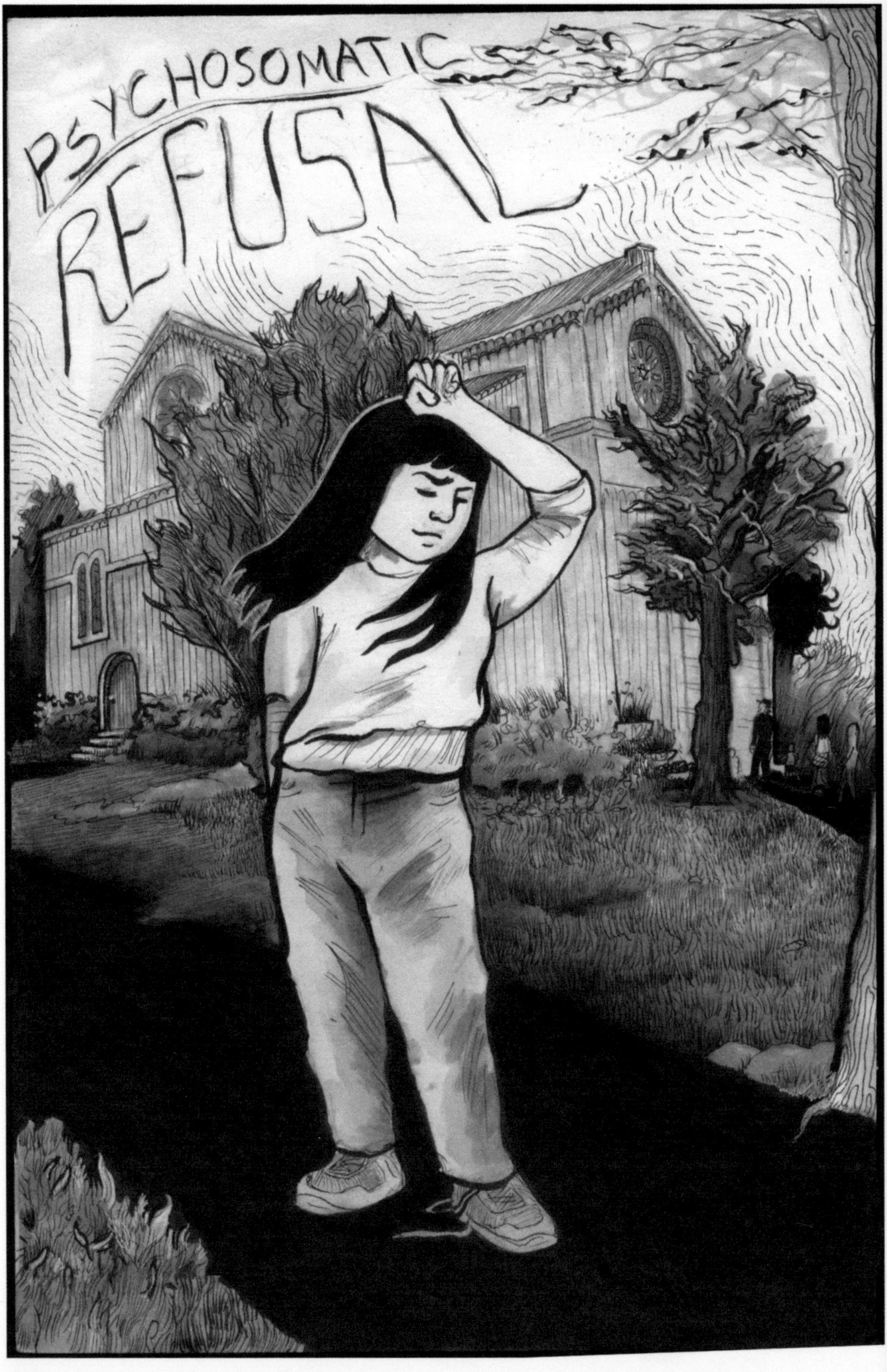
PSYCHOSOMATIC
REFUSAL

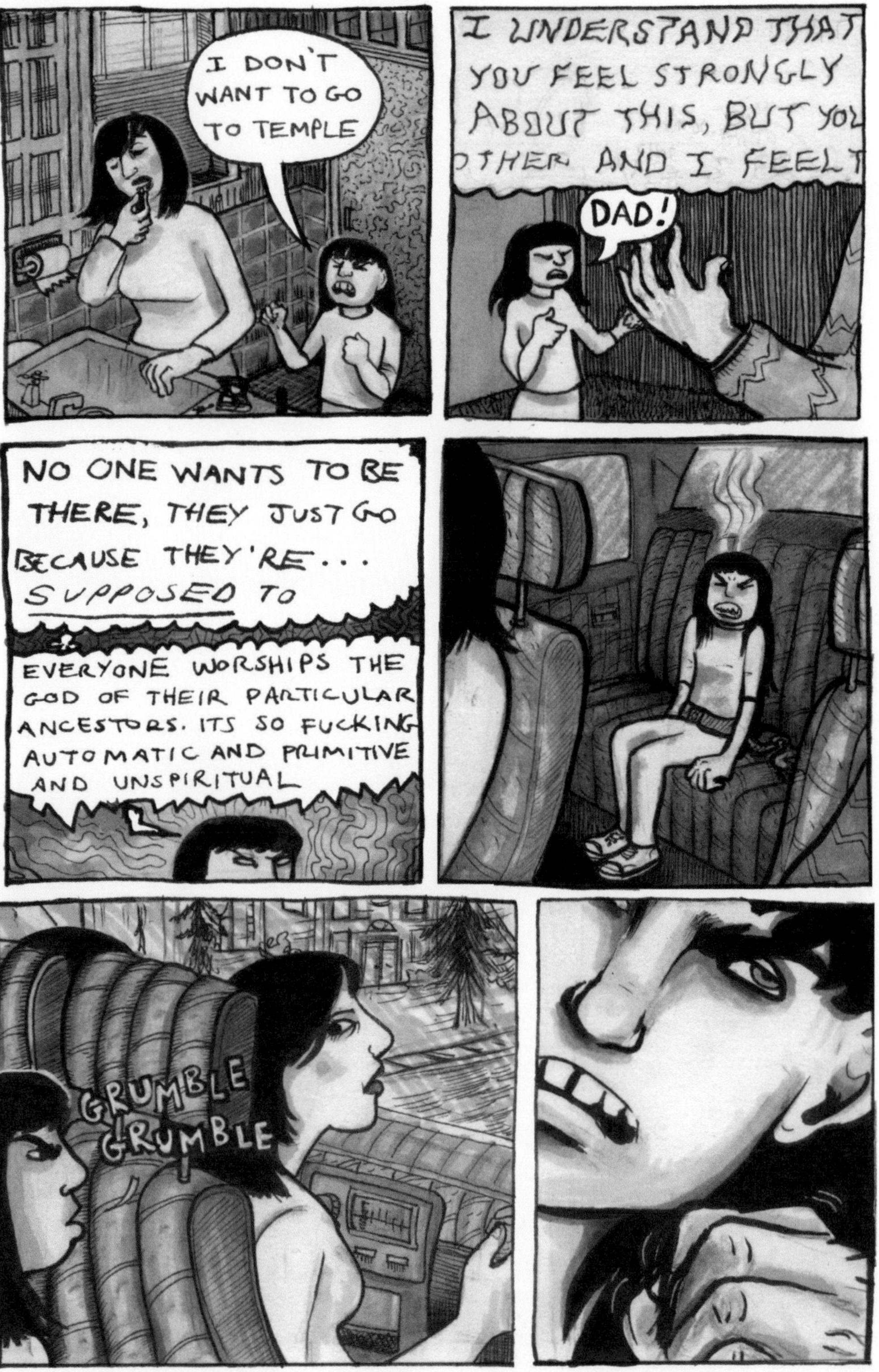
I DON'T WANT TO GO TO TEMPLE
I UNDERSTAND THAT YOU FEEL STRONGLY ABOUT THIS, BUT YOU OTHER AND I FEEL T
DAD!
NO ONE WANTS TO BE THERE, THEY JUST GO BECAUSE THEY'RE... SUPPOSED TO
EVERYONE WORSHIPS THE GOD OF THEIR PARTICULAR ANCESTORS. ITS SO FUCKING AUTOMATIC AND PRIMITIVE AND UNSPIRITUAL
GRUMBLE GRUMBLE

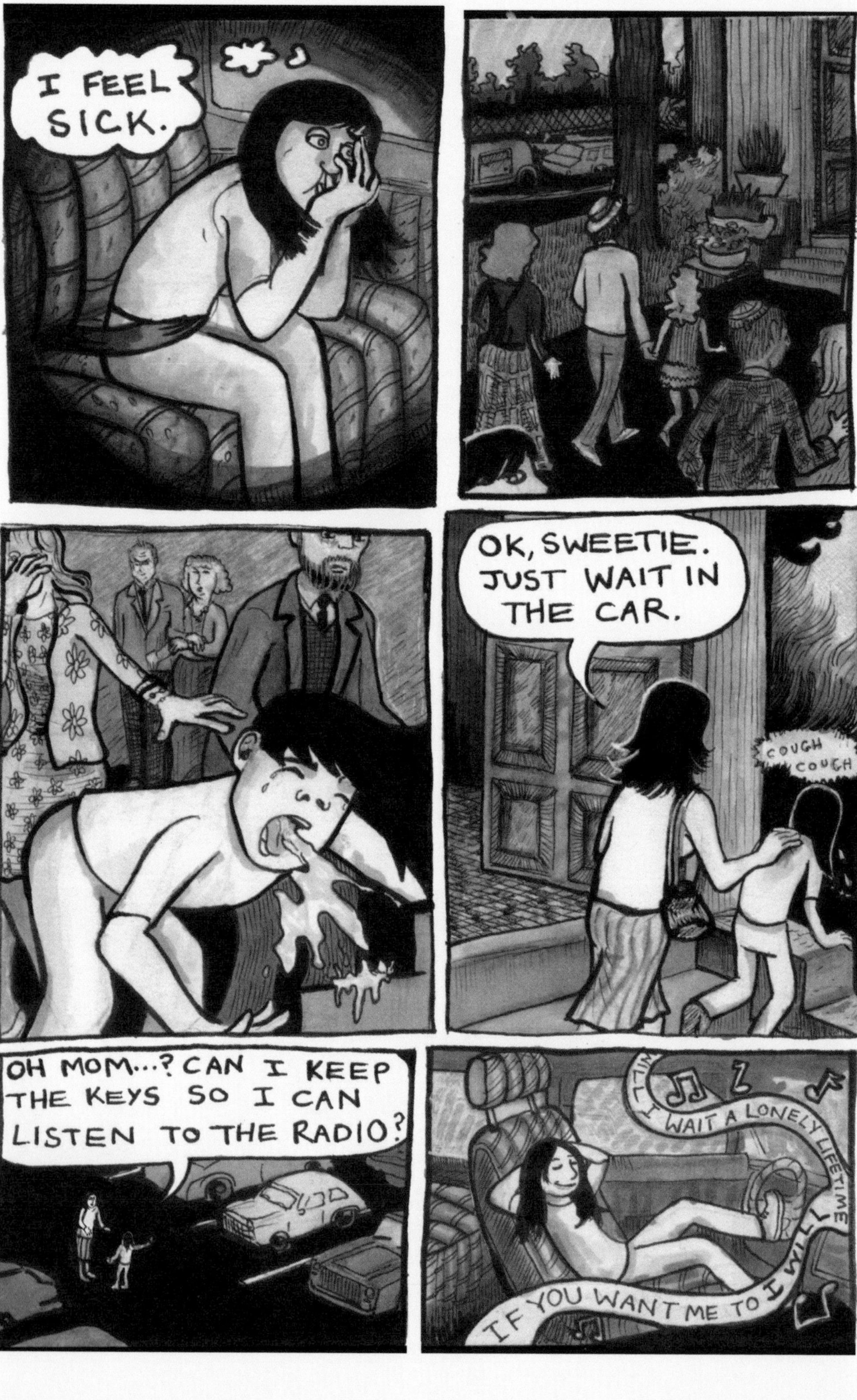
I FEEL SICK.
OK, SWEETIE. JUST WAIT IN THE CAR.
COUGH COUGH
OH MOM...? CAN I KEEP THE KEYS SO I CAN LISTEN TO THE RADIO?
WILL I WAIT A LONELY LIFETIME
IF YOU WANT ME TO I WILL

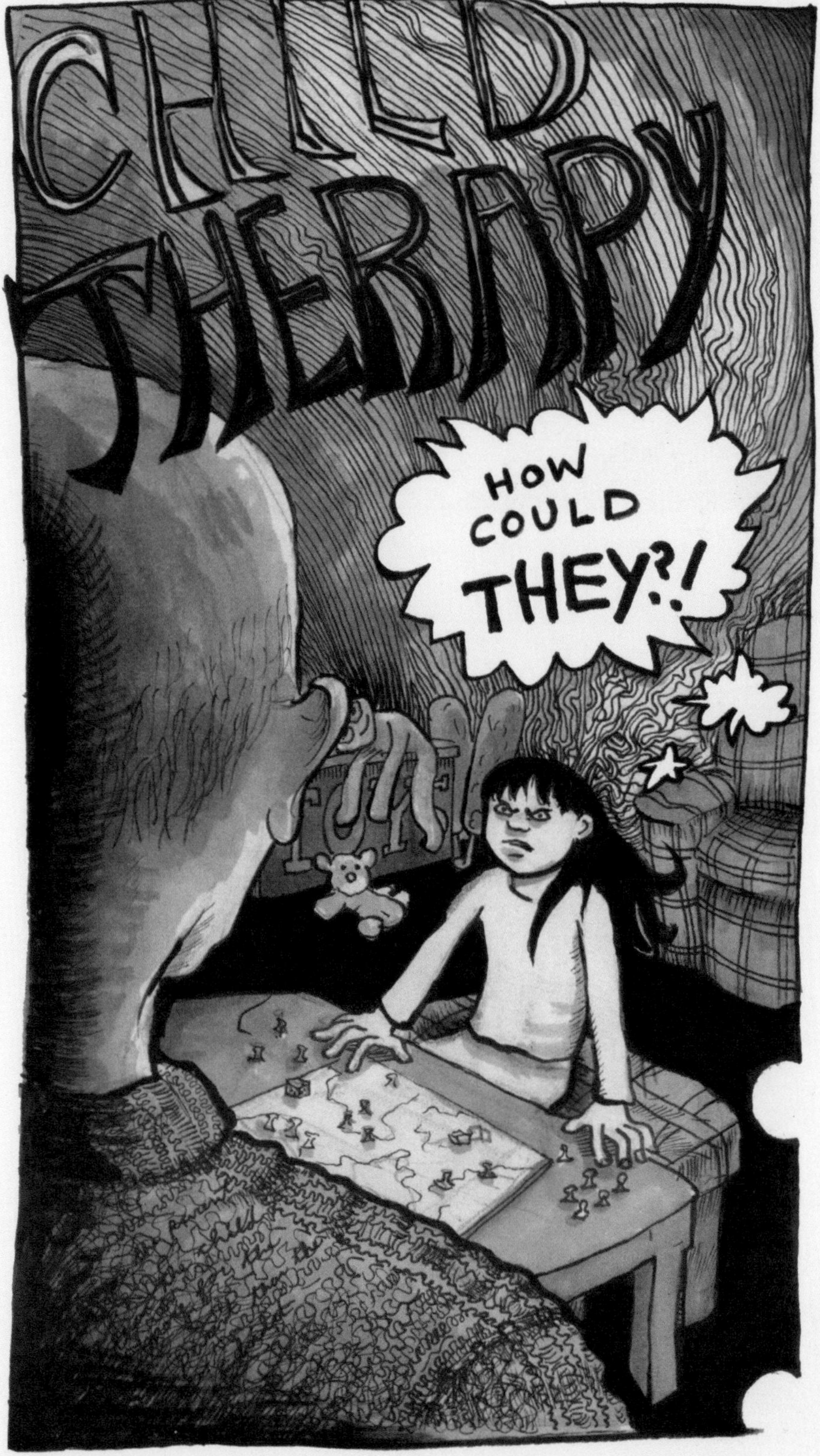
CHILD THERAPY
HOW COULD THEY?!

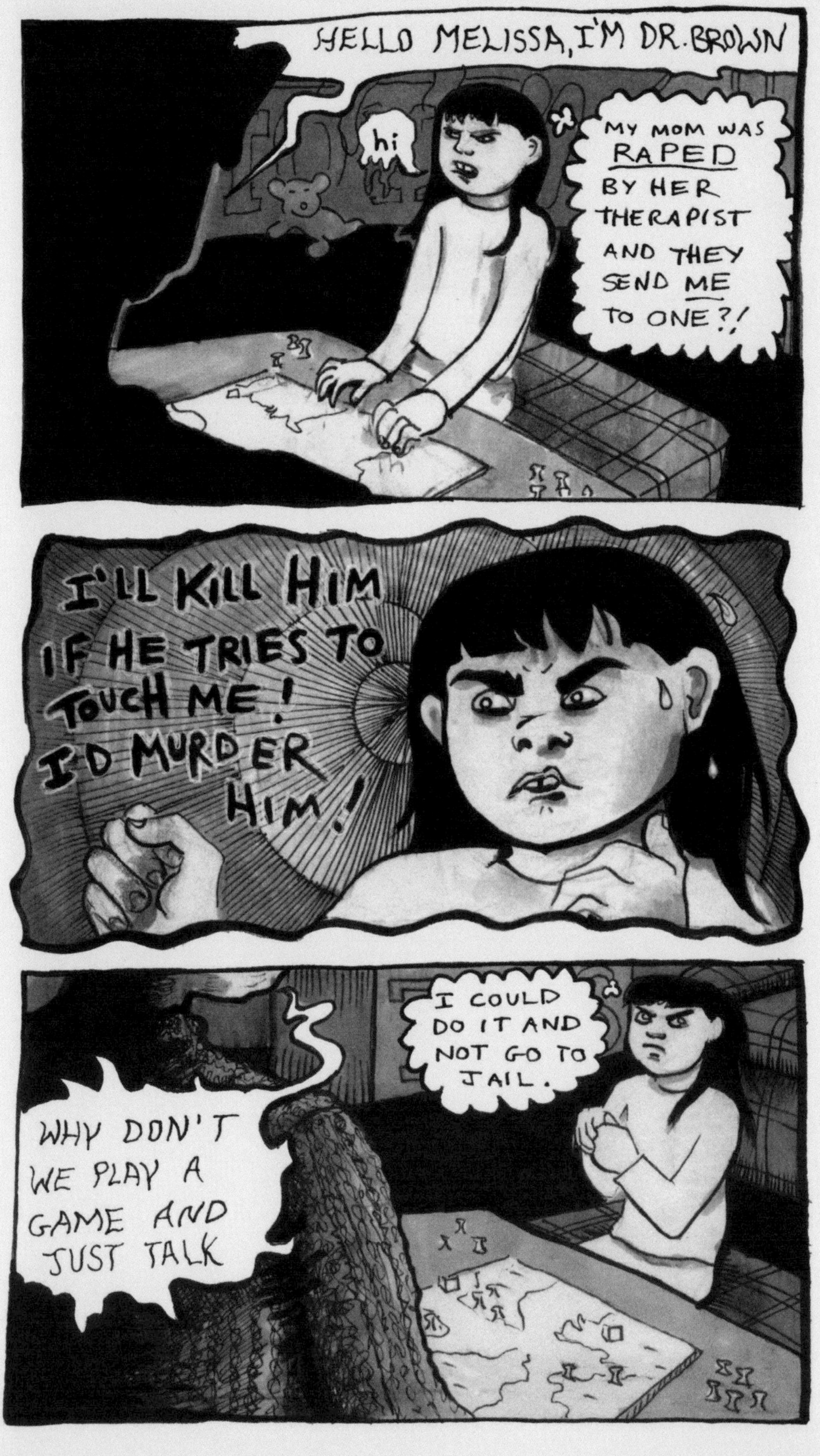
HELLO MELISSA, I'M DR. BROWN
hi
MY MOM WAS RAPED BY HER THERAPIST AND THEY SEND ME TO ONE?!
I'LL KILL HIM IF HE TRIES TO TOUCH ME! I'D MURDER HIM!
I COULD DO IT AND NOT GO TO JAIL.
WHY DON'T WE PLAY A GAME AND JUST TALK

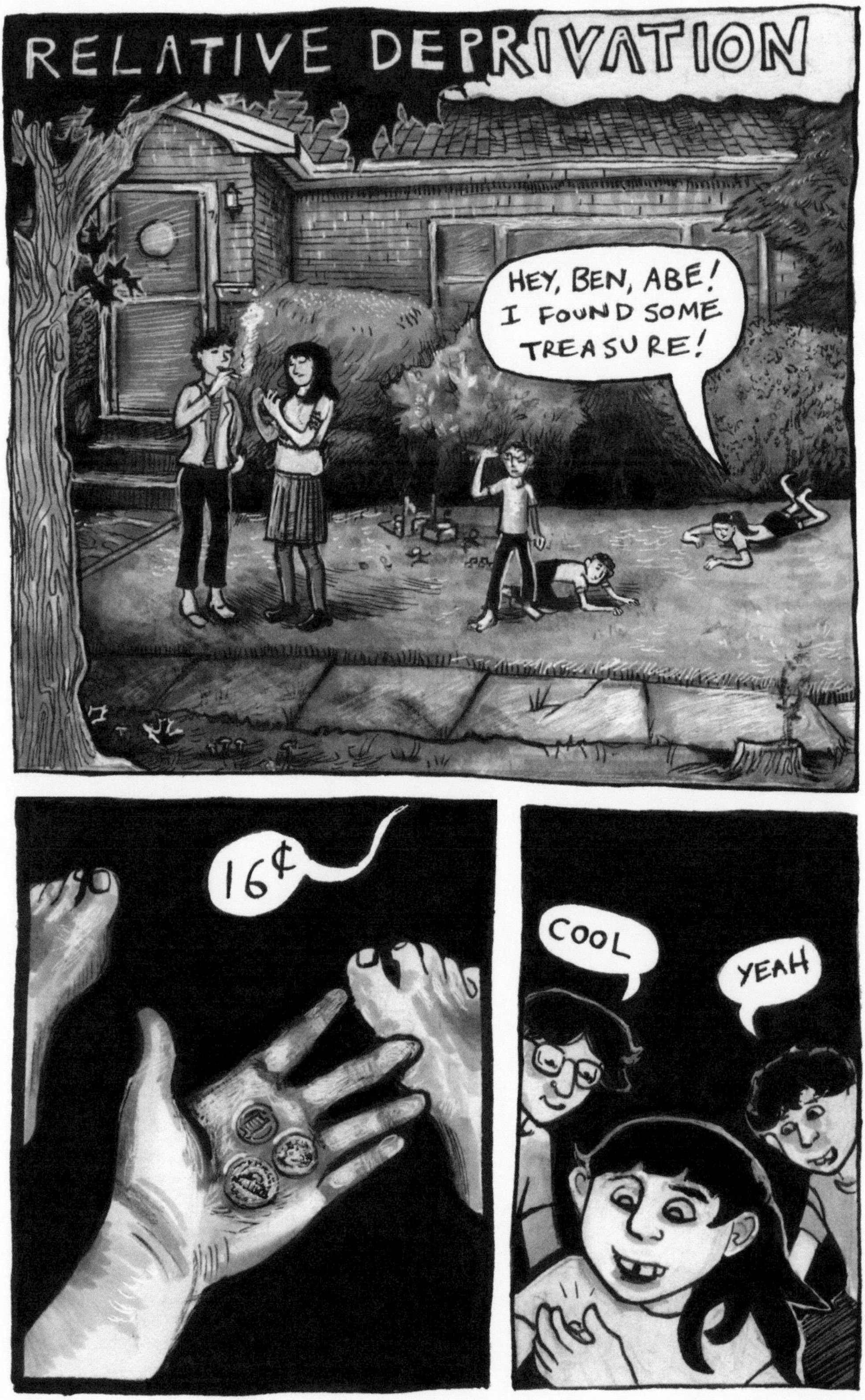
RELATIVE DEPRIVATION
HEY, BEN, ABE! I FOUND SOME TREASURE!
16¢
COOL
YEAH

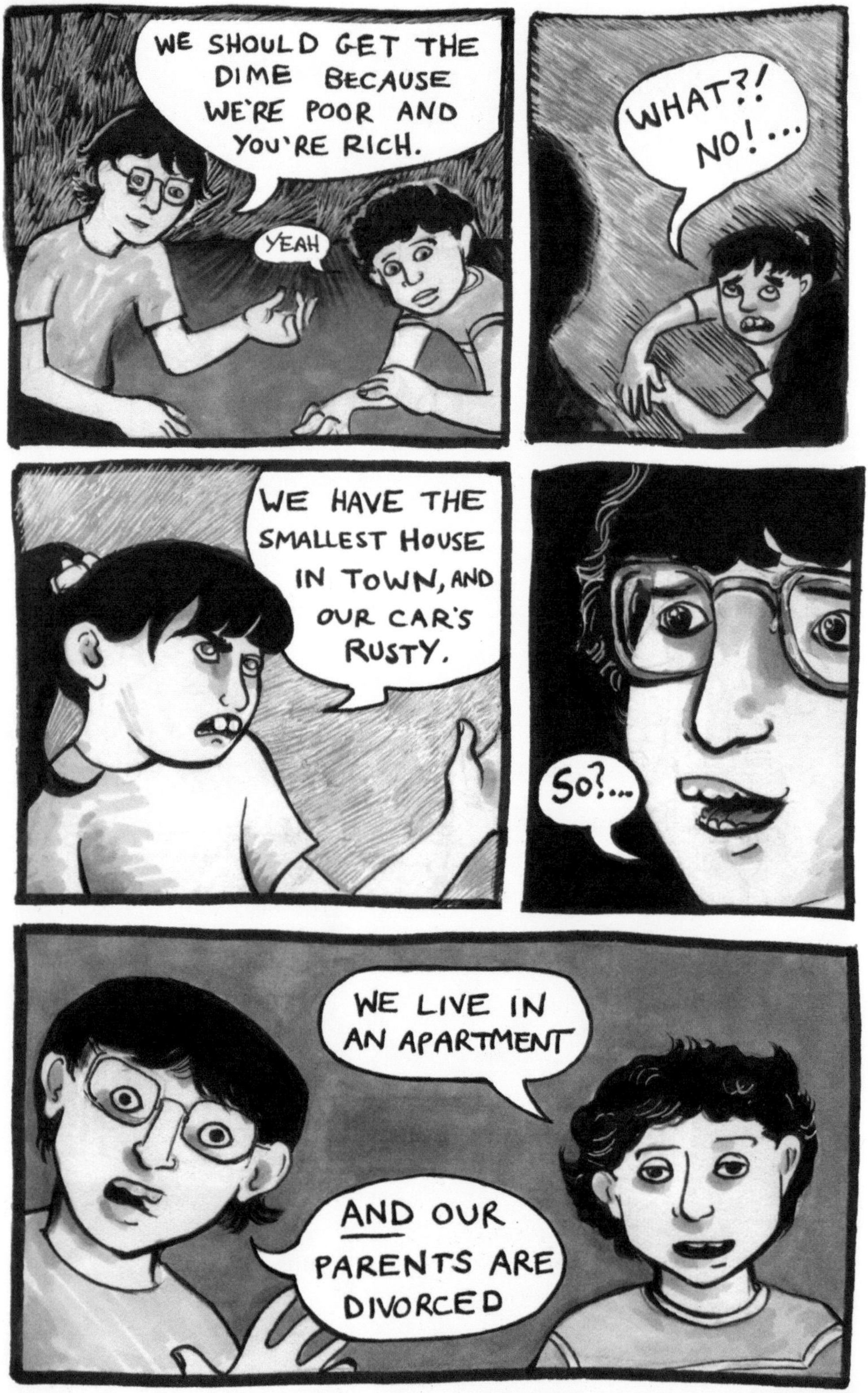
WE SHOULD GET THE DIME BECAUSE WE'RE POOR AND YOU'RE RICH.
YEAH
WHAT?! NO!...
WE HAVE THE SMALLEST HOUSE IN TOWN, AND OUR CAR'S RUSTY.
SO?...
WE LIVE IN AN APARTMENT
AND OUR PARENTS ARE DIVORCED

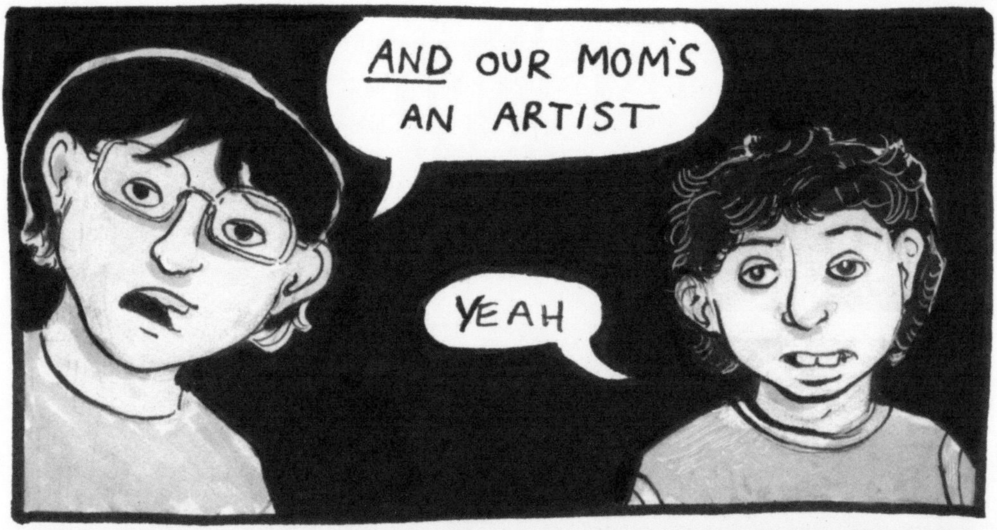
AND OUR MOM'S AN ARTIST
YEAH

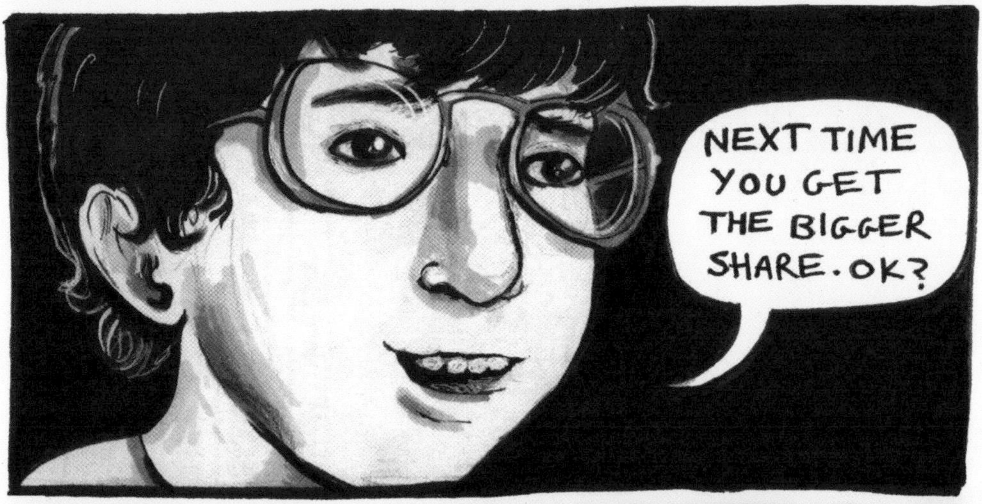
NEXT TIME YOU GET THE BIGGER SHARE. OK?

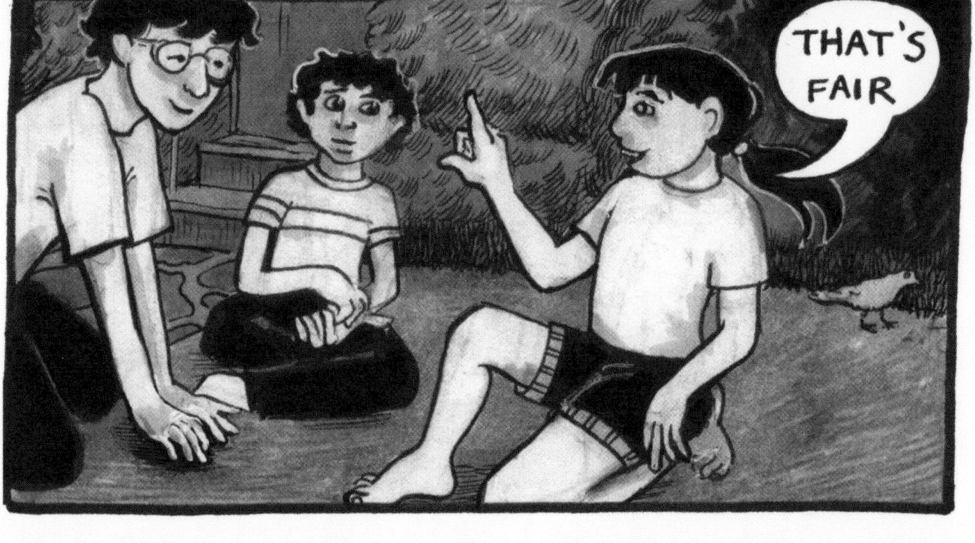
THAT'S FAIR

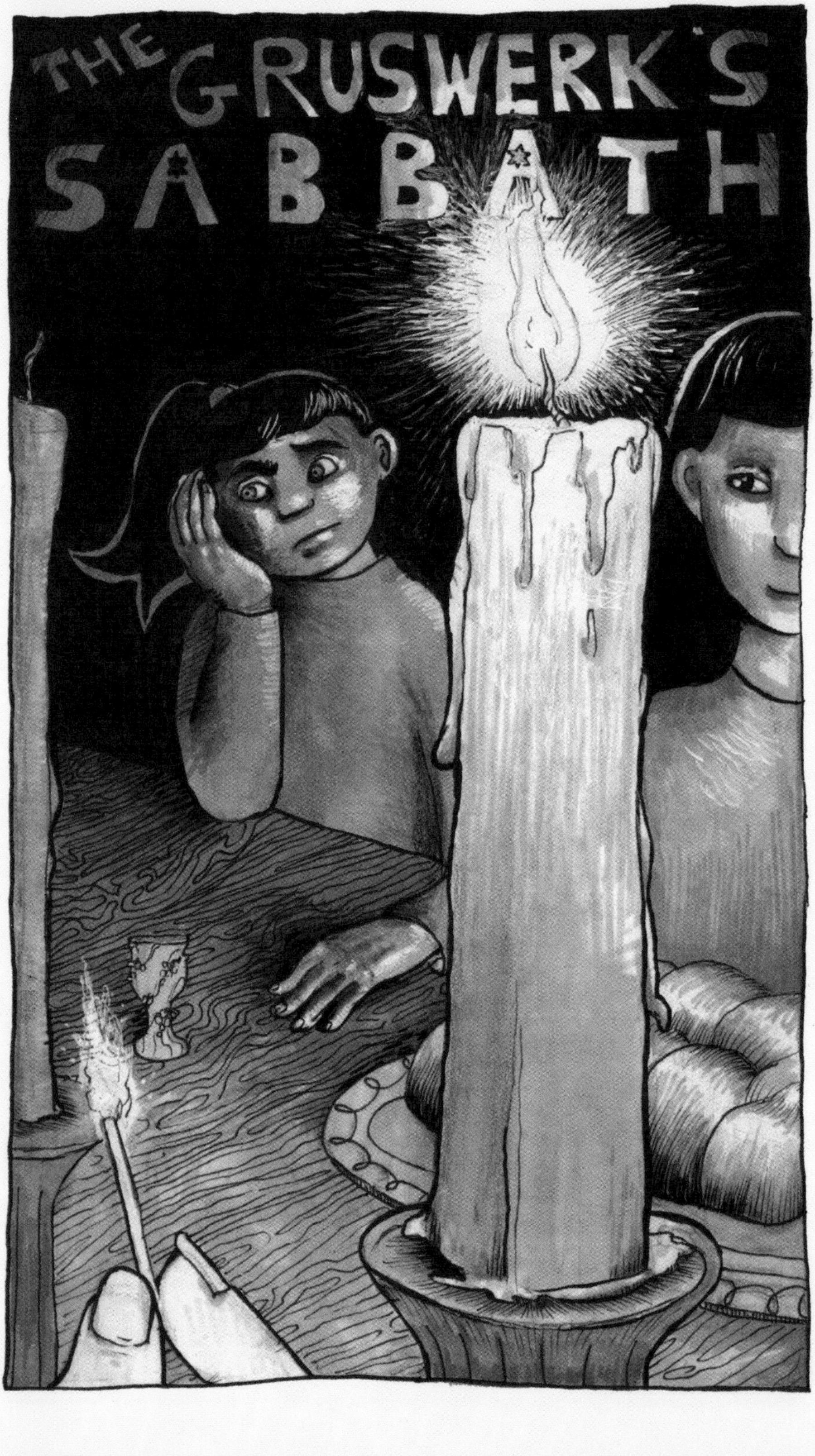
THE GRUSWERK'S
SABBATH

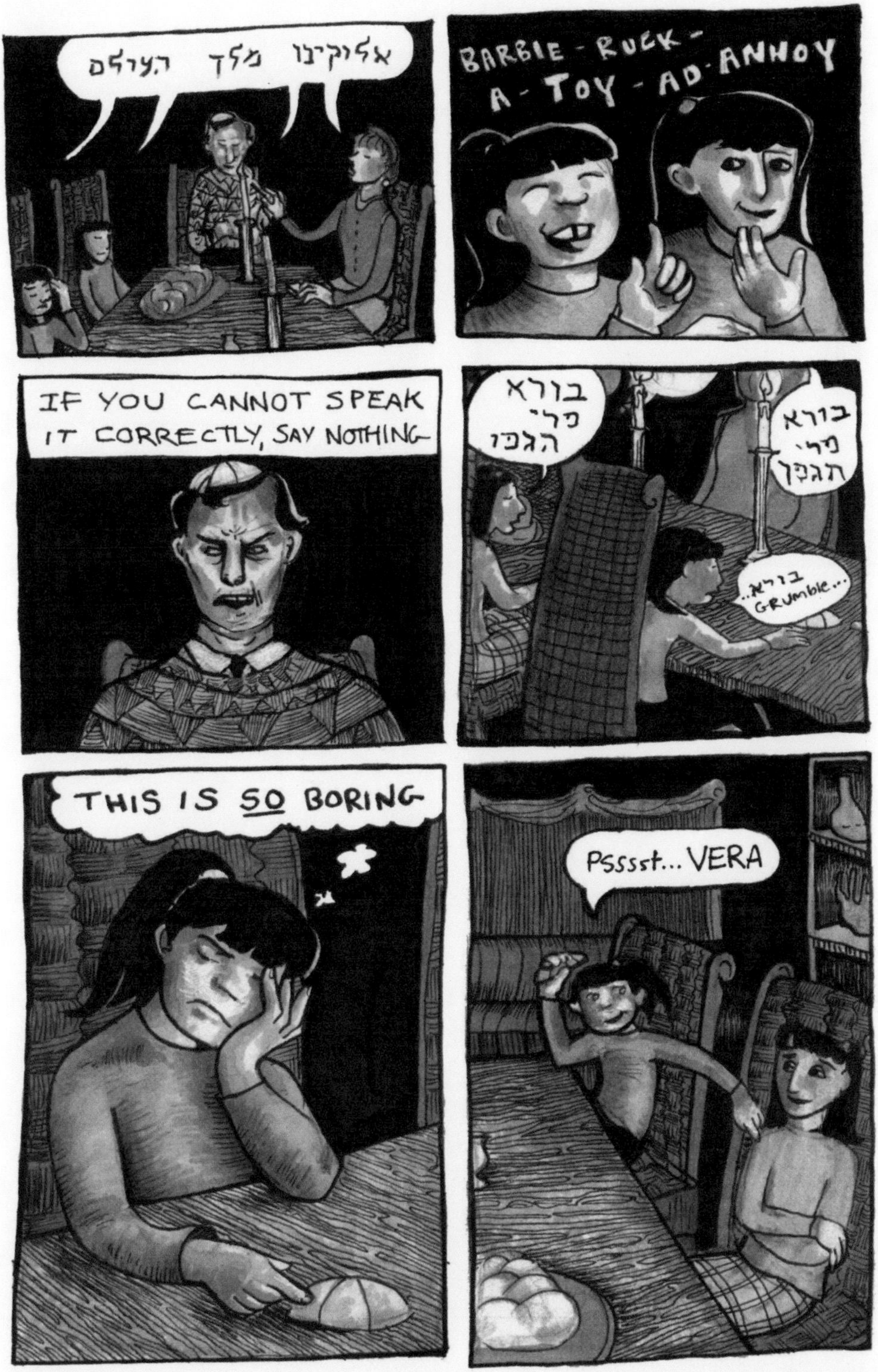
אלוקינו מלך העולם
BARBIE - RUCK - A - TOY - AD - ANNOY
IF YOU CANNOT SPEAK IT CORRECTLY, SAY NOTHING
בורא פרי הגפן
בורא פרי הגפן
..בורא GRUMBLE...
THIS IS SO BORING
PSSSST... VERA

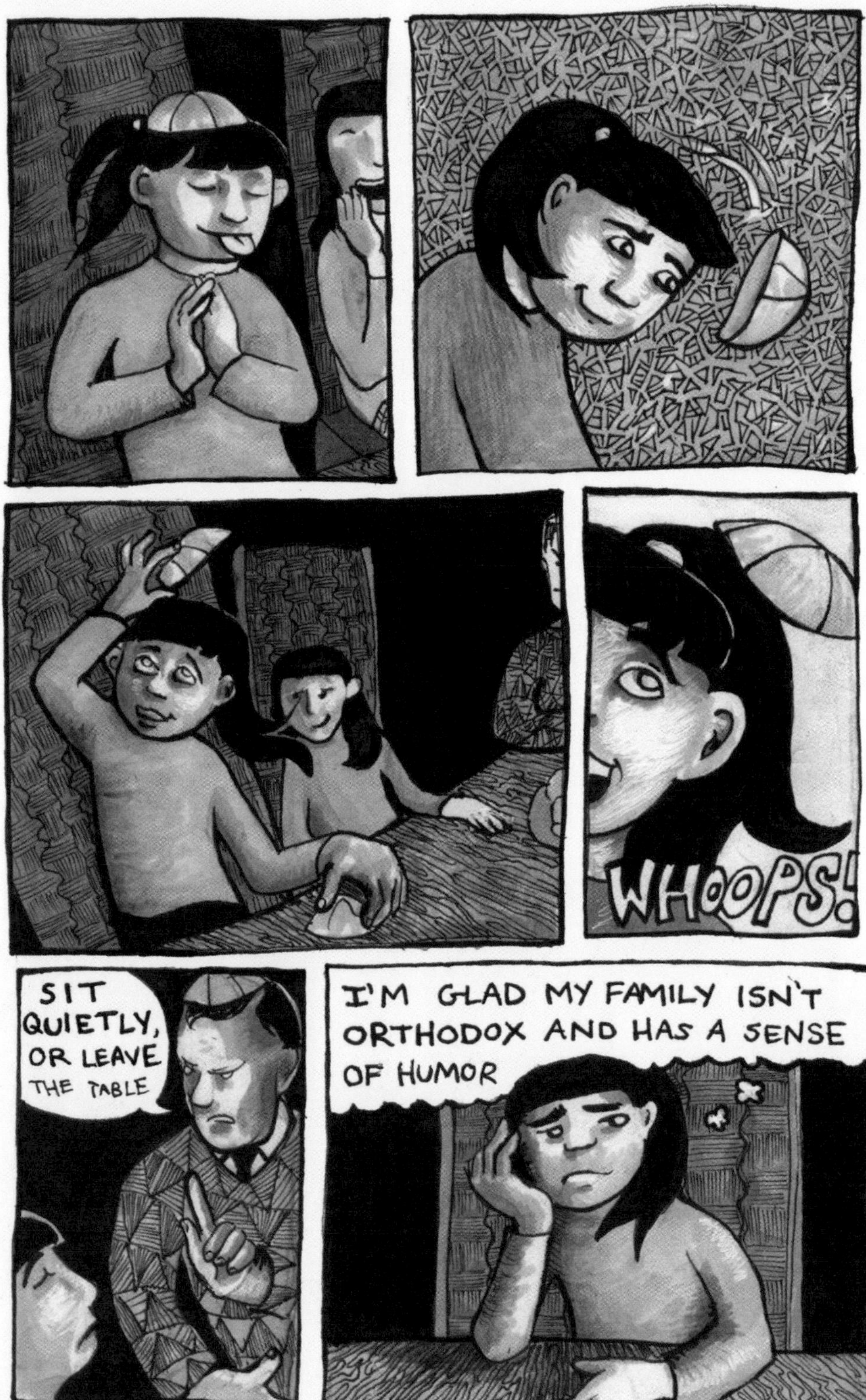
WHOOPS!
SIT QUIETLY, OR LEAVE THE TABLE
I'M GLAD MY FAMILY ISN'T ORTHODOX AND HAS A SENSE OF HUMOR

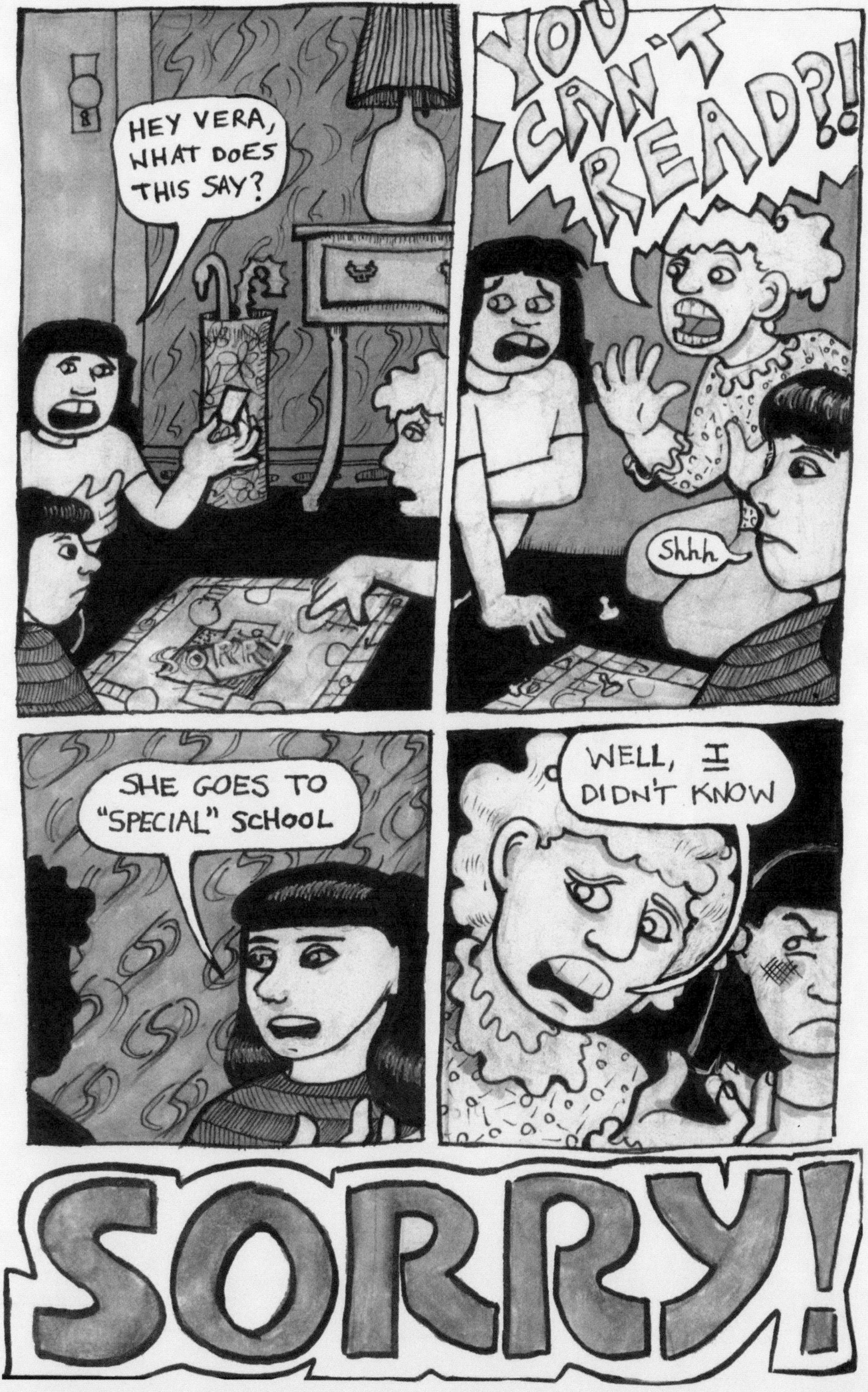
HEY VERA, WHAT DOES THIS SAY?
YOU CAN'T READ?!
Shhh
SHE GOES TO "SPECIAL" SCHOOL
WELL, I DIDN'T KNOW
SORRY!

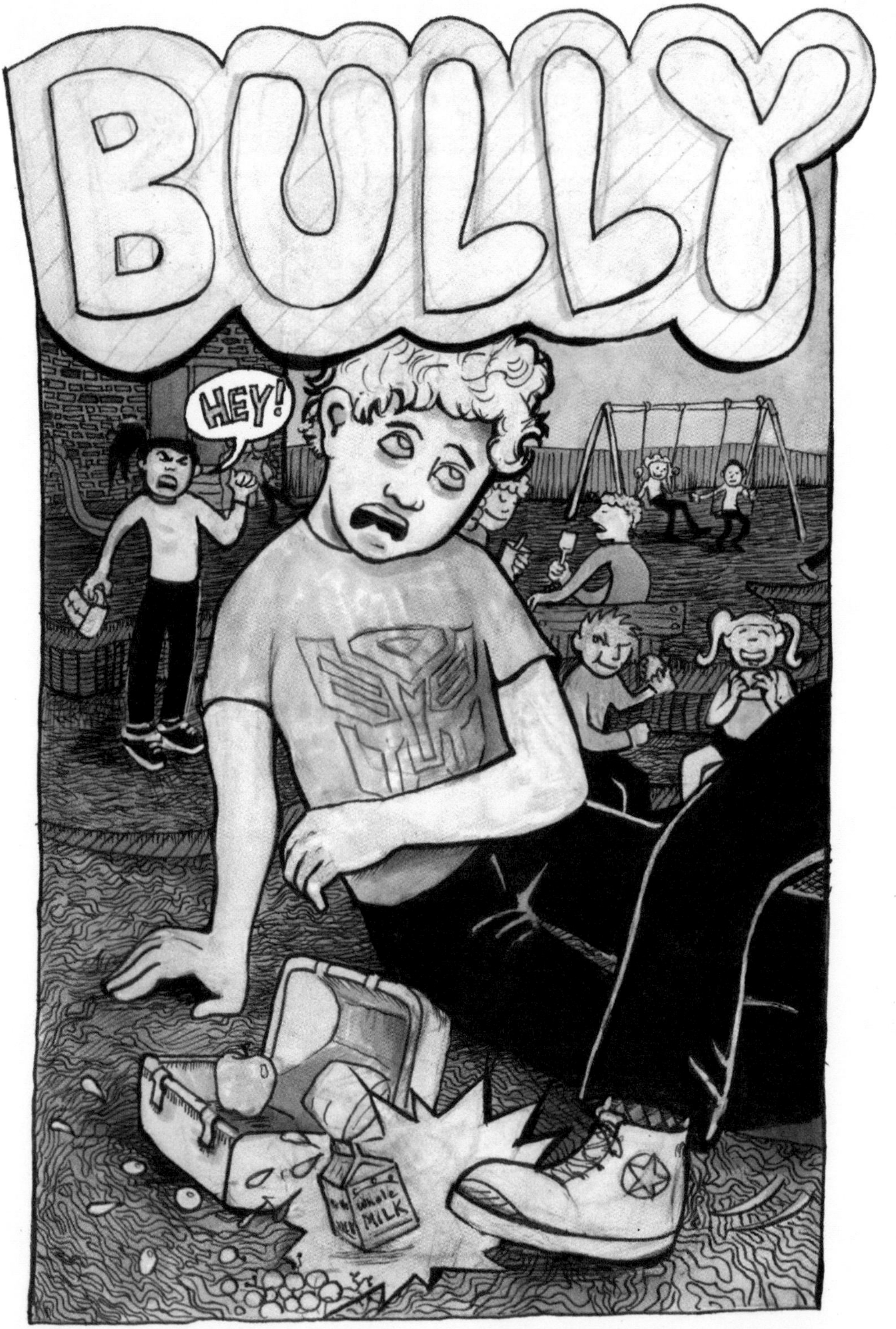
BULLY
HEY!
Whole MILK

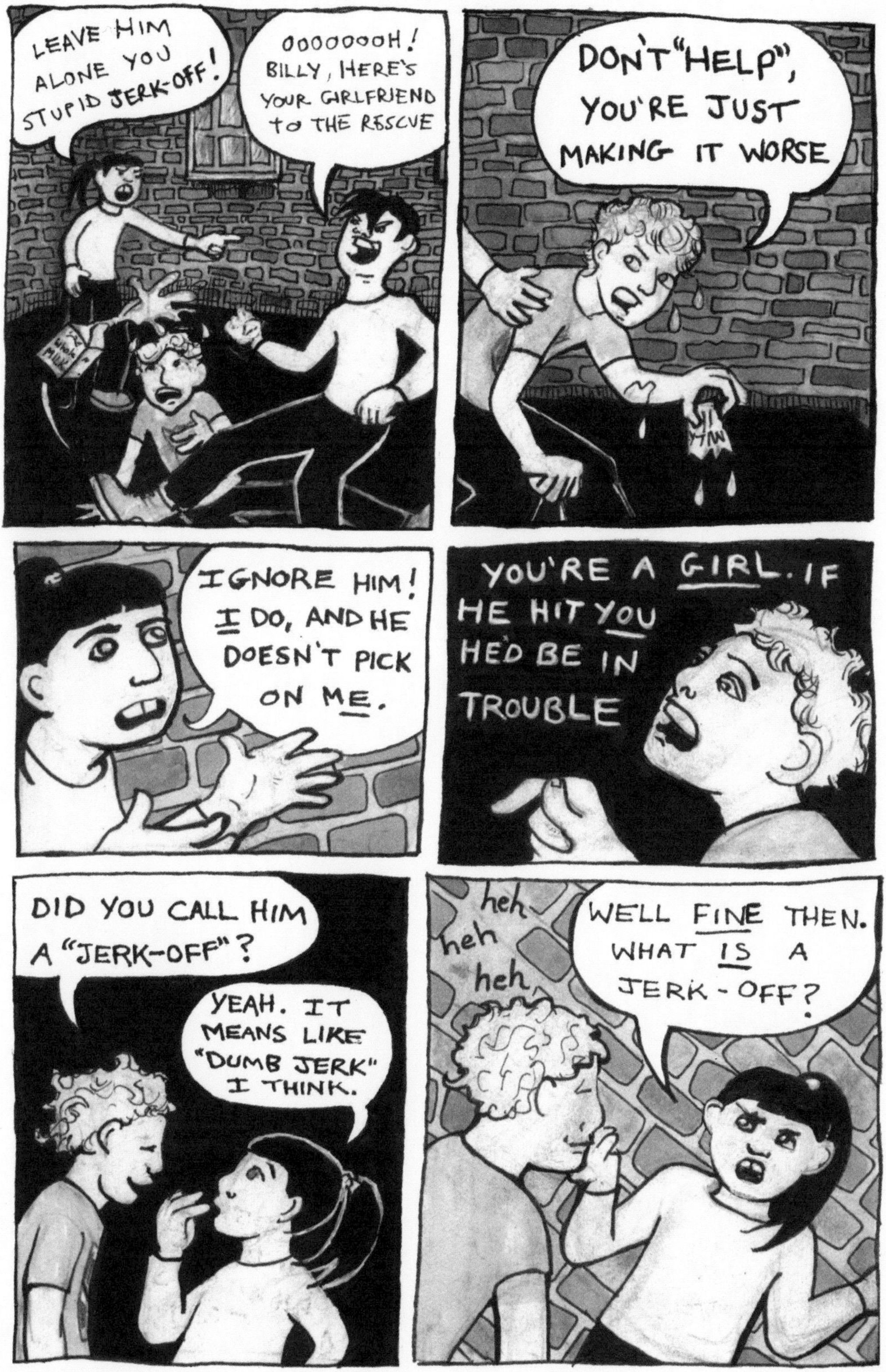
LEAVE HIM ALONE YOU STUPID JERK-OFF!
OOOOOOOH! BILLY, HERE'S YOUR GIRLFRIEND TO THE RESCUE
DON'T "HELP", YOU'RE JUST MAKING IT WORSE
IGNORE HIM! I DO, AND HE DOESN'T PICK ON ME.
YOU'RE A GIRL. IF HE HIT YOU HE'D BE IN TROUBLE
DID YOU CALL HIM A "JERK-OFF"?
YEAH. IT MEANS LIKE "DUMB JERK" I THINK.
heh heh heh,
WELL FINE THEN. WHAT IS A JERK-OFF?

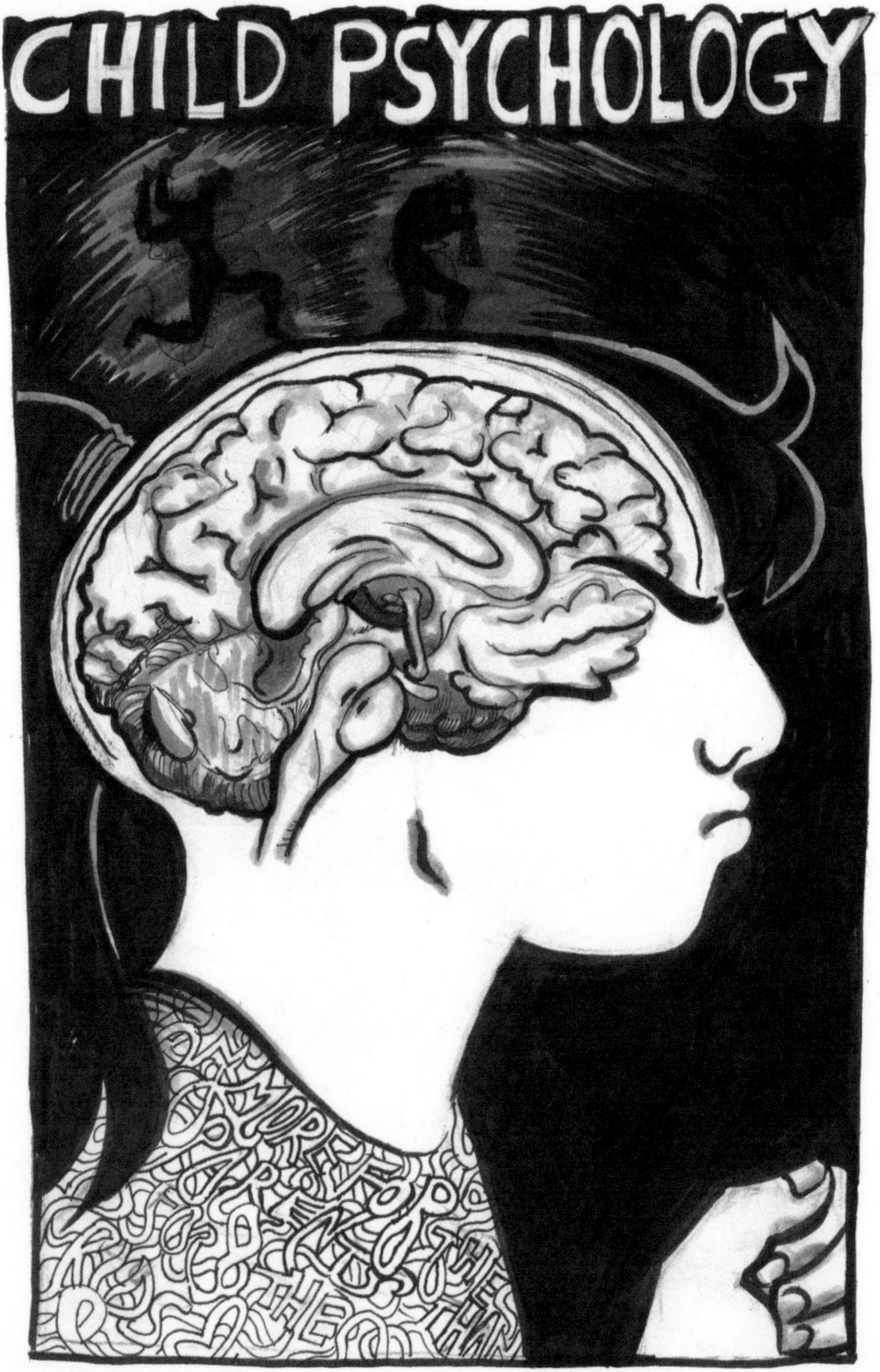
CHILD PSYCHOLOGY

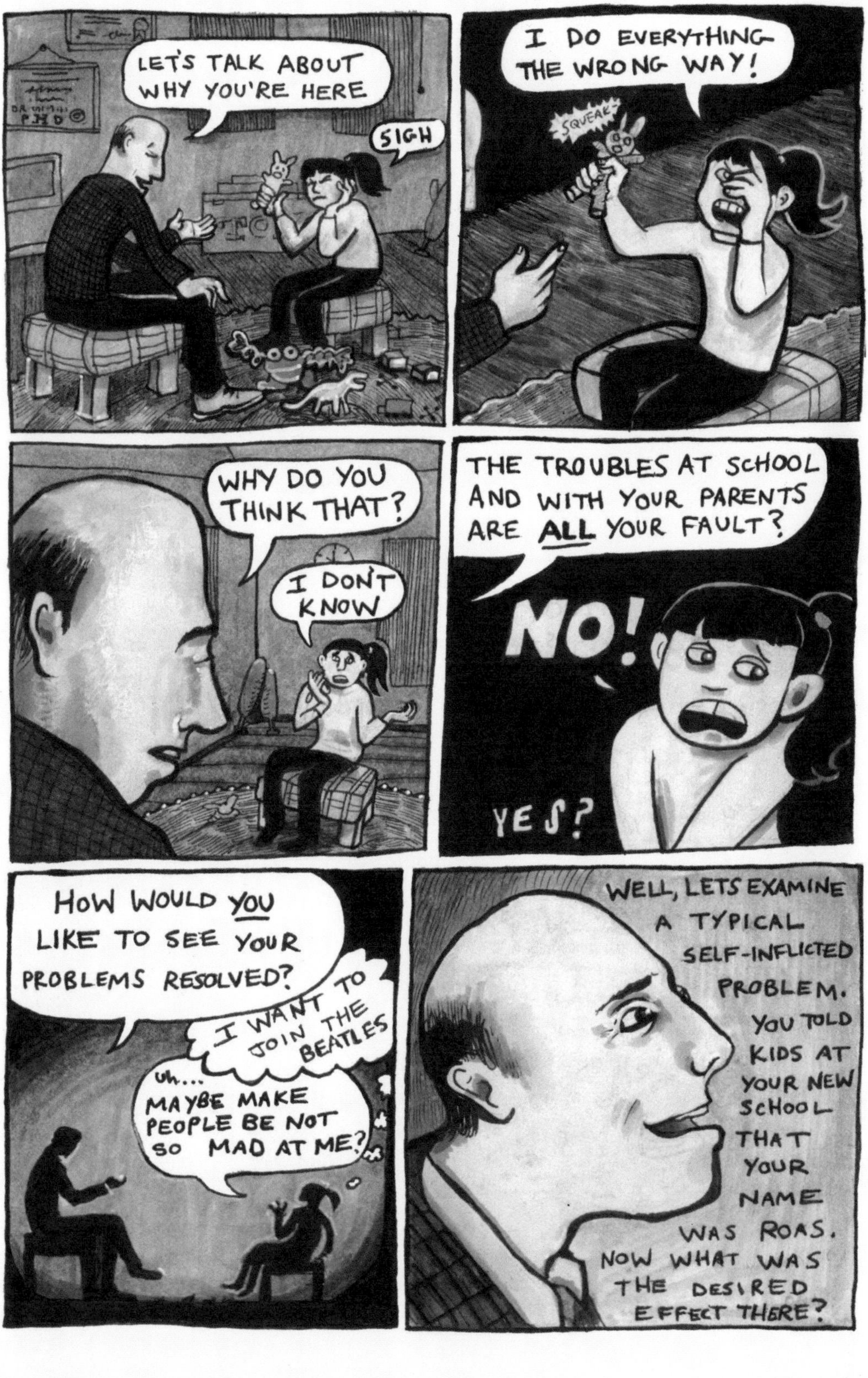
LET'S TALK ABOUT WHY YOU'RE HERE
SIGH
I DO EVERYTHING THE WRONG WAY!
SQUEAK
WHY DO YOU THINK THAT?
I DON'T KNOW
THE TROUBLES AT SCHOOL AND WITH YOUR PARENTS ARE ALL YOUR FAULT?
NO!
YES?
HOW WOULD YOU LIKE TO SEE YOUR PROBLEMS RESOLVED?
I WANT TO JOIN THE BEATLES
uh... MAYBE MAKE PEOPLE BE NOT SO MAD AT ME?
WELL, LETS EXAMINE A TYPICAL SELF-INFLICTED PROBLEM. YOU TOLD KIDS AT YOUR NEW SCHOOL THAT YOUR NAME WAS ROAS. NOW WHAT WAS THE DESIRED EFFECT THERE?

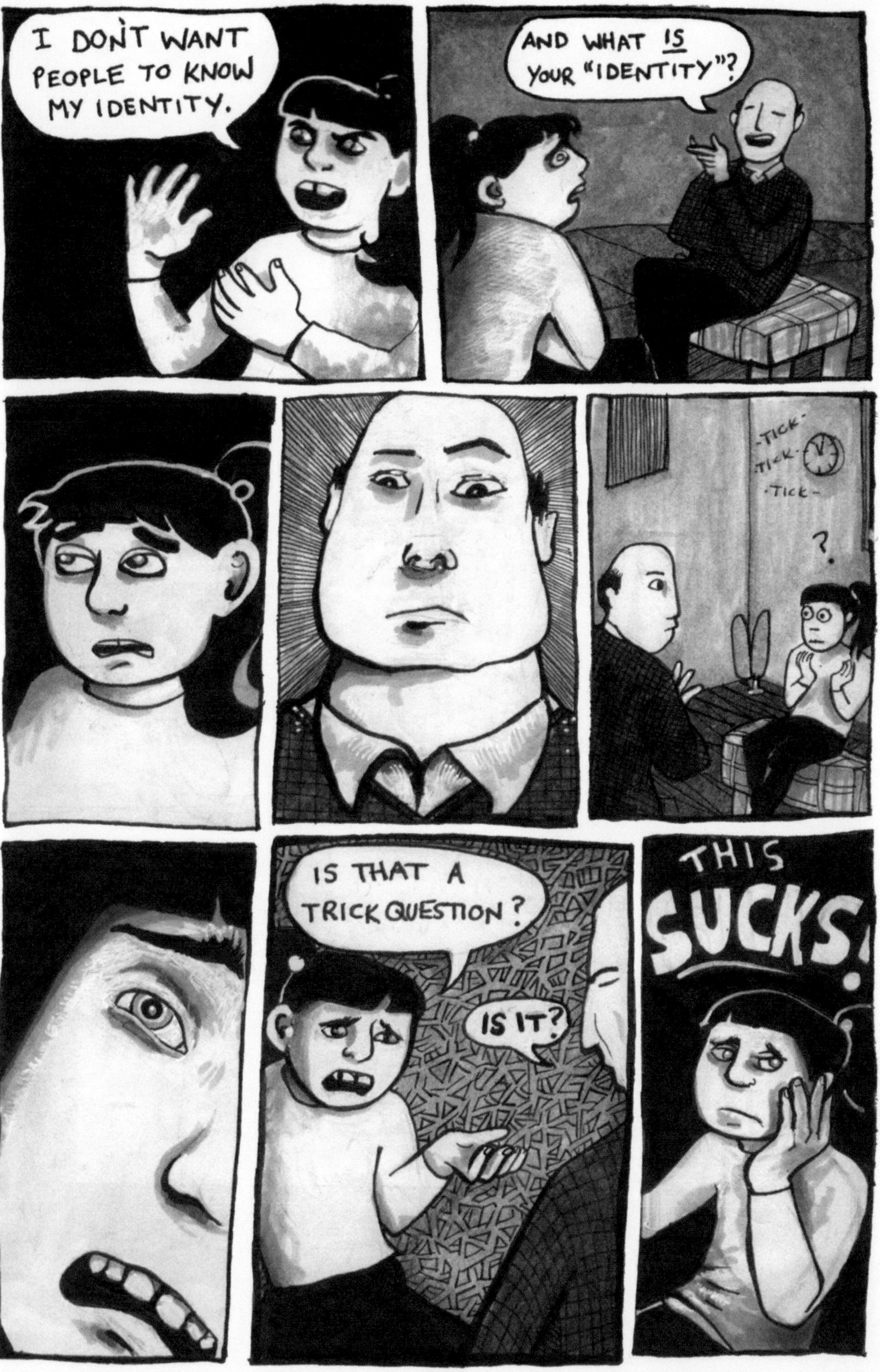
I DON'T WANT PEOPLE TO KNOW MY IDENTITY.
AND WHAT IS YOUR "IDENTITY"?
-TICK- -TICK- -TICK-
?
IS THAT A TRICK QUESTION?
IS IT?
THIS SUCKS!

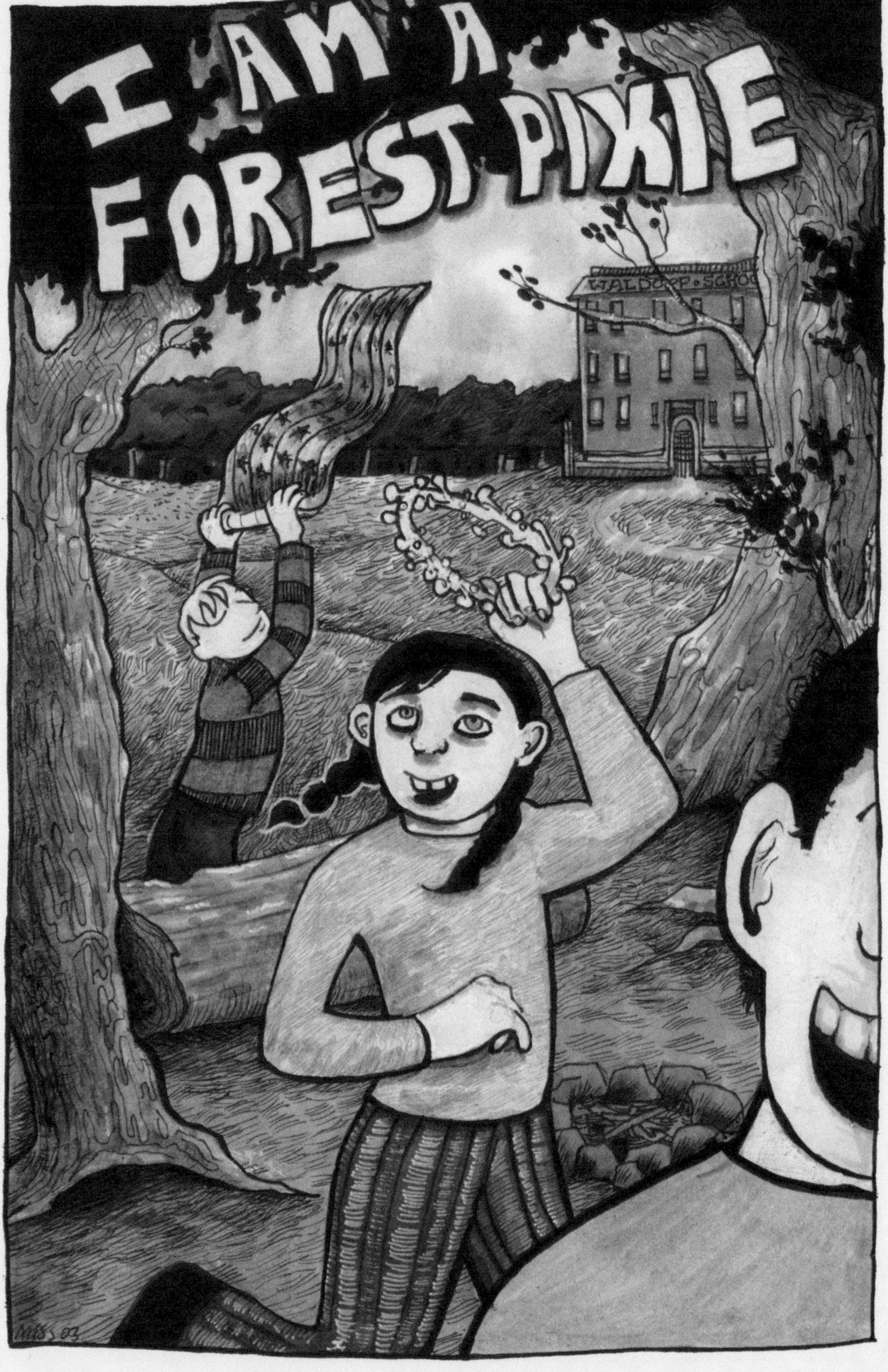
I AM A
FOREST PIXIE
WALDORF • SCHOO

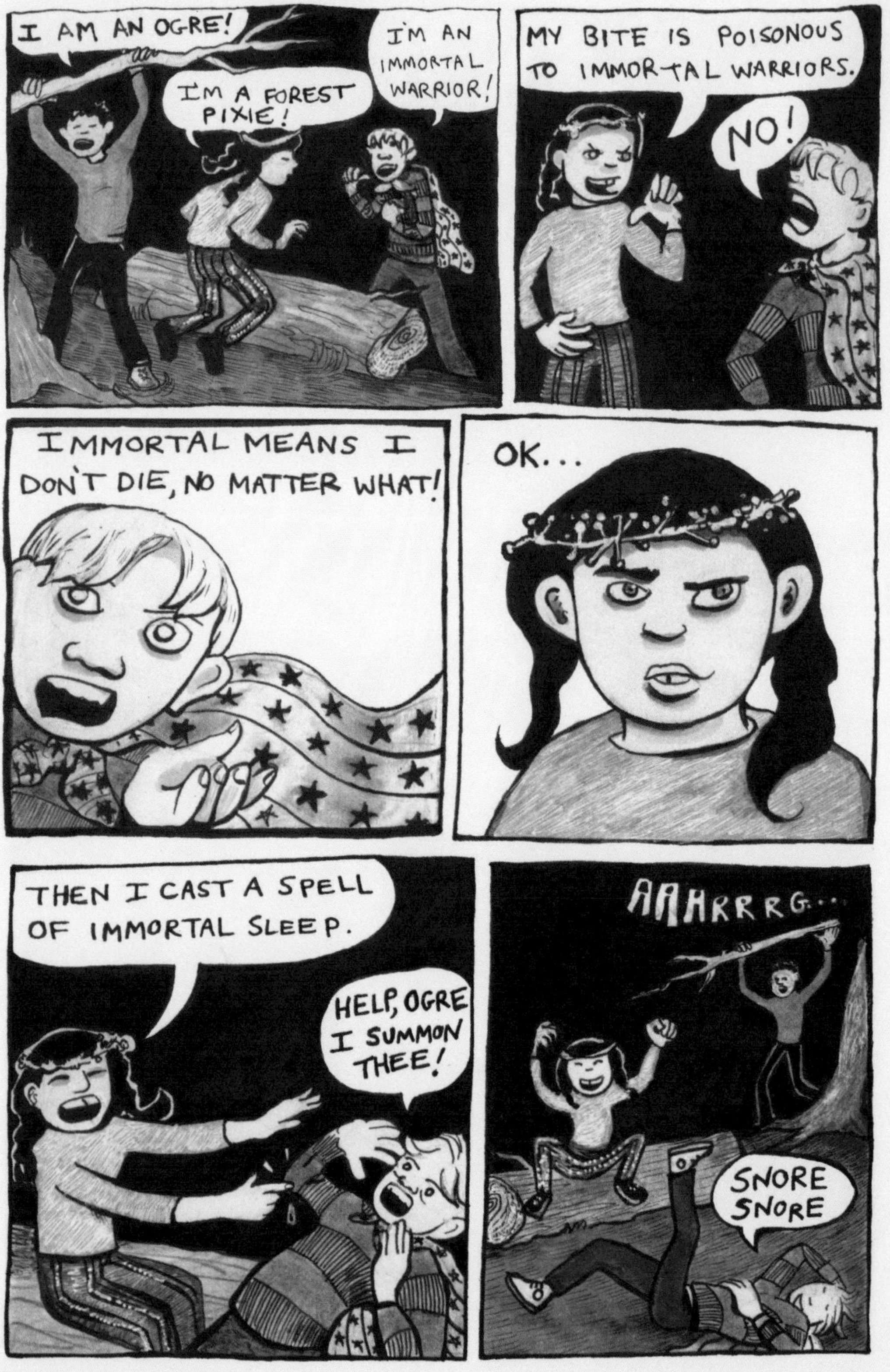
I AM AN OGRE!
I'M A FOREST PIXIE!
I'M AN IMMORTAL WARRIOR!
MY BITE IS POISONOUS TO IMMORTAL WARRIORS.
NO!
IMMORTAL MEANS I DON'T DIE, NO MATTER WHAT!
OK...
THEN I CAST A SPELL OF IMMORTAL SLEEP.
HELP, OGRE I SUMMON THEE!
AAHRRRG...
SNORE SNORE

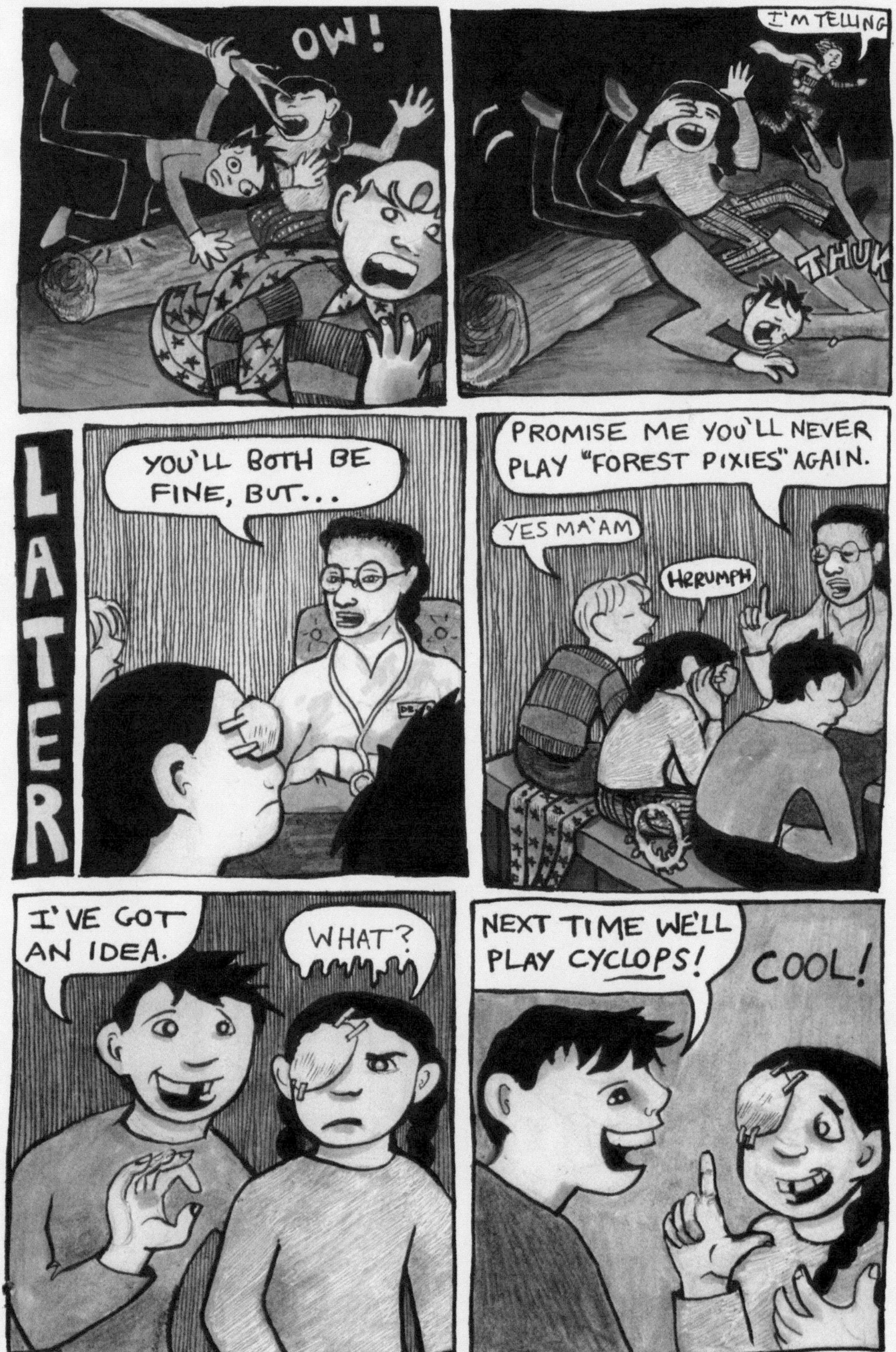
OW!
I'M TELLING
THUK
LATER
YOU'LL BOTH BE FINE, BUT...
PROMISE ME YOU'LL NEVER PLAY "FOREST PIXIES" AGAIN.
YES MA'AM
HRRUMPH
I'VE GOT AN IDEA.
WHAT?
NEXT TIME WE'LL PLAY CYCLOPS!
COOL!

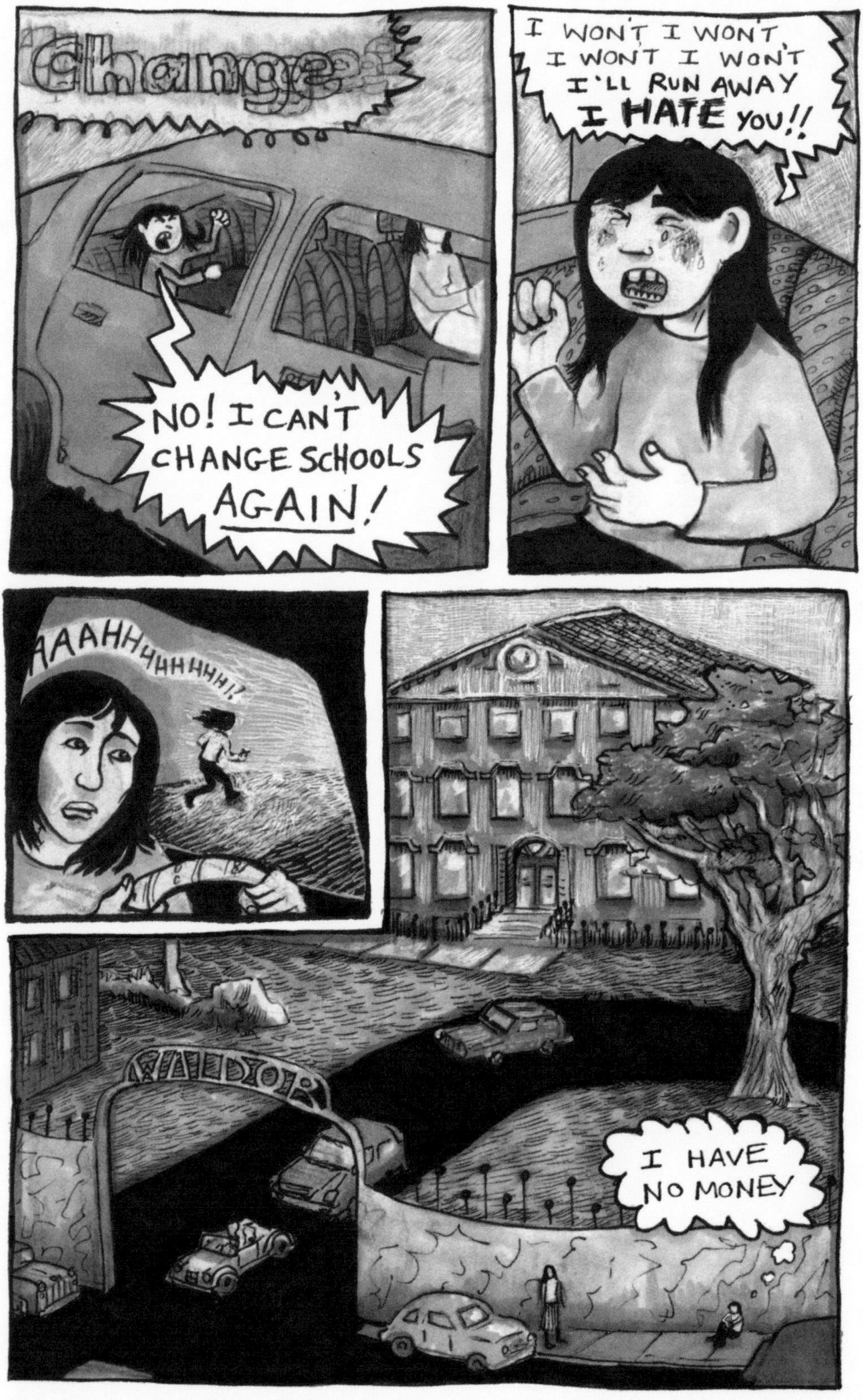
Change
NO! I CAN'T CHANGE SCHOOLS AGAIN!
I WON'T I WON'T I WON'T I WON'T I'LL RUN AWAY I HATE YOU!!
AAAHHHHHHHHH!!
I HAVE NO MONEY

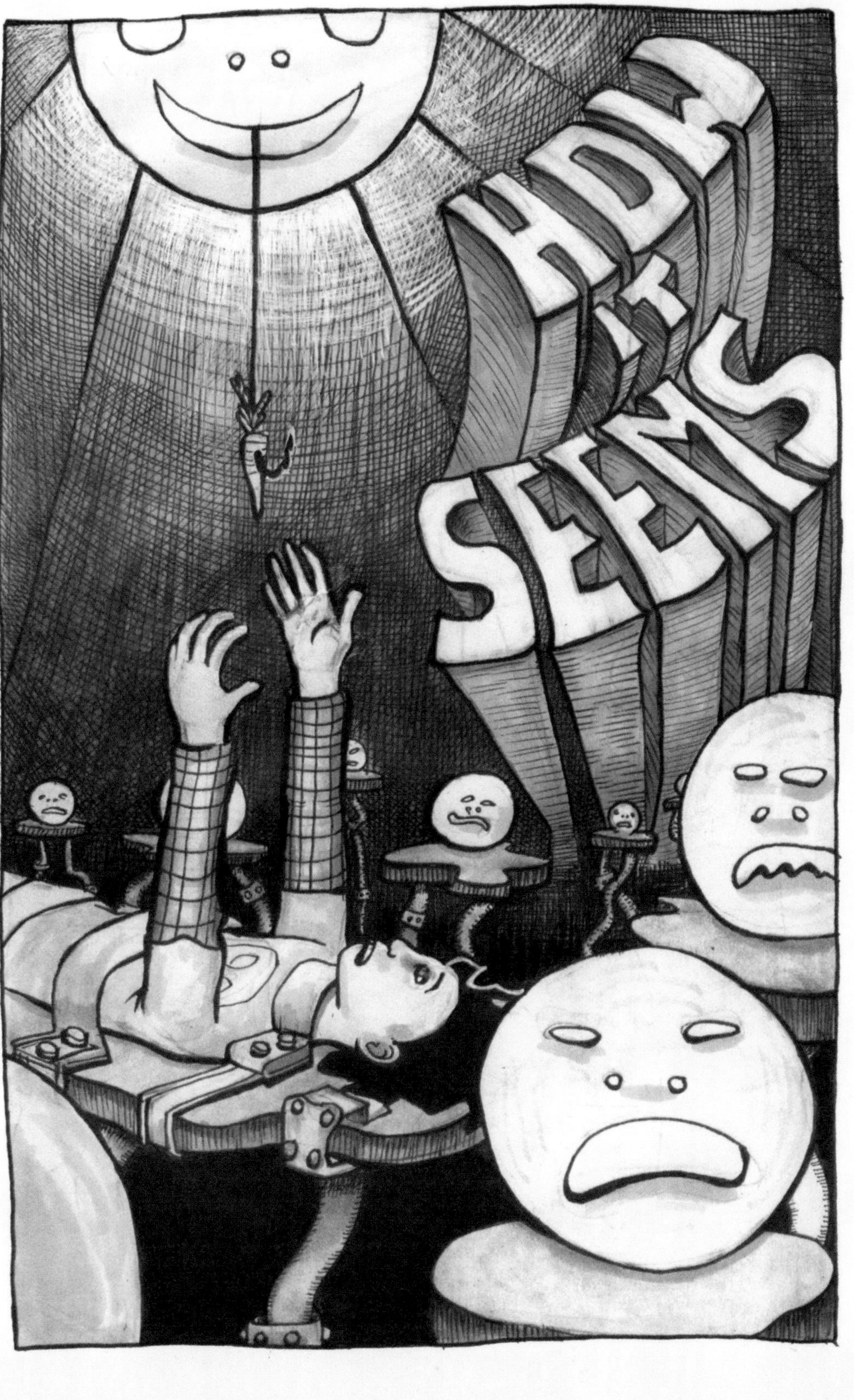
HOW IT SEEMS

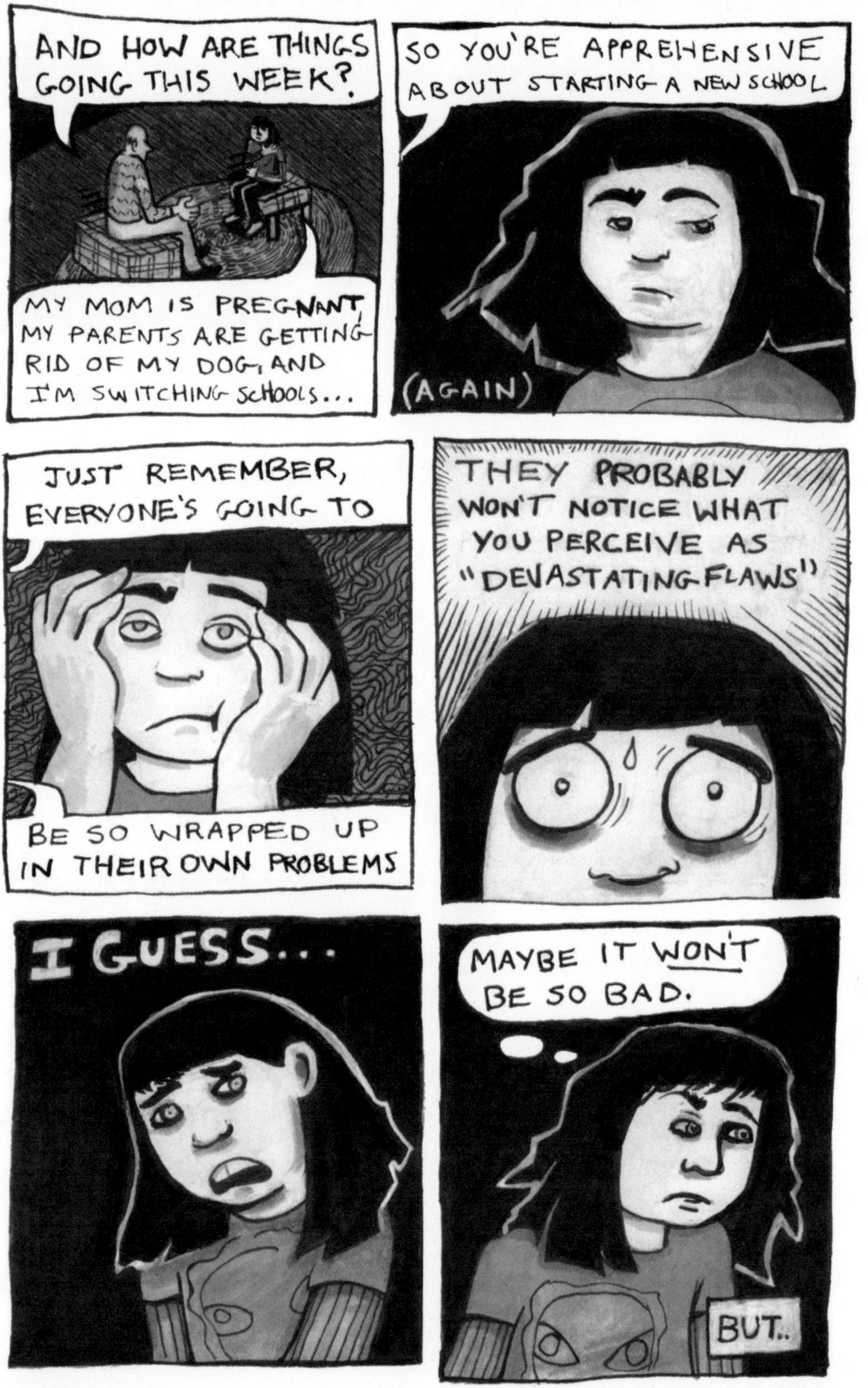
AND HOW ARE THINGS GOING THIS WEEK?
MY MOM IS PREGNANT, MY PARENTS ARE GETTING RID OF MY DOG, AND I'M SWITCHING SCHOOLS...
SO YOU'RE APPREHENSIVE ABOUT STARTING A NEW SCHOOL
(AGAIN)
JUST REMEMBER, EVERYONE'S GOING TO
BE SO WRAPPED UP IN THEIR OWN PROBLEMS
THEY PROBABLY WON'T NOTICE WHAT YOU PERCEIVE AS "DEVASTATING FLAWS"
I GUESS...
MAYBE IT WON'T BE SO BAD.
BUT..

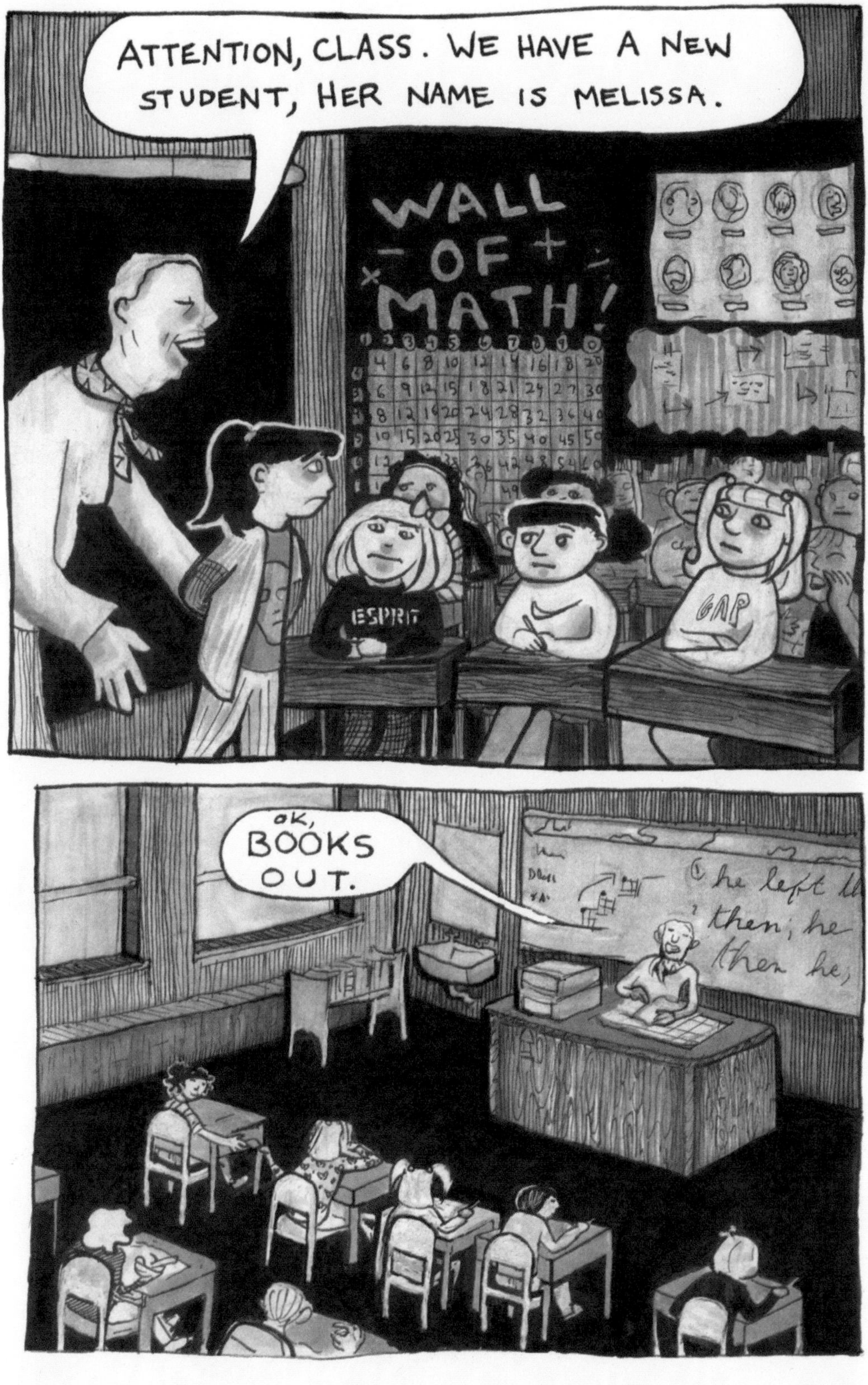
ATTENTION, CLASS. WE HAVE A NEW STUDENT, HER NAME IS MELISSA.
WALL OF MATH!
ESPRIT
GAP
OK, BOOKS OUT.
he left
then; he
then he;

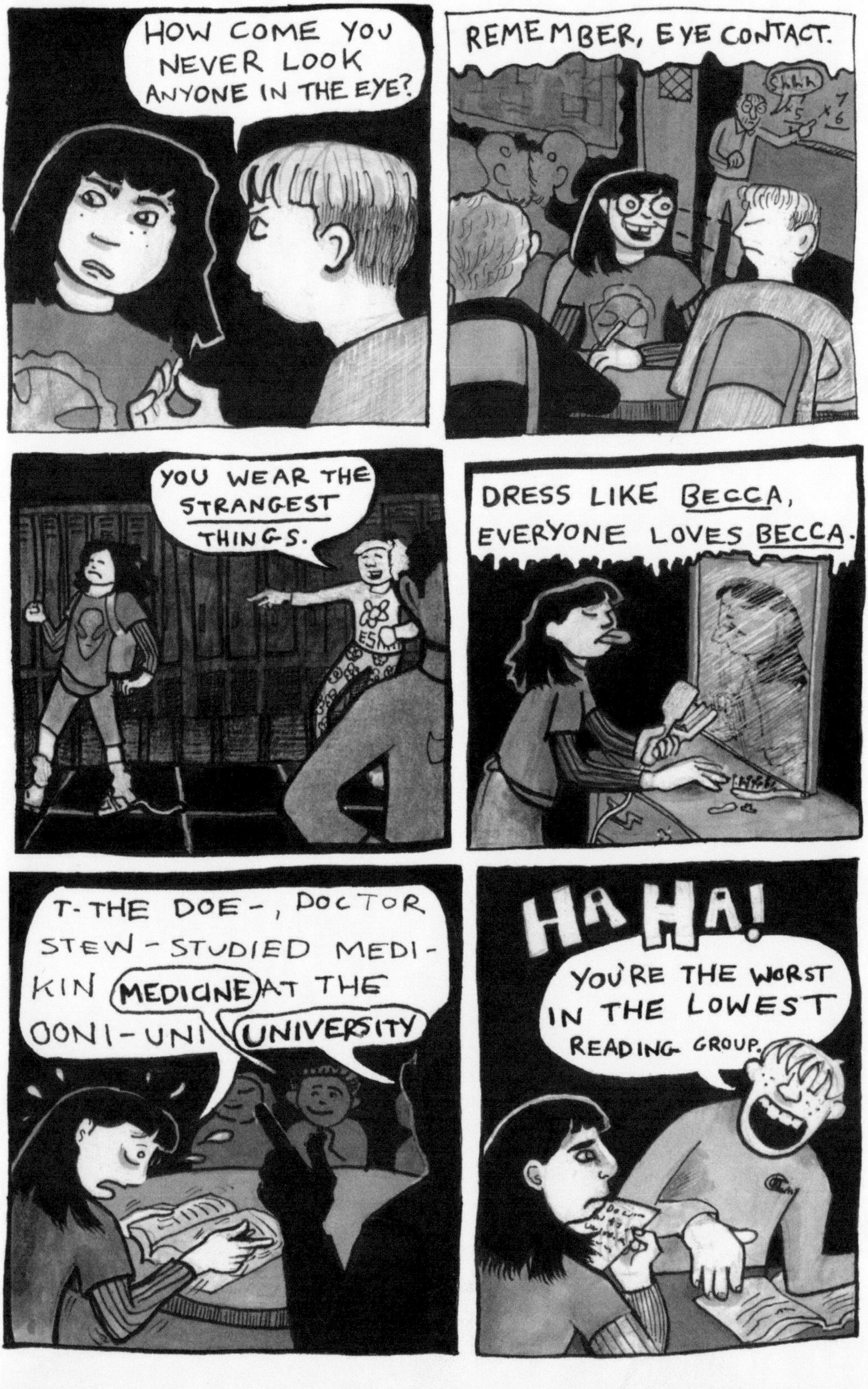
HOW COME YOU NEVER LOOK ANYONE IN THE EYE?
REMEMBER, EYE CONTACT.
Shhh
YOU WEAR THE STRANGEST THINGS.
DRESS LIKE BECCA, EVERYONE LOVES BECCA.
T-THE DOE-, DOCTOR STEW-STUDIED MEDI-KIN MEDICINE AT THE OONI-UNI UNIVERSITY
HAHA!
YOU'RE THE WORST IN THE LOWEST READING GROUP.

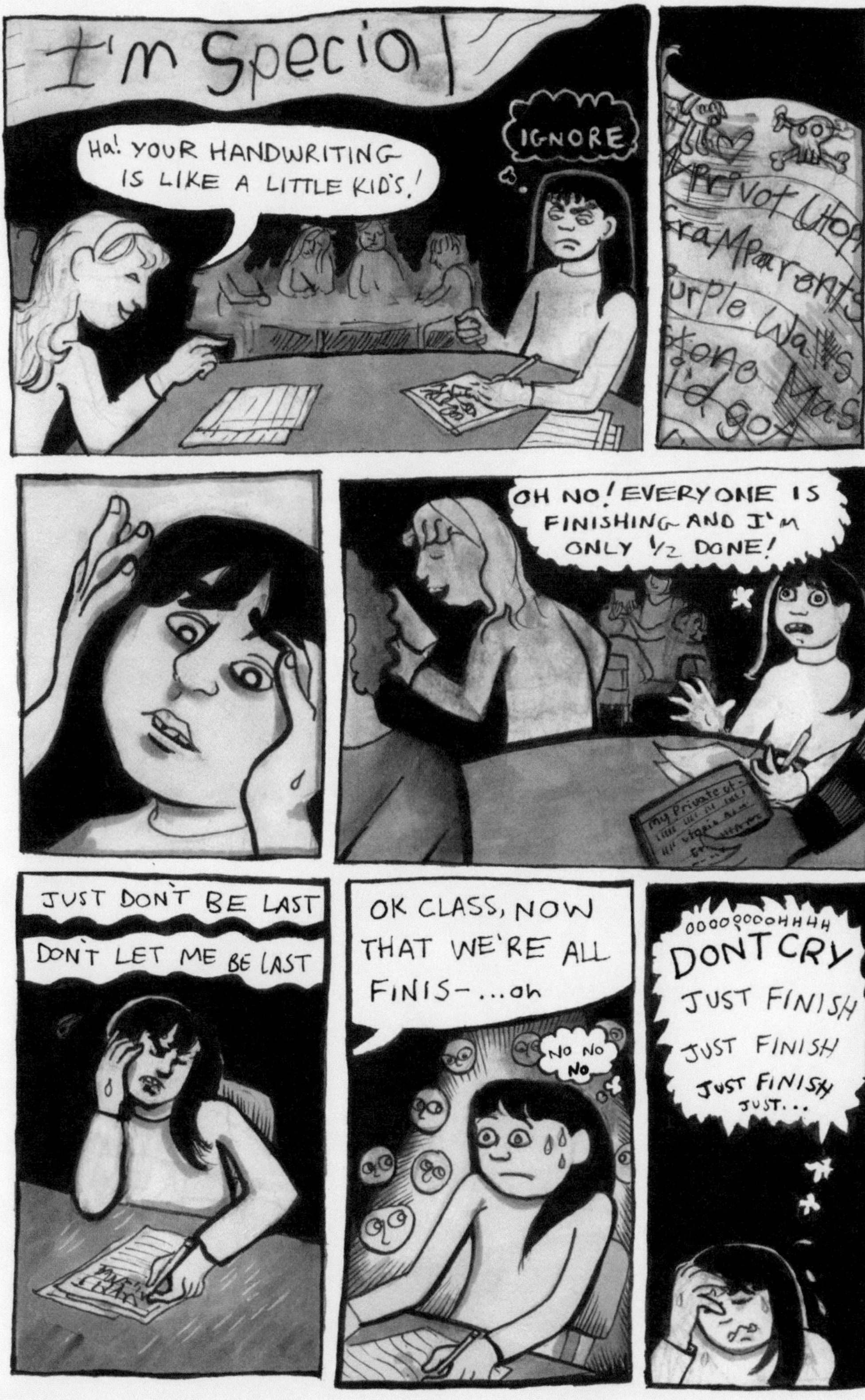
I'm Special
Ha! YOUR HANDWRITING IS LIKE A LITTLE KID'S!
IGNORE
OH NO! EVERYONE IS FINISHING AND I'M ONLY 1/2 DONE!
JUST DON'T BE LAST
DON'T LET ME BE LAST
OK CLASS, NOW THAT WE'RE ALL FINIS-...oh
NO NO NO
OOOOOOOOHHHH
DONT CRY
JUST FINISH
JUST FINISH
JUST FINISH
JUST...

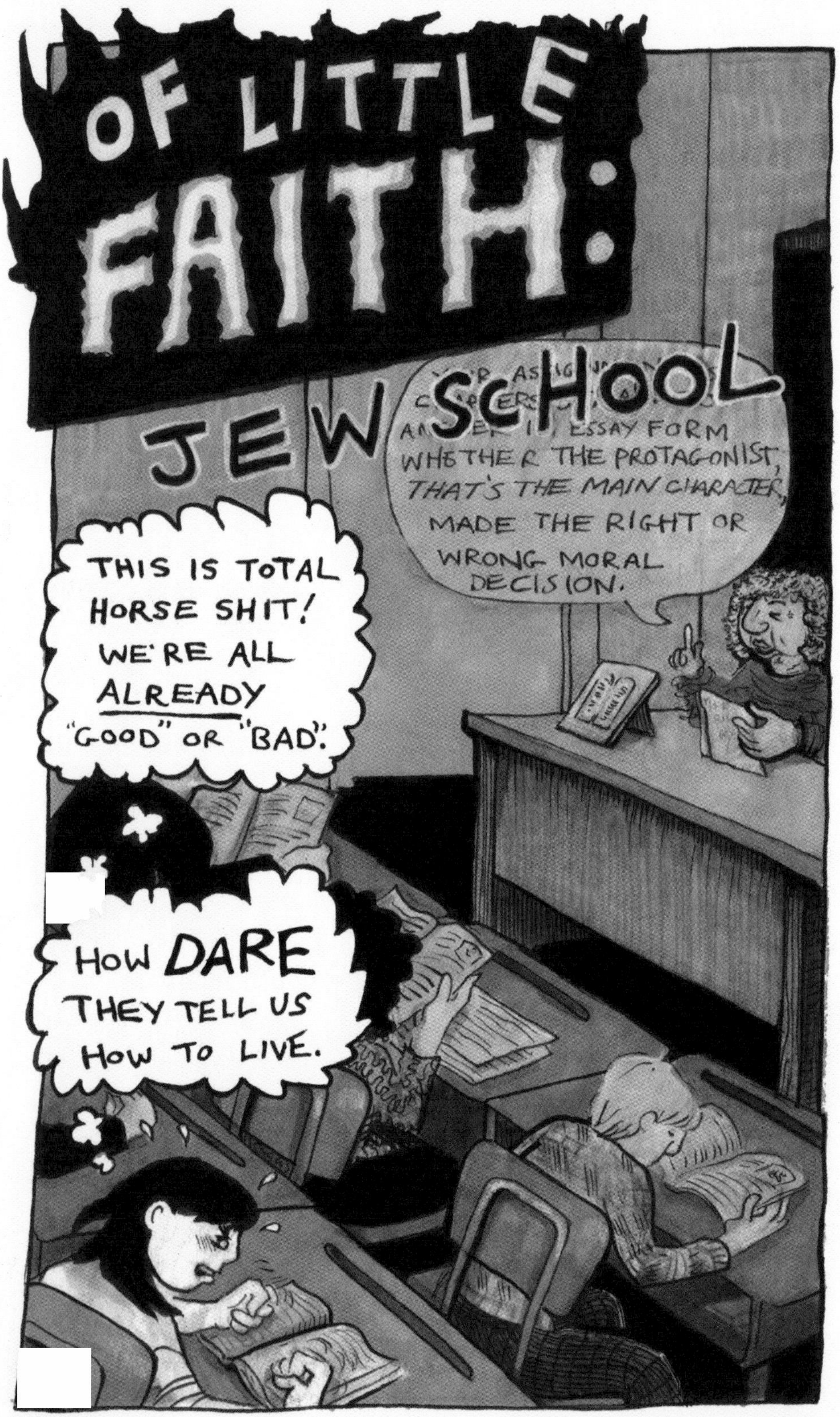
OF LITTLE FAITH:
JEW SCHOOL
ESSAY FORM WHETHER THE PROTAGONIST, THAT'S THE MAIN CHARACTER, MADE THE RIGHT OR WRONG MORAL DECISION.
THIS IS TOTAL HORSE SHIT! WE'RE ALL ALREADY "GOOD" OR "BAD".
HOW DARE THEY TELL US HOW TO LIVE.

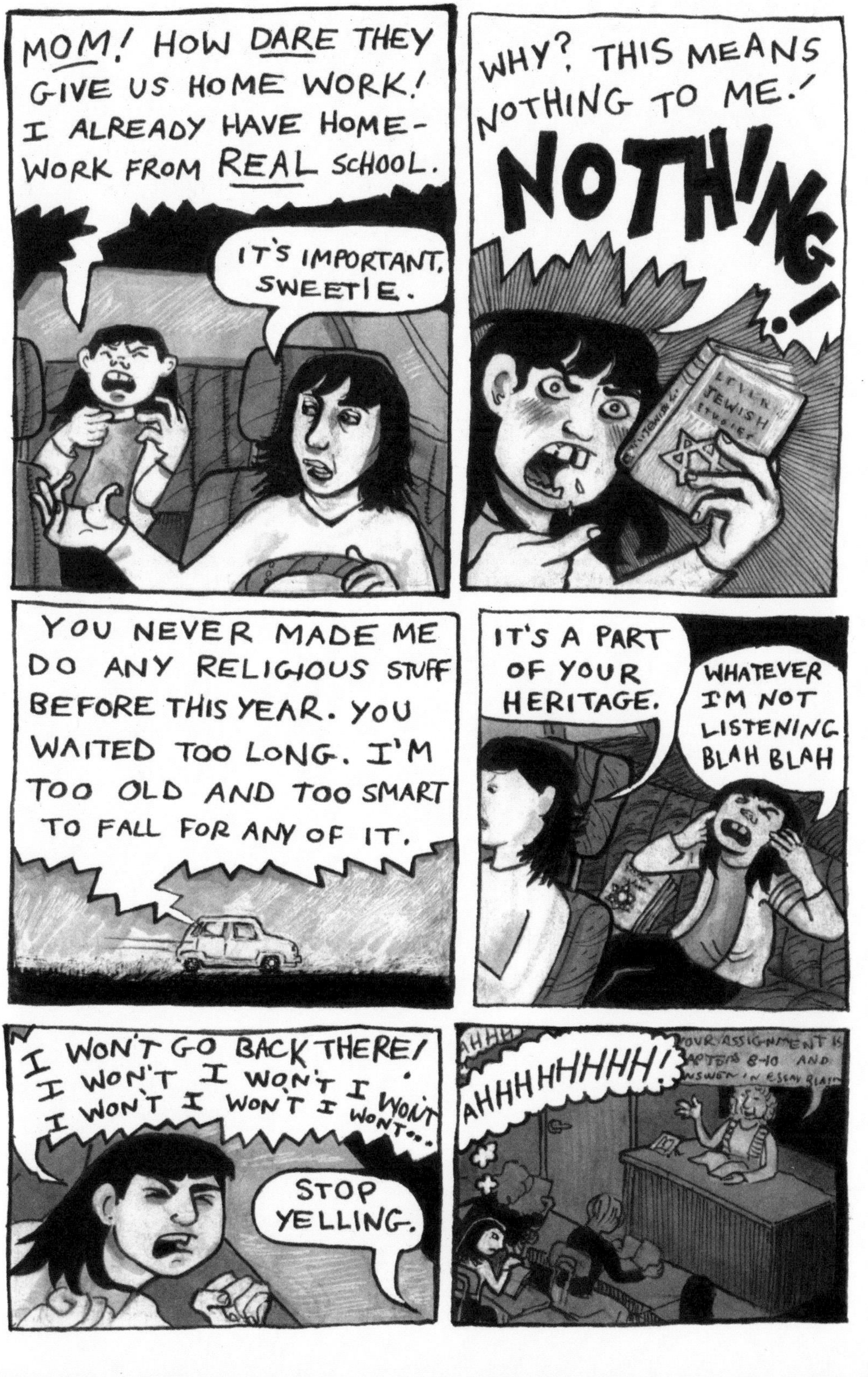
MOM! HOW DARE THEY GIVE US HOME WORK! I ALREADY HAVE HOME-WORK FROM REAL SCHOOL.
IT'S IMPORTANT, SWEETIE.
WHY? THIS MEANS NOTHING TO ME.!
NOTHING!
JEWISH
YOU NEVER MADE ME DO ANY RELIGIOUS STUFF BEFORE THIS YEAR. YOU WAITED TOO LONG. I'M TOO OLD AND TOO SMART TO FALL FOR ANY OF IT.
IT'S A PART OF YOUR HERITAGE.
WHATEVER I'M NOT LISTENING BLAH BLAH
I WON'T GO BACK THERE! I WON'T I WON'T I WON'T I WON'T I WON'T I WONT...
STOP YELLING.
AHHHHHHHHH!
YOUR ASSIGNMENT IS
8-10 AND

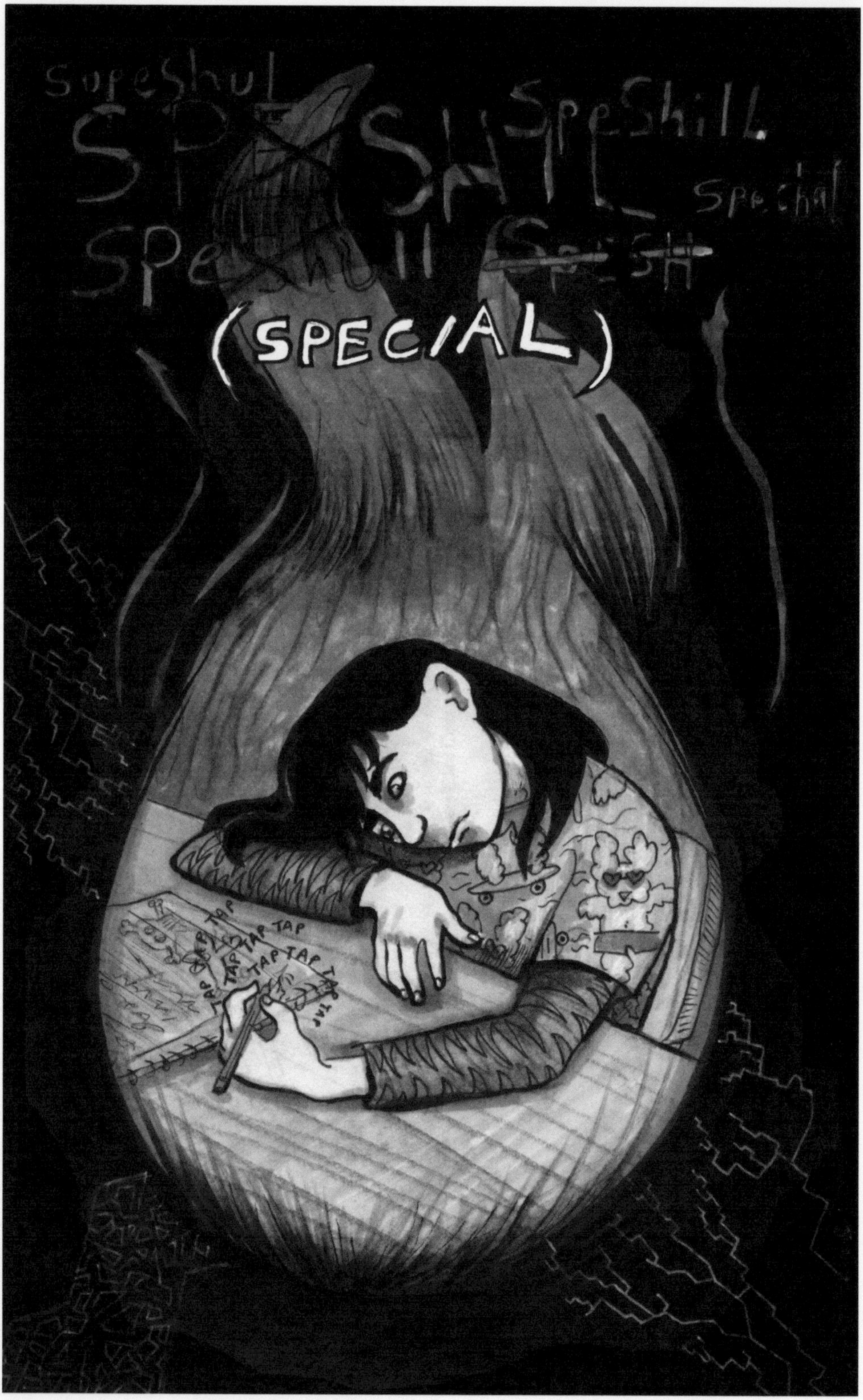
Supeshul
Speshill
Spechal
(SPECIAL)
TAP TAP TAP TAP TAP

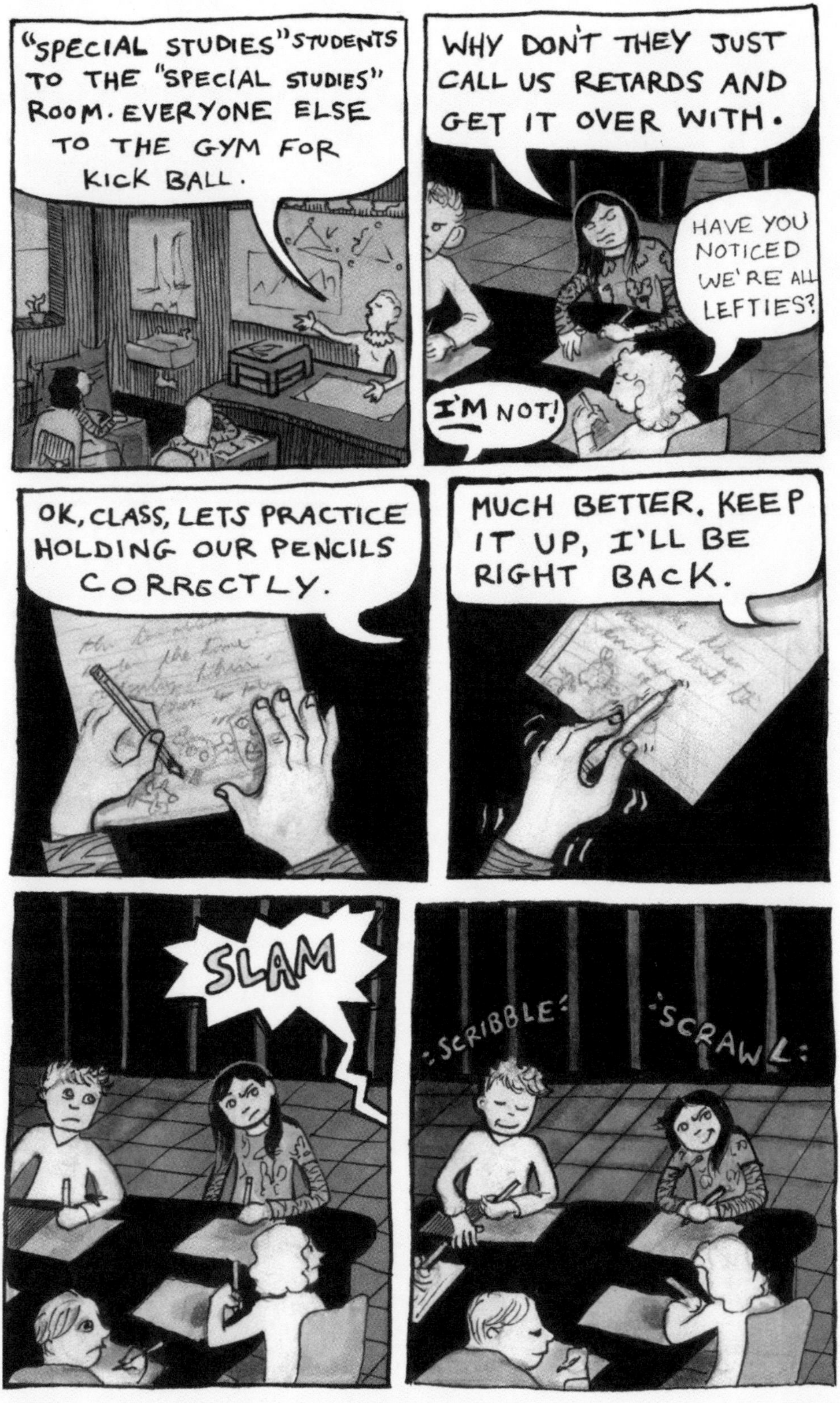
"SPECIAL STUDIES" STUDENTS TO THE "SPECIAL STUDIES" ROOM. EVERYONE ELSE TO THE GYM FOR KICK BALL.
WHY DON'T THEY JUST CALL US RETARDS AND GET IT OVER WITH.
HAVE YOU NOTICED WE'RE ALL LEFTIES?
I'M NOT!
OK, CLASS, LETS PRACTICE HOLDING OUR PENCILS CORRECTLY.
MUCH BETTER. KEEP IT UP, I'LL BE RIGHT BACK.
SLAM
SCRIBBLE
SCRAWL

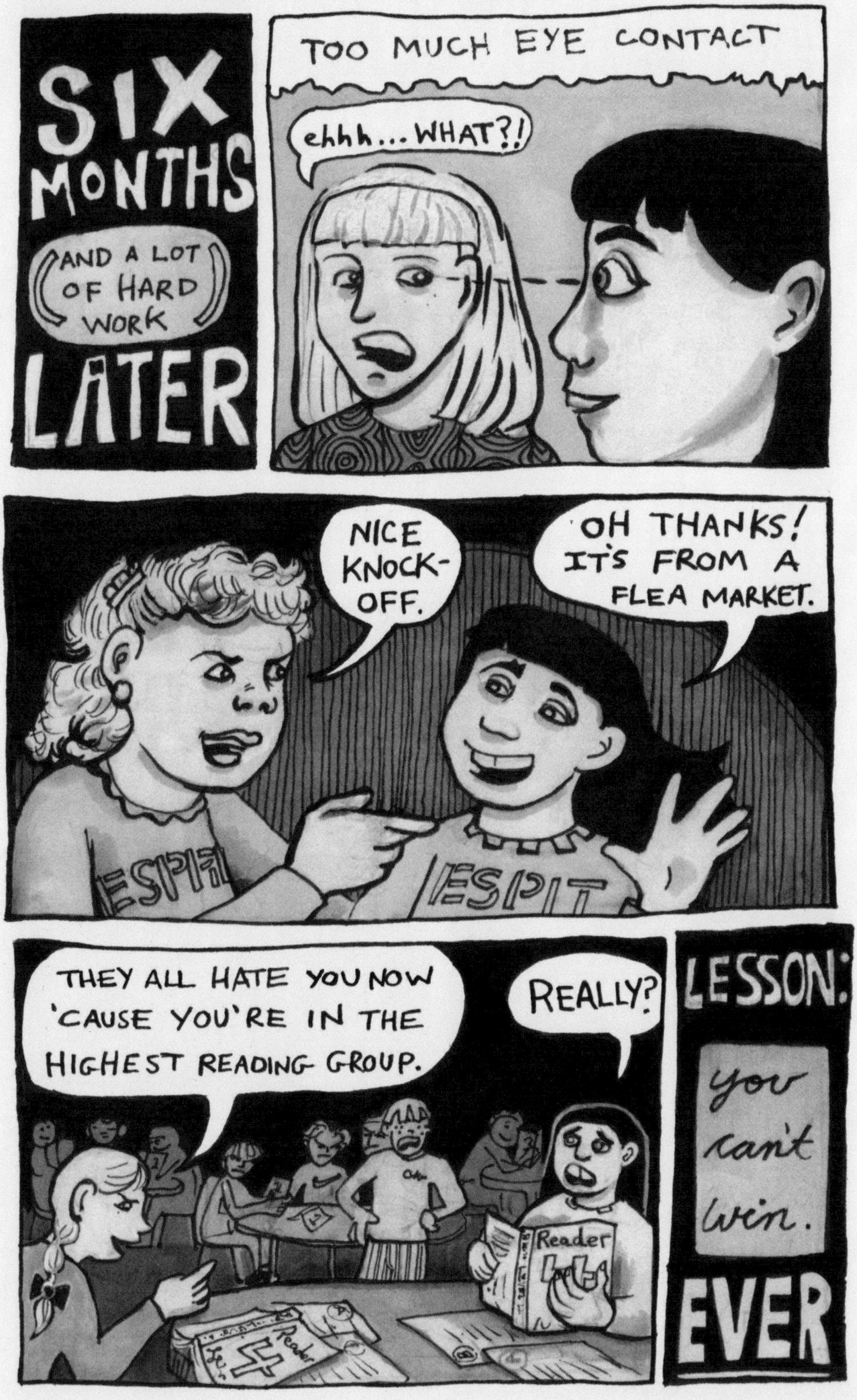
SIX MONTHS
AND A LOT OF HARD WORK
LATER
TOO MUCH EYE CONTACT
ehhh... WHAT?!
NICE KNOCK-OFF.
OH THANKS! IT'S FROM A FLEA MARKET.
ESPIT
THEY ALL HATE YOU NOW 'CAUSE YOU'RE IN THE HIGHEST READING GROUP.
REALLY?
Reader
LESSON:
you can't win.
EVER

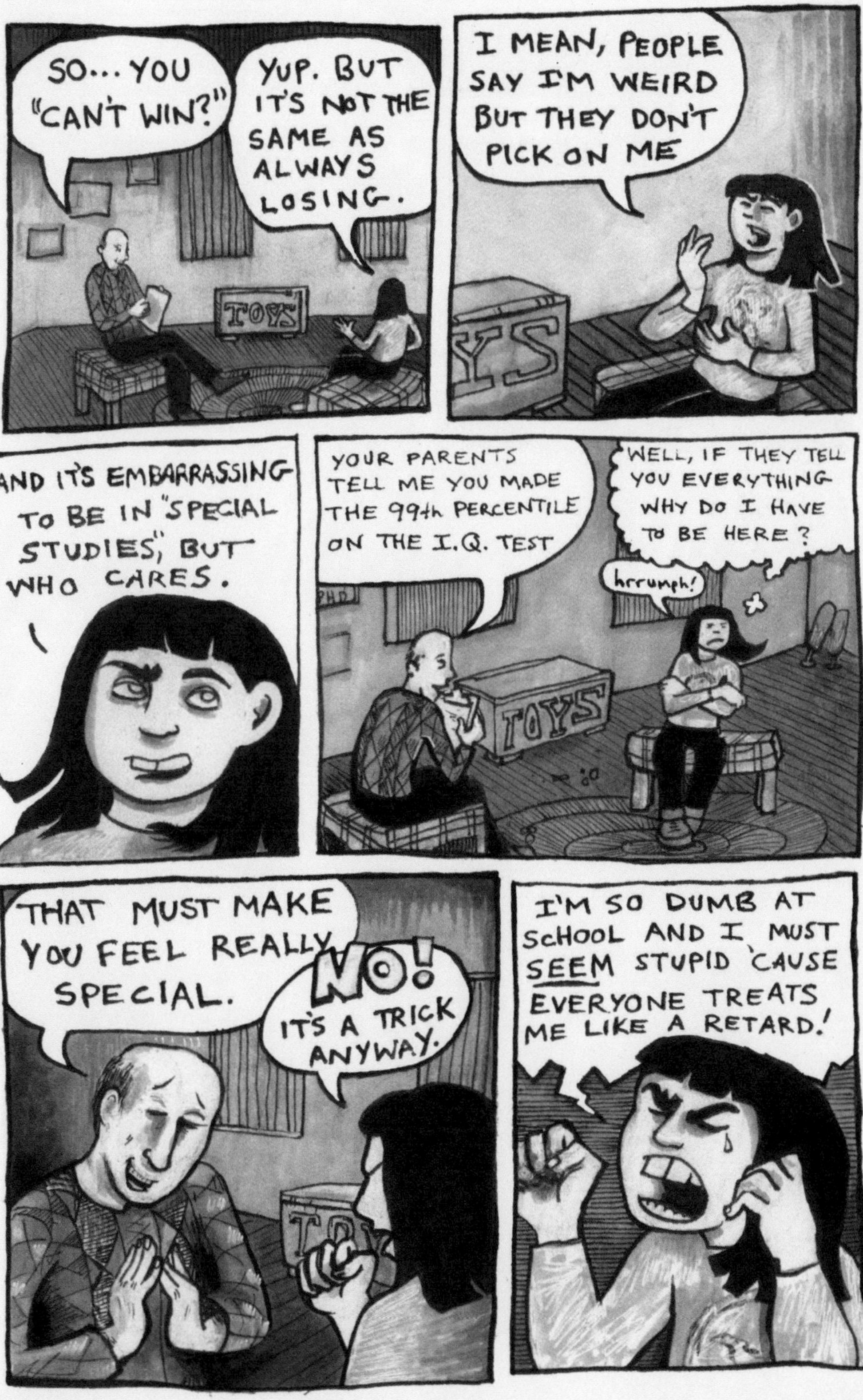
SO... YOU "CAN'T WIN?"
YUP. BUT IT'S NOT THE SAME AS ALWAYS LOSING.
TOYS
I MEAN, PEOPLE SAY I'M WEIRD BUT THEY DON'T PICK ON ME
AND IT'S EMBARRASSING TO BE IN "SPECIAL STUDIES," BUT WHO CARES.
YOUR PARENTS TELL ME YOU MADE THE 99th PERCENTILE ON THE I.Q. TEST
WELL, IF THEY TELL YOU EVERYTHING WHY DO I HAVE TO BE HERE?
hrrumph!
PHD
TOYS
THAT MUST MAKE YOU FEEL REALLY SPECIAL.
NO! IT'S A TRICK ANYWAY.
I'M SO DUMB AT SCHOOL AND I MUST SEEM STUPID 'CAUSE EVERYONE TREATS ME LIKE A RETARD!

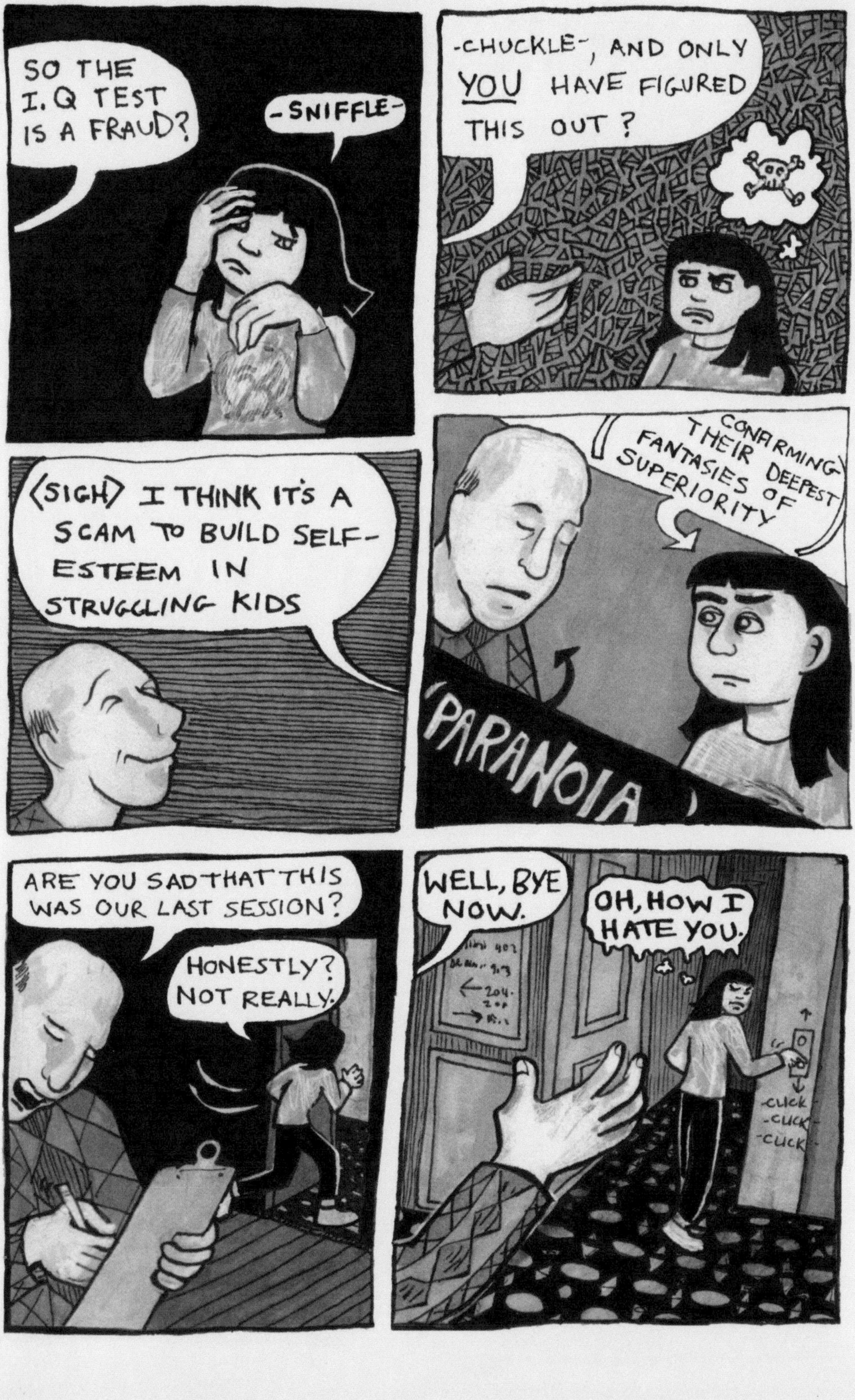
SO THE I.Q TEST IS A FRAUD?
-SNIFFLE-
-CHUCKLE-, AND ONLY YOU HAVE FIGURED THIS OUT?
(SIGH) I THINK IT'S A SCAM TO BUILD SELF-ESTEEM IN STRUGGLING KIDS
CONFIRMING THEIR DEEPEST FANTASIES OF SUPERIORITY
PARANOIA
ARE YOU SAD THAT THIS WAS OUR LAST SESSION?
HONESTLY? NOT REALLY.
WELL, BYE NOW.
OH, HOW I HATE YOU.
-CLICK-
-CLICK-
-CLICK-

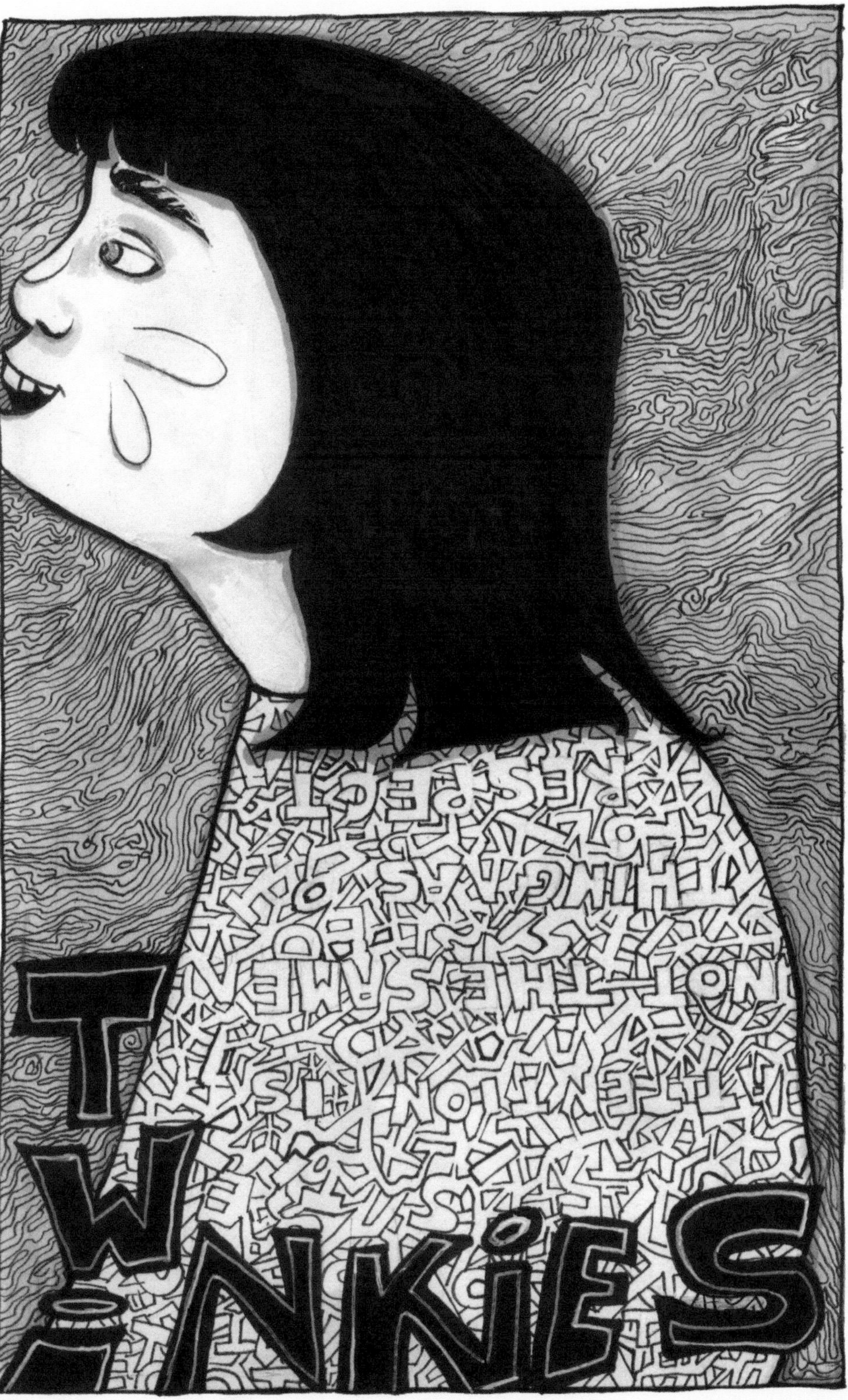
TWINKIES

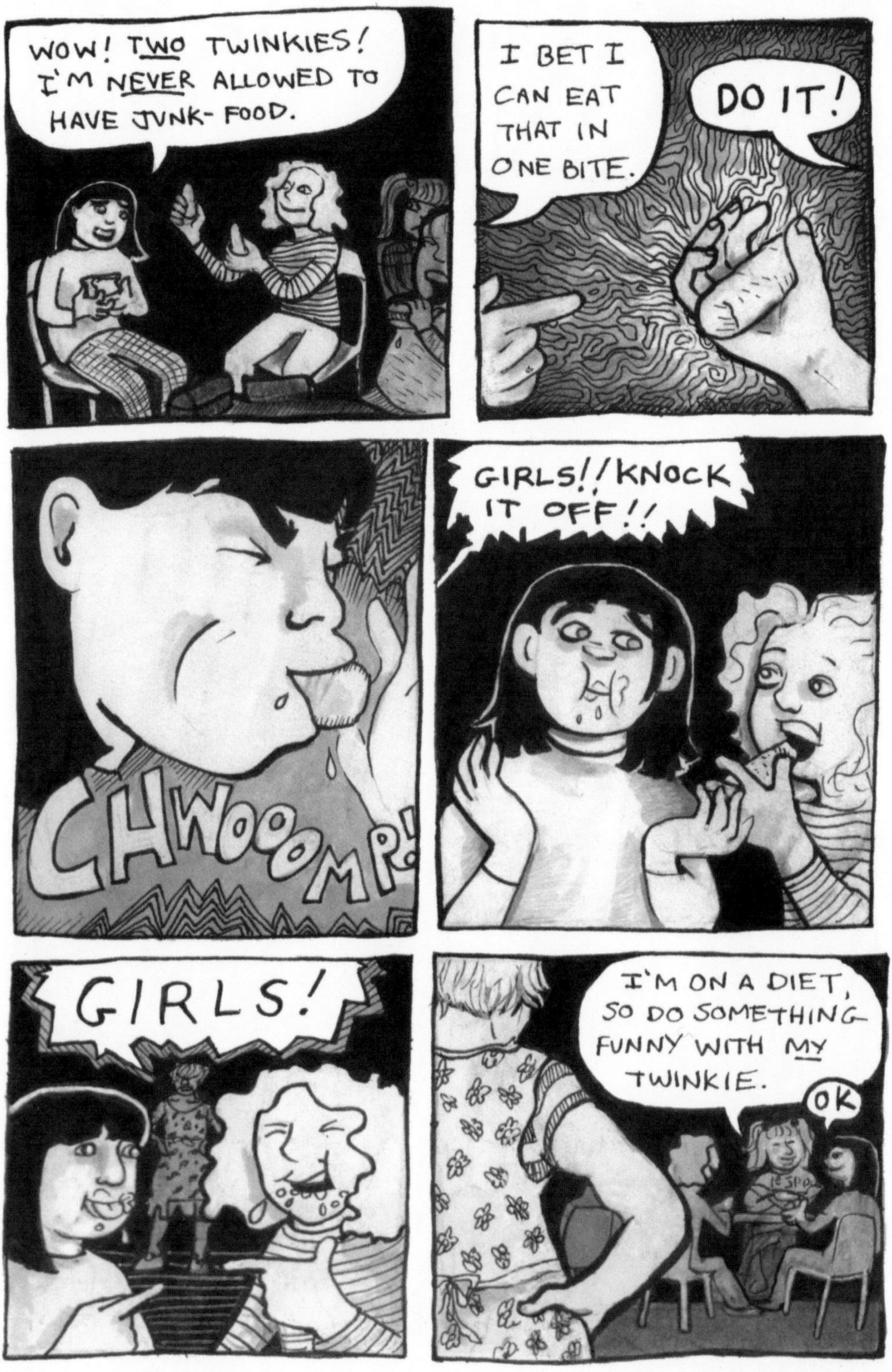
WOW! TWO TWINKIES! I'M NEVER ALLOWED TO HAVE JUNK-FOOD.
I BET I CAN EAT THAT IN ONE BITE.
DO IT!
CHWOOOMP!
GIRLS!! KNOCK IT OFF!!
GIRLS!
I'M ON A DIET, SO DO SOMETHING FUNNY WITH MY TWINKIE.
OK

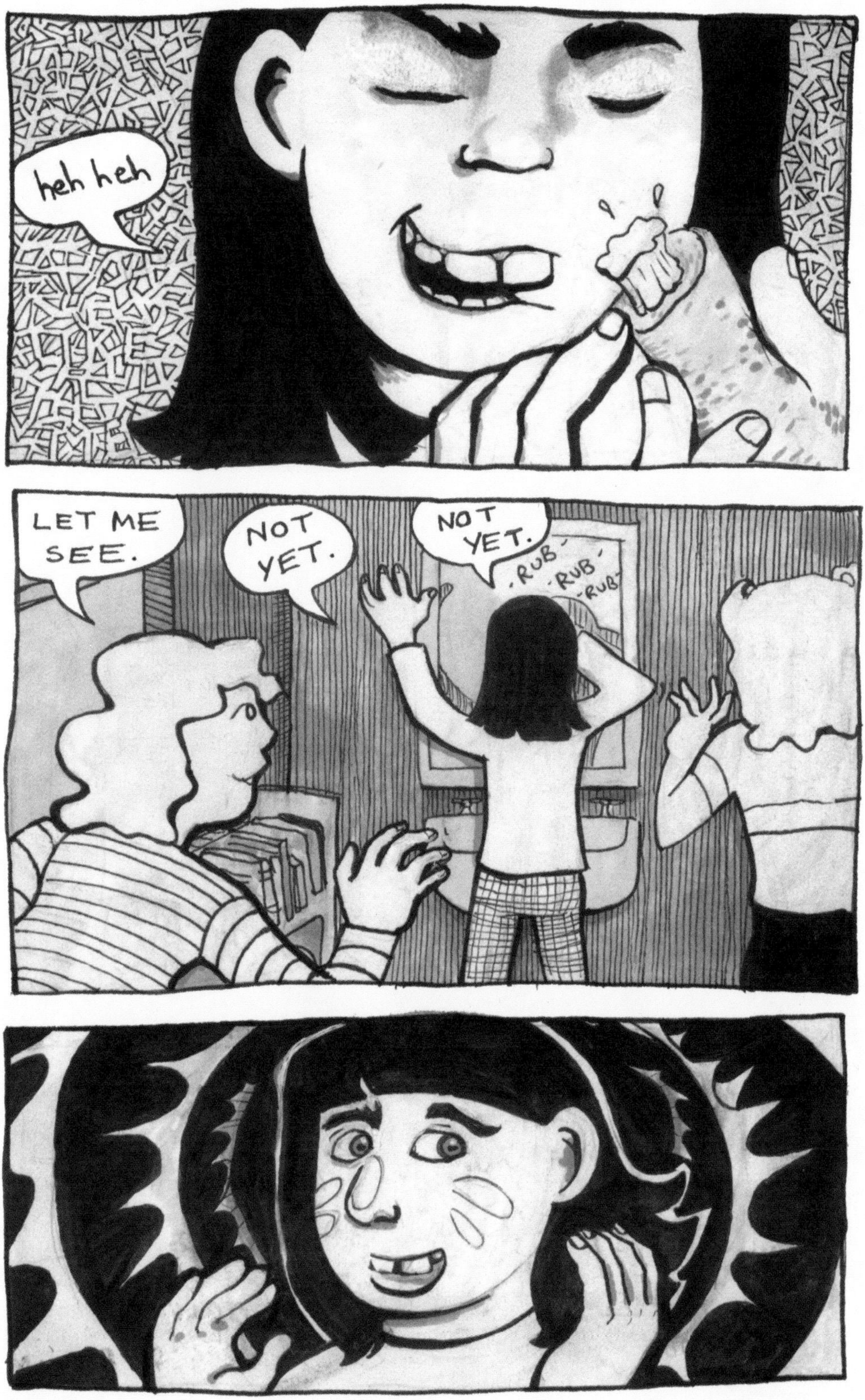
heh heh
LET ME SEE.
NOT YET.
NOT YET.
RUB RUB RUB

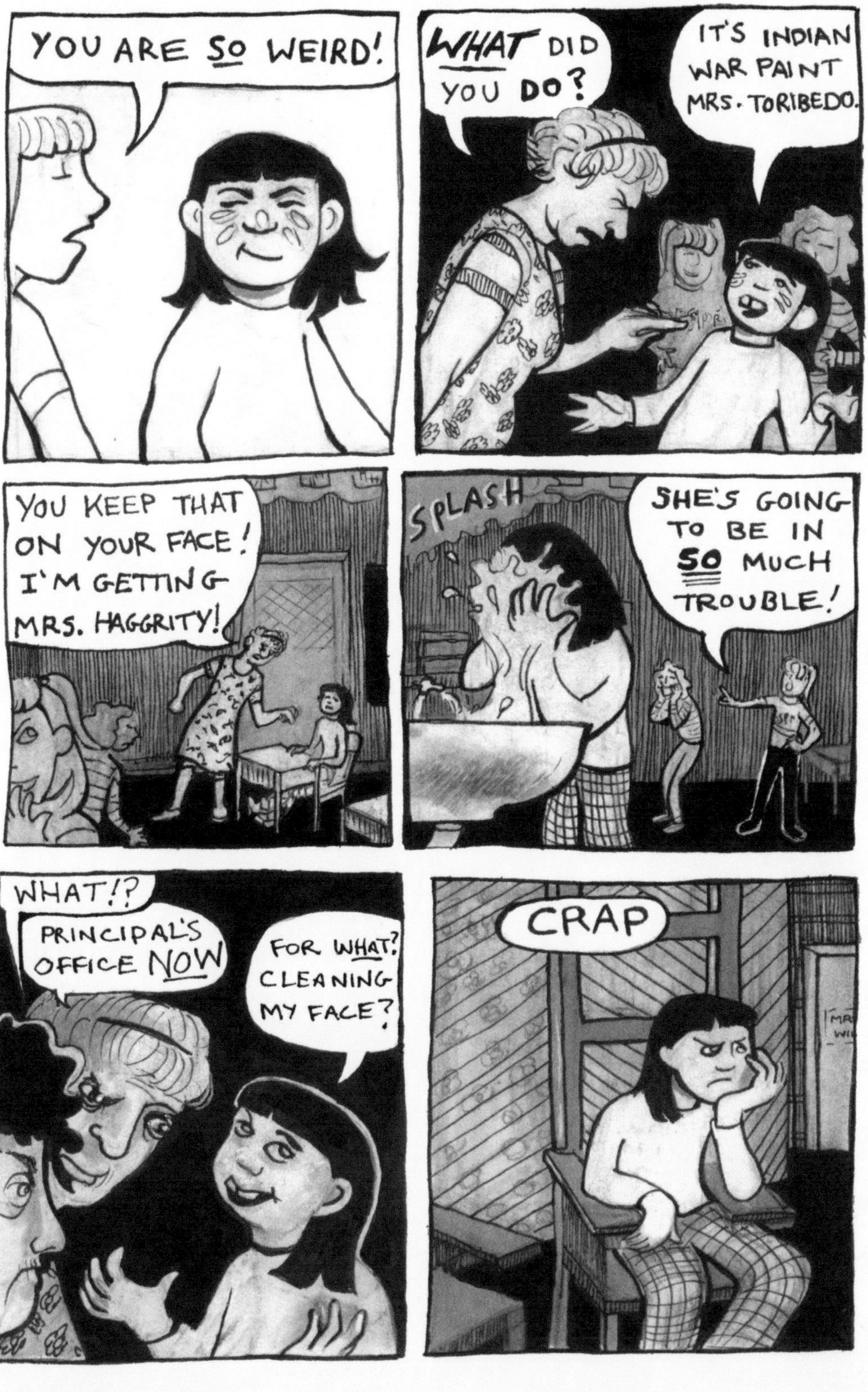
YOU ARE SO WEIRD!
WHAT DID YOU DO?
IT'S INDIAN WAR PAINT MRS. TORIBEDO.
YOU KEEP THAT ON YOUR FACE! I'M GETTING MRS. HAGGRITY!
SPLASH
SHE'S GOING TO BE IN SO MUCH TROUBLE!
WHAT!?
PRINCIPAL'S OFFICE NOW
FOR WHAT? CLEANING MY FACE?
CRAP

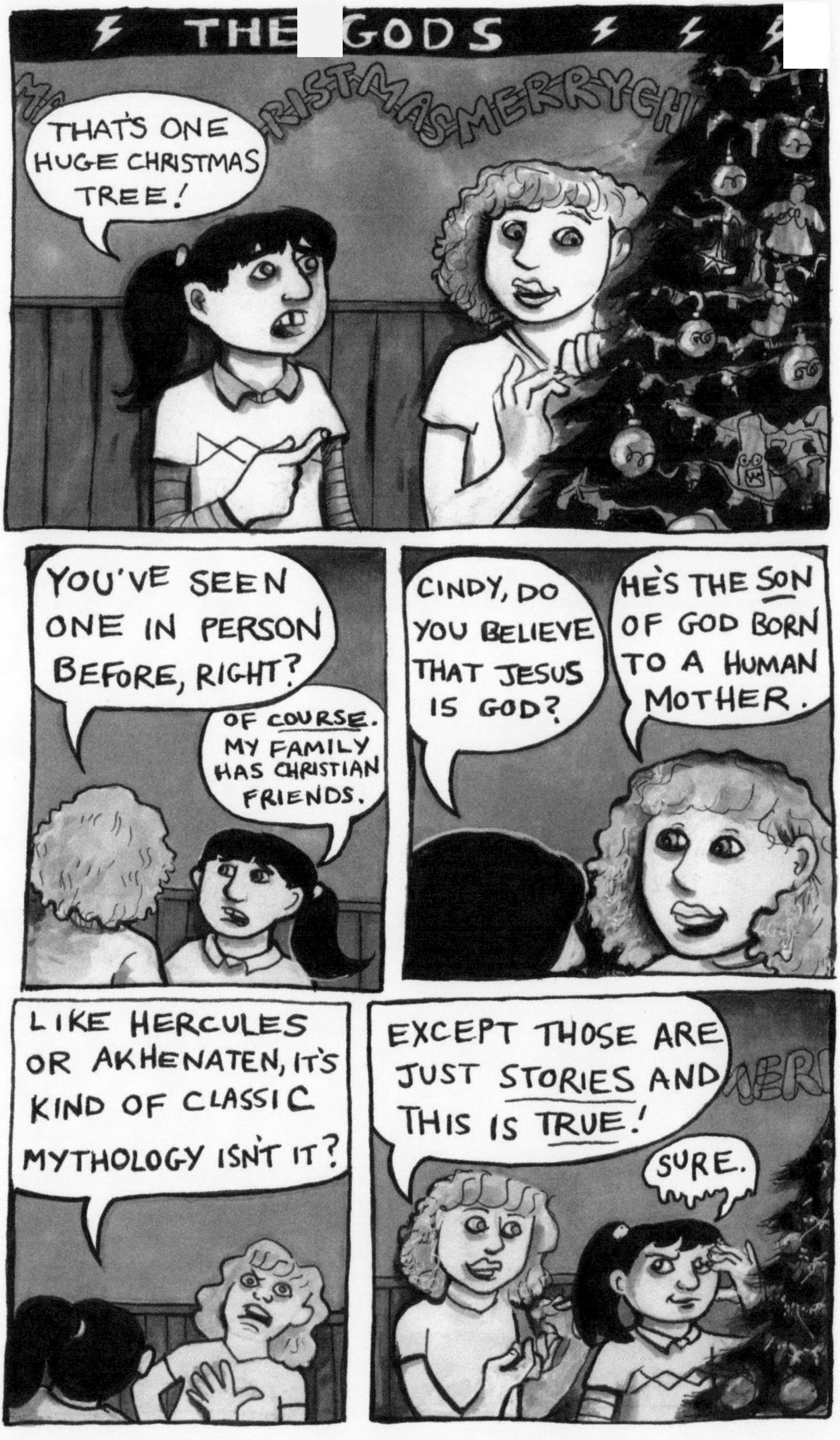
THE GODS
MERRYCHRISTMASMERRYCH
THAT'S ONE HUGE CHRISTMAS TREE!
YOU'VE SEEN ONE IN PERSON BEFORE, RIGHT?
OF COURSE. MY FAMILY HAS CHRISTIAN FRIENDS.
CINDY, DO YOU BELIEVE THAT JESUS IS GOD?
HE'S THE SON OF GOD BORN TO A HUMAN MOTHER.
LIKE HERCULES OR AKHENATEN, IT'S KIND OF CLASSIC MYTHOLOGY ISN'T IT?
EXCEPT THOSE ARE JUST STORIES AND THIS IS TRUE!
SURE.

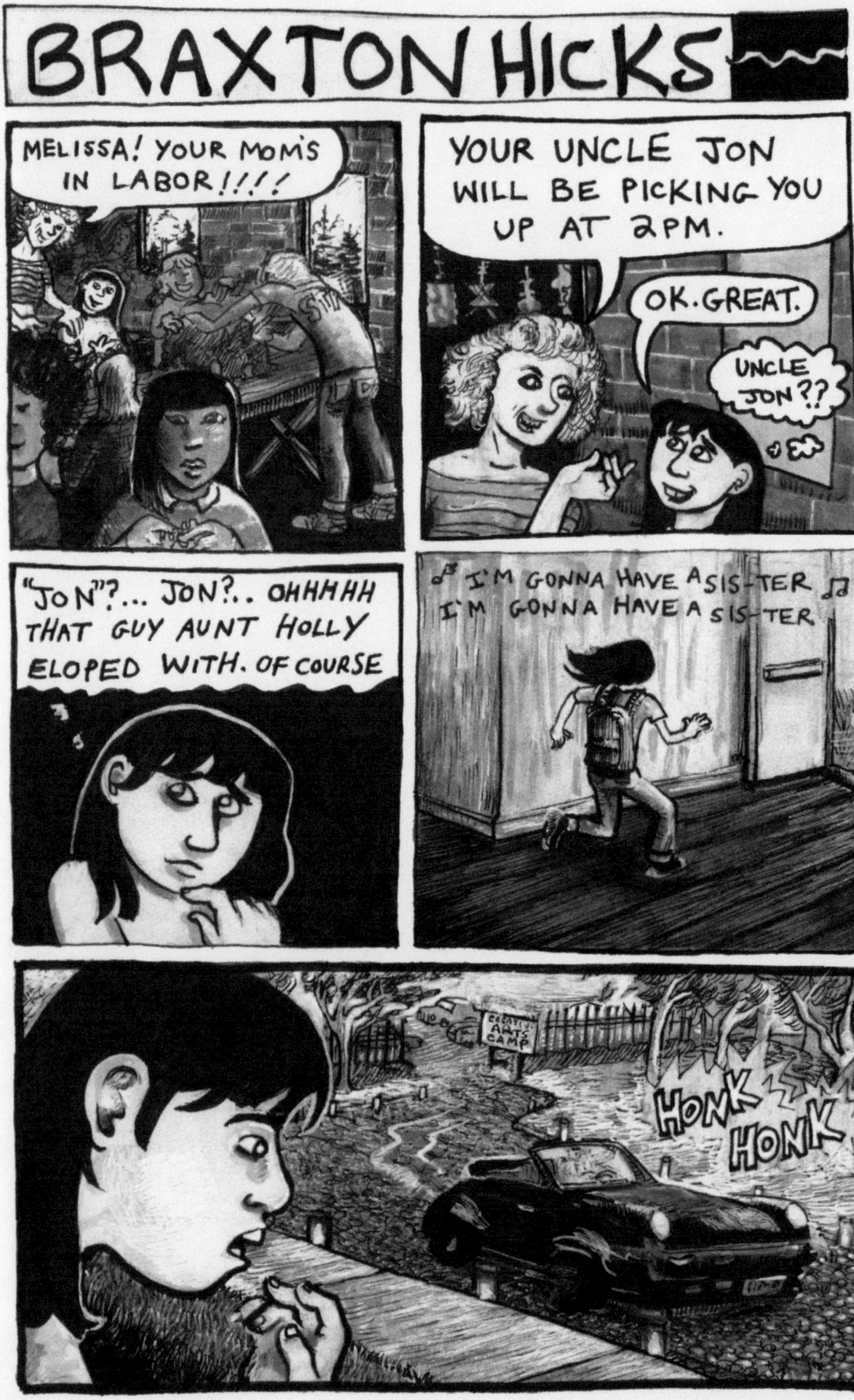
BRAXTON HICKS
MELISSA! YOUR MOM'S IN LABOR!!!!
YOUR UNCLE JON WILL BE PICKING YOU UP AT 2PM.
OK. GREAT.
UNCLE JON??
"JON"?... JON?.. OHHHHH THAT GUY AUNT HOLLY ELOPED WITH. OF COURSE
I'M GONNA HAVE A SIS-TER
I'M GONNA HAVE A SIS-TER
ARTS CAMP
HONK HONK

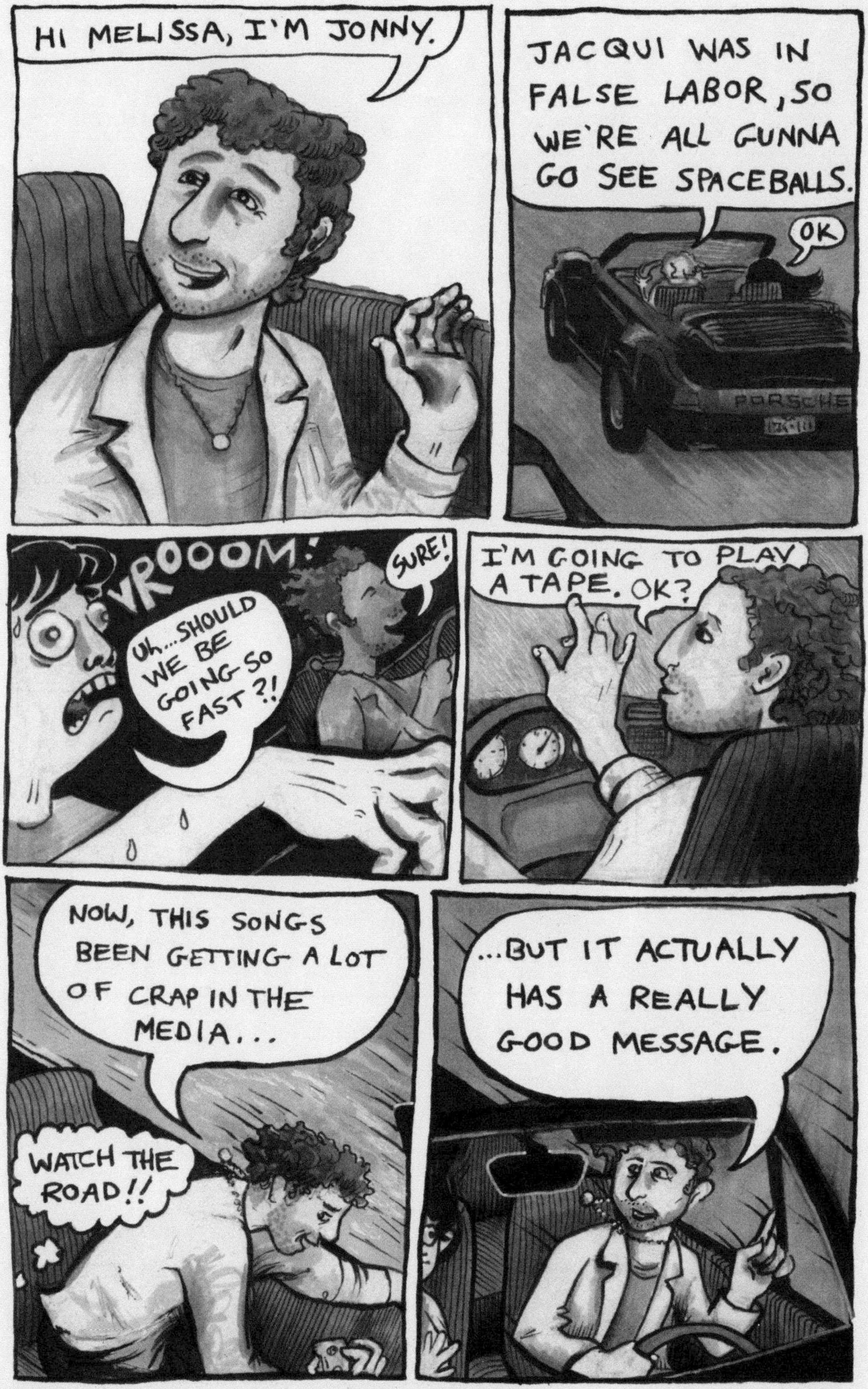
HI MELISSA, I'M JONNY.
JACQUI WAS IN FALSE LABOR, SO WE'RE ALL GUNNA GO SEE SPACEBALLS.
OK
PORSCHE
VROOOM!
SURE!
Uh...SHOULD WE BE GOING SO FAST?!
I'M GOING TO PLAY A TAPE. OK?
NOW, THIS SONGS BEEN GETTING A LOT OF CRAP IN THE MEDIA...
WATCH THE ROAD!!
...BUT IT ACTUALLY HAS A REALLY GOOD MESSAGE.

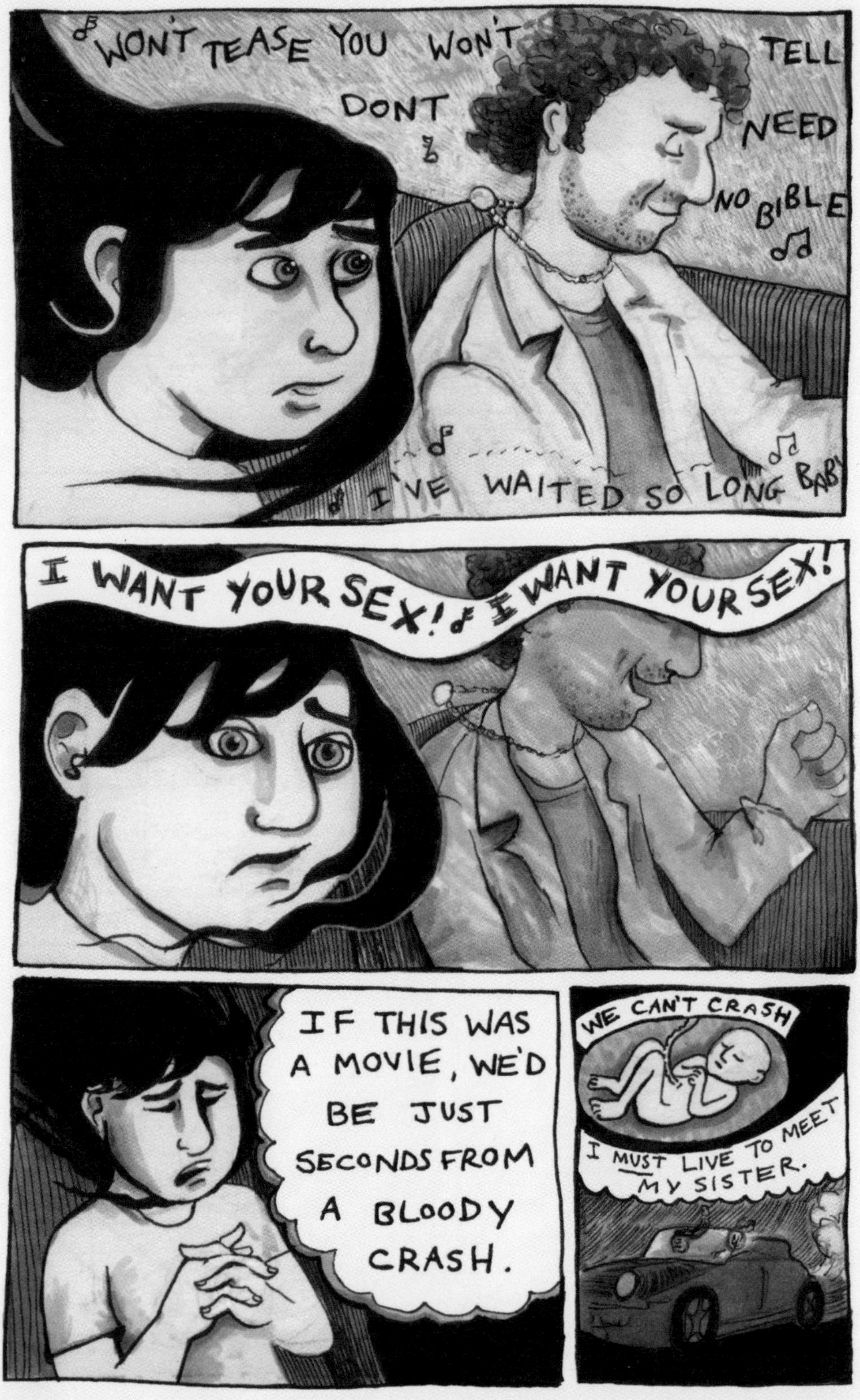
WON'T TEASE YOU WON'T TELL
DONT NEED NO BIBLE
I'VE WAITED SO LONG BABY
I WANT YOUR SEX! I WANT YOUR SEX!
IF THIS WAS A MOVIE, WE'D BE JUST SECONDS FROM A BLOODY CRASH.
WE CAN'T CRASH
I MUST LIVE TO MEET MY SISTER.

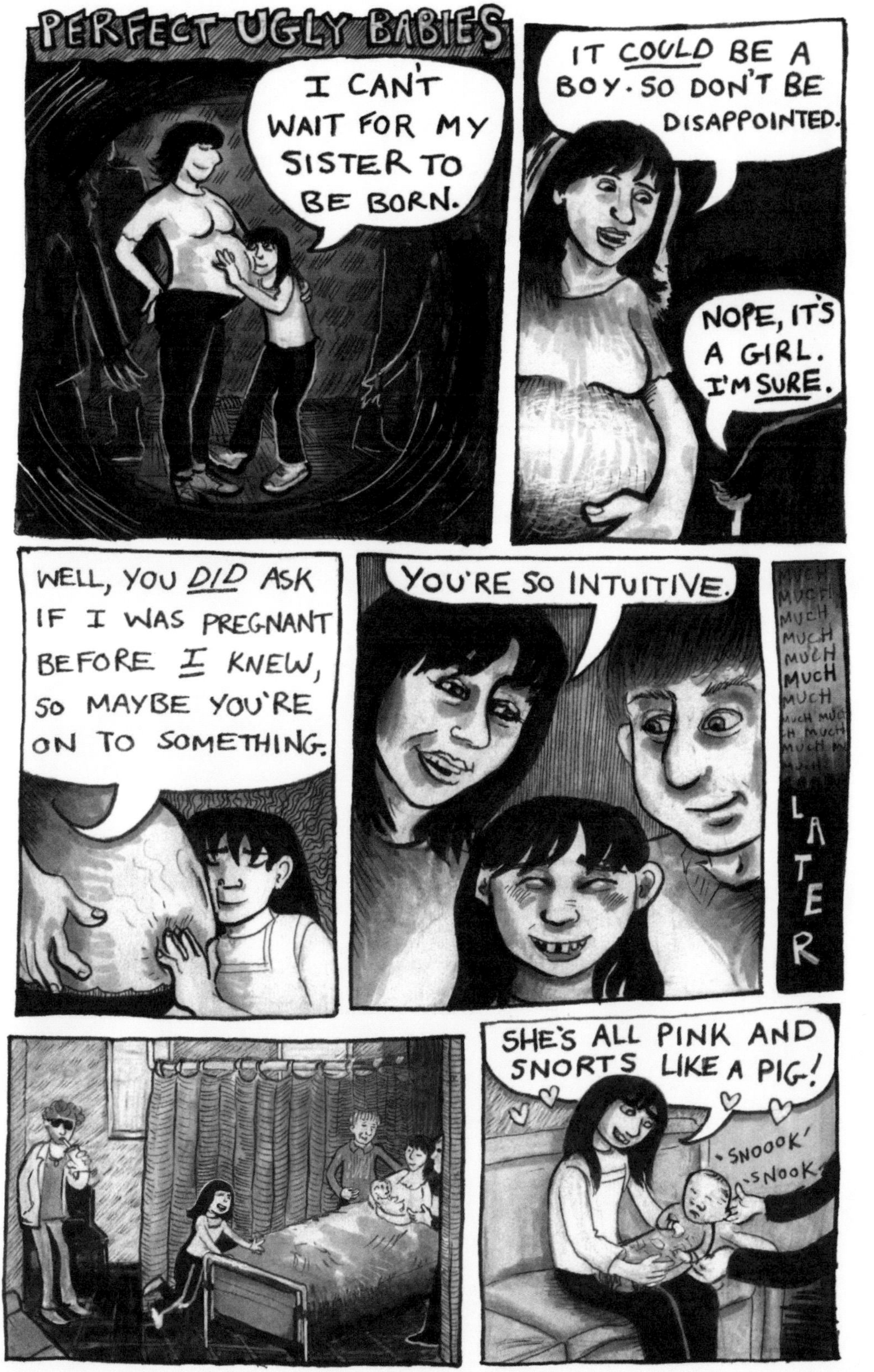
PERFECT UGLY BABIES
I CAN'T WAIT FOR MY SISTER TO BE BORN.
IT COULD BE A BOY. SO DON'T BE DISAPPOINTED.
NOPE, IT'S A GIRL. I'M SURE.
WELL, YOU DID ASK IF I WAS PREGNANT BEFORE I KNEW, SO MAYBE YOU'RE ON TO SOMETHING.
YOU'RE SO INTUITIVE.
LATER
SHE'S ALL PINK AND SNORTS LIKE A PIG!
SNOOOK'
SNOOK

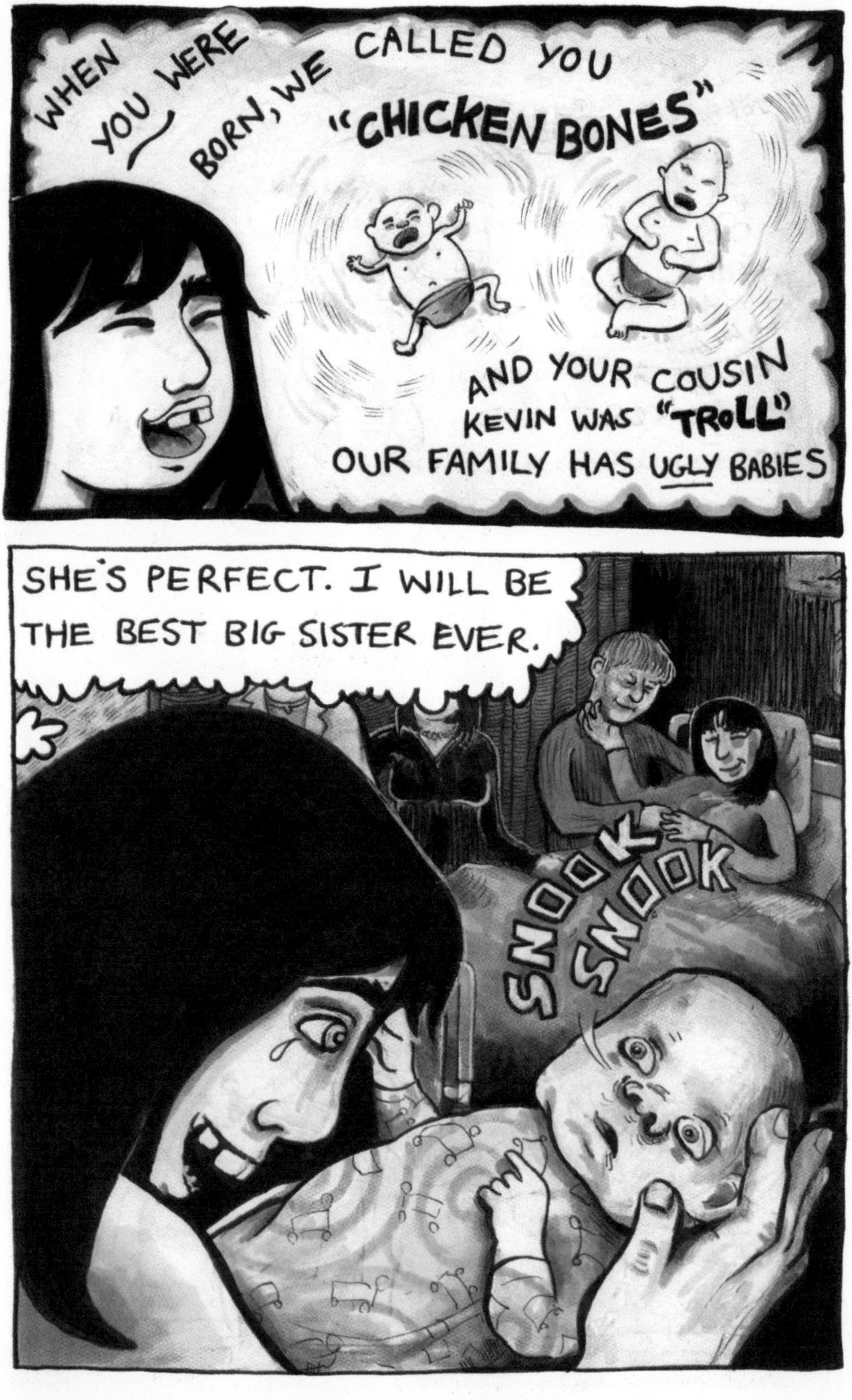
WHEN YOU WERE BORN, WE CALLED YOU "CHICKEN BONES"
AND YOUR COUSIN KEVIN WAS "TROLL"
OUR FAMILY HAS UGLY BABIES
SHE'S PERFECT. I WILL BE THE BEST BIG SISTER EVER.
SNOOK
SNOOK

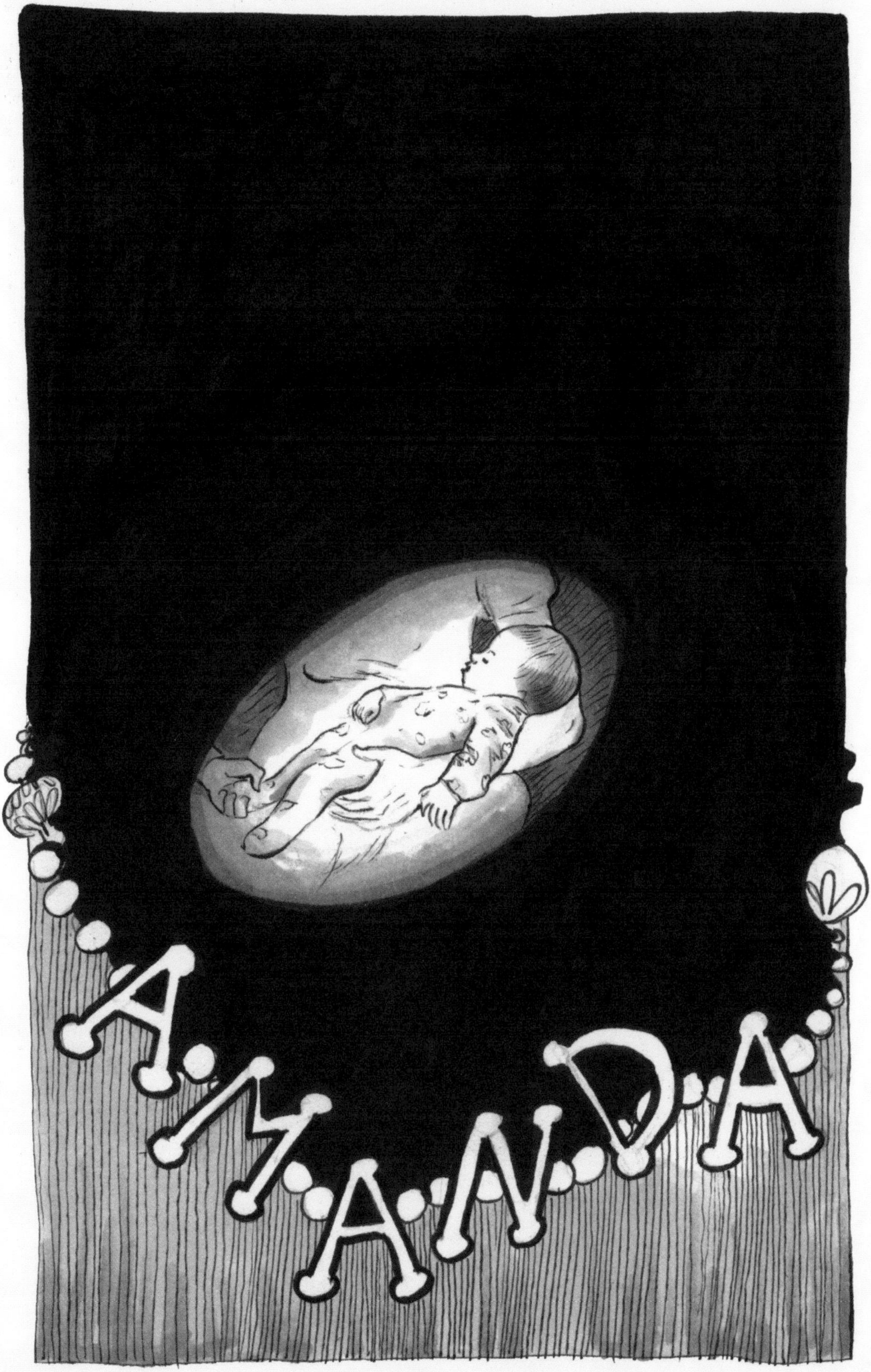
AMANDA

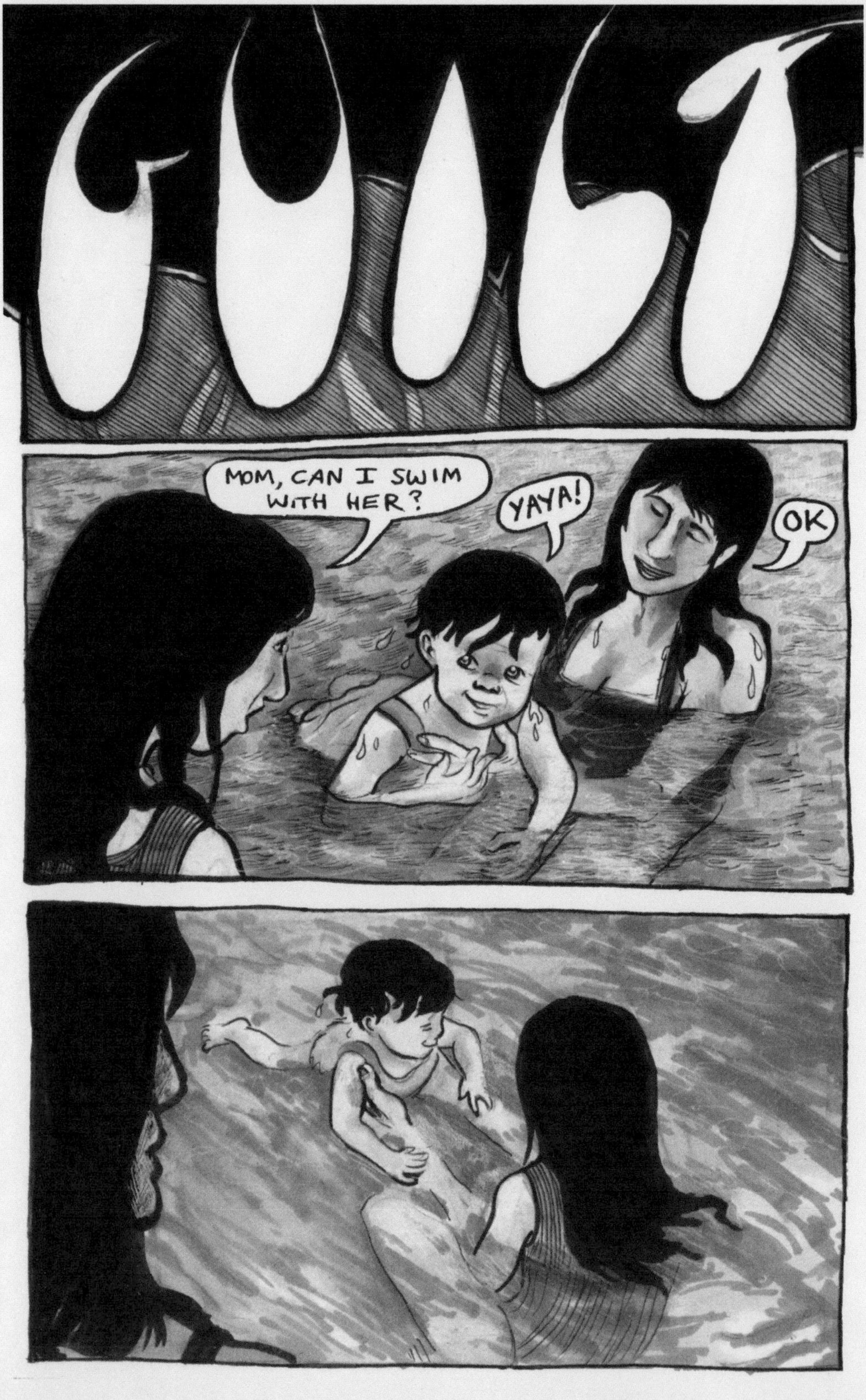
MOM, CAN I SWIM WITH HER?
YAYA!
OK

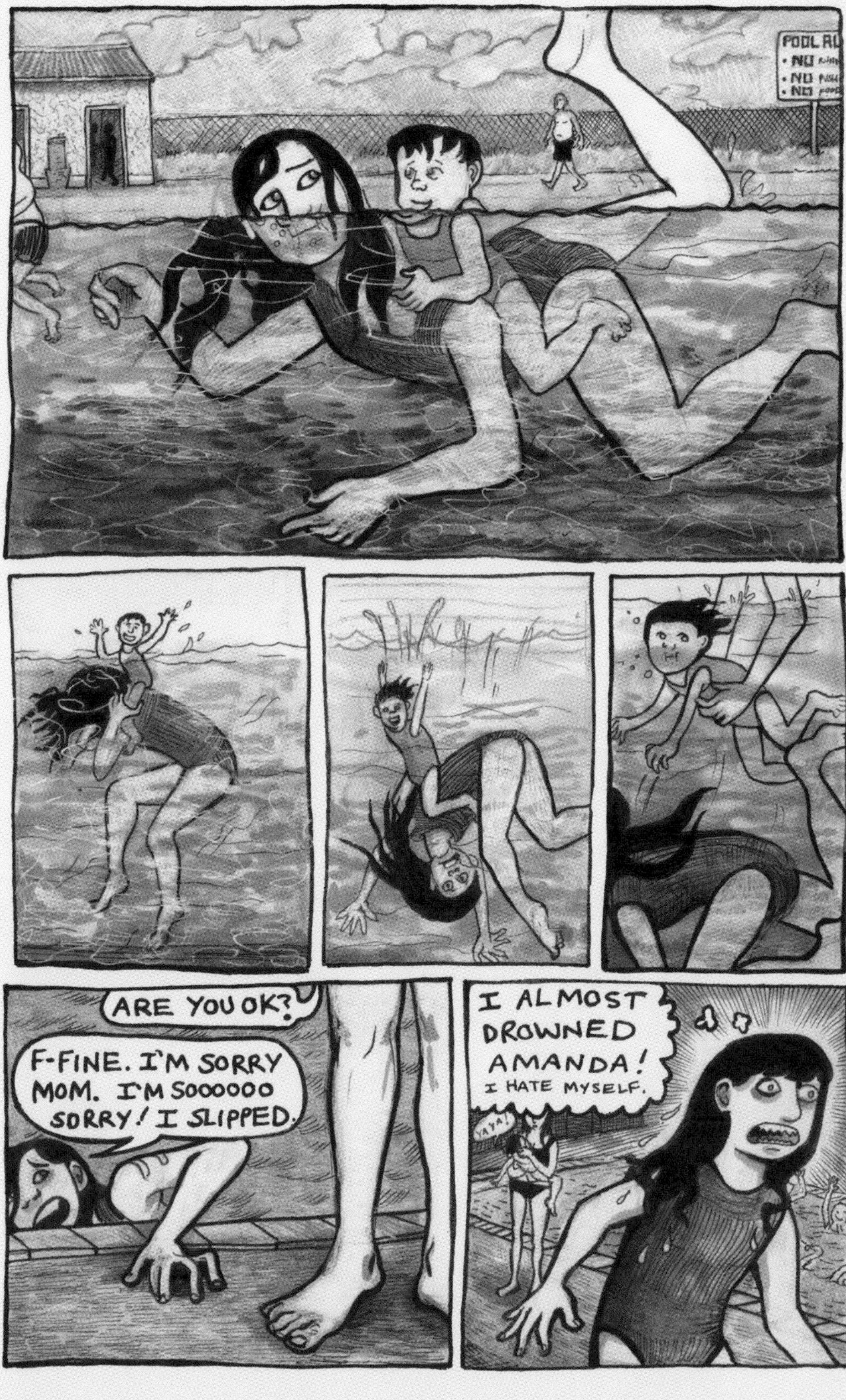
ARE YOU OK?
F-FINE. I'M SORRY MOM. I'M SOOOOOO SORRY! I SLIPPED.
I ALMOST DROWNED AMANDA!
I HATE MYSELF.
YA YA!

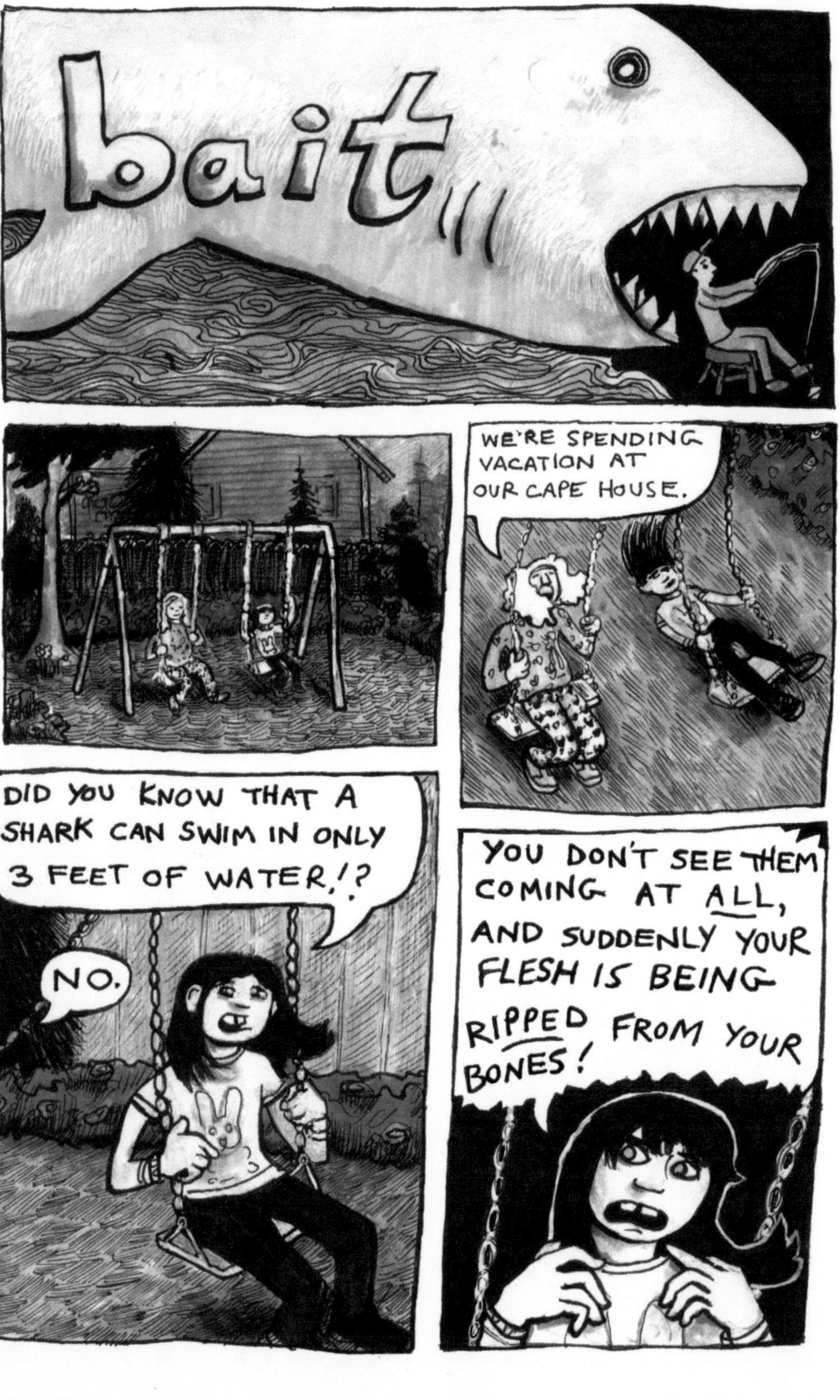
bait
WE'RE SPENDING VACATION AT OUR CAPE HOUSE.
DID YOU KNOW THAT A SHARK CAN SWIM IN ONLY 3 FEET OF WATER!?
NO.
YOU DON'T SEE THEM COMING AT ALL, AND SUDDENLY YOUR FLESH IS BEING RIPPED FROM YOUR BONES!

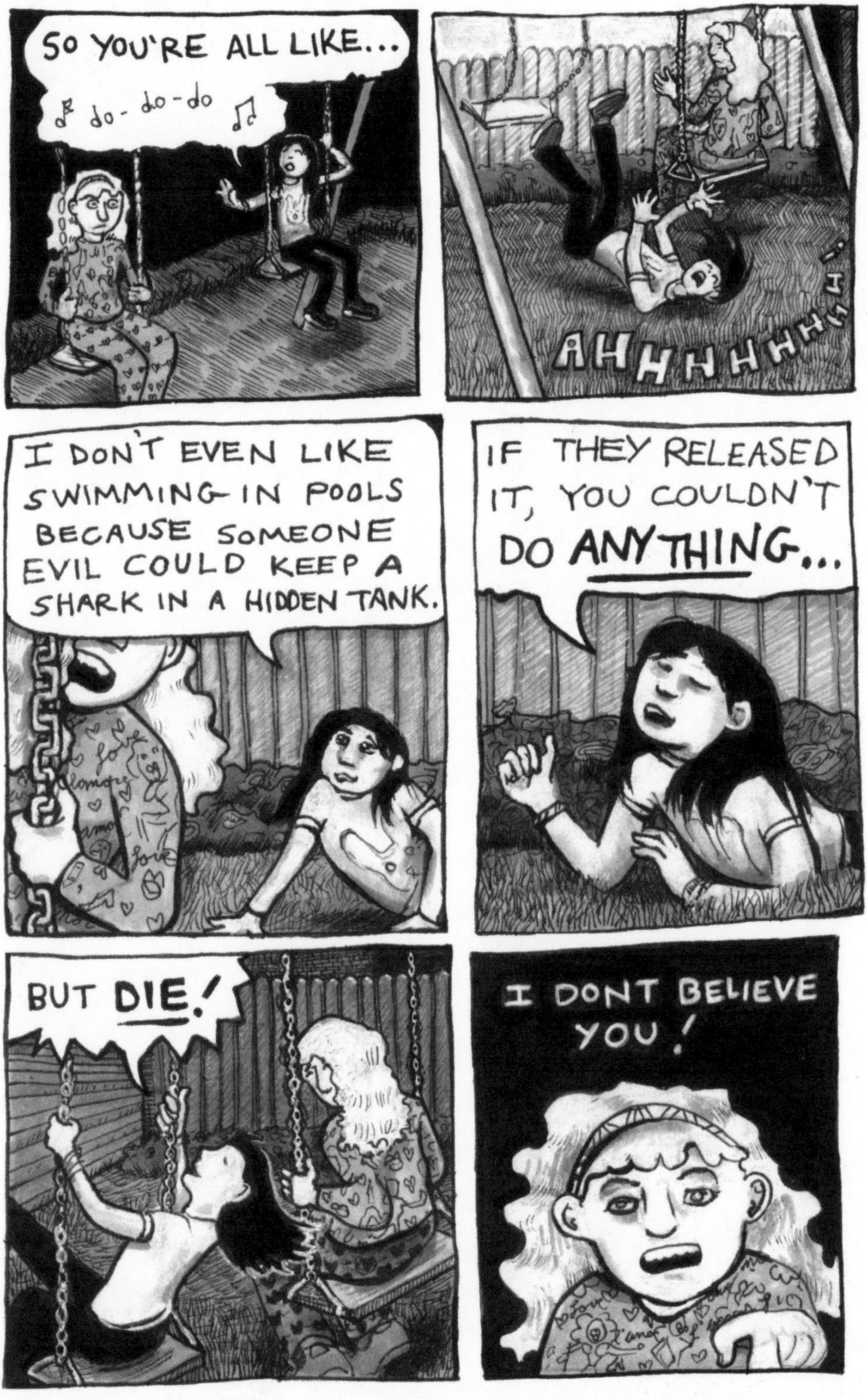
SO YOU'RE ALL LIKE...
do-do-do
AHHHHHHHH!
I DON'T EVEN LIKE SWIMMING IN POOLS BECAUSE SOMEONE EVIL COULD KEEP A SHARK IN A HIDDEN TANK.
IF THEY RELEASED IT, YOU COULDN'T DO ANYTHING...
BUT DIE!
I DONT BELIEVE YOU!

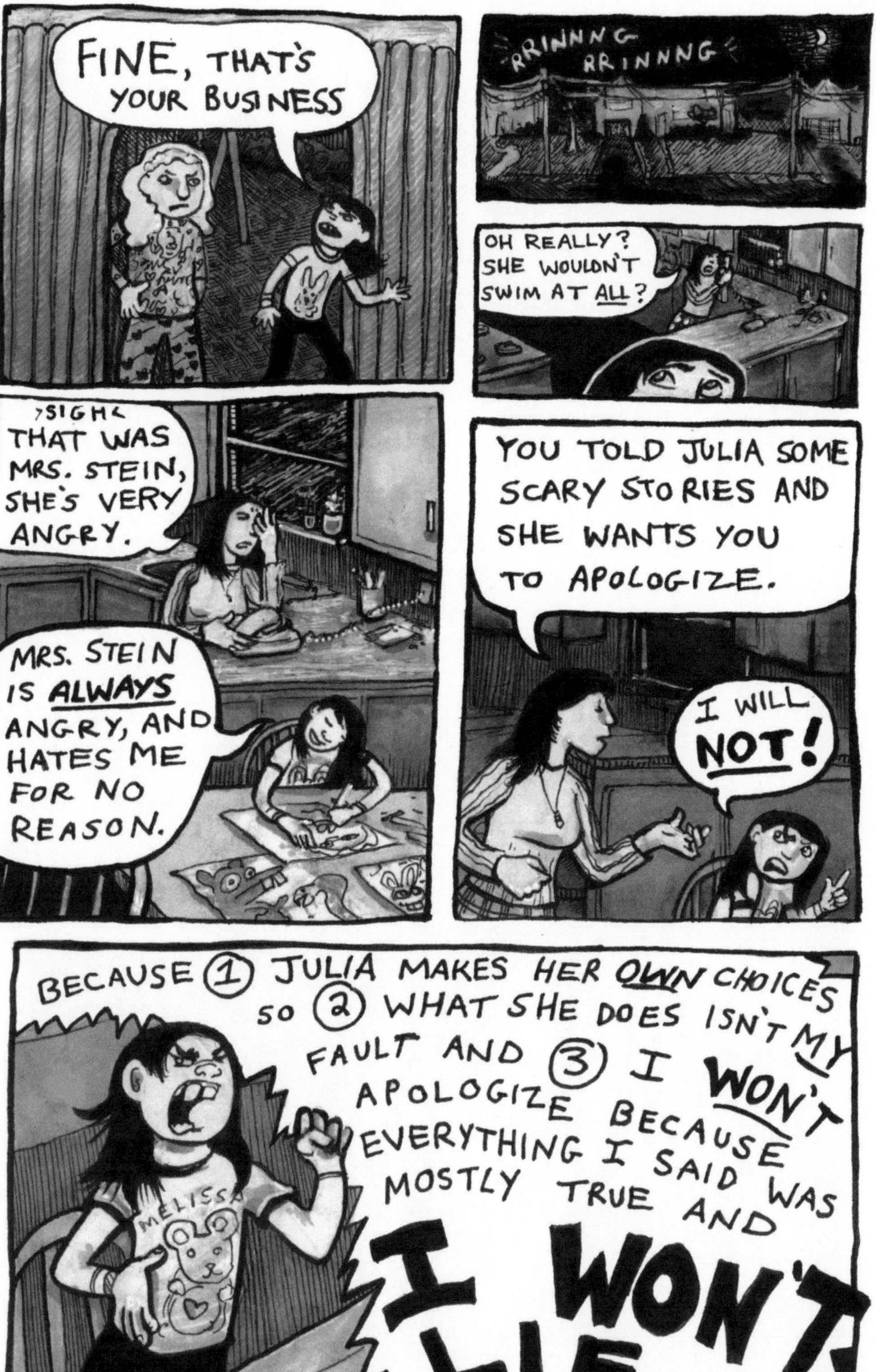
FINE, THAT'S YOUR BUSINESS
RRINNNG RRINNNG
OH REALLY? SHE WOULDN'T SWIM AT ALL?
>SIGH<
THAT WAS MRS. STEIN, SHE'S VERY ANGRY.
MRS. STEIN IS ALWAYS ANGRY, AND HATES ME FOR NO REASON.
YOU TOLD JULIA SOME SCARY STORIES AND SHE WANTS YOU TO APOLOGIZE.
I WILL NOT!
BECAUSE (1) JULIA MAKES HER OWN CHOICES SO (2) WHAT SHE DOES ISN'T MY FAULT AND (3) I WON'T APOLOGIZE BECAUSE EVERYTHING I SAID WAS MOSTLY TRUE AND
I WON'T LIE.
MELISSA

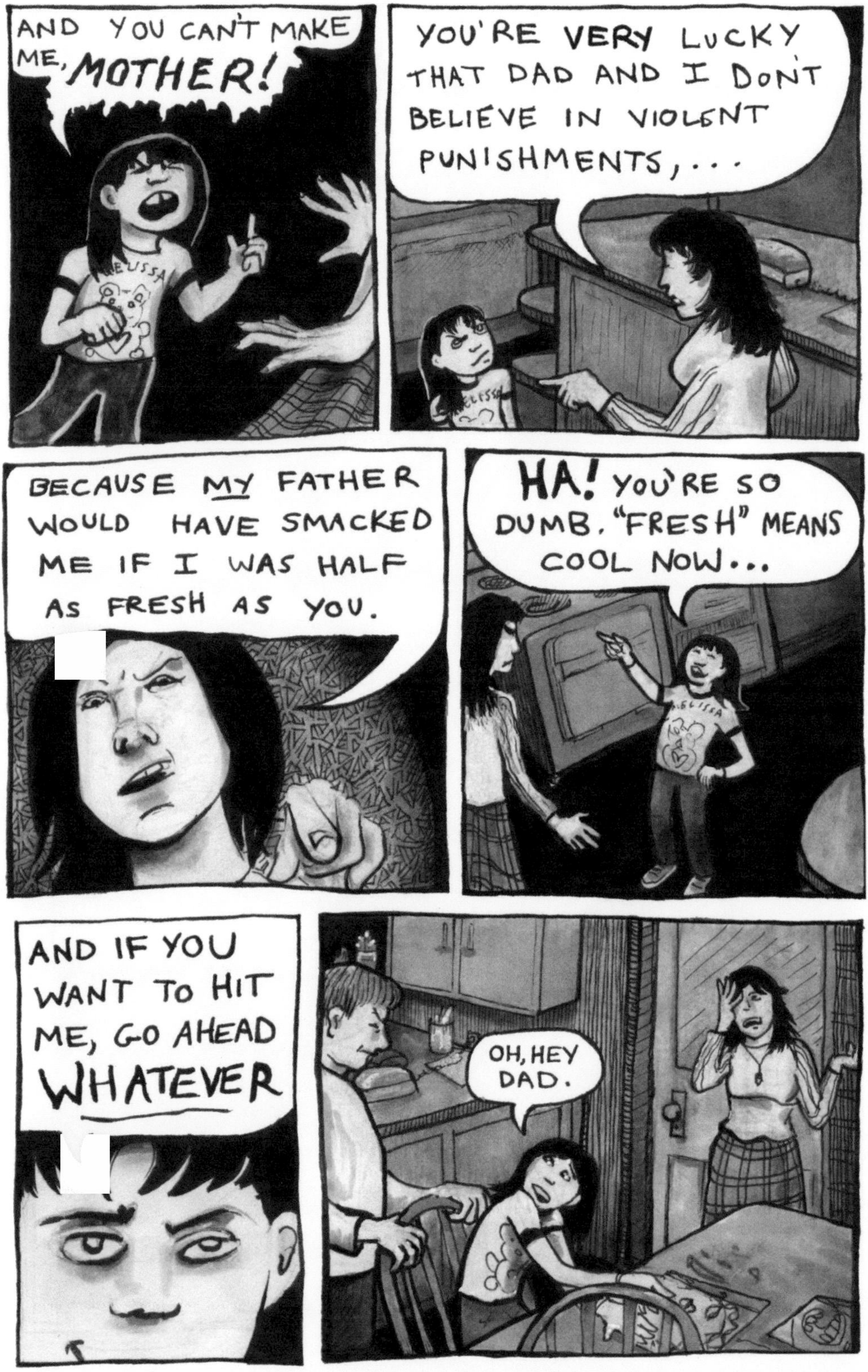
AND YOU CAN'T MAKE ME, MOTHER!
YOU'RE VERY LUCKY THAT DAD AND I DON'T BELIEVE IN VIOLENT PUNISHMENTS, . . .
MELISSA
BECAUSE MY FATHER WOULD HAVE SMACKED ME IF I WAS HALF AS FRESH AS YOU.
HA! YOU'RE SO DUMB. "FRESH" MEANS COOL NOW...
AND IF YOU WANT TO HIT ME, GO AHEAD WHATEVER
OH, HEY DAD.

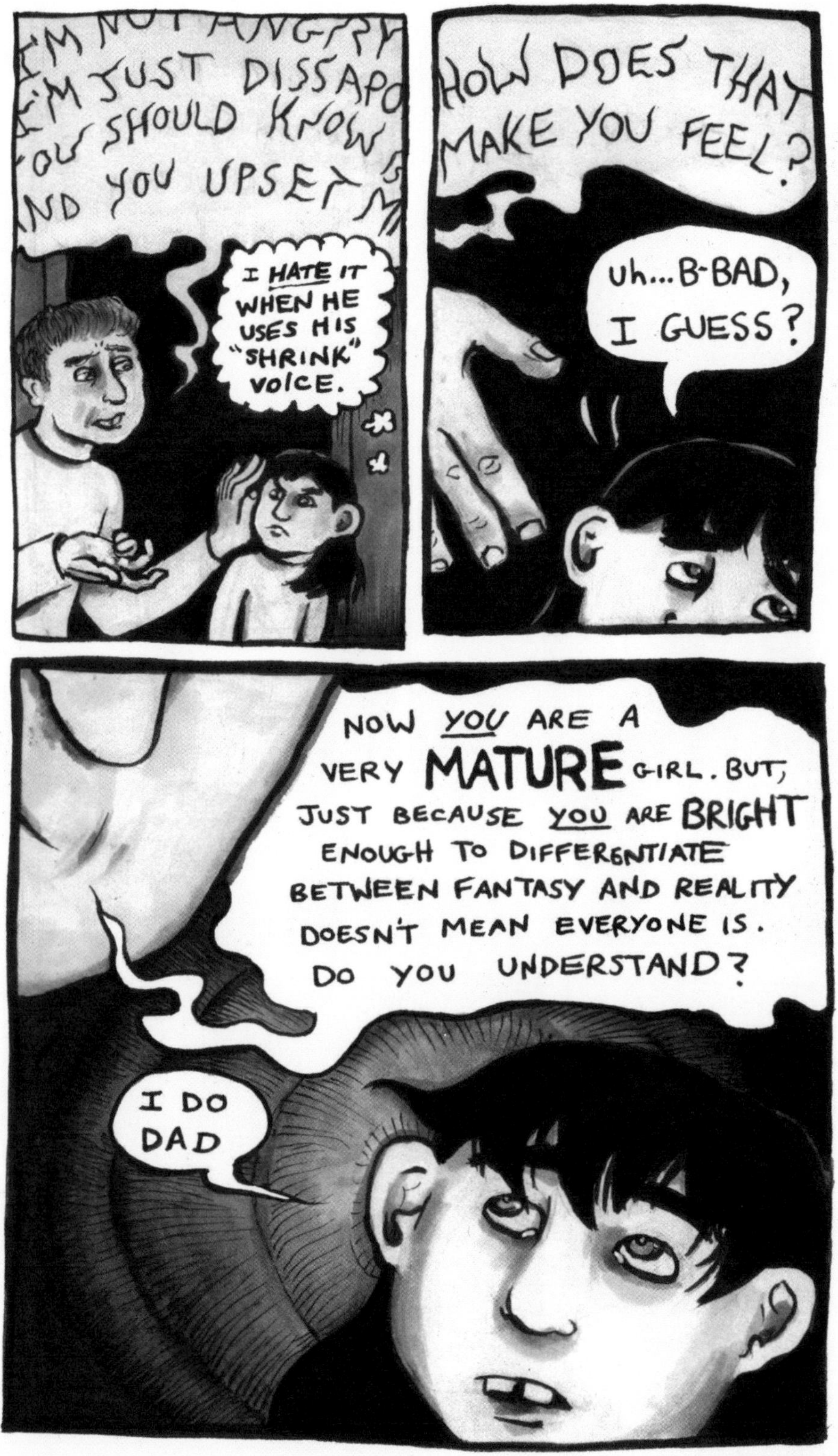
I'M NOT ANGRY
I'M JUST DISSAPO
OU SHOULD KNOW
ND YOU UPSET M
I HATE IT WHEN HE USES HIS "SHRINK" VOICE.
HOW DOES THAT MAKE YOU FEEL?
Uh... B-BAD, I GUESS?
NOW YOU ARE A VERY MATURE GIRL. BUT, JUST BECAUSE YOU ARE BRIGHT ENOUGH TO DIFFERENTIATE BETWEEN FANTASY AND REALITY DOESN'T MEAN EVERYONE IS. DO YOU UNDERSTAND?
I DO DAD

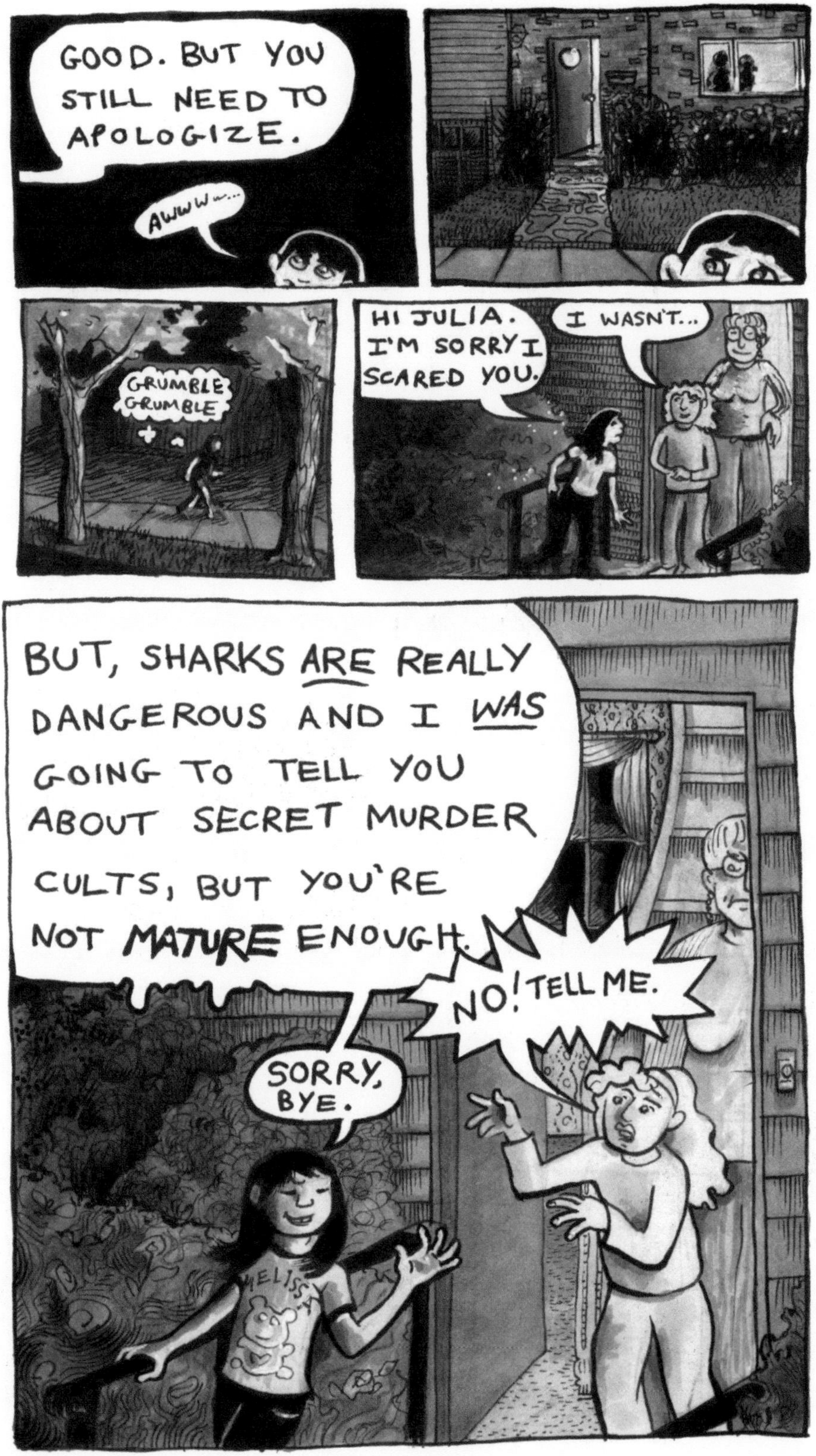
GOOD. BUT YOU STILL NEED TO APOLOGIZE.
AWWW...
GRUMBLE GRUMBLE
HI JULIA. I'M SORRY I SCARED YOU.
I WASN'T...
BUT, SHARKS ARE REALLY DANGEROUS AND I WAS GOING TO TELL YOU ABOUT SECRET MURDER CULTS, BUT YOU'RE NOT MATURE ENOUGH.
SORRY, BYE.
NO! TELL ME.
MELISSA

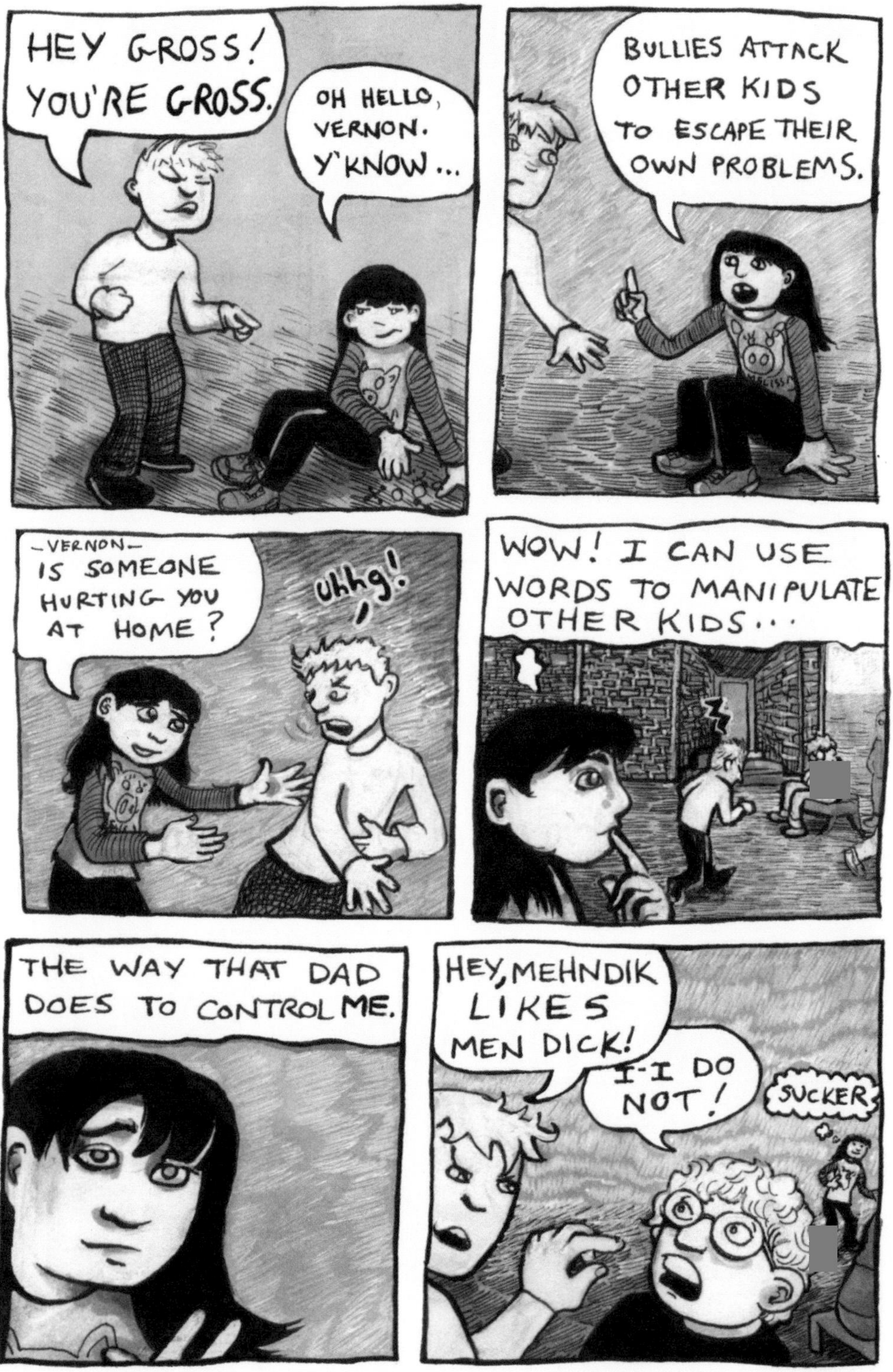
HEY GROSS! YOU'RE GROSS.
OH HELLO, VERNON. Y'KNOW...
BULLIES ATTACK OTHER KIDS TO ESCAPE THEIR OWN PROBLEMS.
-VERNON- IS SOMEONE HURTING YOU AT HOME?
uhhg!
WOW! I CAN USE WORDS TO MANIPULATE OTHER KIDS...
THE WAY THAT DAD DOES TO CONTROL ME.
HEY, MEHNDIK LIKES MEN DICK!
I-I DO NOT!
SUCKER

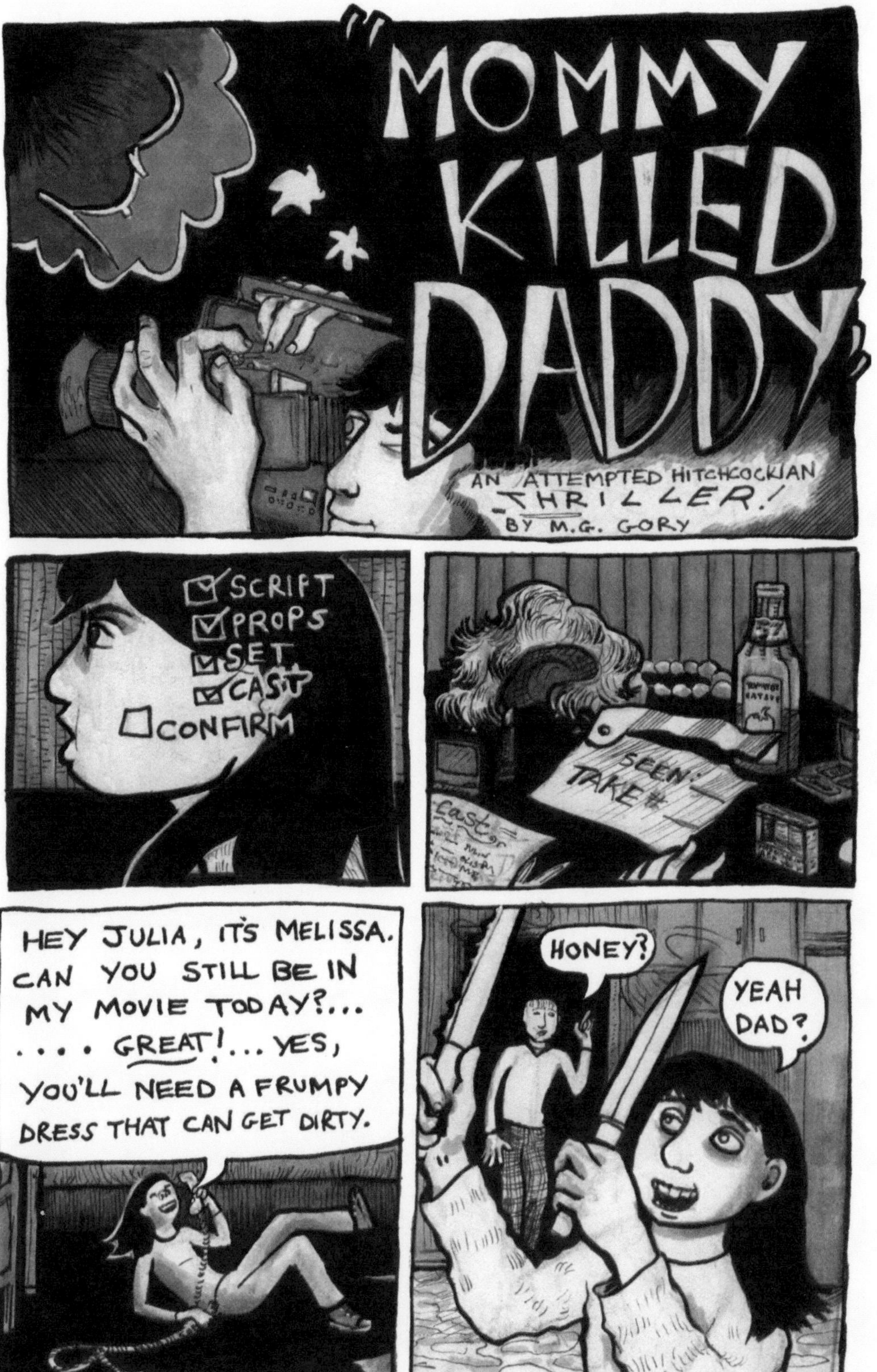
"MOMMY KILLED DADDY"
AN ATTEMPTED HITCHCOCKIAN THRILLER!
BY M.G. GORY
SCRIPT
PROPS
SET
CAST
CONFIRM
SEEN:
TAKE#
CAST
HEY JULIA, IT'S MELISSA. CAN YOU STILL BE IN MY MOVIE TODAY?... .... GREAT!... YES, YOU'LL NEED A FRUMPY DRESS THAT CAN GET DIRTY.
HONEY?
YEAH DAD?

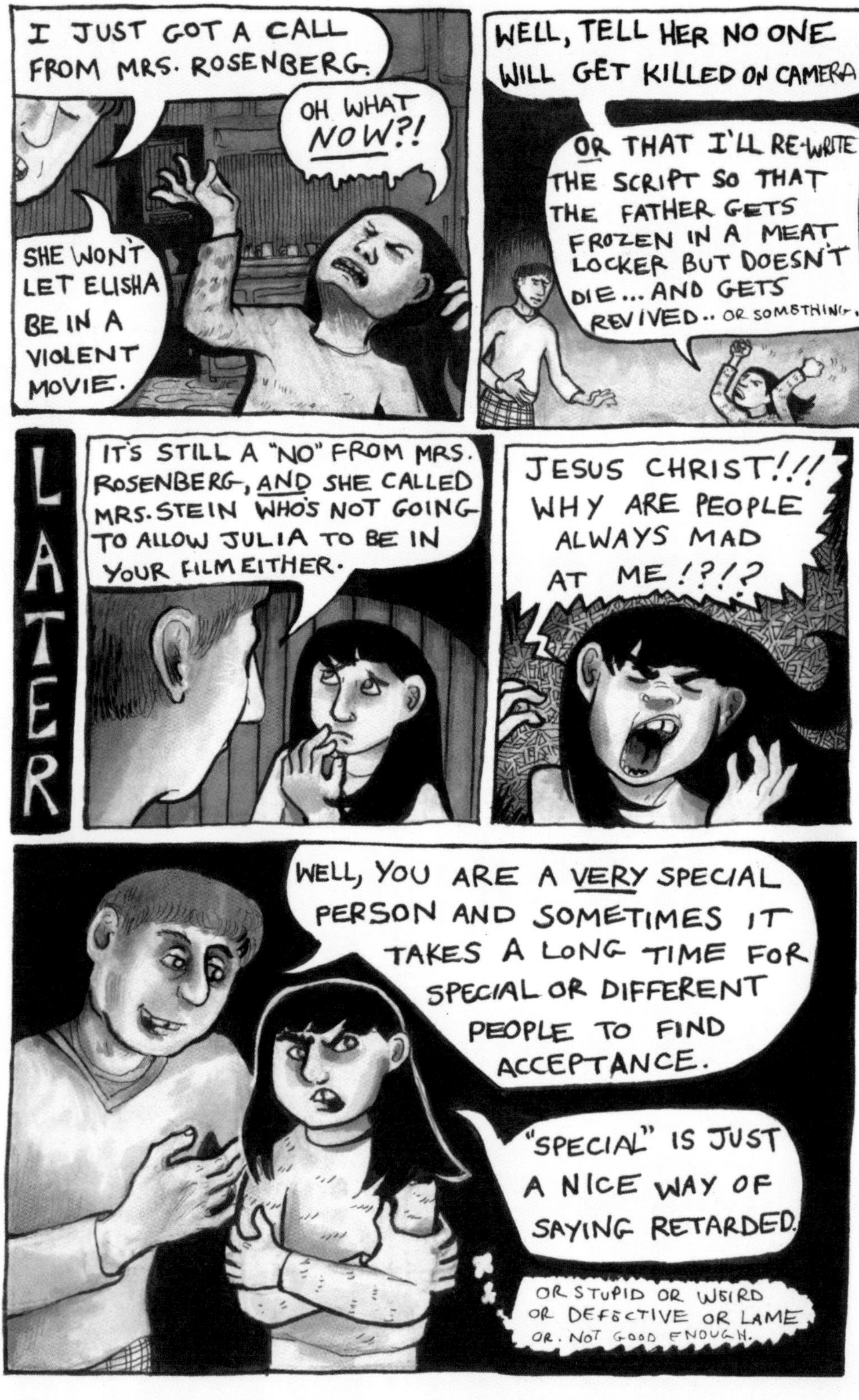
I JUST GOT A CALL FROM MRS. ROSENBERG.
OH WHAT NOW?!
SHE WON'T LET ELISHA BE IN A VIOLENT MOVIE.
WELL, TELL HER NO ONE WILL GET KILLED ON CAMERA
OR THAT I'LL RE-WRITE THE SCRIPT SO THAT THE FATHER GETS FROZEN IN A MEAT LOCKER BUT DOESN'T DIE... AND GETS REVIVED.. OR SOMETHING.
LATER
IT'S STILL A "NO" FROM MRS. ROSENBERG, AND SHE CALLED MRS. STEIN WHO'S NOT GOING TO ALLOW JULIA TO BE IN YOUR FILM EITHER.
JESUS CHRIST!!! WHY ARE PEOPLE ALWAYS MAD AT ME!?!?
WELL, YOU ARE A VERY SPECIAL PERSON AND SOMETIMES IT TAKES A LONG TIME FOR SPECIAL OR DIFFERENT PEOPLE TO FIND ACCEPTANCE.
"SPECIAL" IS JUST A NICE WAY OF SAYING RETARDED.
OR STUPID OR WEIRD OR DEFECTIVE OR LAME OR. NOT GOOD ENOUGH.

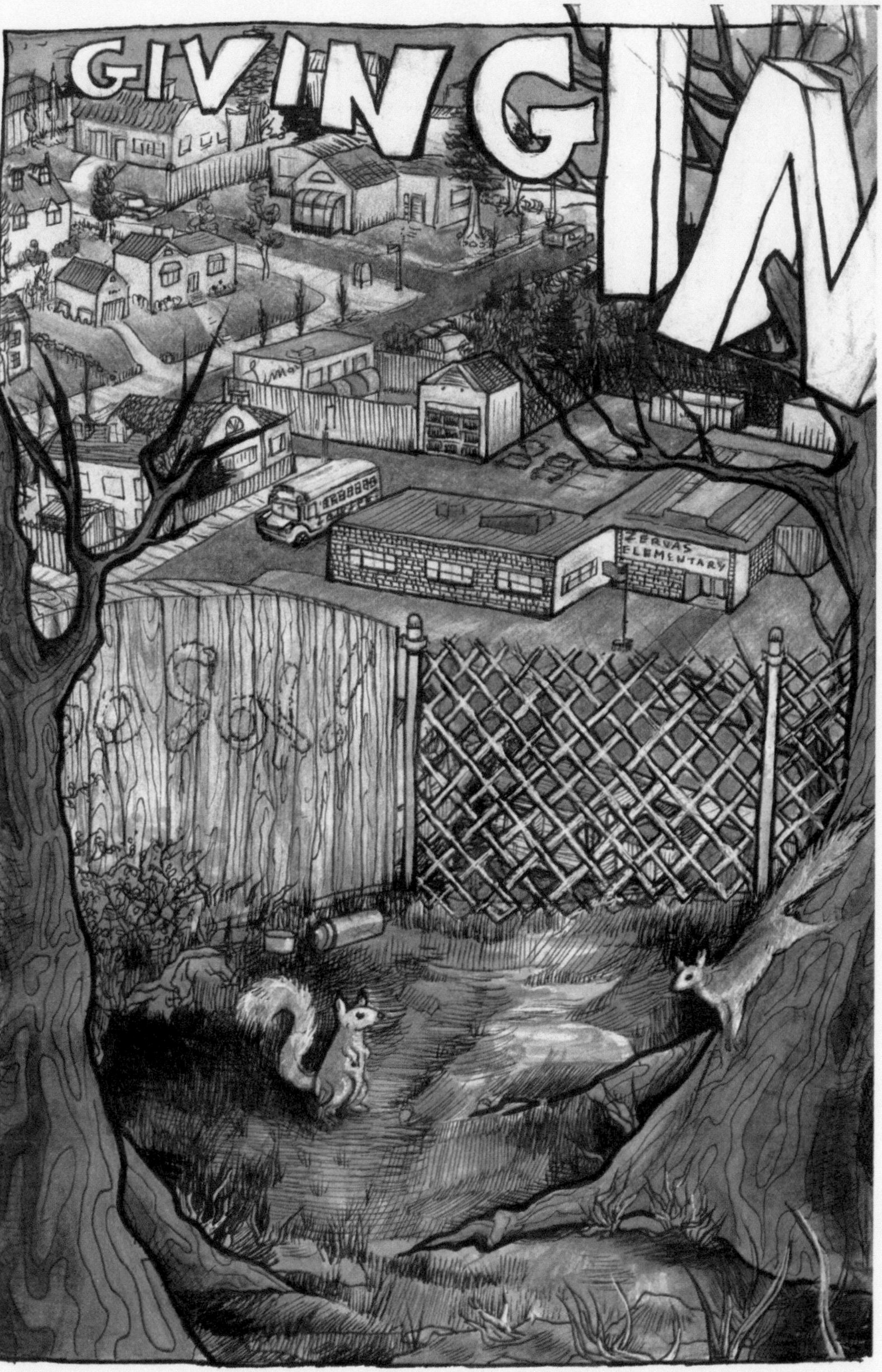
GIVING GIAN
ZERVAS ELEMENTARY

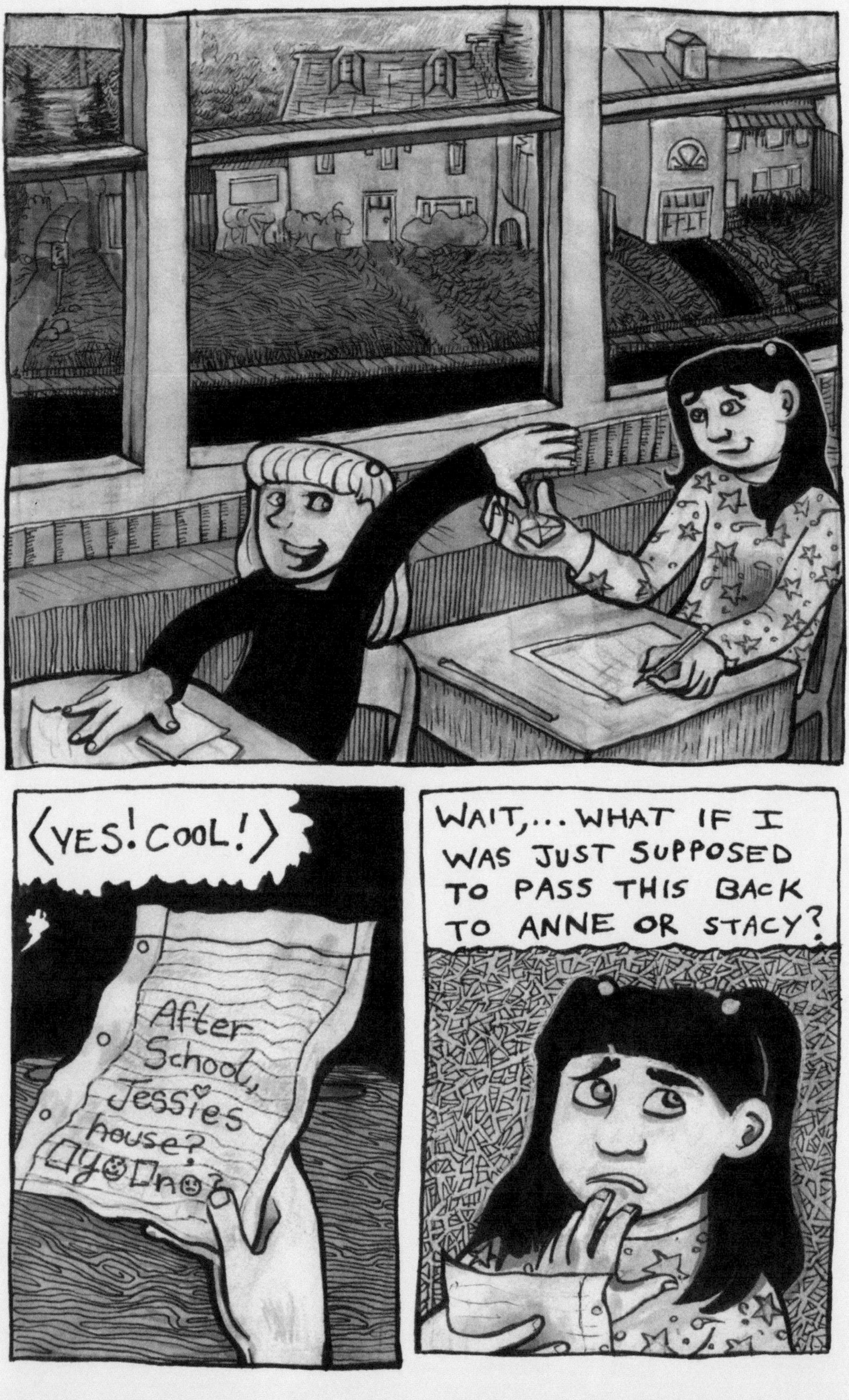
<YES! COOL!>
After School, Jessies house? ☐y ☐no?
WAIT,... WHAT IF I WAS JUST SUPPOSED TO PASS THIS BACK TO ANNE OR STACY?

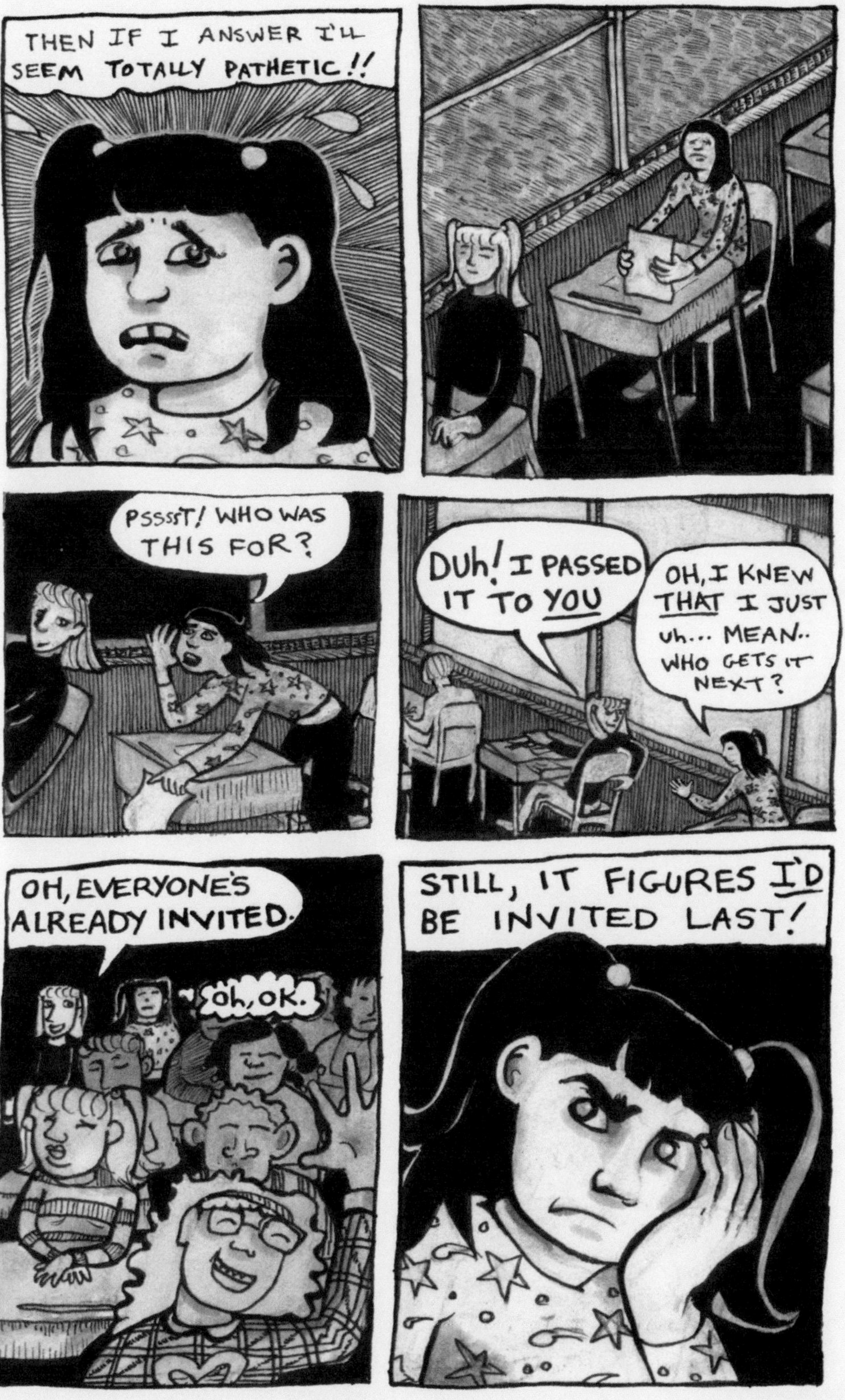
THEN IF I ANSWER I'LL SEEM TOTALLY PATHETIC!!
PSSSST! WHO WAS THIS FOR?
DUH! I PASSED IT TO YOU
OH, I KNEW THAT I JUST uh... MEAN.. WHO GETS IT NEXT?
OH, EVERYONE'S ALREADY INVITED.
oh, OK.
STILL, IT FIGURES I'D BE INVITED LAST!

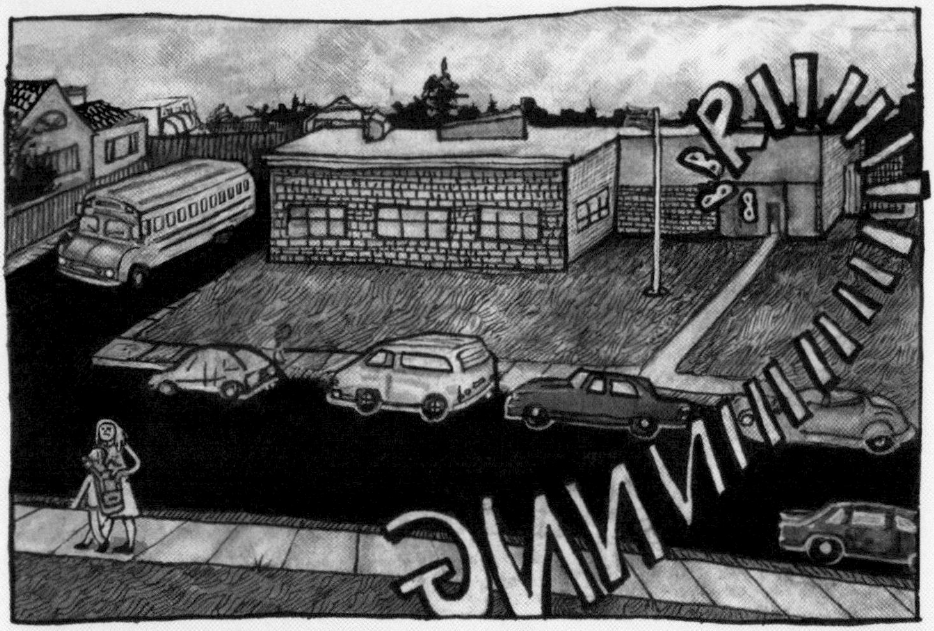
BRIIIIIIIIIIIINNNNG

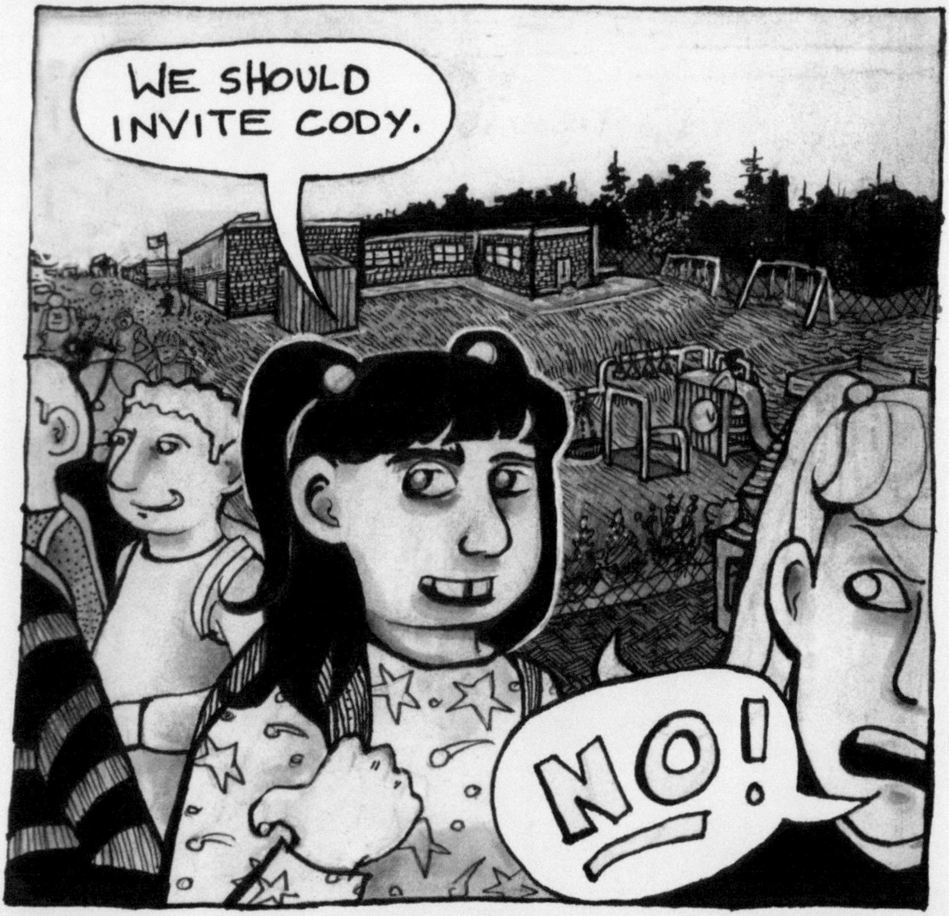
WE SHOULD INVITE CODY.
NO!

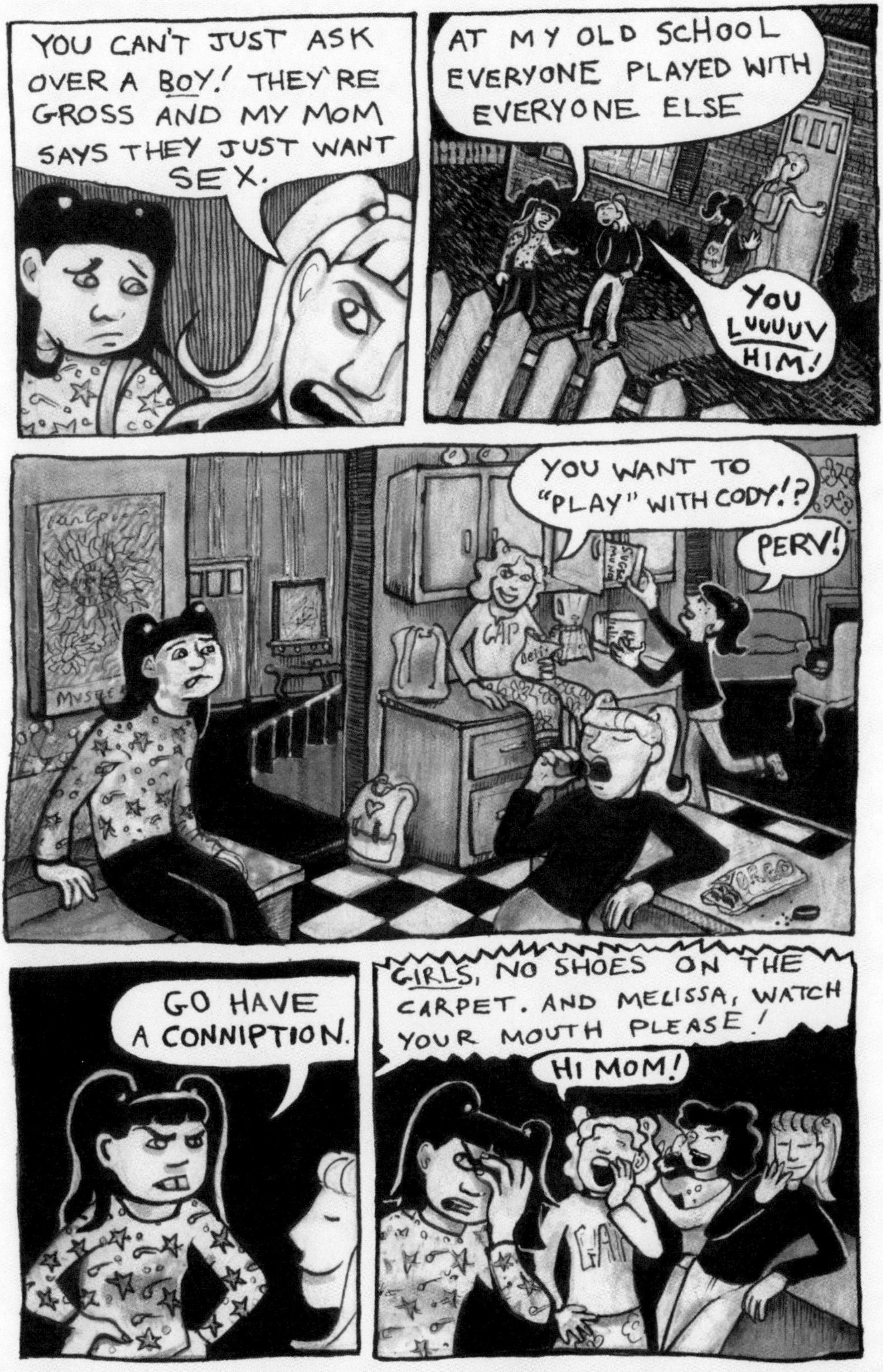

YOU CAN'T JUST ASK OVER A BOY! THEY'RE GROSS AND MY MOM SAYS THEY JUST WANT SEX.
AT MY OLD SCHOOL EVERYONE PLAYED WITH EVERYONE ELSE
YOU LUUUUV HIM!
YOU WANT TO "PLAY" WITH CODY!?
PERV!
OREO
GO HAVE A CONNIPTION.
GIRLS, NO SHOES ON THE CARPET. AND MELISSA, WATCH YOUR MOUTH PLEASE!
HI MOM!

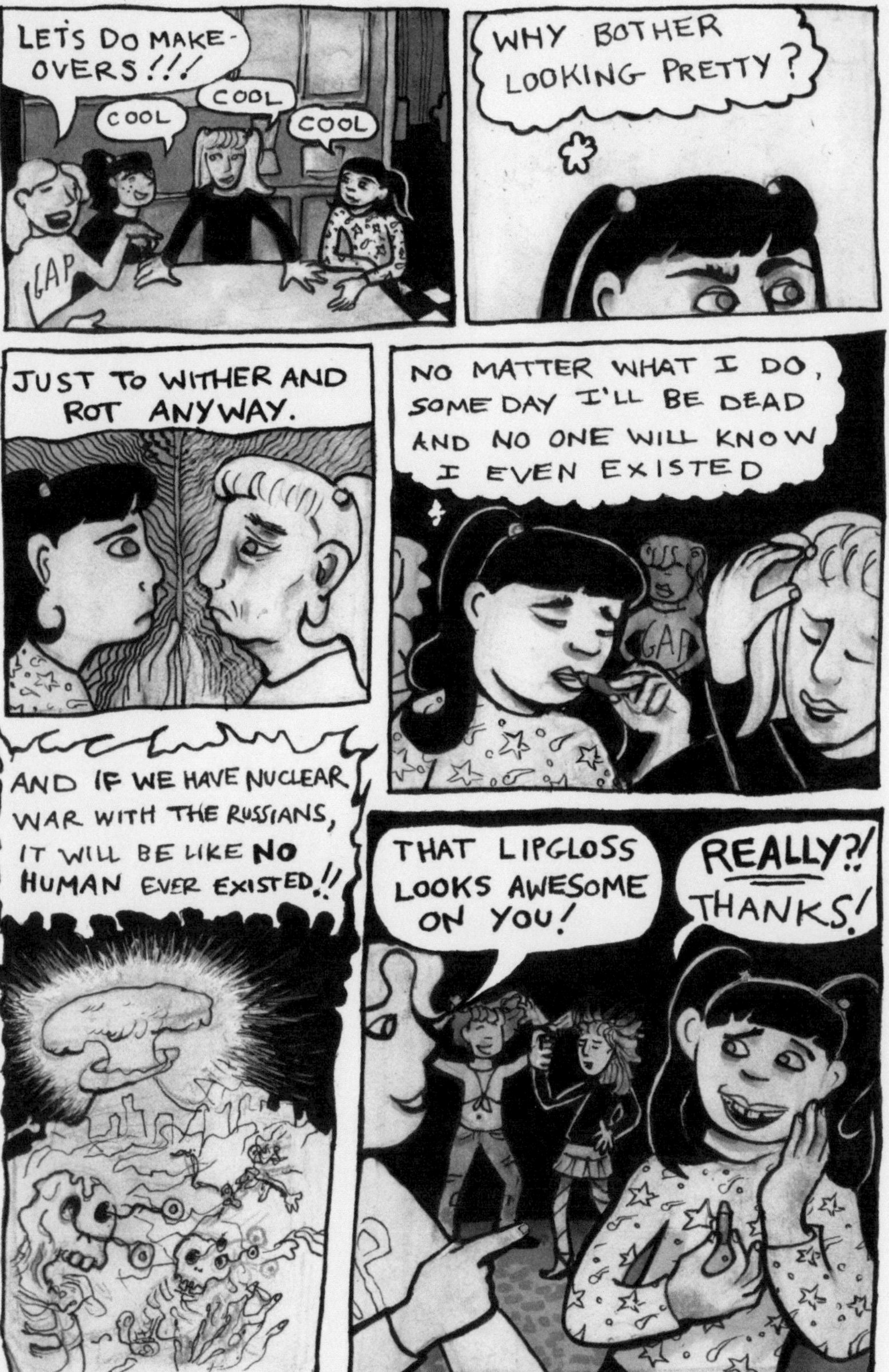
LET'S DO MAKE-OVERS!!!
COOL
COOL
COOL
GAP
WHY BOTHER LOOKING PRETTY?
JUST TO WITHER AND ROT ANYWAY.
NO MATTER WHAT I DO, SOME DAY I'LL BE DEAD AND NO ONE WILL KNOW I EVEN EXISTED
GAP
AND IF WE HAVE NUCLEAR WAR WITH THE RUSSIANS, IT WILL BE LIKE NO HUMAN EVER EXISTED!!
THAT LIPGLOSS LOOKS AWESOME ON YOU!
REALLY?! THANKS!

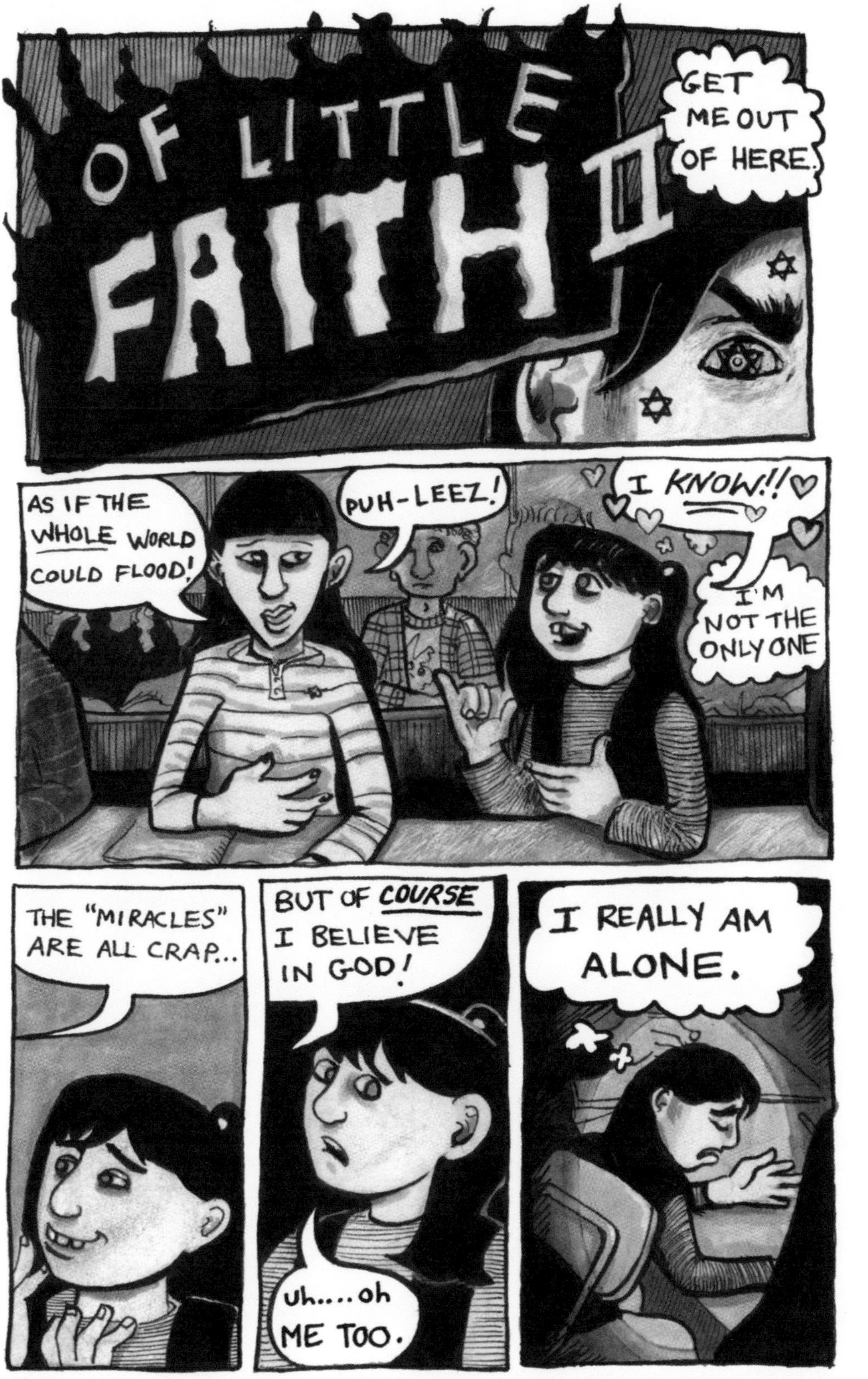
OF LITTLE FAITH II
GET ME OUT OF HERE.
AS IF THE WHOLE WORLD COULD FLOOD!
PUH-LEEZ!
I KNOW!!
I'M NOT THE ONLY ONE
THE "MIRACLES" ARE ALL CRAP...
BUT OF COURSE I BELIEVE IN GOD!
uh....oh ME TOO.
I REALLY AM ALONE.

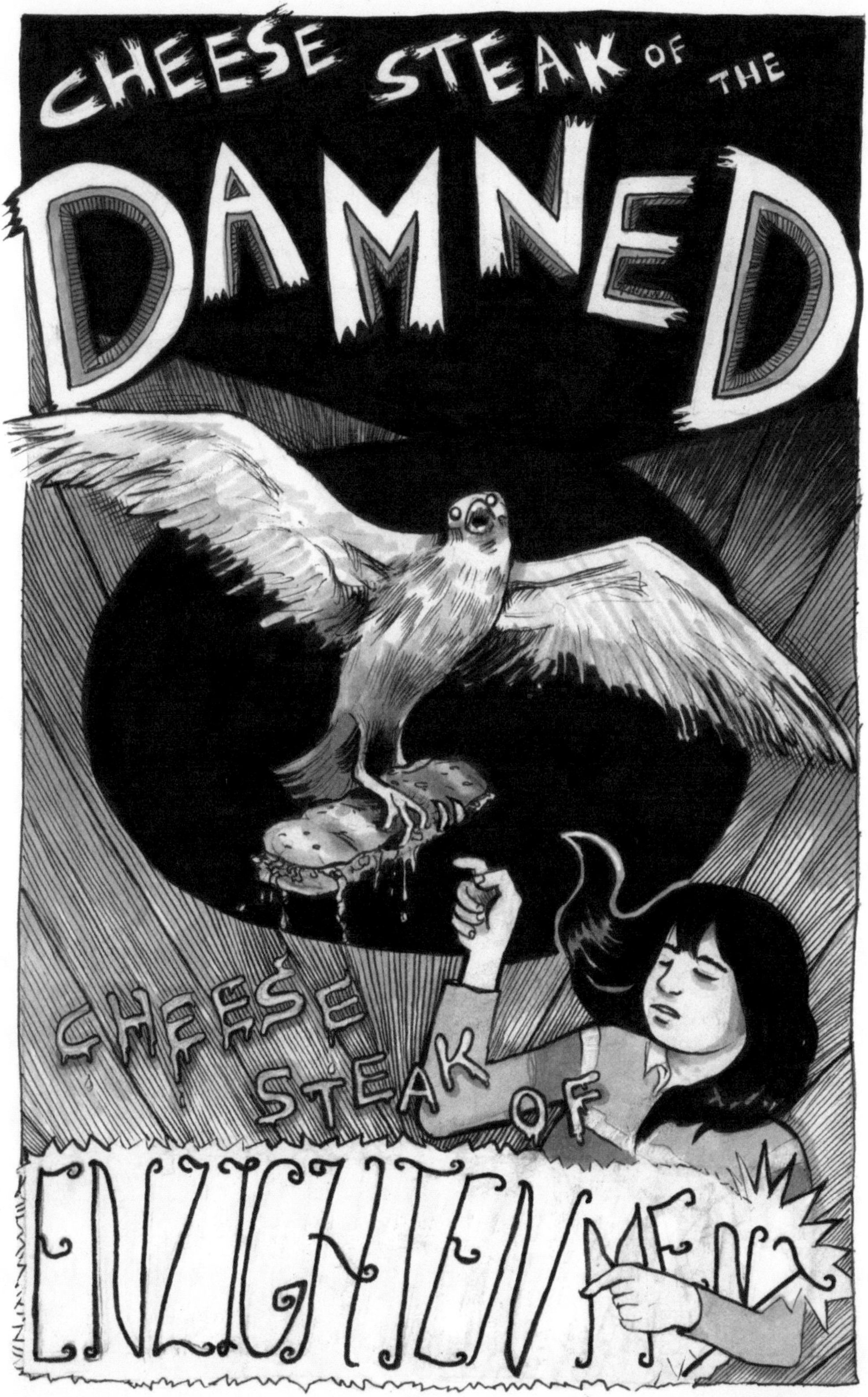
CHEESE STEAK OF THE
DAMNED
CHEESE STEAK OF
ENLIGHTENMENT

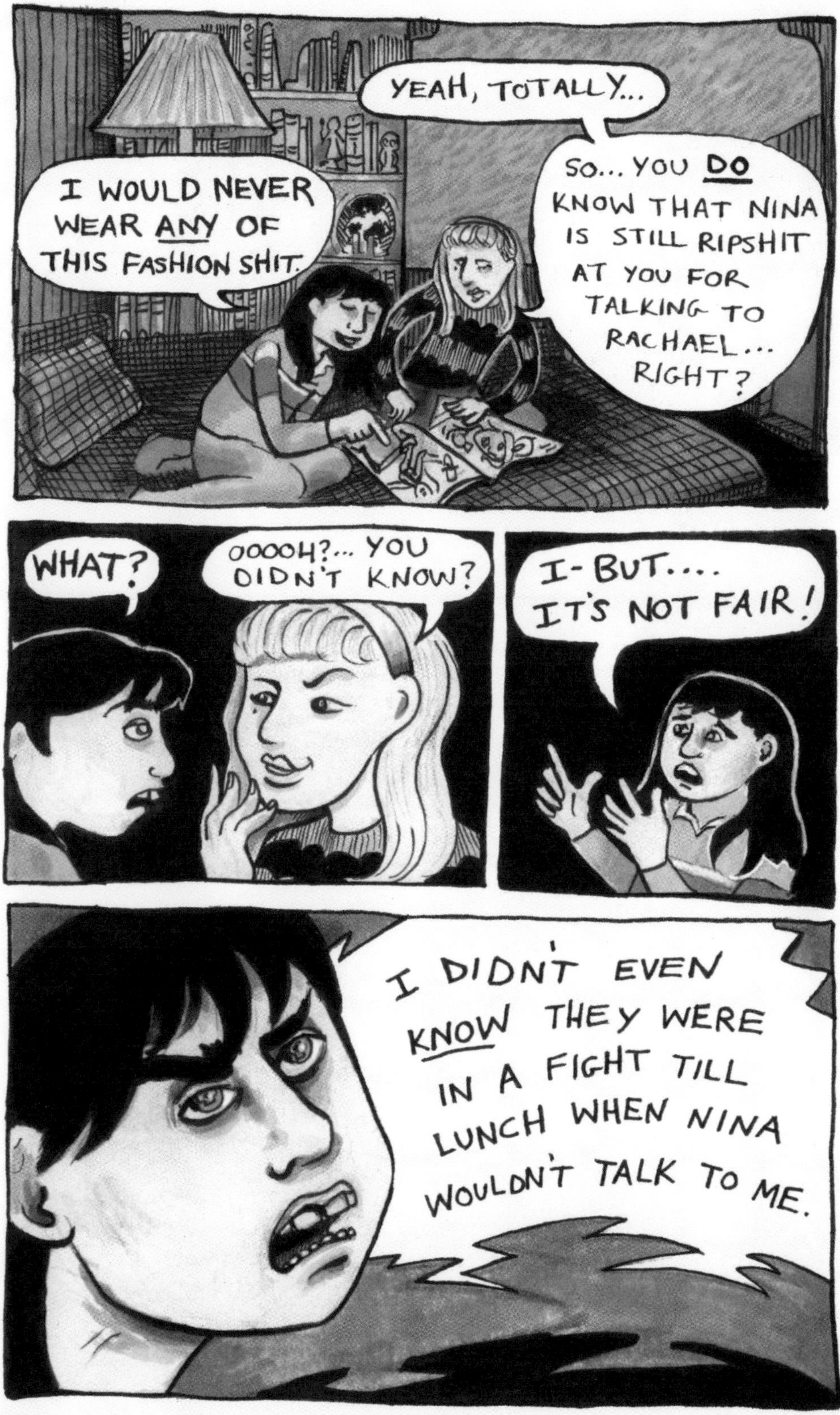
YEAH, TOTALLY...
I WOULD NEVER WEAR ANY OF THIS FASHION SHIT.
SO... YOU DO KNOW THAT NINA IS STILL RIPSHIT AT YOU FOR TALKING TO RACHAEL... RIGHT?
WHAT?
OOOOH?... YOU DIDN'T KNOW?
I- BUT.... IT'S NOT FAIR!
I DIDN'T EVEN KNOW THEY WERE IN A FIGHT TILL LUNCH WHEN NINA WOULDN'T TALK TO ME.

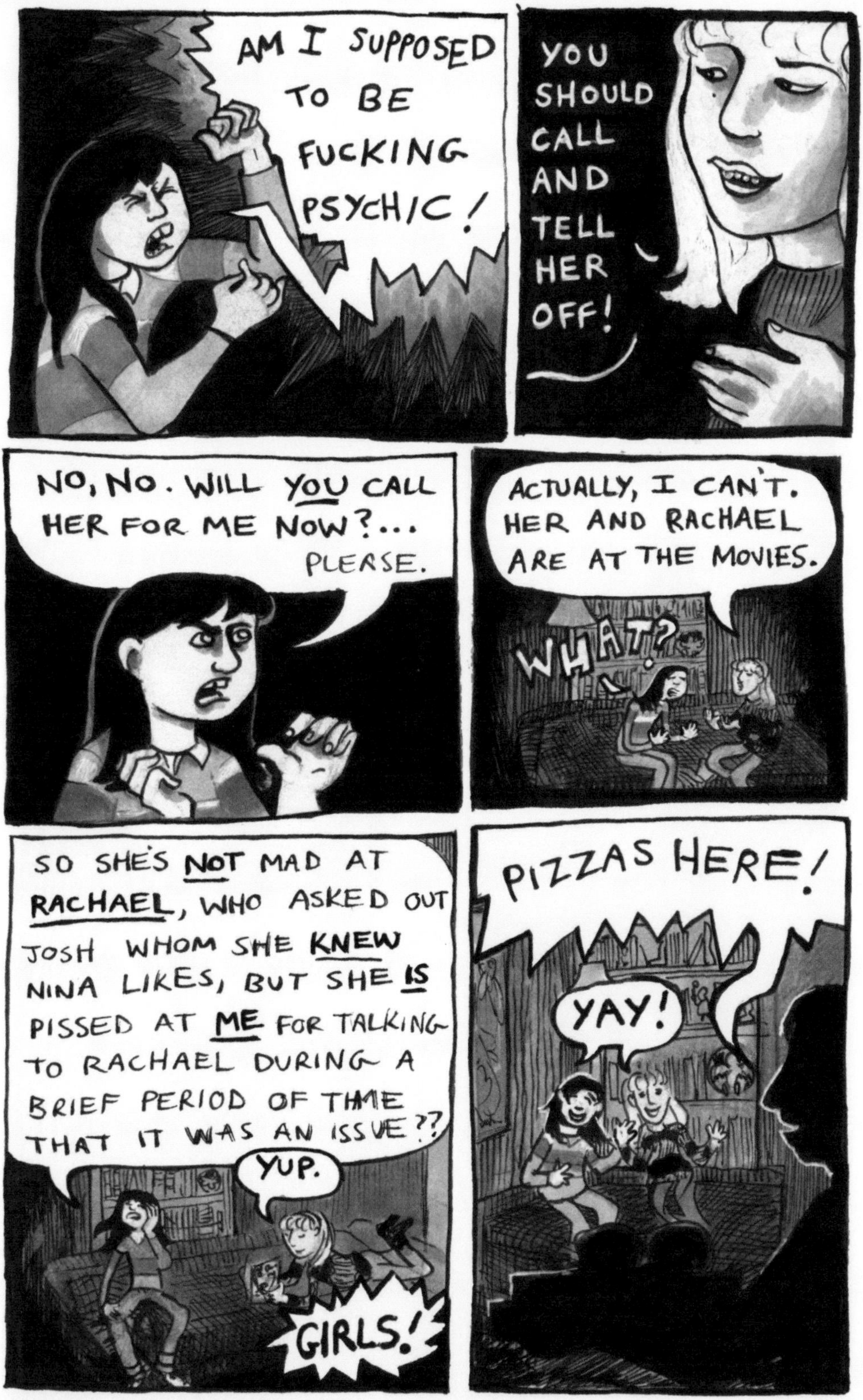
AM I SUPPOSED TO BE FUCKING PSYCHIC!
YOU SHOULD CALL AND TELL HER OFF!
NO, NO. WILL YOU CALL HER FOR ME NOW?... PLEASE.
ACTUALLY, I CAN'T. HER AND RACHAEL ARE AT THE MOVIES.
WHAT?
SO SHE'S NOT MAD AT RACHAEL, WHO ASKED OUT JOSH WHOM SHE KNEW NINA LIKES, BUT SHE IS PISSED AT ME FOR TALKING TO RACHAEL DURING A BRIEF PERIOD OF TIME THAT IT WAS AN ISSUE??
YUP.
GIRLS!
PIZZAS HERE!
YAY!

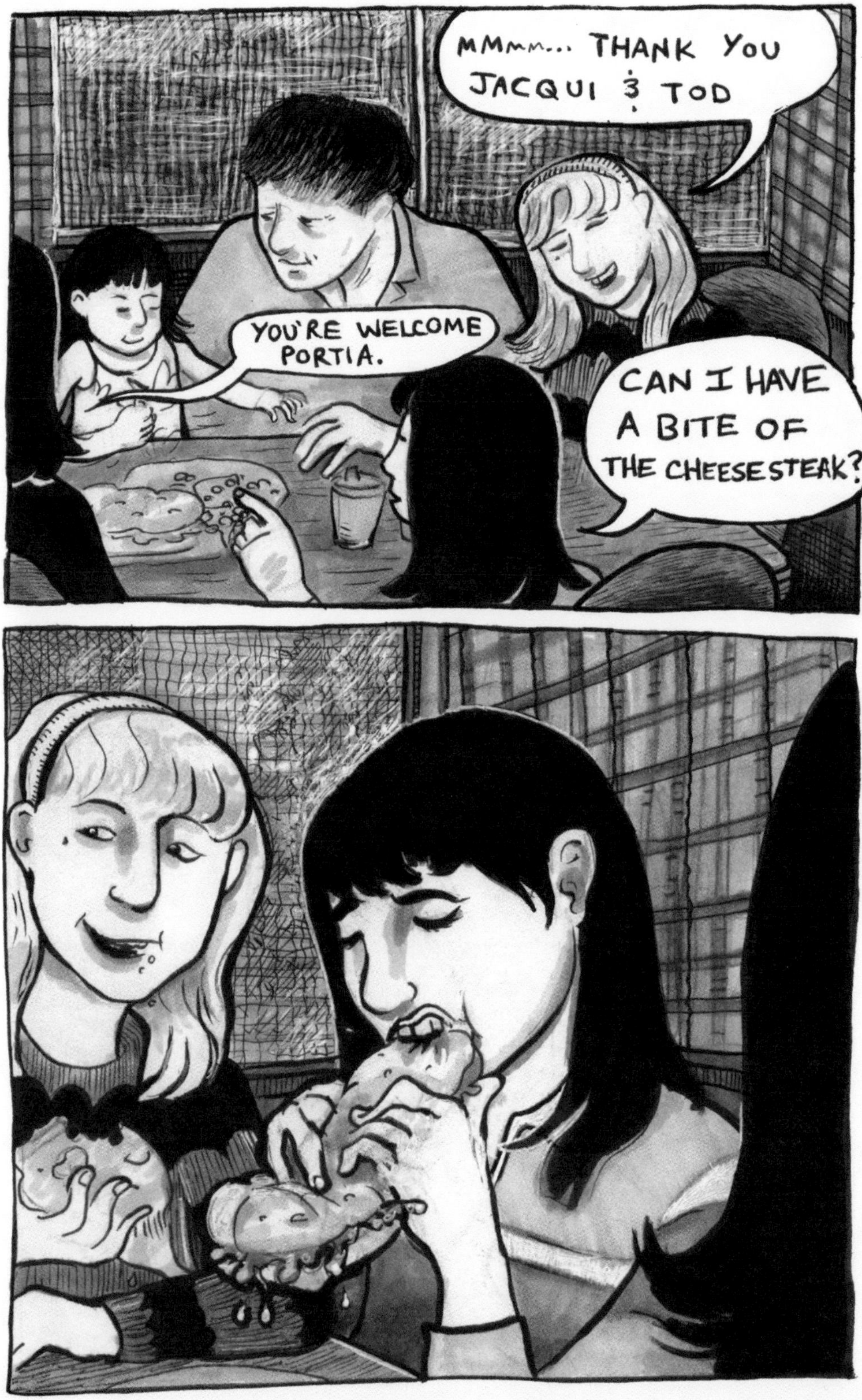
MMMM... THANK YOU JACQUI & TOD
YOU'RE WELCOME PORTIA.
CAN I HAVE A BITE OF THE CHEESESTEAK?

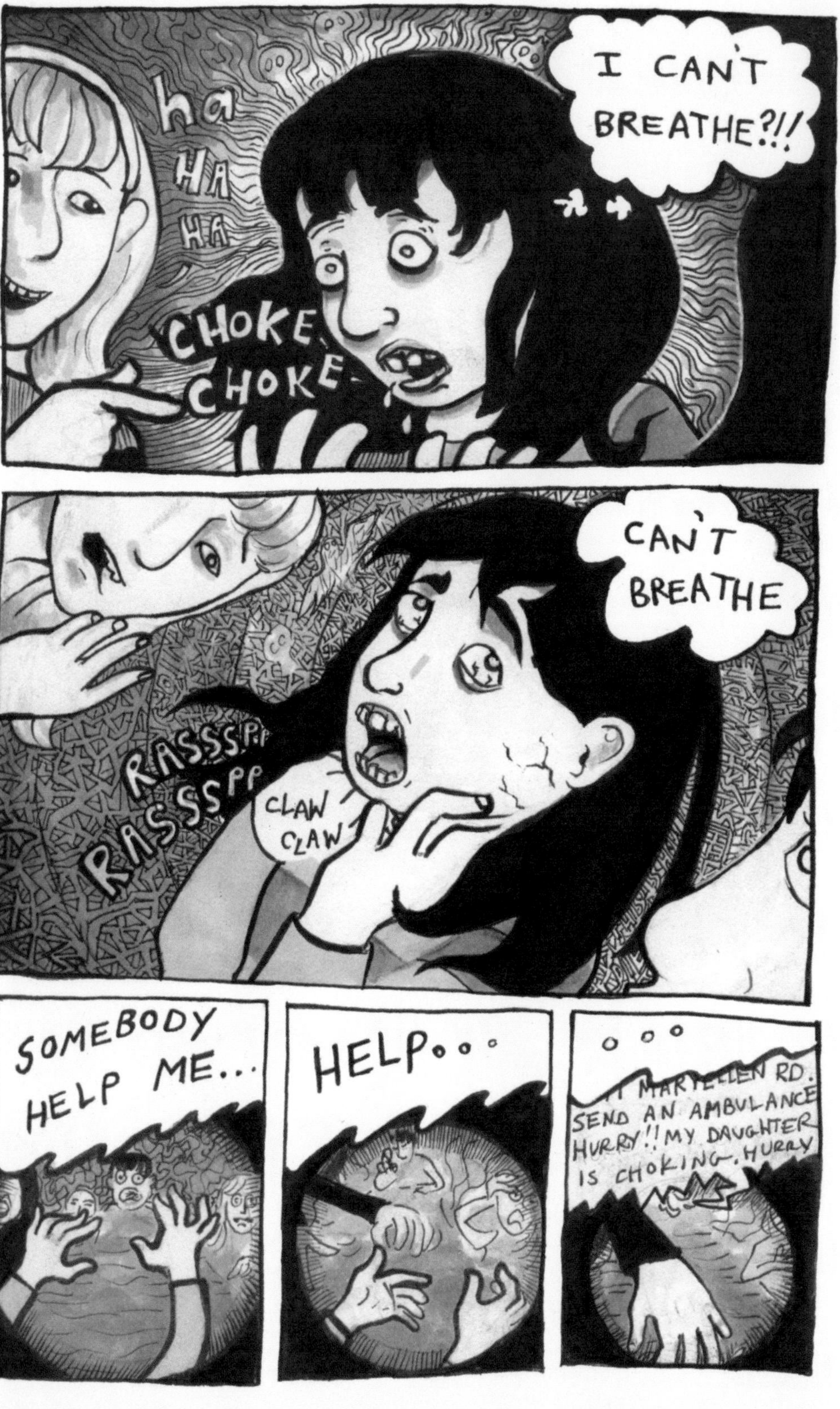
ha
HA
HA
CHOKE
CHOKE
I CAN'T BREATHE?!!
CAN'T BREATHE
RASSSPP
RASSSPP
CLAW CLAW
SOMEBODY HELP ME...
HELP...
...
MARYELLEN RD. SEND AN AMBULANCE HURRY!! MY DAUGHTER IS CHOKING. HURRY

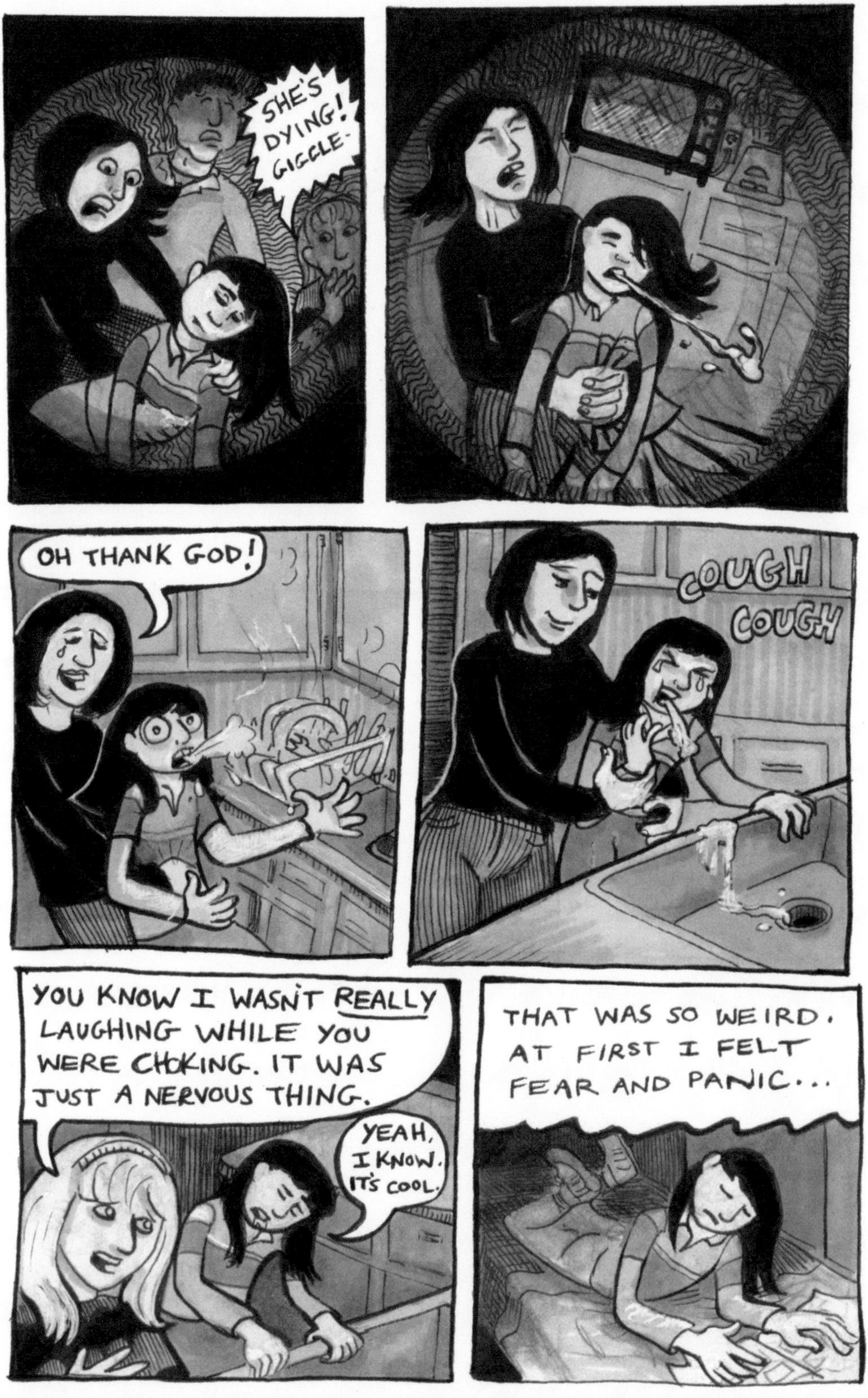
SHE'S DYING! GIGGLE-
OH THANK GOD!
COUGH
COUGH
YOU KNOW I WASN'T REALLY LAUGHING WHILE YOU WERE CHOKING. IT WAS JUST A NERVOUS THING.
YEAH, I KNOW. IT'S COOL.
THAT WAS SO WEIRD. AT FIRST I FELT FEAR AND PANIC...

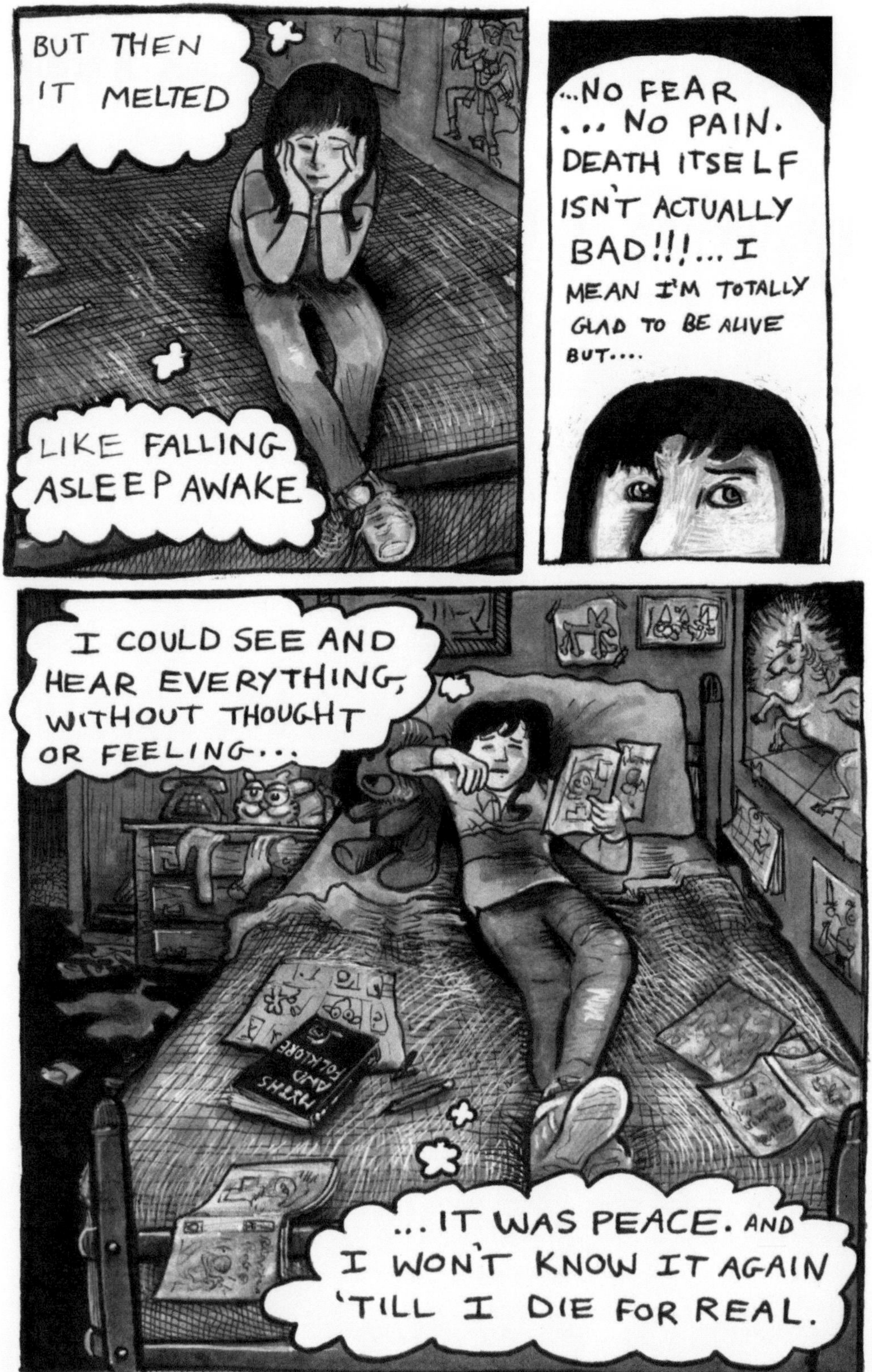
BUT THEN IT MELTED
LIKE FALLING ASLEEP AWAKE
...NO FEAR ... NO PAIN. DEATH ITSELF ISN'T ACTUALLY BAD!!!... I MEAN I'M TOTALLY GLAD TO BE ALIVE BUT....
I COULD SEE AND HEAR EVERYTHING, WITHOUT THOUGHT OR FEELING...
MYTHS AND FOLKLORE
...IT WAS PEACE. AND I WON'T KNOW IT AGAIN 'TILL I DIE FOR REAL.

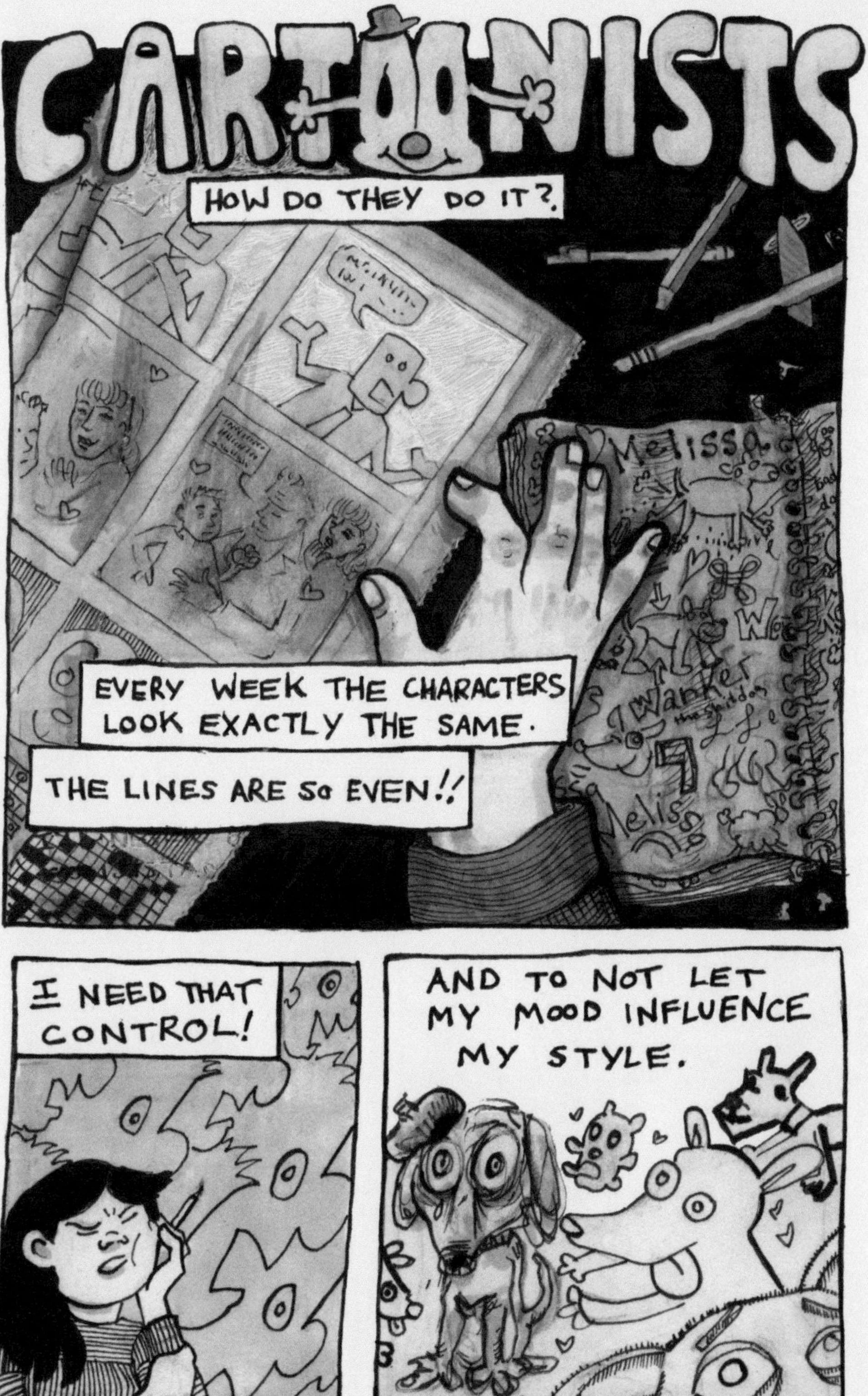
CARTOONISTS
HOW DO THEY DO IT?
EVERY WEEK THE CHARACTERS LOOK EXACTLY THE SAME.
THE LINES ARE SO EVEN!!
I NEED THAT CONTROL!
AND TO NOT LET MY MOOD INFLUENCE MY STYLE.

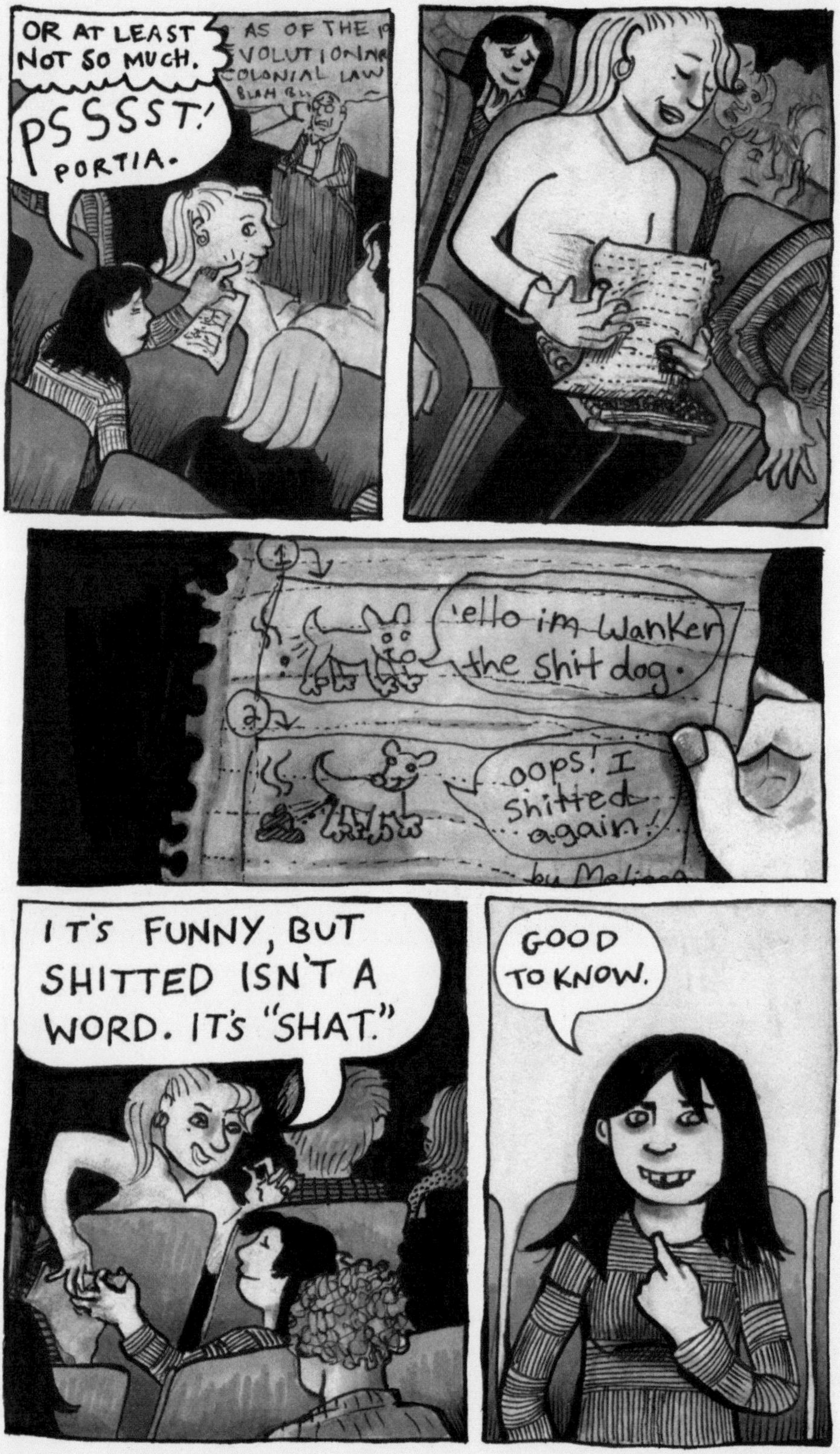
OR AT LEAST NOT SO MUCH.
PSSSST! PORTIA.
'ello im Wanker the shit dog.
oops! I shitted again!
IT'S FUNNY, BUT SHITTED ISN'T A WORD. IT'S "SHAT."
GOOD TO KNOW.

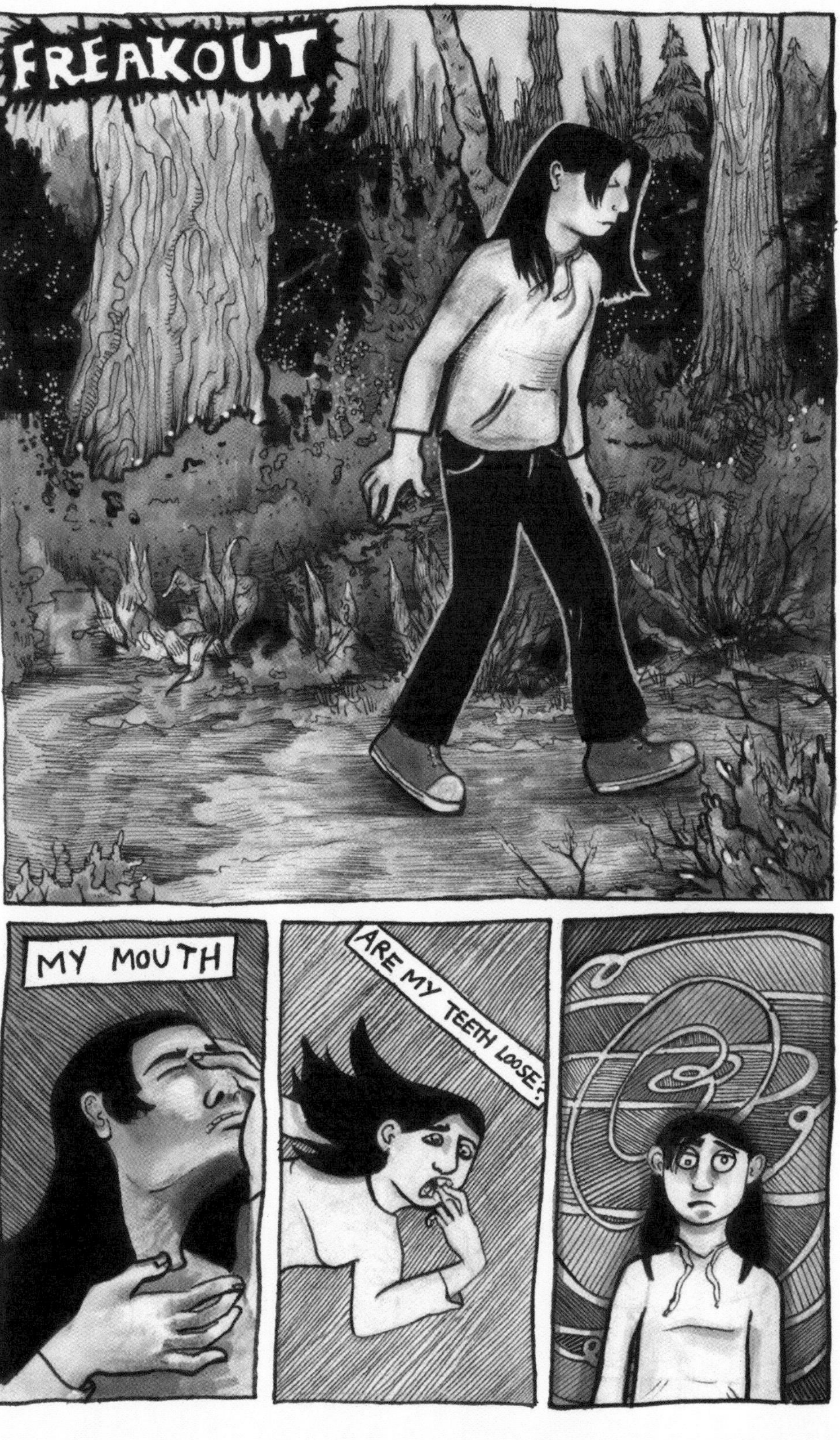
FREAKOUT
MY MOUTH
ARE MY TEETH LOOSE?

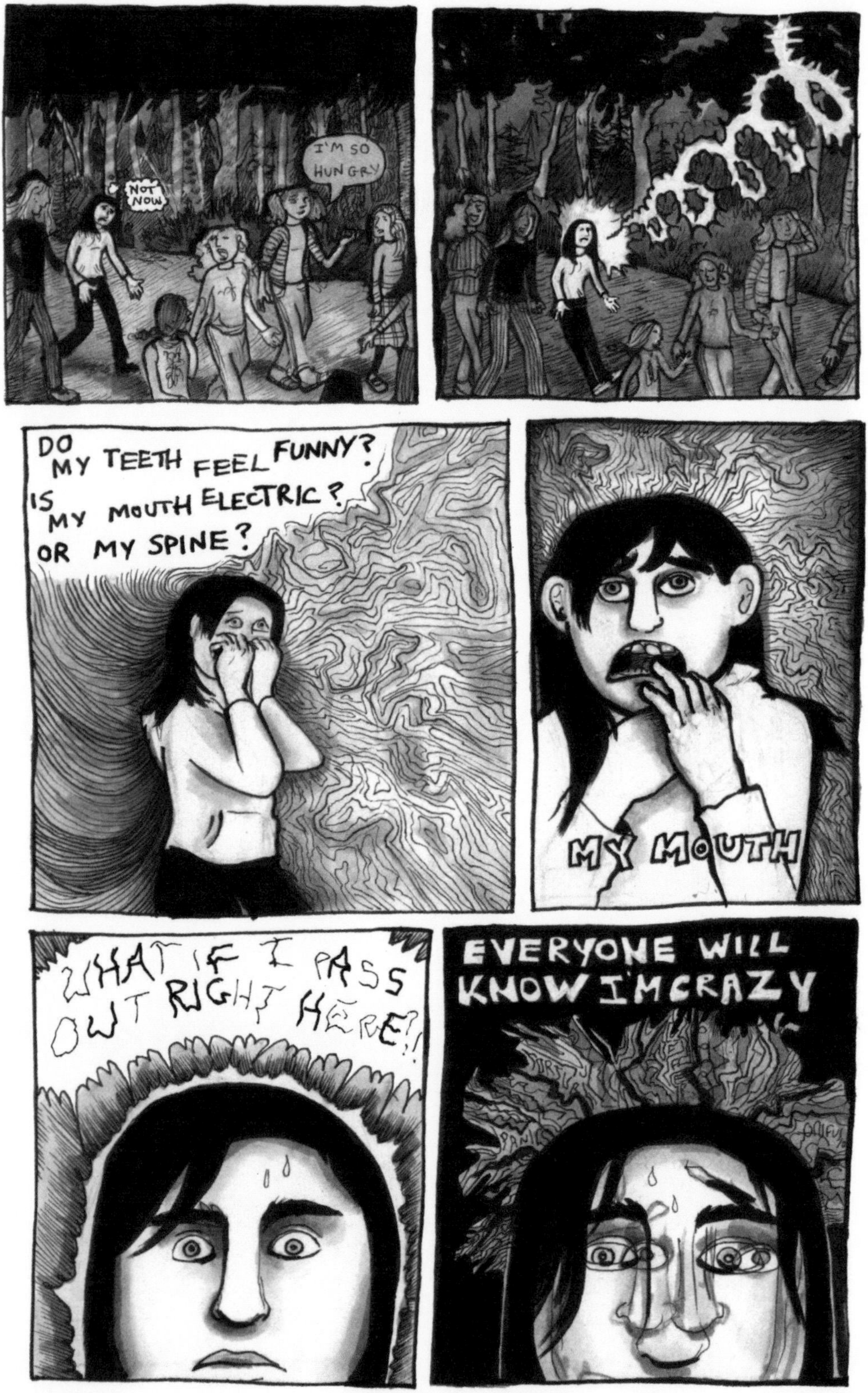
NOT NOW
I'M SO HUNGRY
DO MY TEETH FEEL FUNNY?
IS MY MOUTH ELECTRIC?
OR MY SPINE?
MY MOUTH
WHAT IF I PASS OUT RIGHT HERE?!
EVERYONE WILL KNOW I'M CRAZY

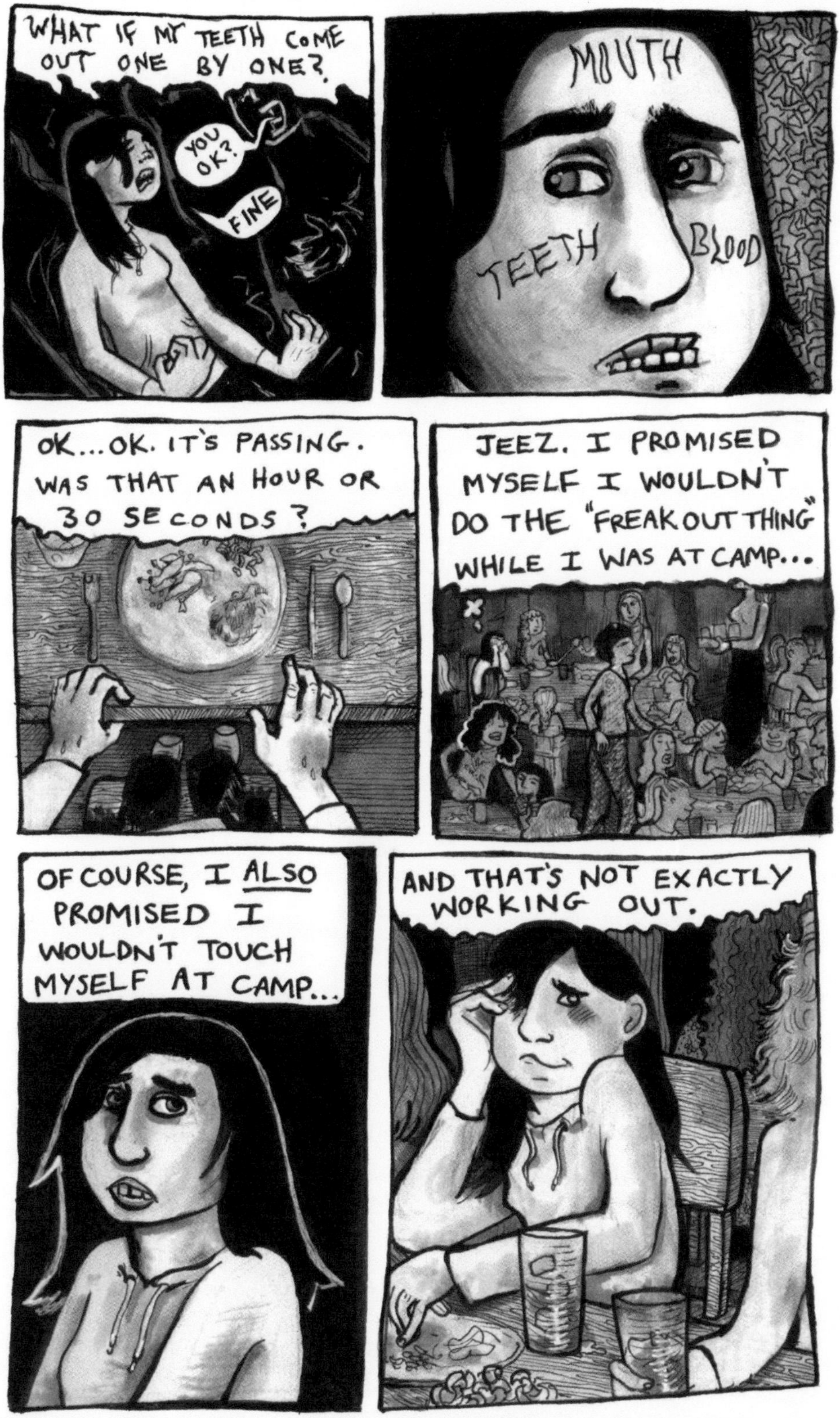
WHAT IF MY TEETH COME OUT ONE BY ONE?
YOU OK?
FINE
MOUTH
TEETH
BLOOD
OK...OK. IT'S PASSING. WAS THAT AN HOUR OR 30 SECONDS?
JEEZ. I PROMISED MYSELF I WOULDN'T DO THE "FREAKOUT THING" WHILE I WAS AT CAMP...
OF COURSE, I ALSO PROMISED I WOULDN'T TOUCH MYSELF AT CAMP...
AND THAT'S NOT EXACTLY WORKING OUT.

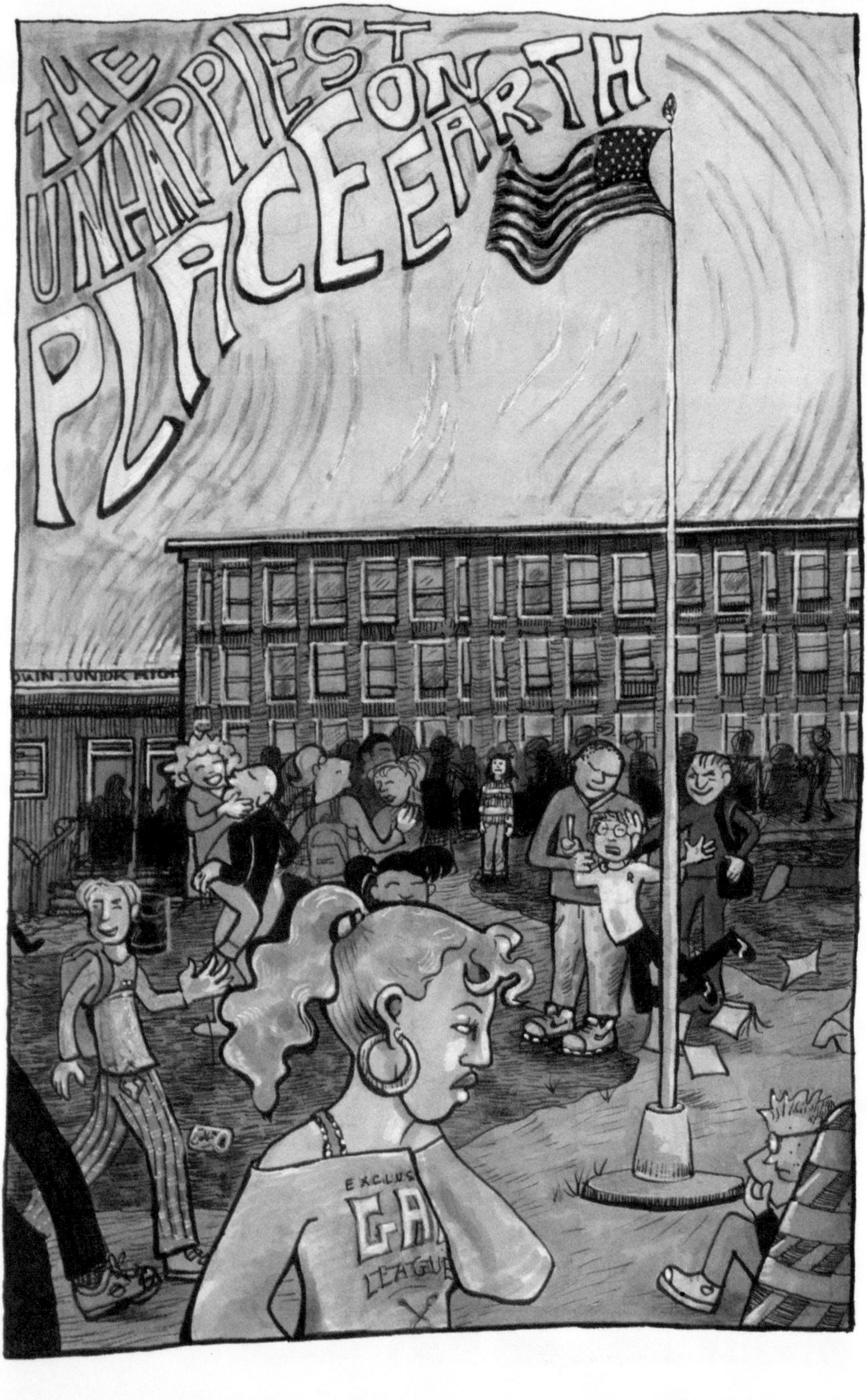
THE UNHAPPIEST PLACE ON EARTH

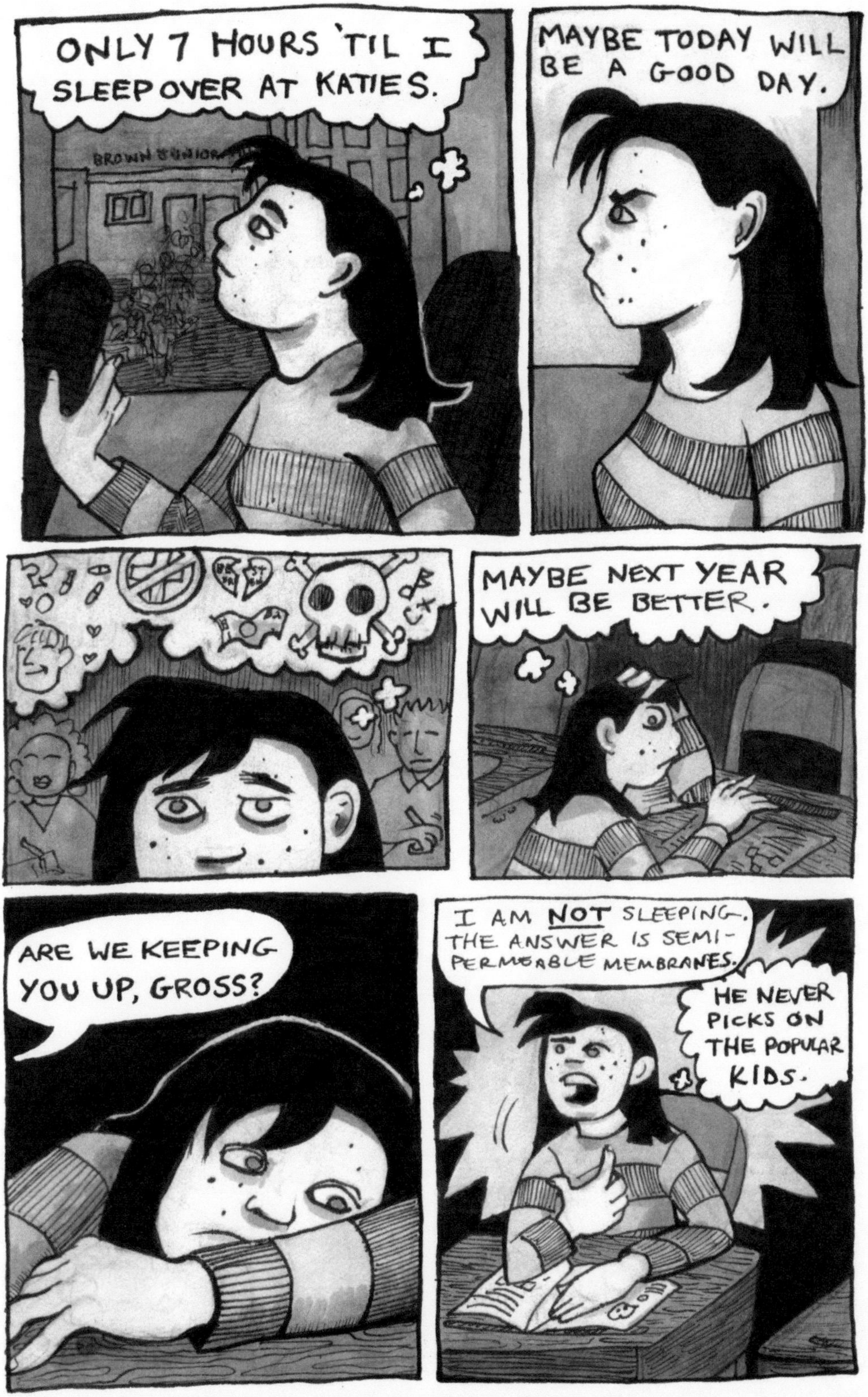
ONLY 7 HOURS 'TIL I SLEEPOVER AT KATIES.
BROWN
MAYBE TODAY WILL BE A GOOD DAY.
MAYBE NEXT YEAR WILL BE BETTER.
ARE WE KEEPING YOU UP, GROSS?
I AM NOT SLEEPING. THE ANSWER IS SEMI-PERMEABLE MEMBRANES.
HE NEVER PICKS ON THE POPULAR KIDS.

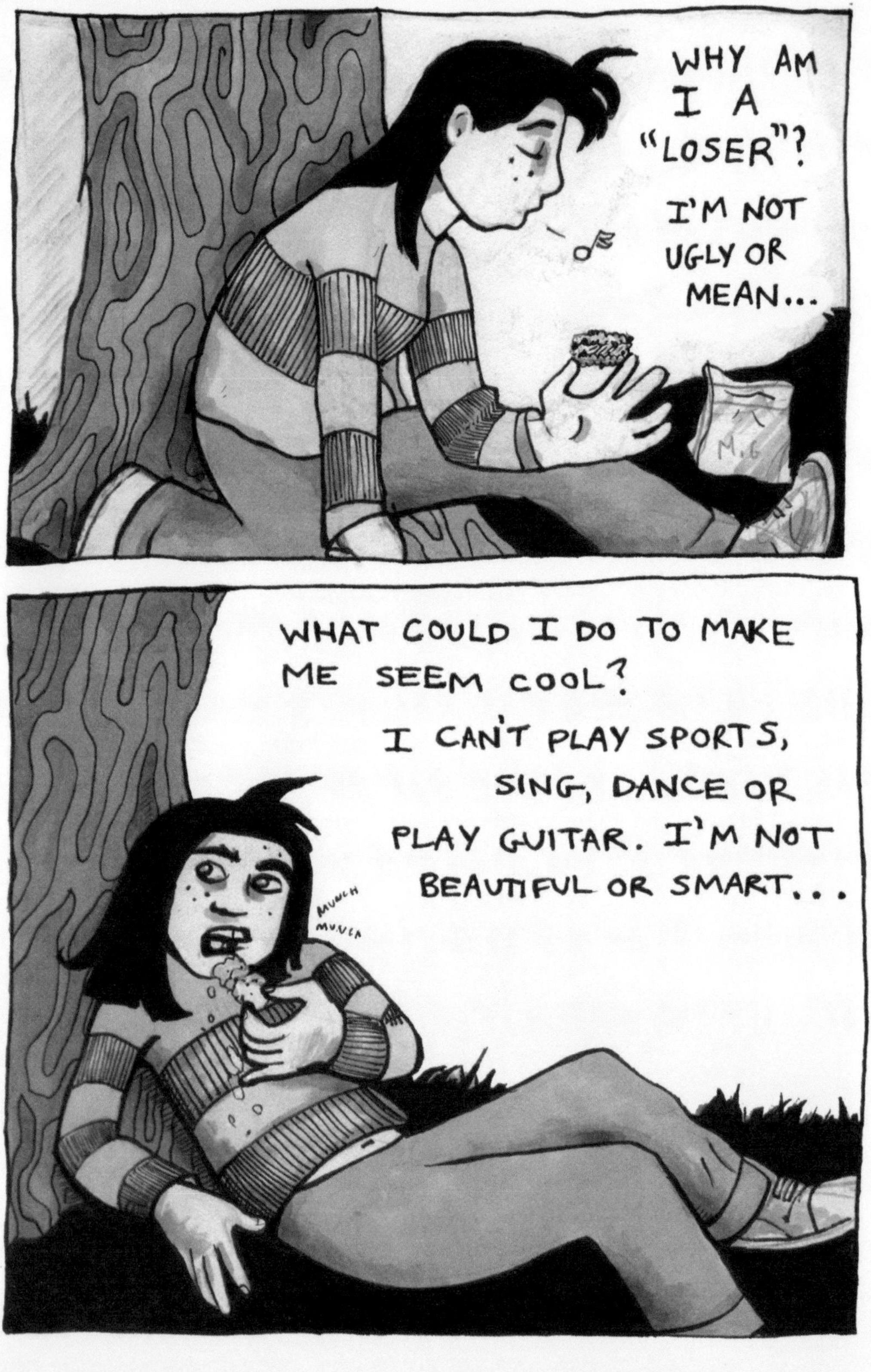
WHY AM I A "LOSER"? I'M NOT UGLY OR MEAN...
WHAT COULD I DO TO MAKE ME SEEM COOL? I CAN'T PLAY SPORTS, SING, DANCE OR PLAY GUITAR. I'M NOT BEAUTIFUL OR SMART...
MUNCH MUNCH

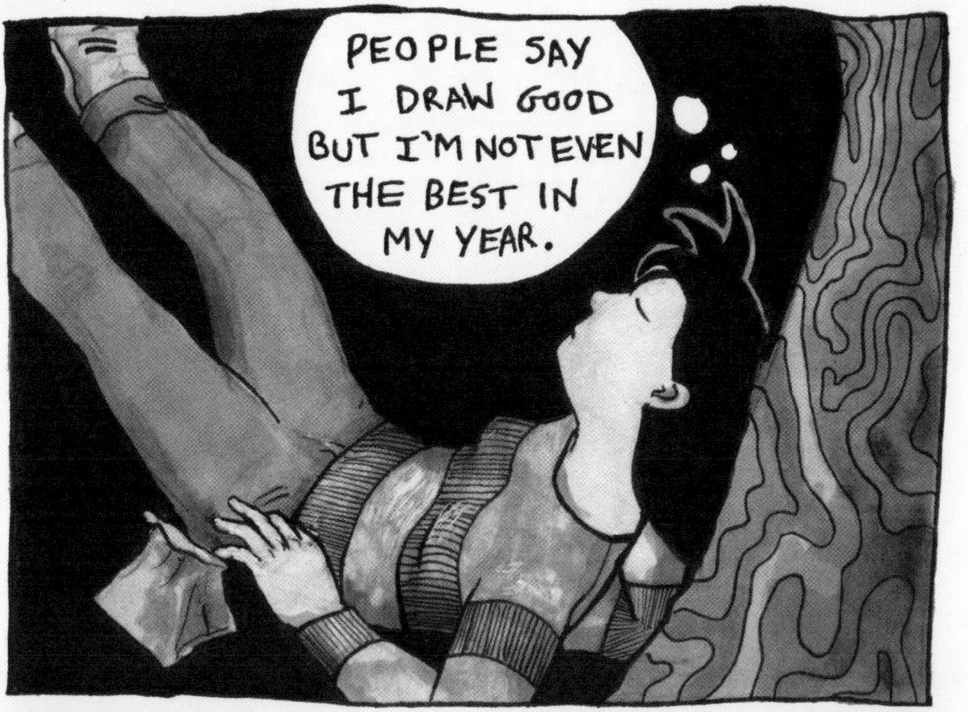
PEOPLE SAY I DRAW GOOD BUT I'M NOT EVEN THE BEST IN MY YEAR.

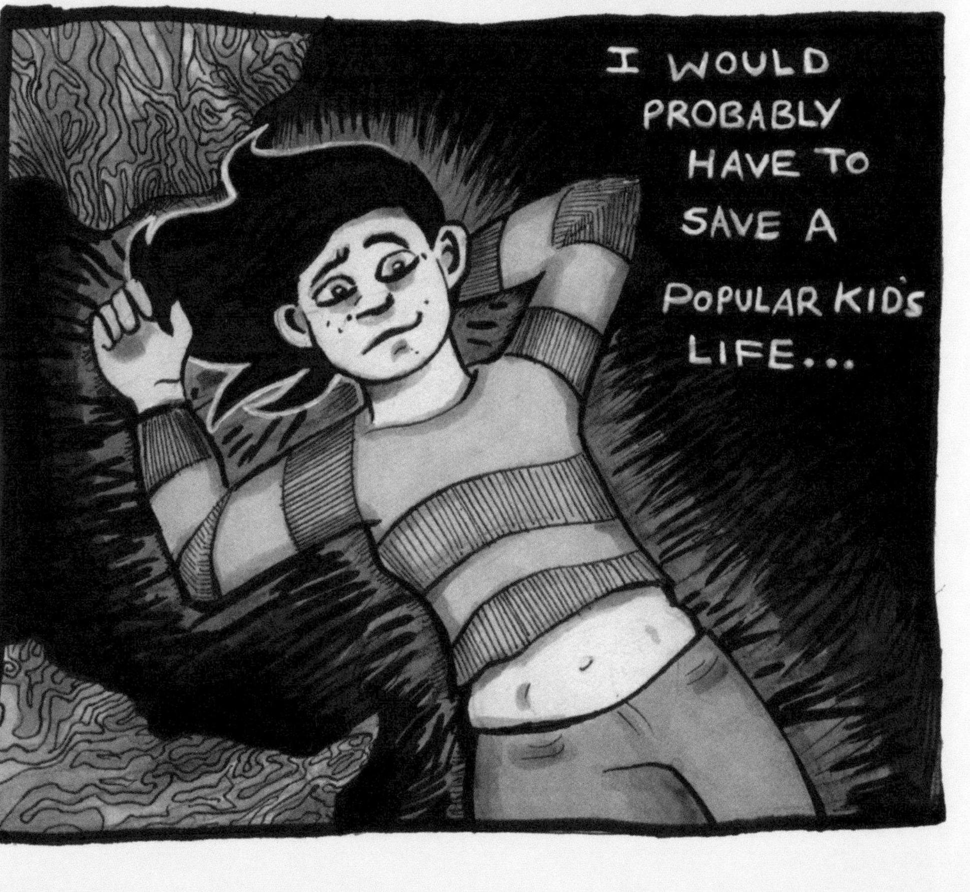
I WOULD PROBABLY HAVE TO SAVE A POPULAR KID'S LIFE...

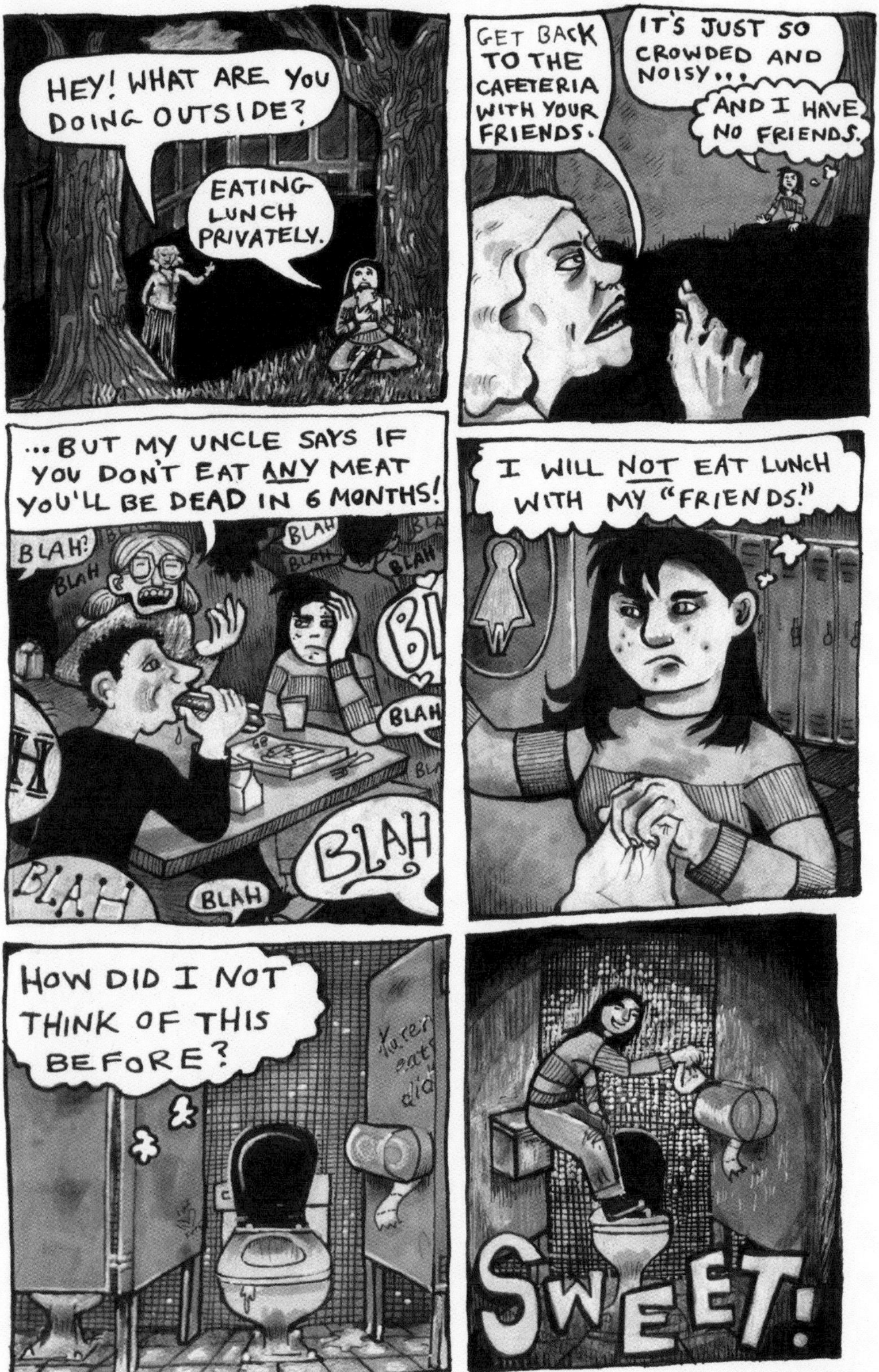
HEY! WHAT ARE YOU DOING OUTSIDE?
EATING LUNCH PRIVATELY.
GET BACK TO THE CAFETERIA WITH YOUR FRIENDS.
IT'S JUST SO CROWDED AND NOISY...
AND I HAVE NO FRIENDS.
...BUT MY UNCLE SAYS IF YOU DON'T EAT ANY MEAT YOU'LL BE DEAD IN 6 MONTHS!
BLAH?
BLAH
BLAH
BLAH
BLAH
BLAH
BLAH
BLAH
BLAH
I WILL NOT EAT LUNCH WITH MY "FRIENDS."
HOW DID I NOT THINK OF THIS BEFORE?
SWEET!

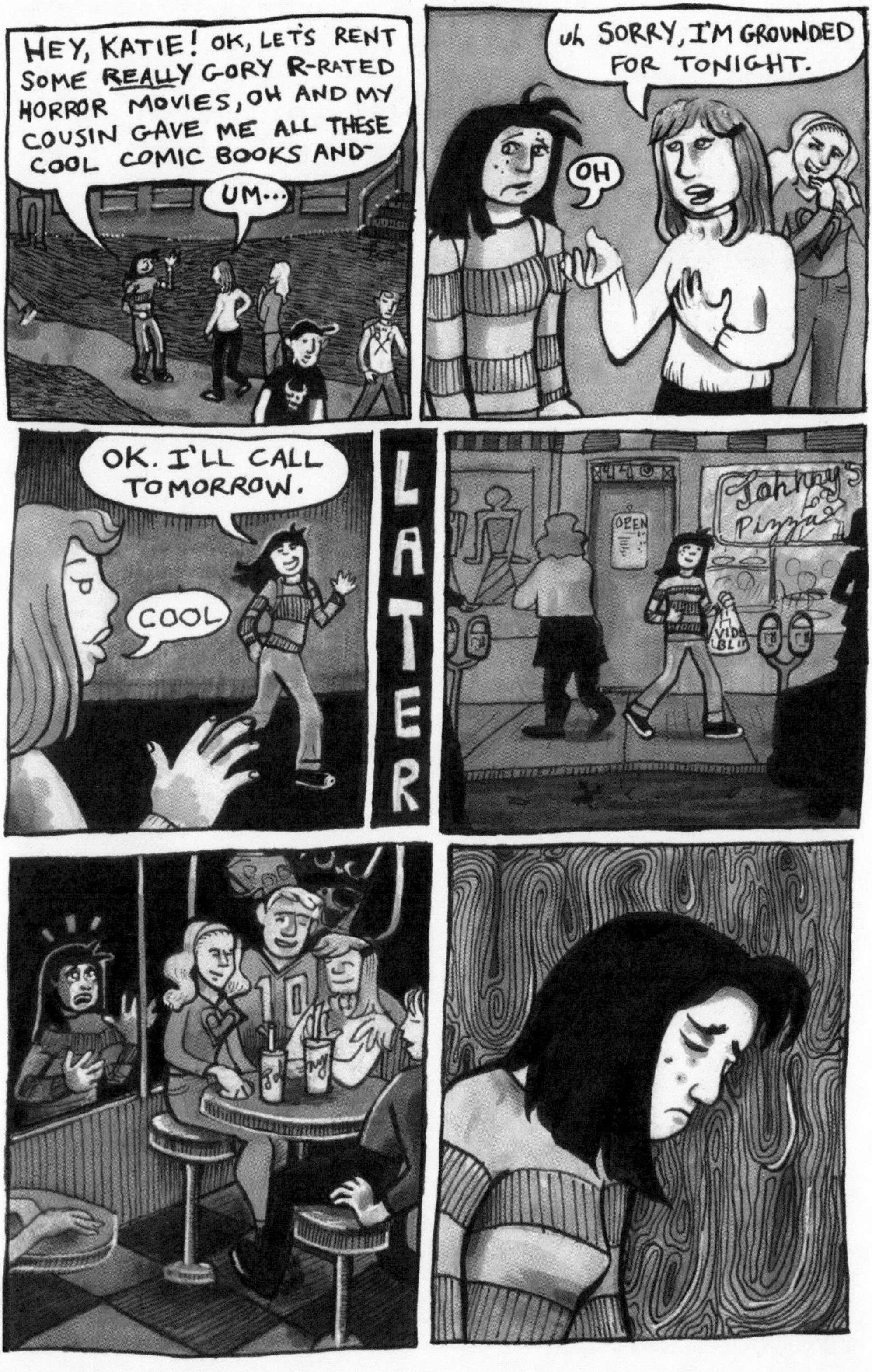
HEY, KATIE! OK, LET'S RENT SOME REALLY GORY R-RATED HORROR MOVIES, OH AND MY COUSIN GAVE ME ALL THESE COOL COMIC BOOKS AND-
UM...
uh SORRY, I'M GROUNDED FOR TONIGHT.
OH
OK. I'LL CALL TOMORROW.
COOL
LATER
OPEN
Johnny's Pizza

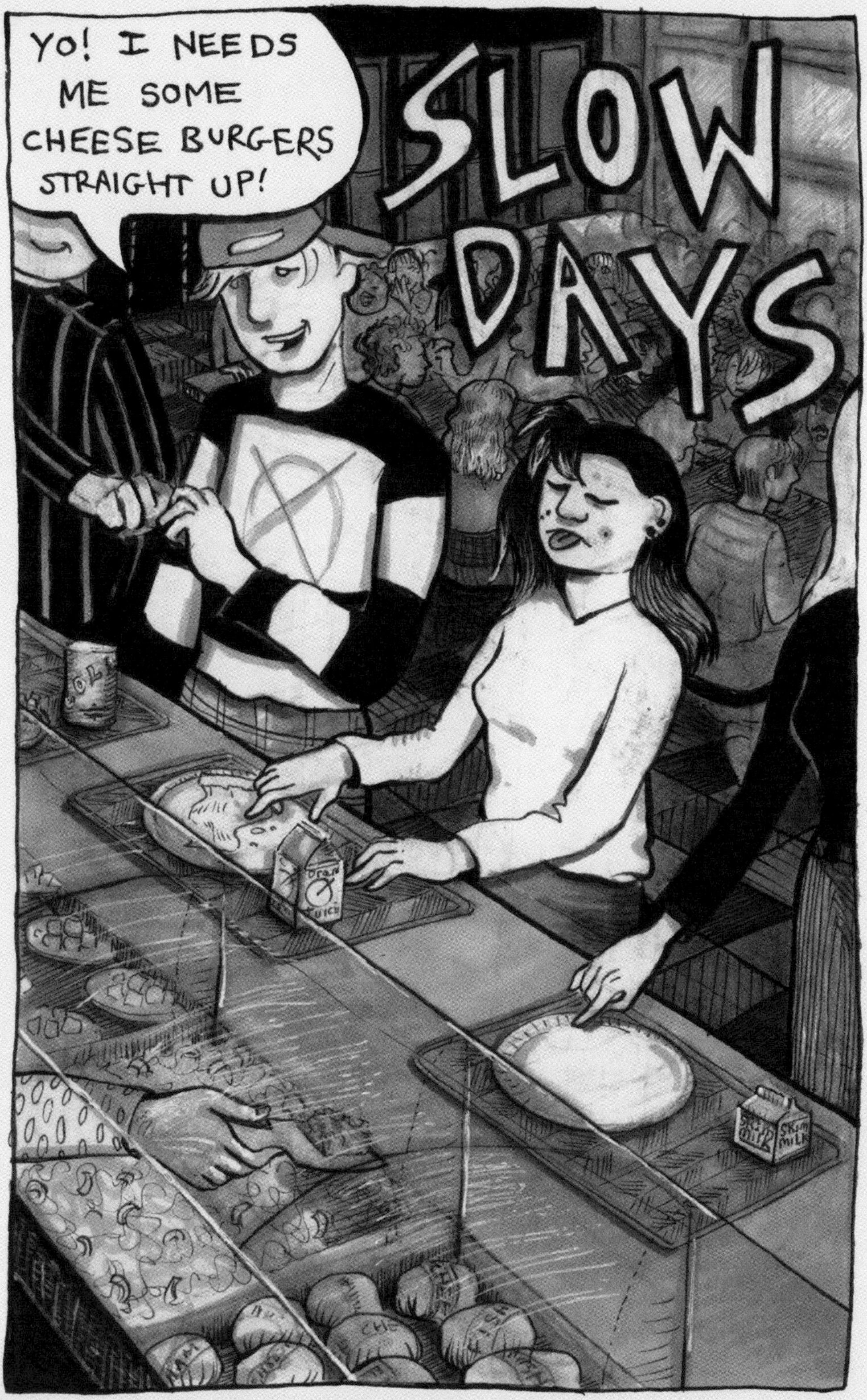
YO! I NEEDS ME SOME CHEESE BURGERS STRAIGHT UP!
SLOW DAYS
SKIM MILK

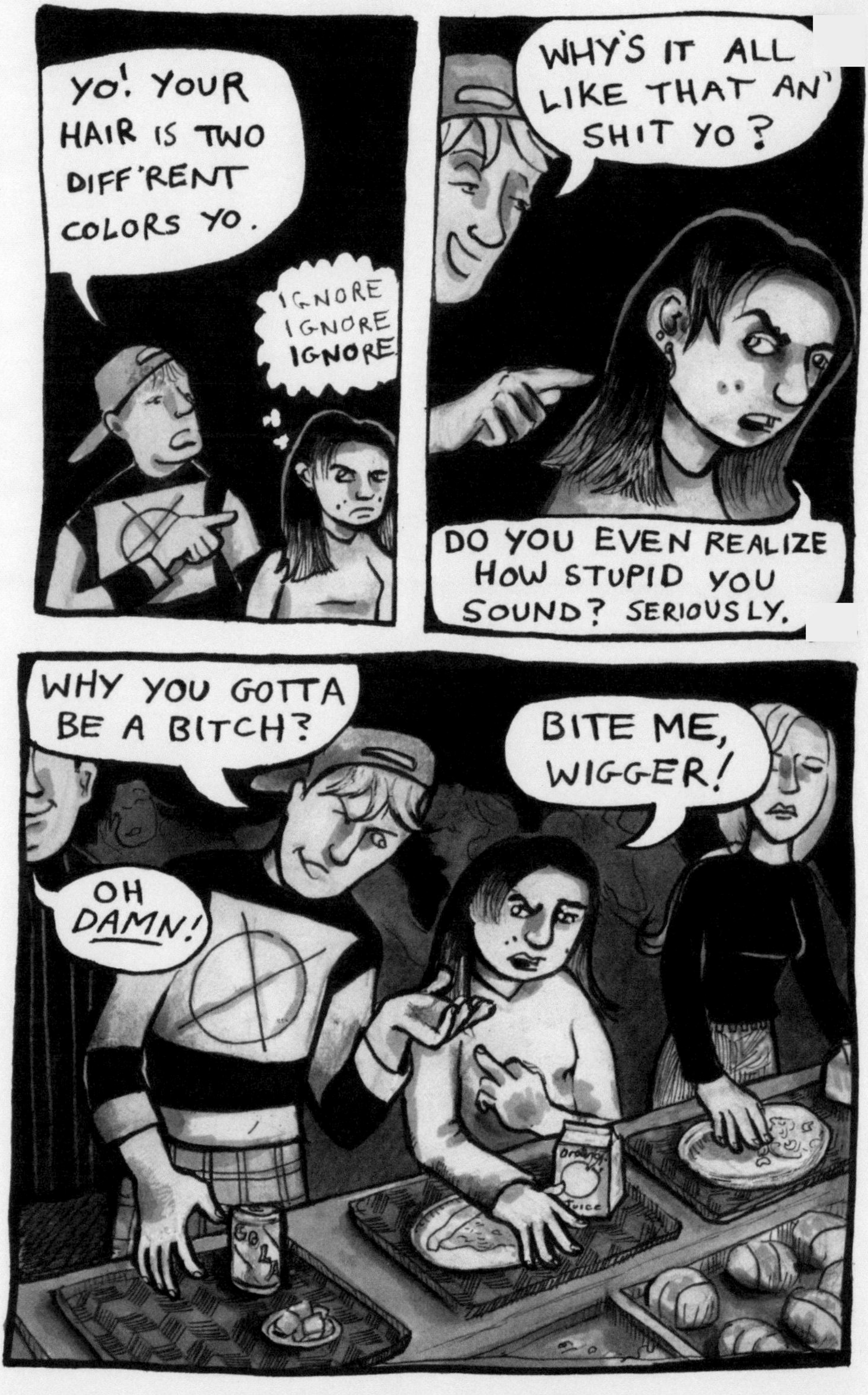
YO! YOUR HAIR IS TWO DIFF'RENT COLORS YO.
IGNORE IGNORE IGNORE
WHY'S IT ALL LIKE THAT AN' SHIT YO?
DO YOU EVEN REALIZE HOW STUPID YOU SOUND? SERIOUSLY.
WHY YOU GOTTA BE A BITCH?
BITE ME, WIGGER!
OH DAMN!

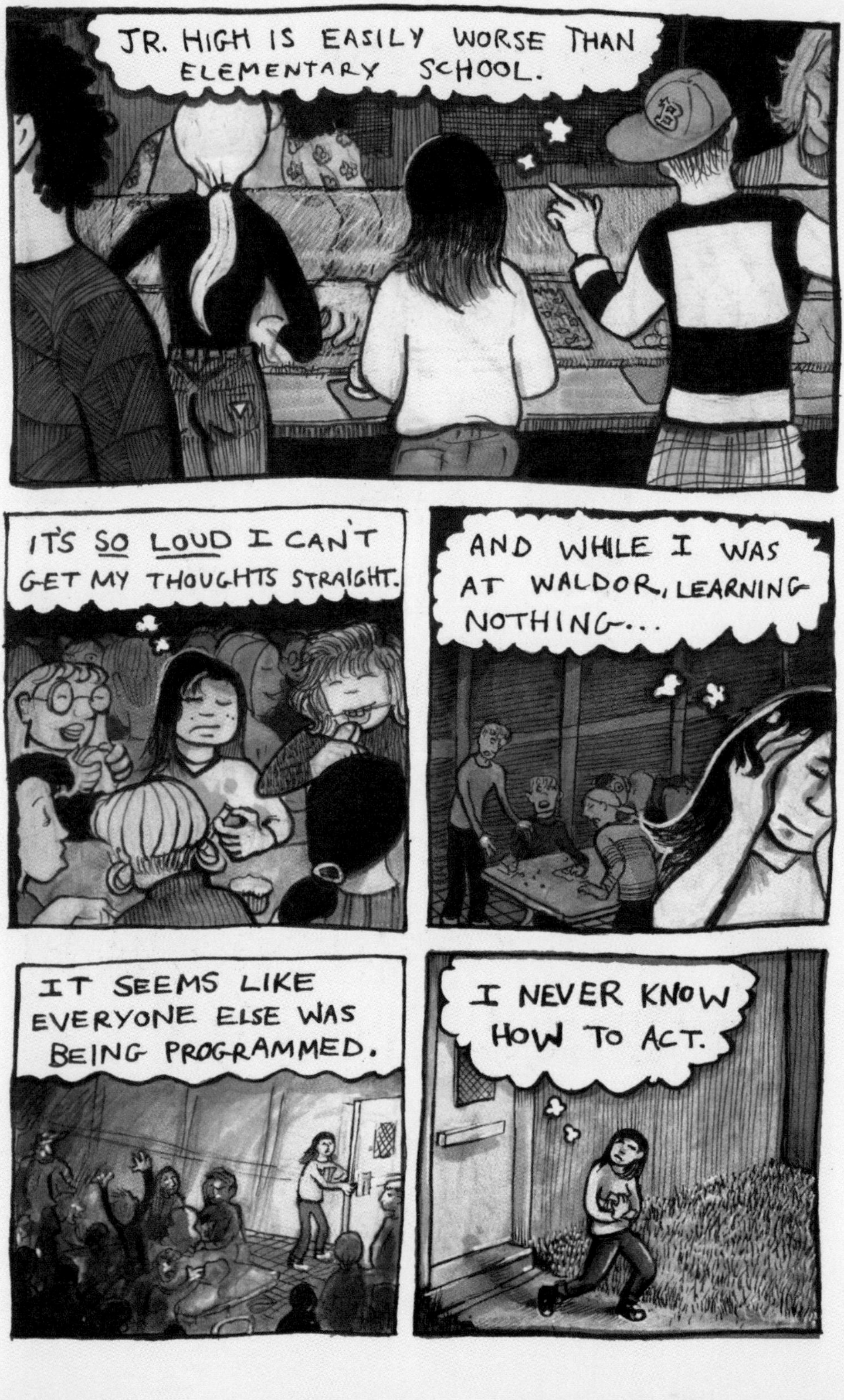
JR. HIGH IS EASILY WORSE THAN ELEMENTARY SCHOOL.
IT'S SO LOUD I CAN'T GET MY THOUGHTS STRAIGHT.
AND WHILE I WAS AT WALDOR, LEARNING NOTHING...
IT SEEMS LIKE EVERYONE ELSE WAS BEING PROGRAMMED.
I NEVER KNOW HOW TO ACT.

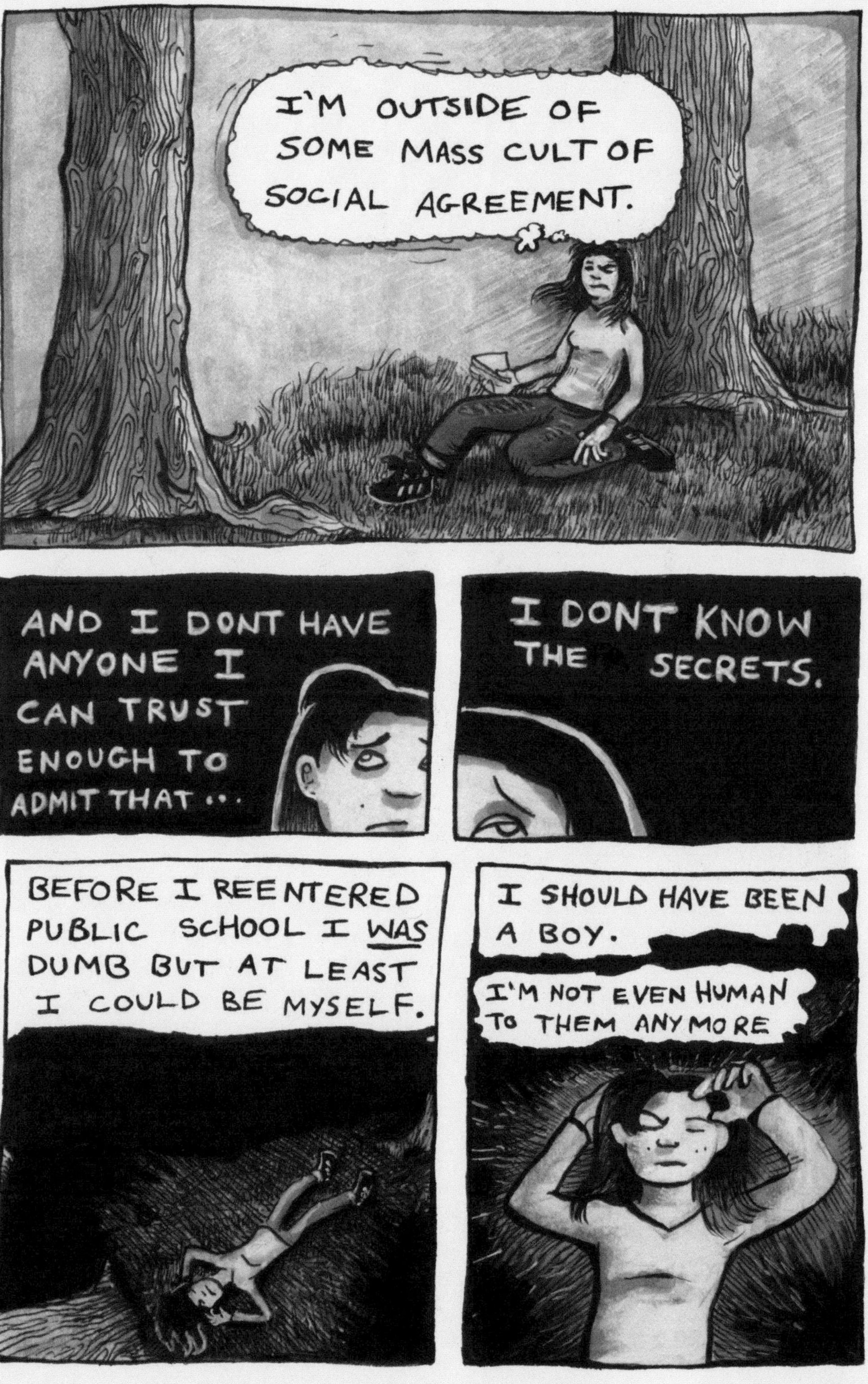
I'M OUTSIDE OF SOME MASS CULT OF SOCIAL AGREEMENT.
AND I DONT HAVE ANYONE I CAN TRUST ENOUGH TO ADMIT THAT...
I DONT KNOW THE SECRETS.
BEFORE I REENTERED PUBLIC SCHOOL I WAS DUMB BUT AT LEAST I COULD BE MYSELF.
I SHOULD HAVE BEEN A BOY.
I'M NOT EVEN HUMAN TO THEM ANYMORE

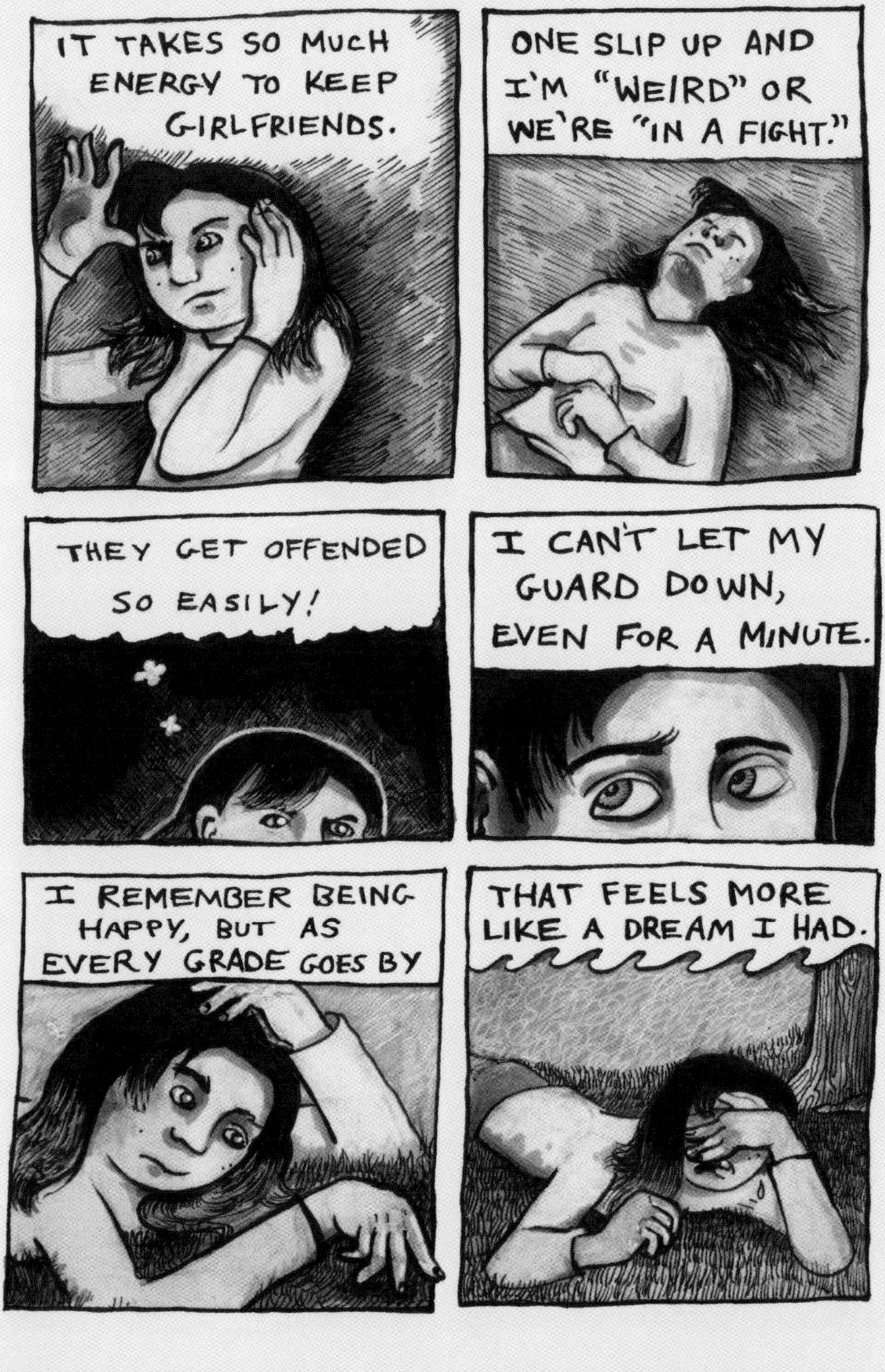
IT TAKES SO MUCH ENERGY TO KEEP GIRLFRIENDS.
ONE SLIP UP AND I'M "WEIRD" OR WE'RE "IN A FIGHT."
THEY GET OFFENDED SO EASILY!
I CAN'T LET MY GUARD DOWN, EVEN FOR A MINUTE.
I REMEMBER BEING HAPPY, BUT AS EVERY GRADE GOES BY
THAT FEELS MORE LIKE A DREAM I HAD.

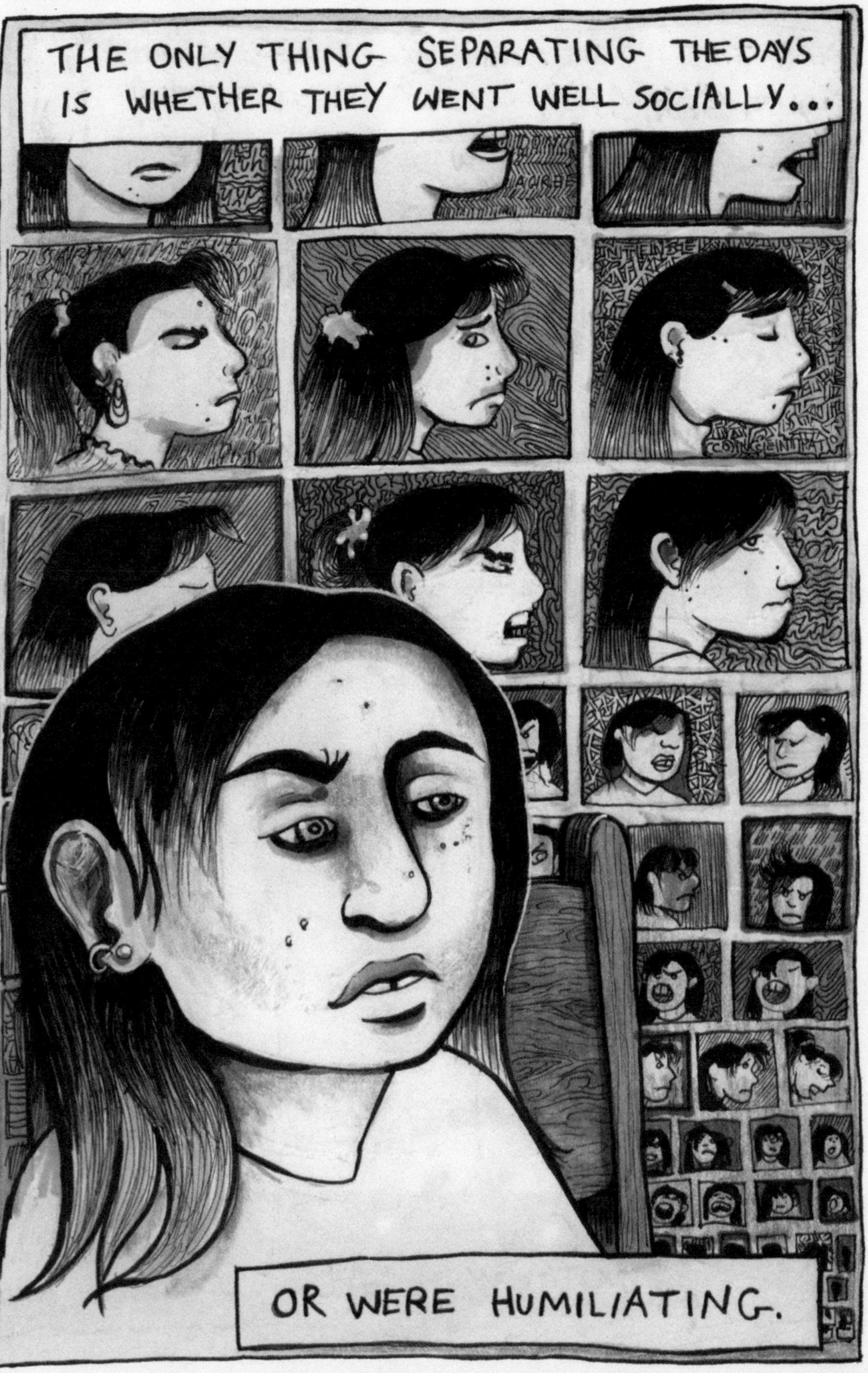
THE ONLY THING SEPARATING THE DAYS IS WHETHER THEY WENT WELL SOCIALLY...
OR WERE HUMILIATING.

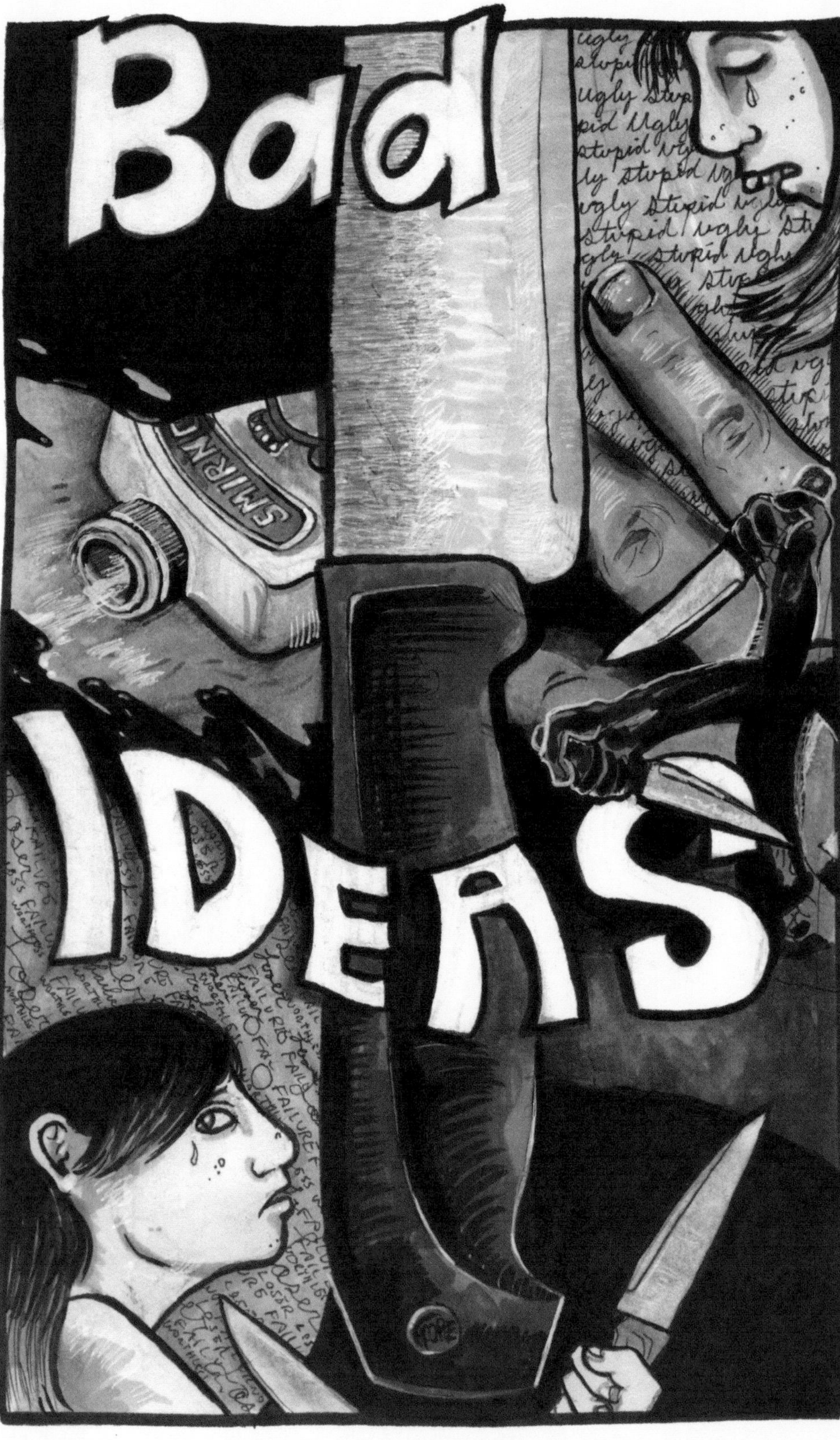
Bad
IDEAS

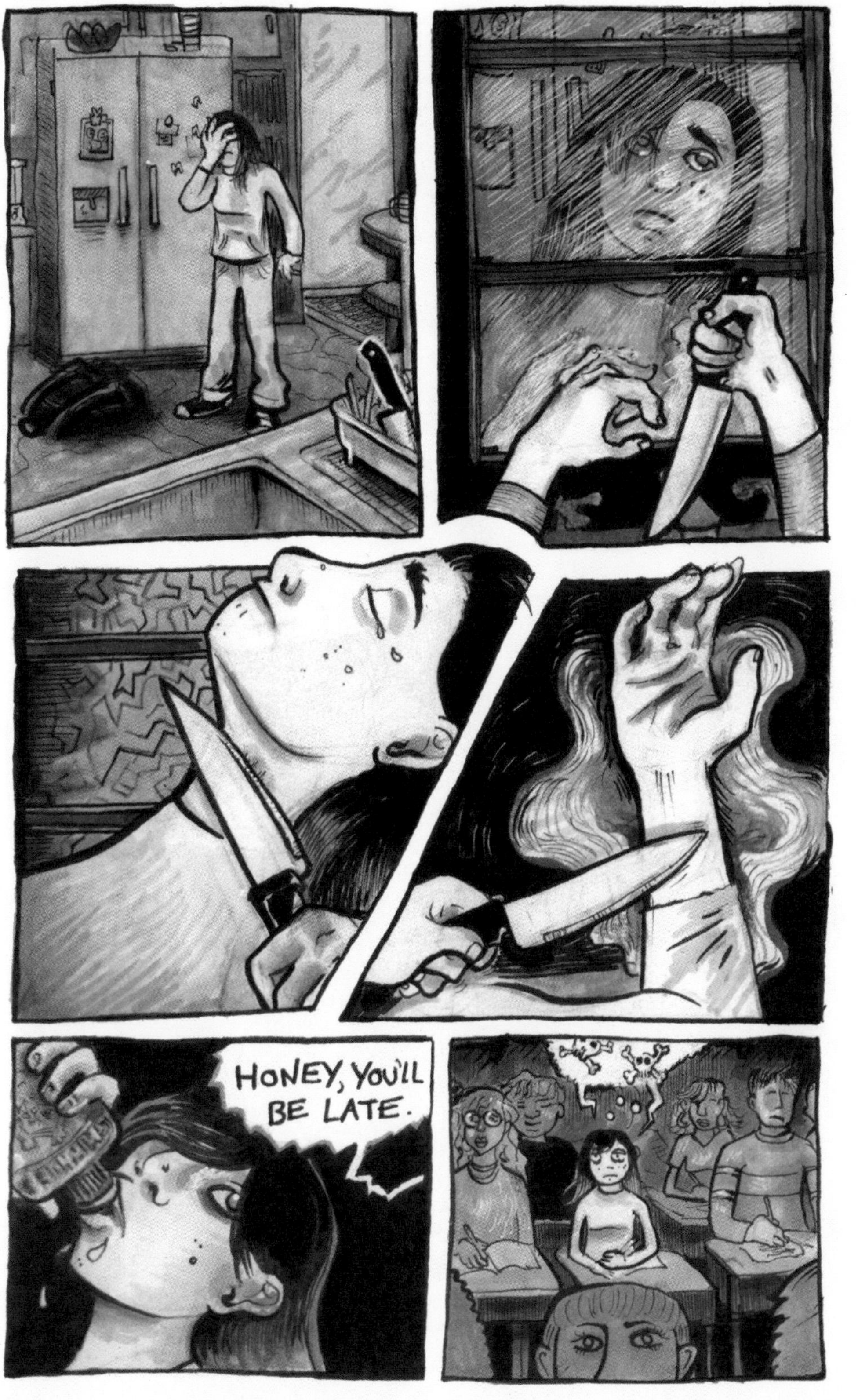
HONEY, YOU'LL BE LATE.

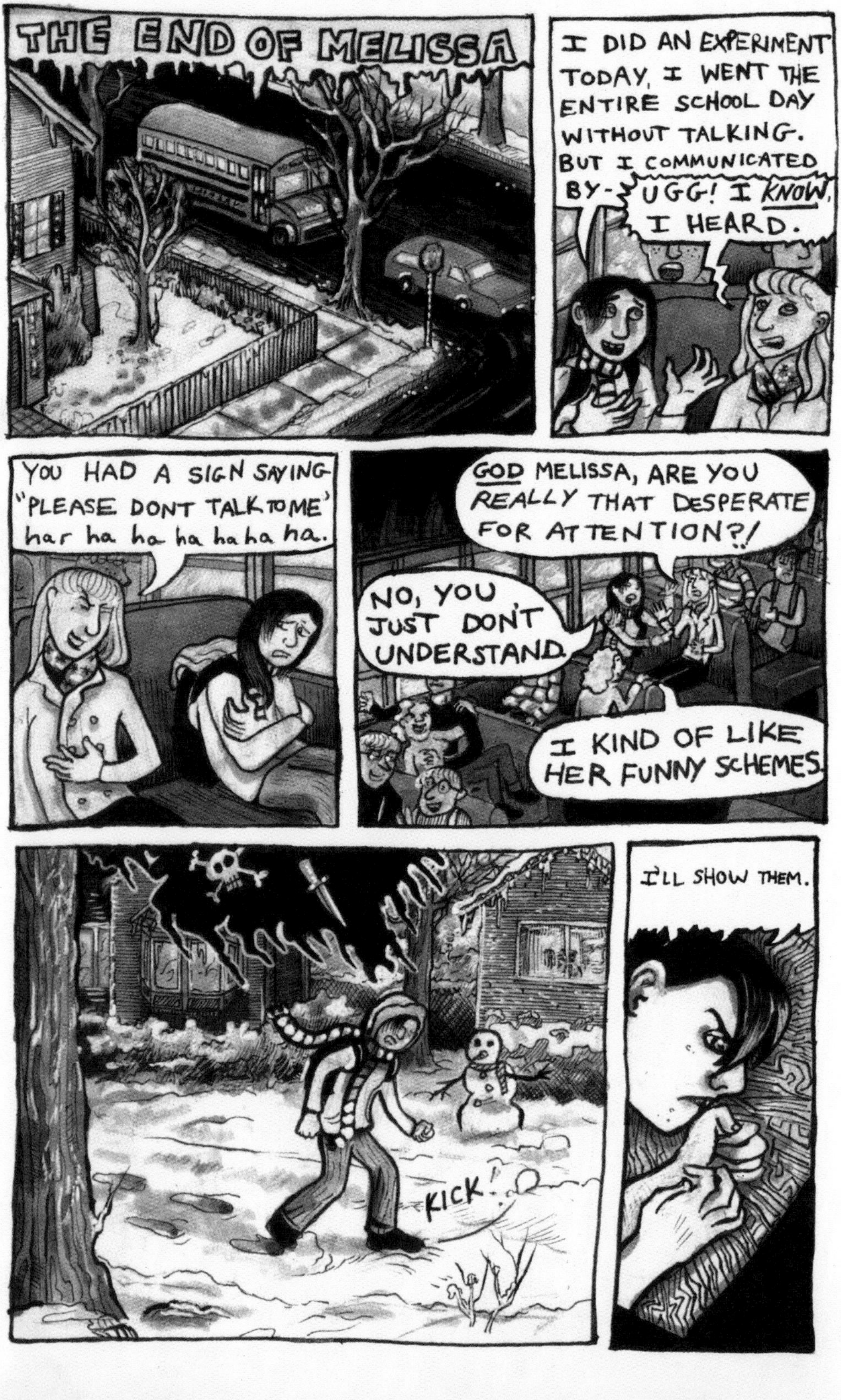
THE END OF MELISSA
I DID AN EXPERIMENT TODAY, I WENT THE ENTIRE SCHOOL DAY WITHOUT TALKING. BUT I COMMUNICATED BY-
UGG! I KNOW, I HEARD.
YOU HAD A SIGN SAYING "PLEASE DONT TALK TO ME" har ha ha ha ha ha ha.
GOD MELISSA, ARE YOU REALLY THAT DESPERATE FOR ATTENTION?!
NO, YOU JUST DON'T UNDERSTAND.
I KIND OF LIKE HER FUNNY SCHEMES.
KICK!
I'LL SHOW THEM.

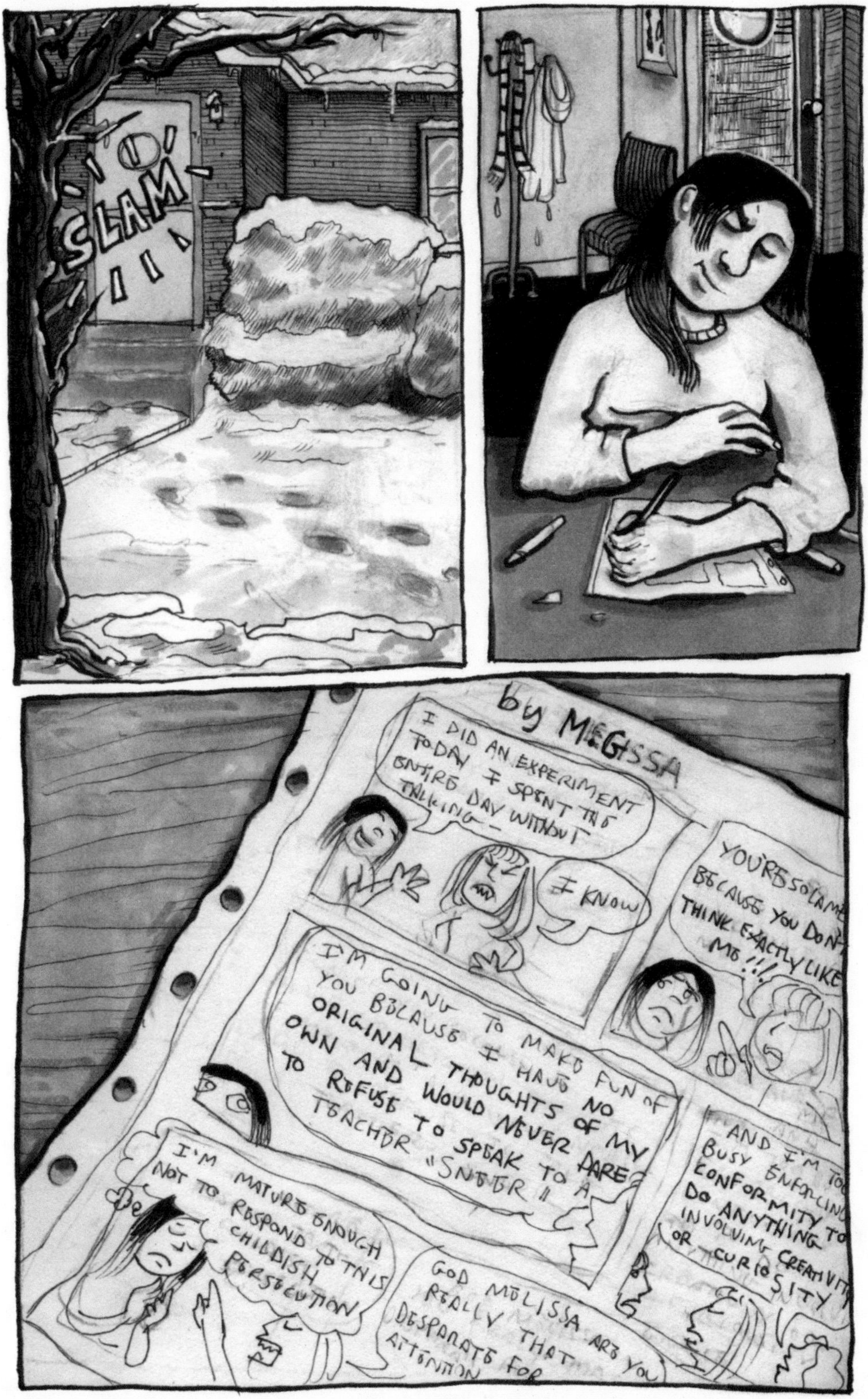
SLAM
by MELISSA
I DID AN EXPERIMENT TODAY I SPENT THE ENTIRE DAY WITHOUT TALKING—
I KNOW
I'M GOING TO MAKE FUN OF YOU BECAUSE I HAVE NO ORIGINAL THOUGHTS OF MY OWN AND WOULD NEVER DARE TO REFUSE TO SPEAK TO A TEACHER "SNEER"
I'M MATURE ENOUGH NOT TO RESPOND TO THIS CHILDISH PERSECUTION
GOD MELISSA ARE YOU REALLY THAT DESPARATE FOR ATTENTION
YOU'RE SO LAME BECAUSE YOU DON'T THINK EXACTLY LIKE ME!!!
AND I'M TOO BUSY ENFORCING CONFORMITY TO DO ANYTHING INVOLVING CREATIVITY OR CURIOSITY

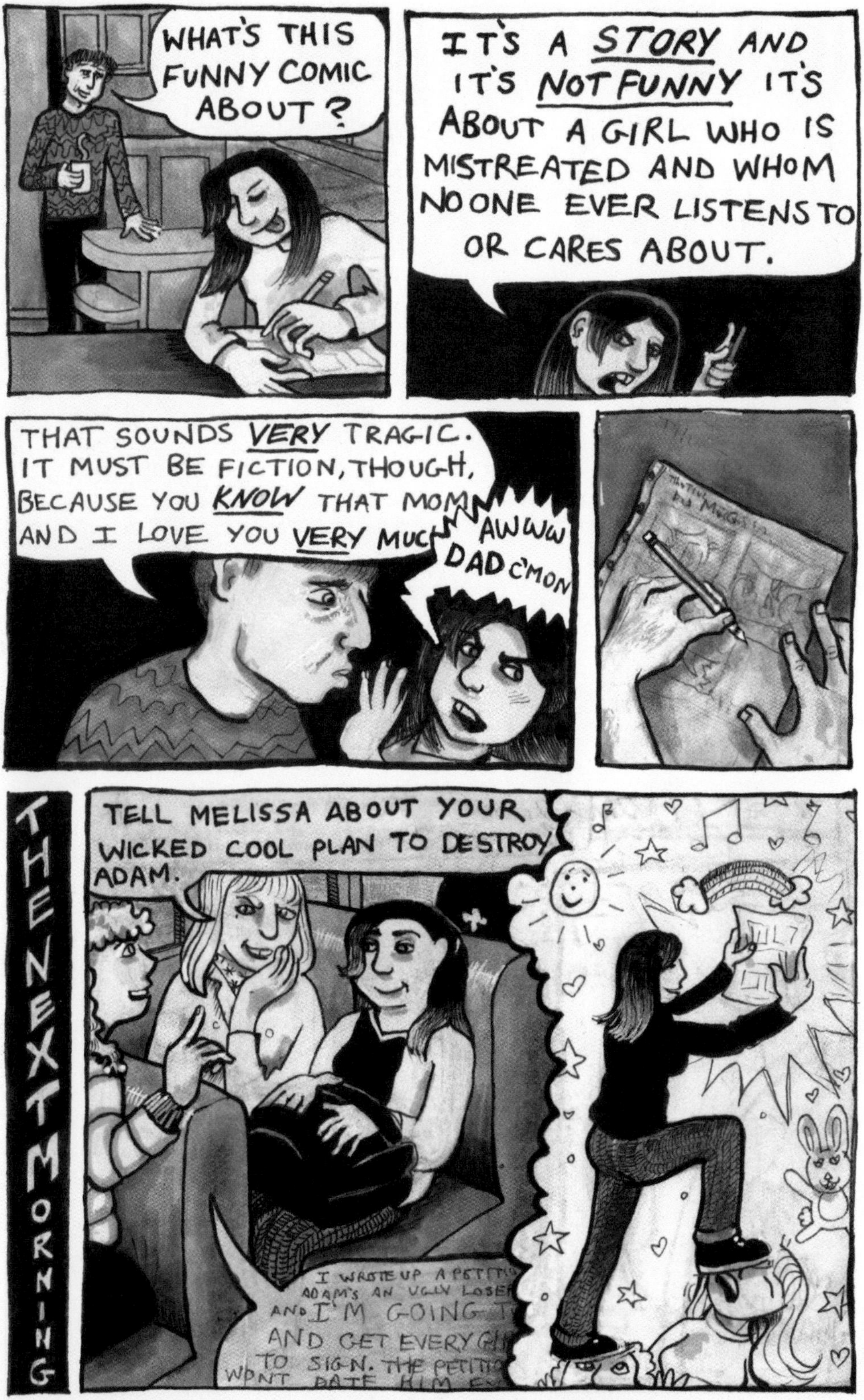
WHAT'S THIS FUNNY COMIC ABOUT?
IT'S A STORY AND IT'S NOT FUNNY IT'S ABOUT A GIRL WHO IS MISTREATED AND WHOM NO ONE EVER LISTENS TO OR CARES ABOUT.
THAT SOUNDS VERY TRAGIC. IT MUST BE FICTION, THOUGH, BECAUSE YOU KNOW THAT MOM AND I LOVE YOU VERY MUC
AWWW DAD C'MON
THE NEXT MORNING
TELL MELISSA ABOUT YOUR WICKED COOL PLAN TO DESTROY ADAM.
I WROTE UP A PETITI
ADAM'S AN UGLY LOSE
AND I'M GOING T
AND GET EVERY G
TO SIGN. THE PETITIO
WONT DATE HIM

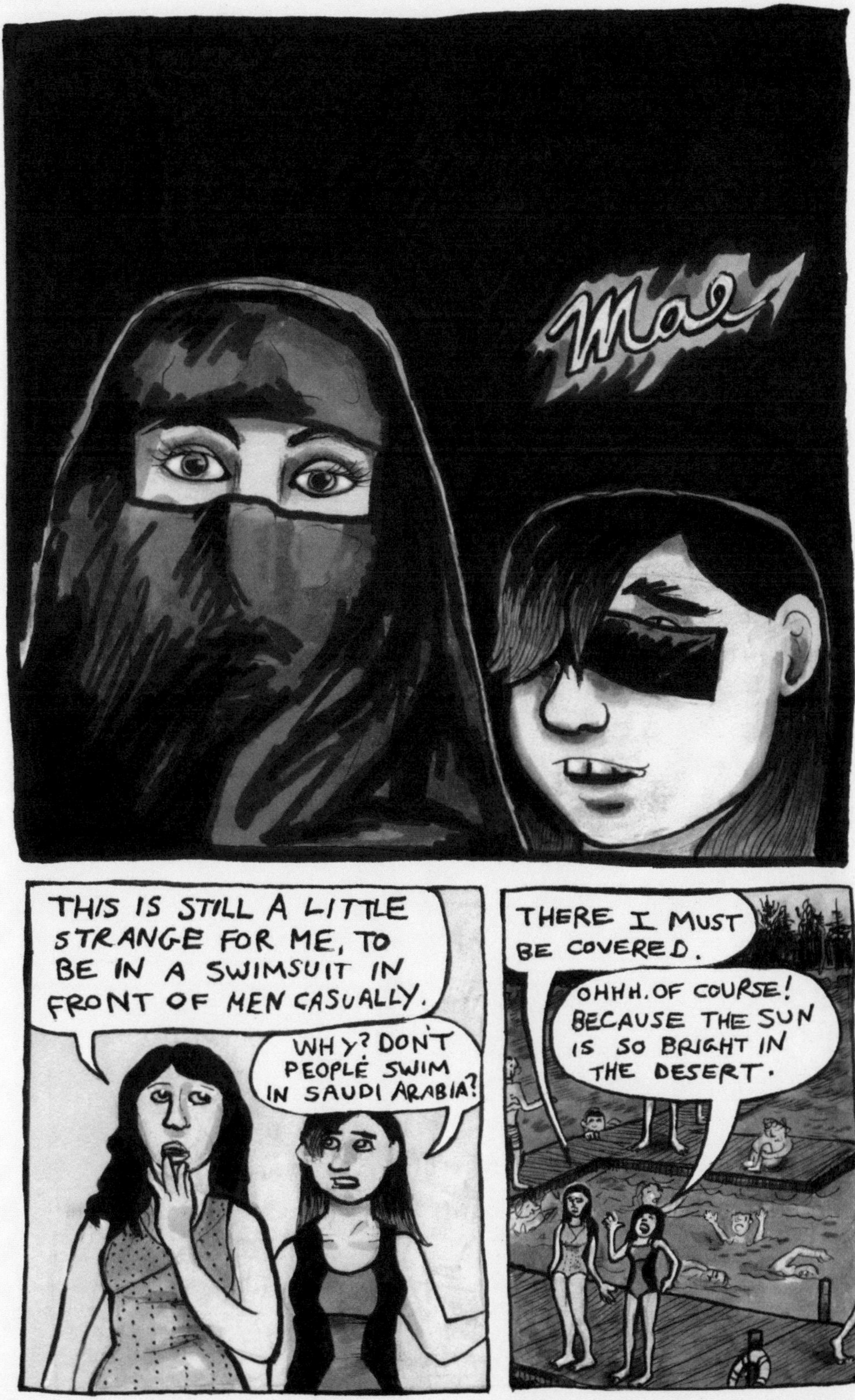
Mae
THIS IS STILL A LITTLE STRANGE FOR ME, TO BE IN A SWIMSUIT IN FRONT OF MEN CASUALLY.
WHY? DON'T PEOPLE SWIM IN SAUDI ARABIA?
THERE I MUST BE COVERED.
OHHH. OF COURSE! BECAUSE THE SUN IS SO BRIGHT IN THE DESERT.

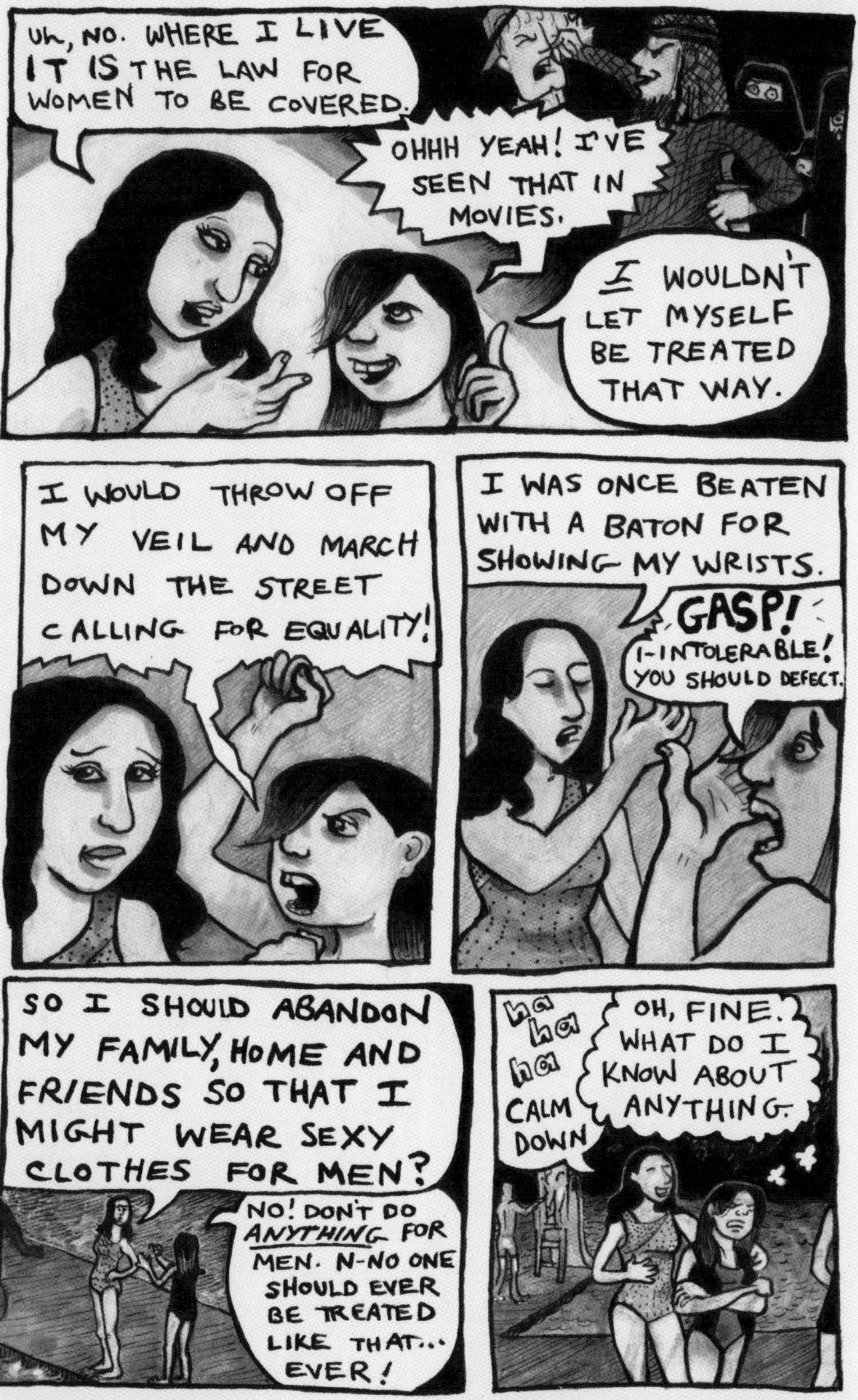
UH, NO. WHERE I LIVE IT IS THE LAW FOR WOMEN TO BE COVERED.
OHHH YEAH! I'VE SEEN THAT IN MOVIES.
I WOULDN'T LET MYSELF BE TREATED THAT WAY.
I WOULD THROW OFF MY VEIL AND MARCH DOWN THE STREET CALLING FOR EQUALITY!
I WAS ONCE BEATEN WITH A BATON FOR SHOWING MY WRISTS.
GASP!
I-INTOLERABLE! YOU SHOULD DEFECT.
SO I SHOULD ABANDON MY FAMILY, HOME AND FRIENDS SO THAT I MIGHT WEAR SEXY CLOTHES FOR MEN?
NO! DON'T DO ANYTHING FOR MEN. N-NO ONE SHOULD EVER BE TREATED LIKE THAT... EVER!
ha ha ha
CALM DOWN
OH, FINE. WHAT DO I KNOW ABOUT ANYTHING.

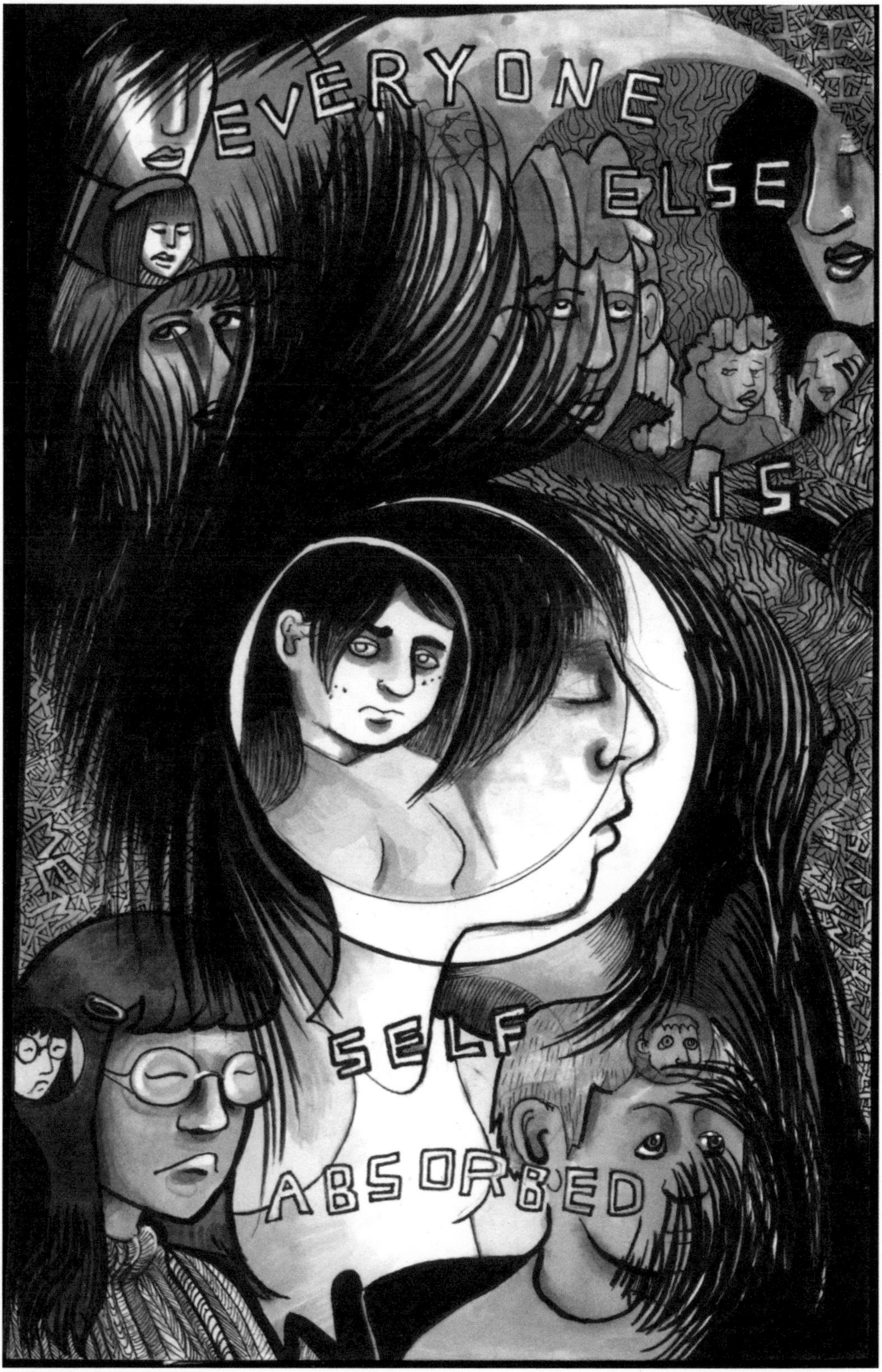
EVERYONE
ELSE
IS
SELF
ABSORBED

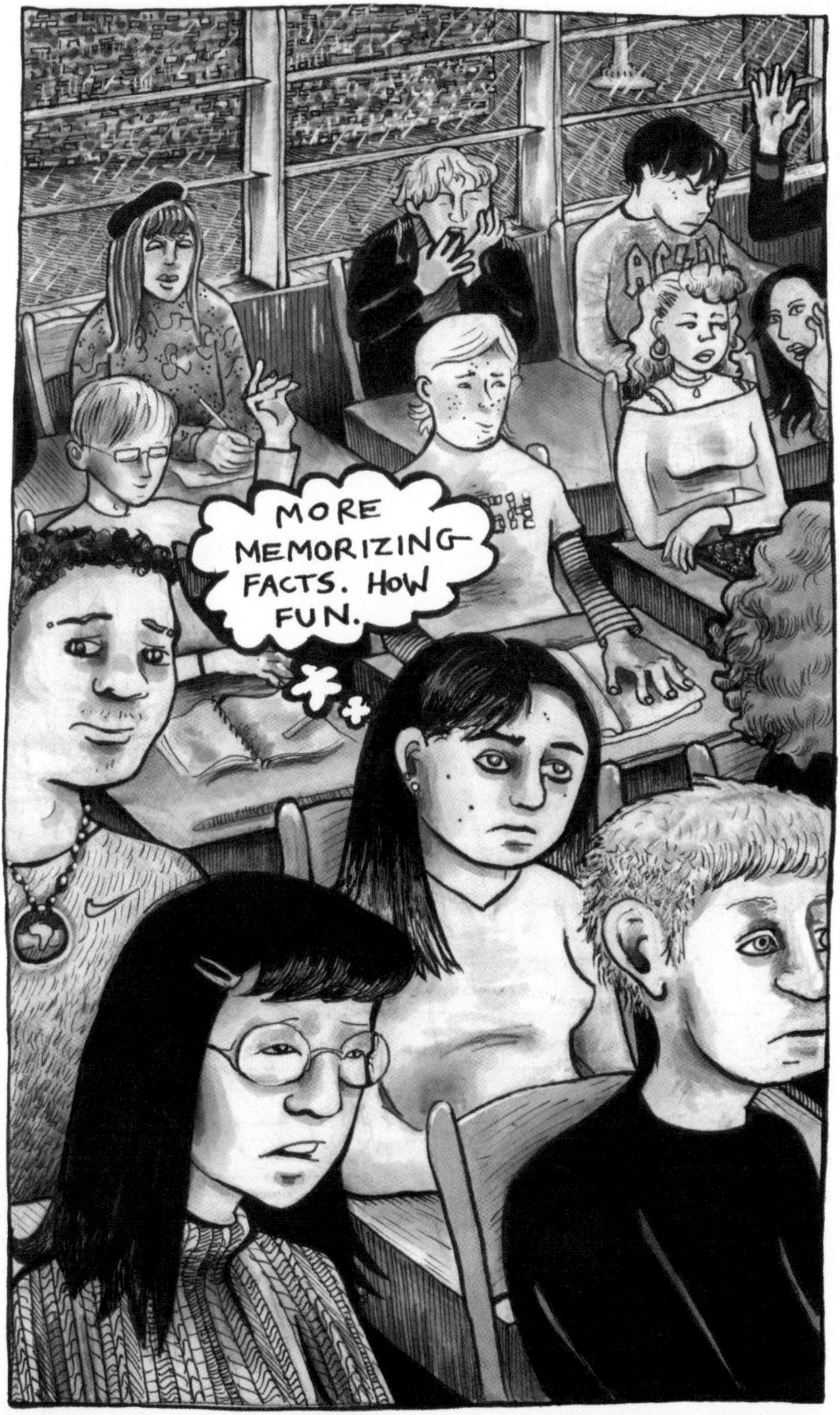
MORE MEMORIZING FACTS. HOW FUN.

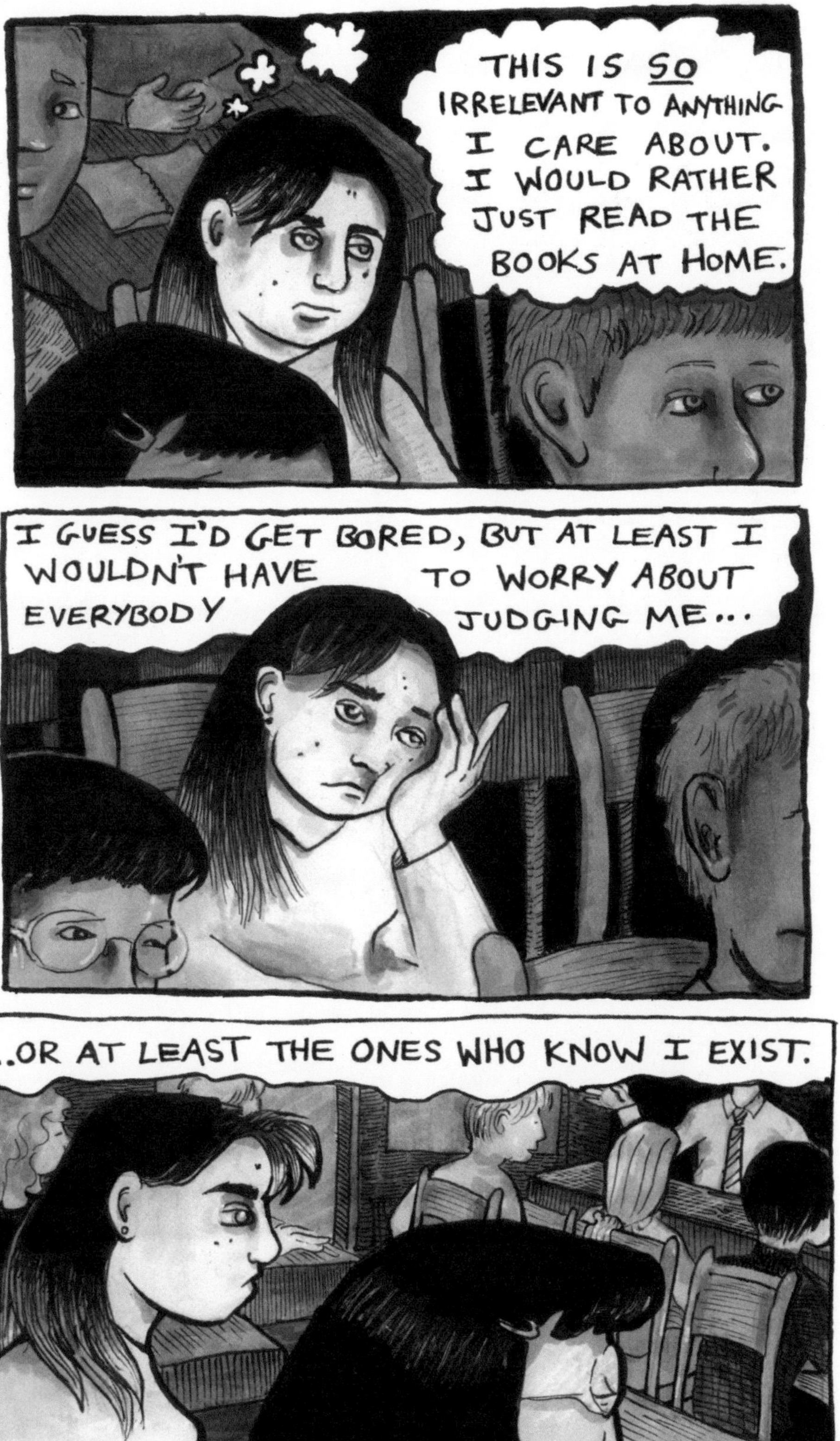
THIS IS SO IRRELEVANT TO ANYTHING I CARE ABOUT. I WOULD RATHER JUST READ THE BOOKS AT HOME.
I GUESS I'D GET BORED, BUT AT LEAST I WOULDN'T HAVE TO WORRY ABOUT EVERYBODY JUDGING ME...
..OR AT LEAST THE ONES WHO KNOW I EXIST.

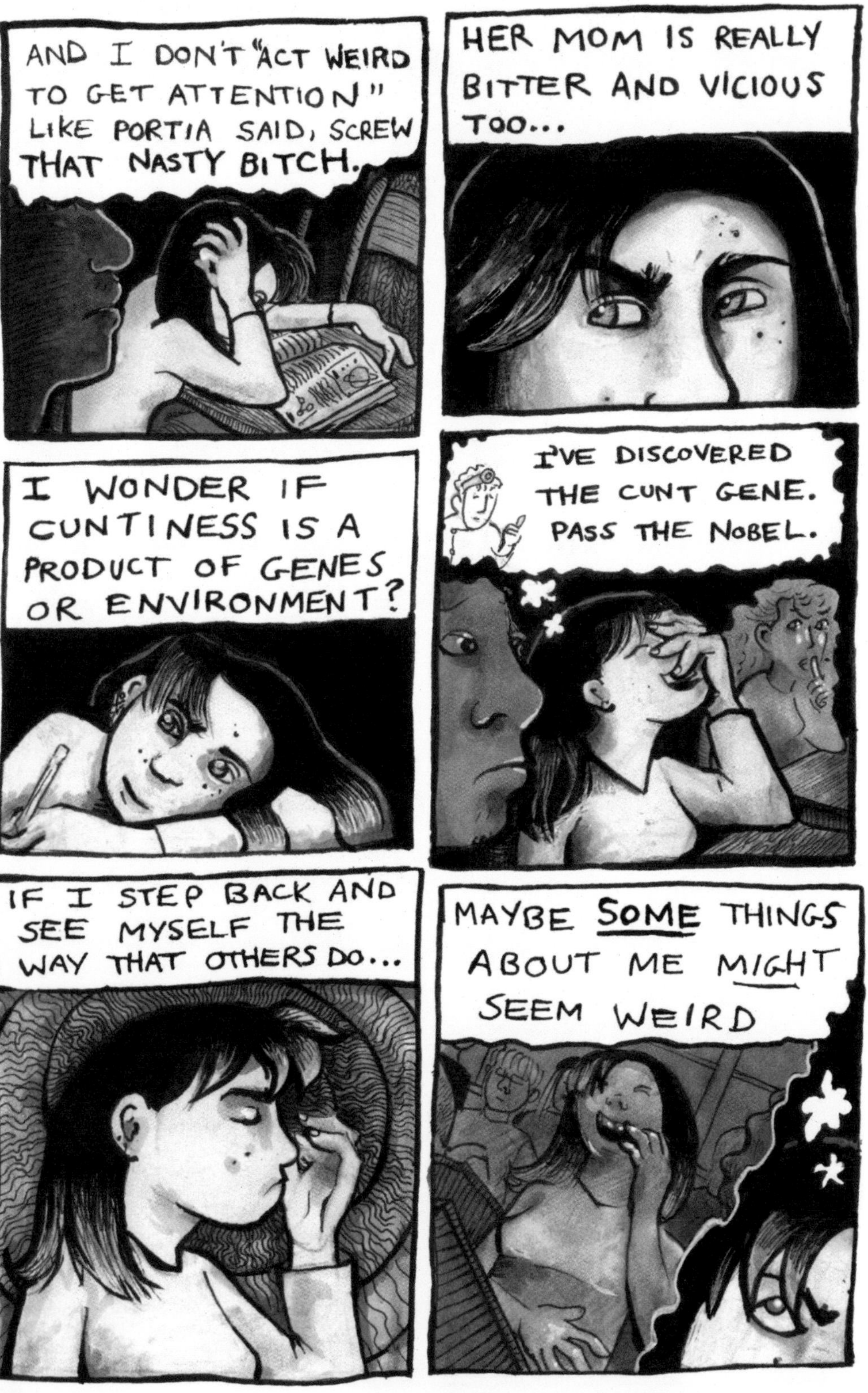
AND I DON'T "ACT WEIRD TO GET ATTENTION" LIKE PORTIA SAID, SCREW THAT NASTY BITCH.
HER MOM IS REALLY BITTER AND VICIOUS TOO...
I WONDER IF CUNTINESS IS A PRODUCT OF GENES OR ENVIRONMENT?
I'VE DISCOVERED THE CUNT GENE. PASS THE NOBEL.
IF I STEP BACK AND SEE MYSELF THE WAY THAT OTHERS DO...
MAYBE SOME THINGS ABOUT ME MIGHT SEEM WEIRD

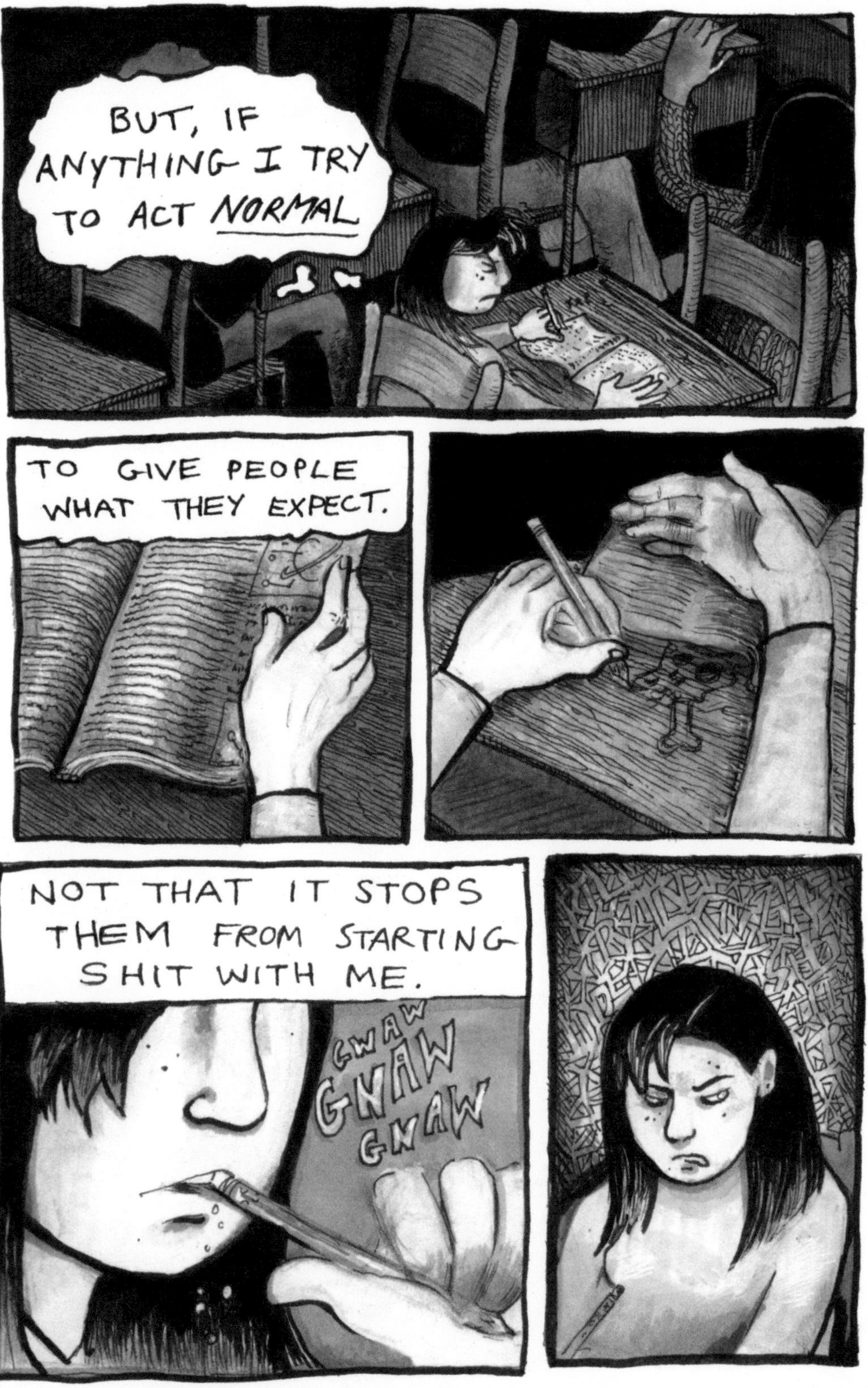

BUT, IF ANYTHING I TRY TO ACT NORMAL
TO GIVE PEOPLE WHAT THEY EXPECT.
NOT THAT IT STOPS THEM FROM STARTING SHIT WITH ME.
GNAW GNAW GNAW

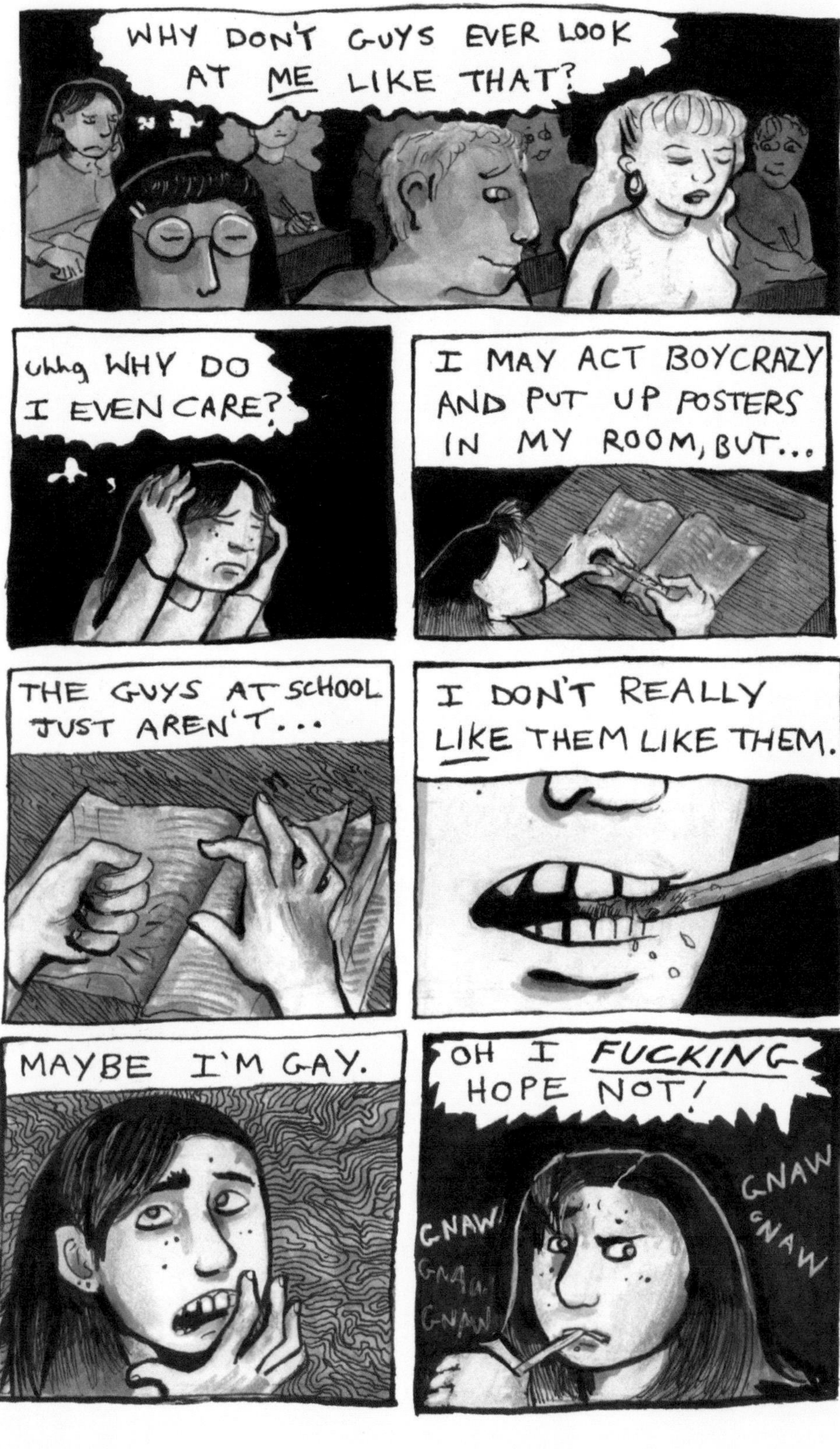
WHY DON'T GUYS EVER LOOK AT ME LIKE THAT?
uhhg WHY DO I EVEN CARE?
I MAY ACT BOYCRAZY AND PUT UP POSTERS IN MY ROOM, BUT...
THE GUYS AT SCHOOL JUST AREN'T...
I DON'T REALLY LIKE THEM LIKE THEM.
MAYBE I'M GAY.
OH I FUCKING HOPE NOT!
GNAW GNAW
GNAW GNAW GNAW

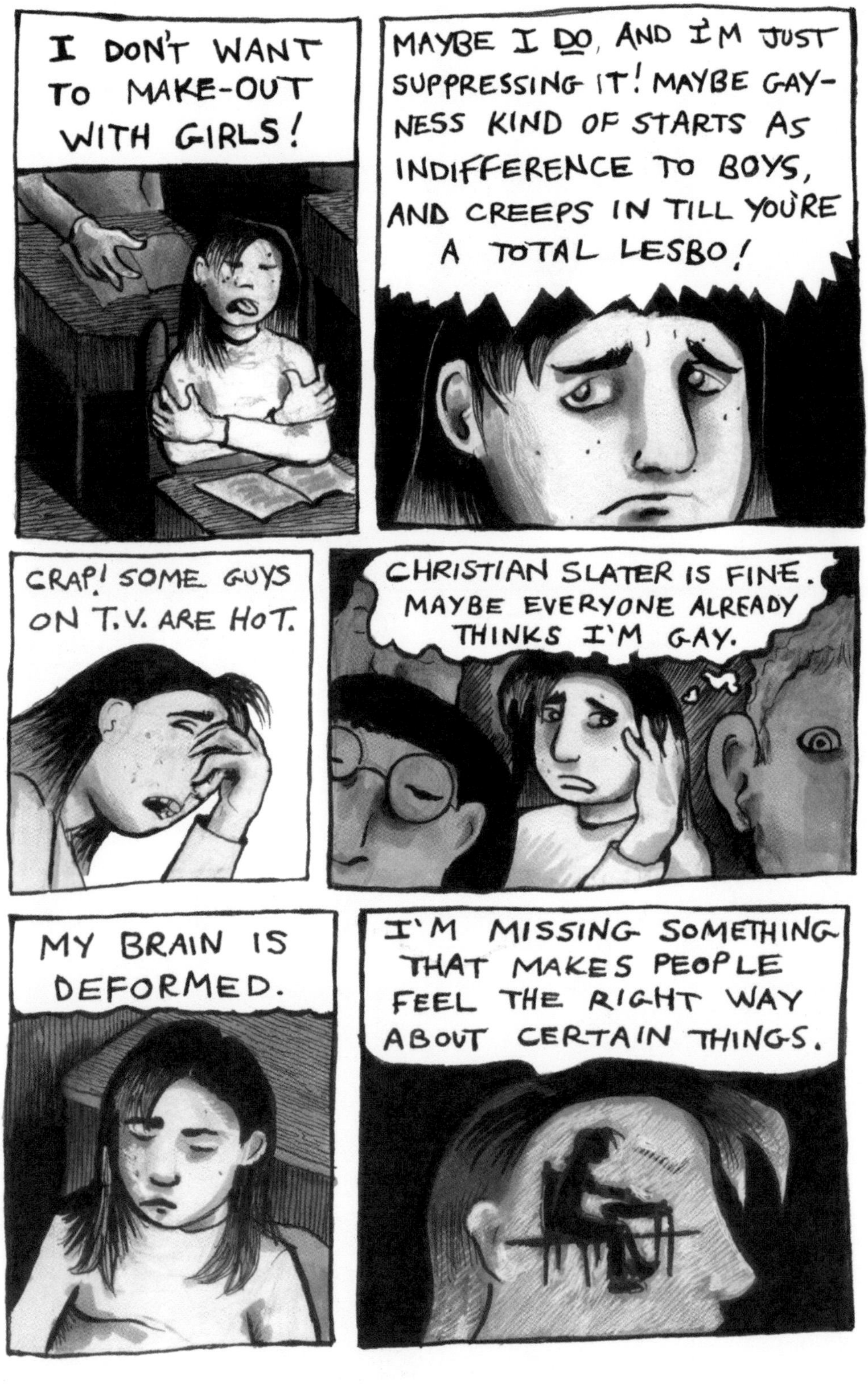
I DON'T WANT TO MAKE-OUT WITH GIRLS!
MAYBE I DO, AND I'M JUST SUPPRESSING IT! MAYBE GAY-NESS KIND OF STARTS AS INDIFFERENCE TO BOYS, AND CREEPS IN TILL YOU'RE A TOTAL LESBO!
CRAP! SOME GUYS ON T.V. ARE HOT.
CHRISTIAN SLATER IS FINE. MAYBE EVERYONE ALREADY THINKS I'M GAY.
MY BRAIN IS DEFORMED.
I'M MISSING SOMETHING THAT MAKES PEOPLE FEEL THE RIGHT WAY ABOUT CERTAIN THINGS.

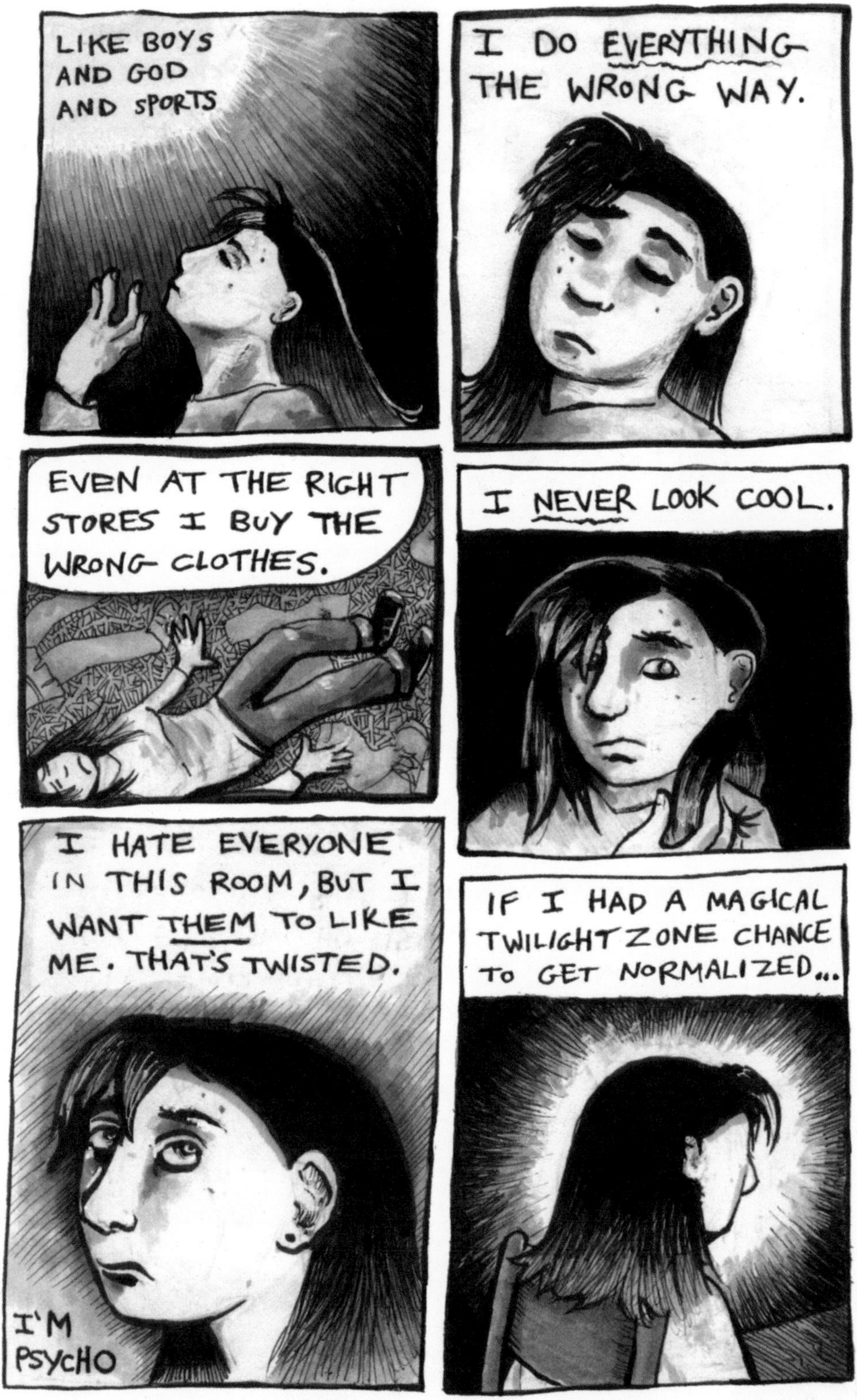
LIKE BOYS AND GOD AND SPORTS
I DO EVERYTHING THE WRONG WAY.
EVEN AT THE RIGHT STORES I BUY THE WRONG CLOTHES.
I NEVER LOOK COOL.
I HATE EVERYONE IN THIS ROOM, BUT I WANT THEM TO LIKE ME. THAT'S TWISTED.
I'M PSYCHO
IF I HAD A MAGICAL TWILIGHT ZONE CHANCE TO GET NORMALIZED...

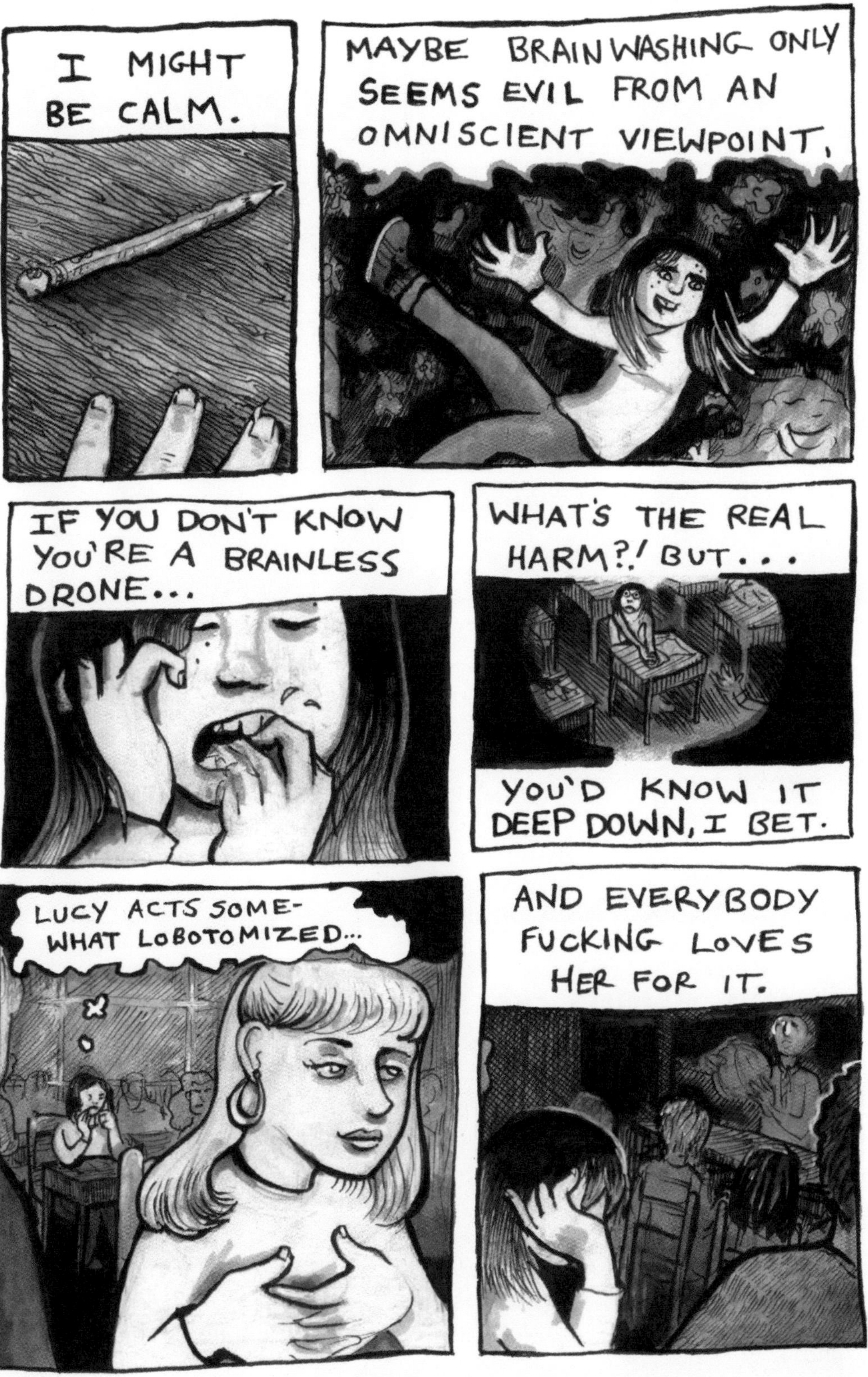
I MIGHT BE CALM.
MAYBE BRAINWASHING ONLY SEEMS EVIL FROM AN OMNISCIENT VIEWPOINT,
IF YOU DON'T KNOW YOU'RE A BRAINLESS DRONE...
WHAT'S THE REAL HARM?! BUT...
YOU'D KNOW IT DEEP DOWN, I BET.
LUCY ACTS SOME-WHAT LOBOTOMIZED...
AND EVERYBODY FUCKING LOVES HER FOR IT.

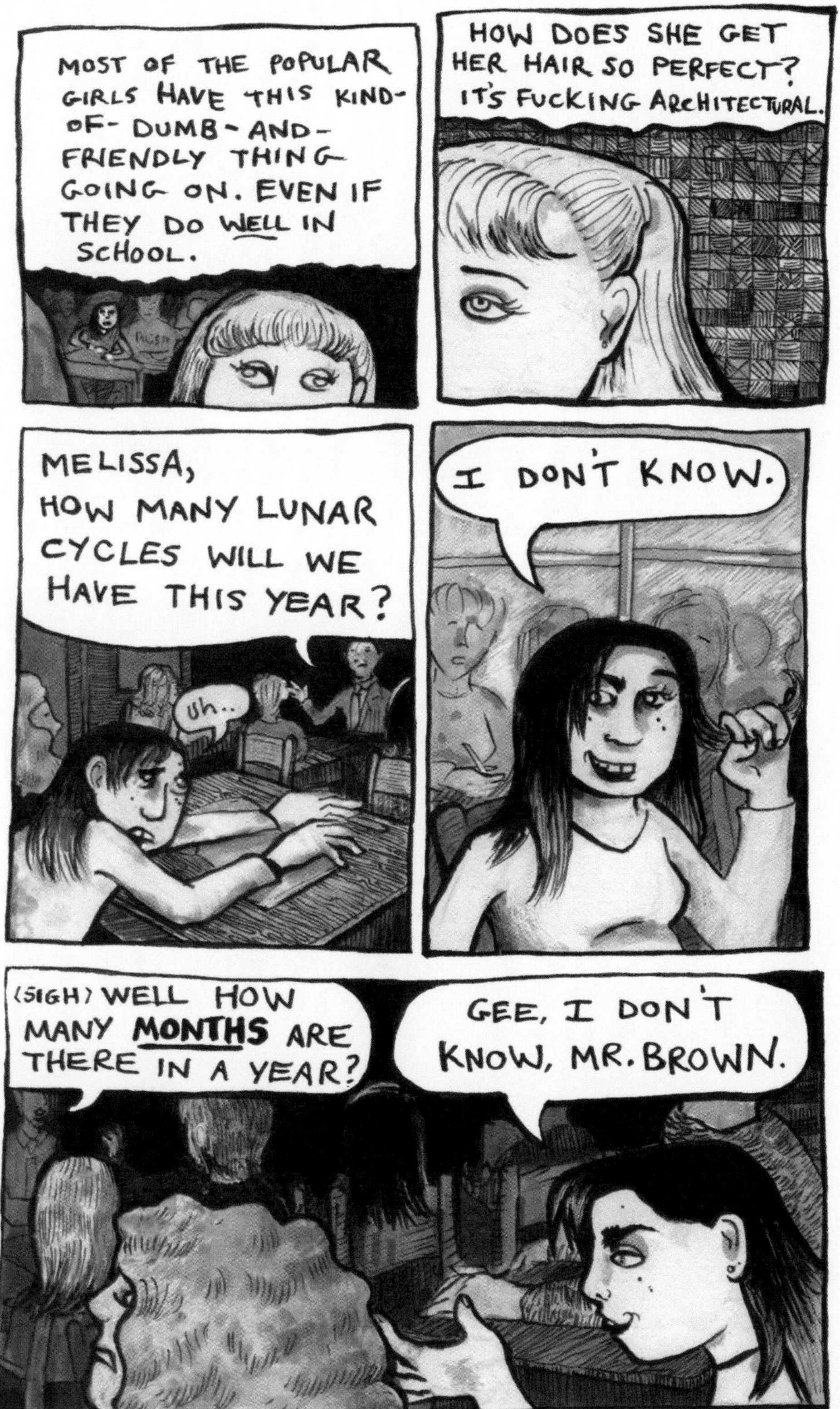
MOST OF THE POPULAR GIRLS HAVE THIS KIND-OF-DUMB-AND-FRIENDLY THING GOING ON. EVEN IF THEY DO WELL IN SCHOOL.
HOW DOES SHE GET HER HAIR SO PERFECT? IT'S FUCKING ARCHITECTURAL.
MELISSA, HOW MANY LUNAR CYCLES WILL WE HAVE THIS YEAR?
Uh..
I DON'T KNOW.
(SIGH) WELL HOW MANY MONTHS ARE THERE IN A YEAR?
GEE, I DON'T KNOW, MR. BROWN.

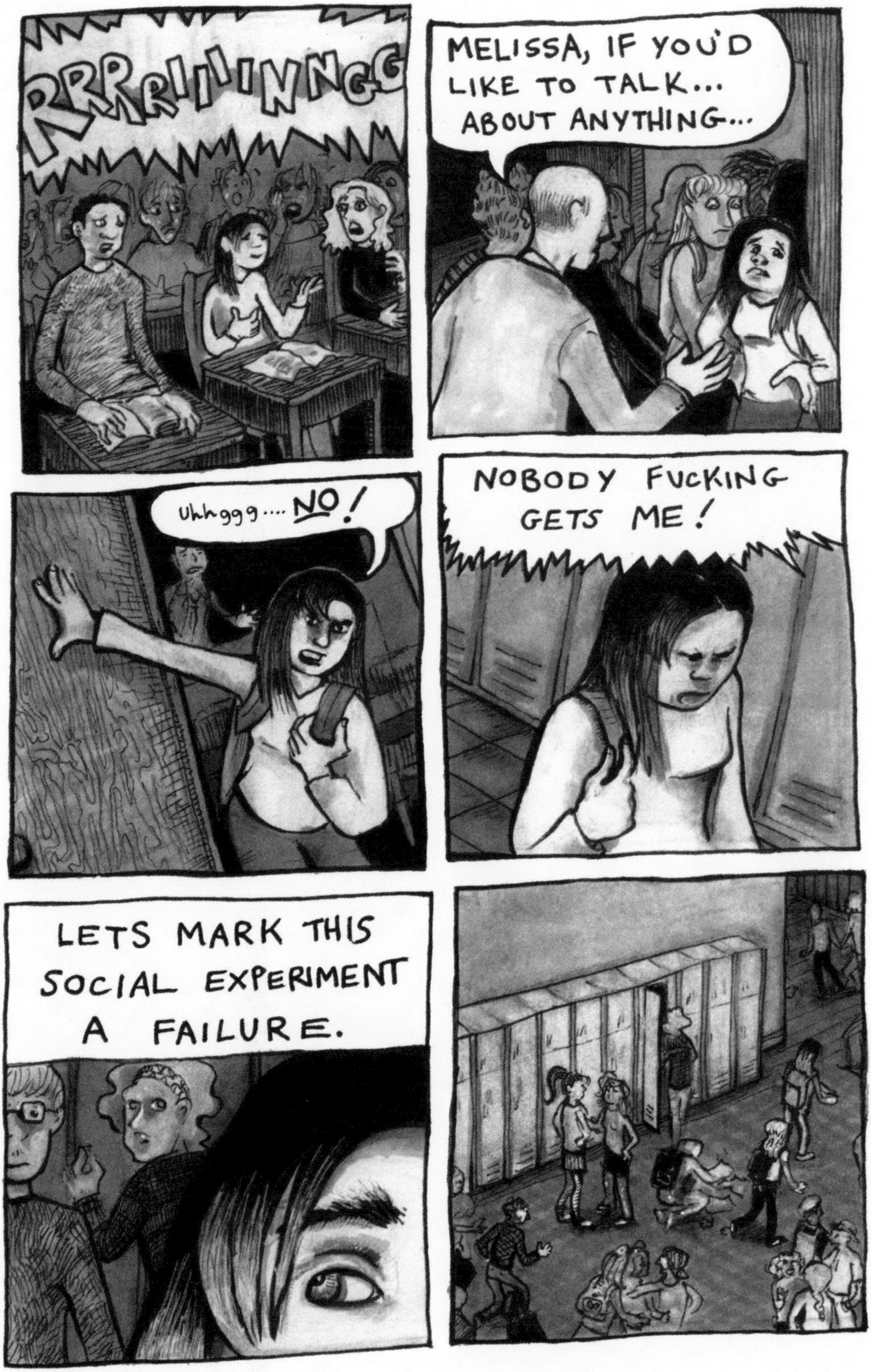
RRRRIIIINNGG
MELISSA, IF YOU'D LIKE TO TALK... ABOUT ANYTHING...
Uhhggg.... NO!
NOBODY FUCKING GETS ME!
LETS MARK THIS SOCIAL EXPERIMENT A FAILURE.

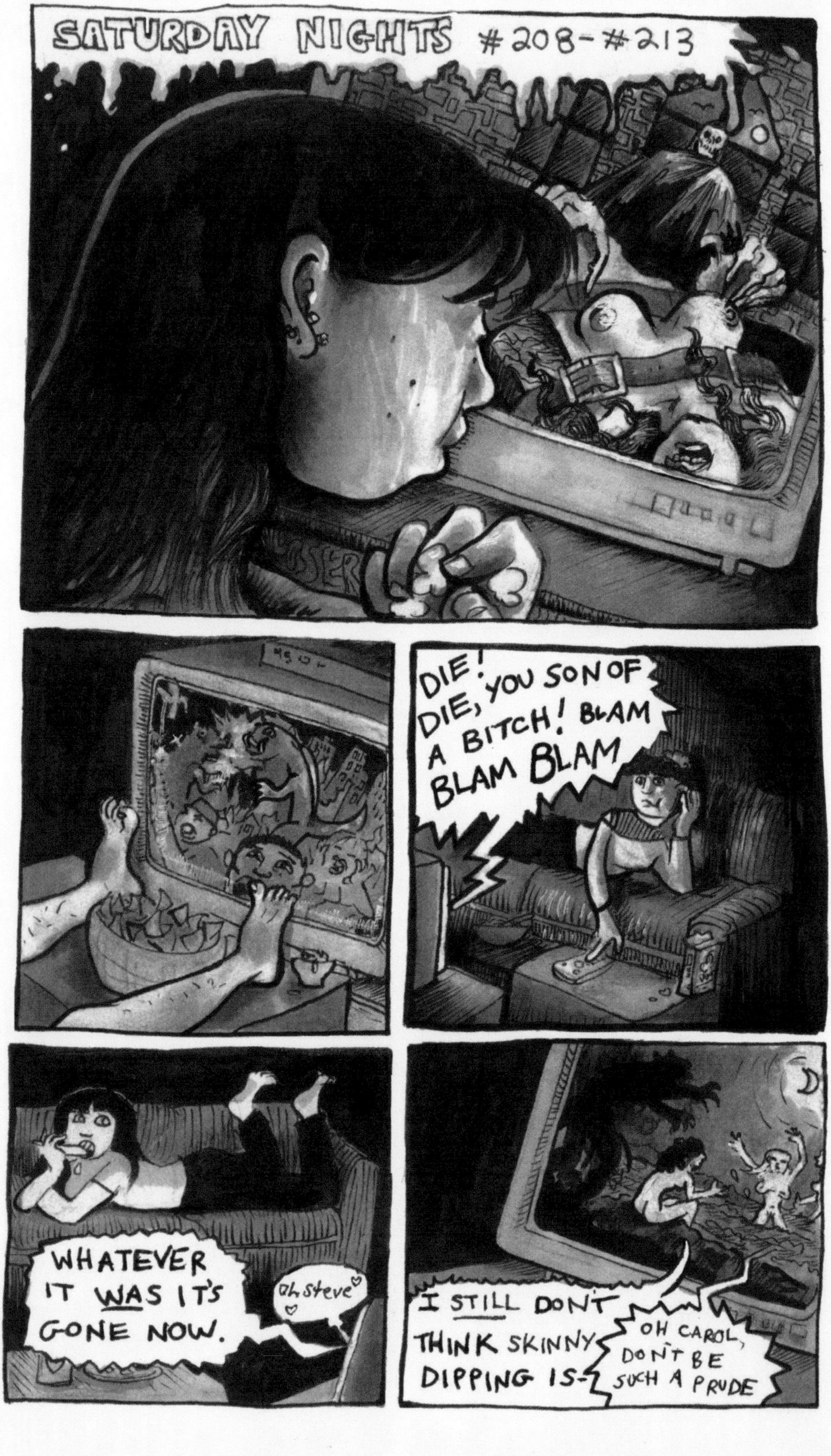
SATURDAY NIGHTS #208-#213
DIE! DIE, YOU SON OF A BITCH! BLAM BLAM BLAM
WHATEVER IT WAS IT'S GONE NOW.
oh steve
I STILL DON'T THINK SKINNY DIPPING IS-
OH CAROL, DON'T BE SUCH A PRUDE

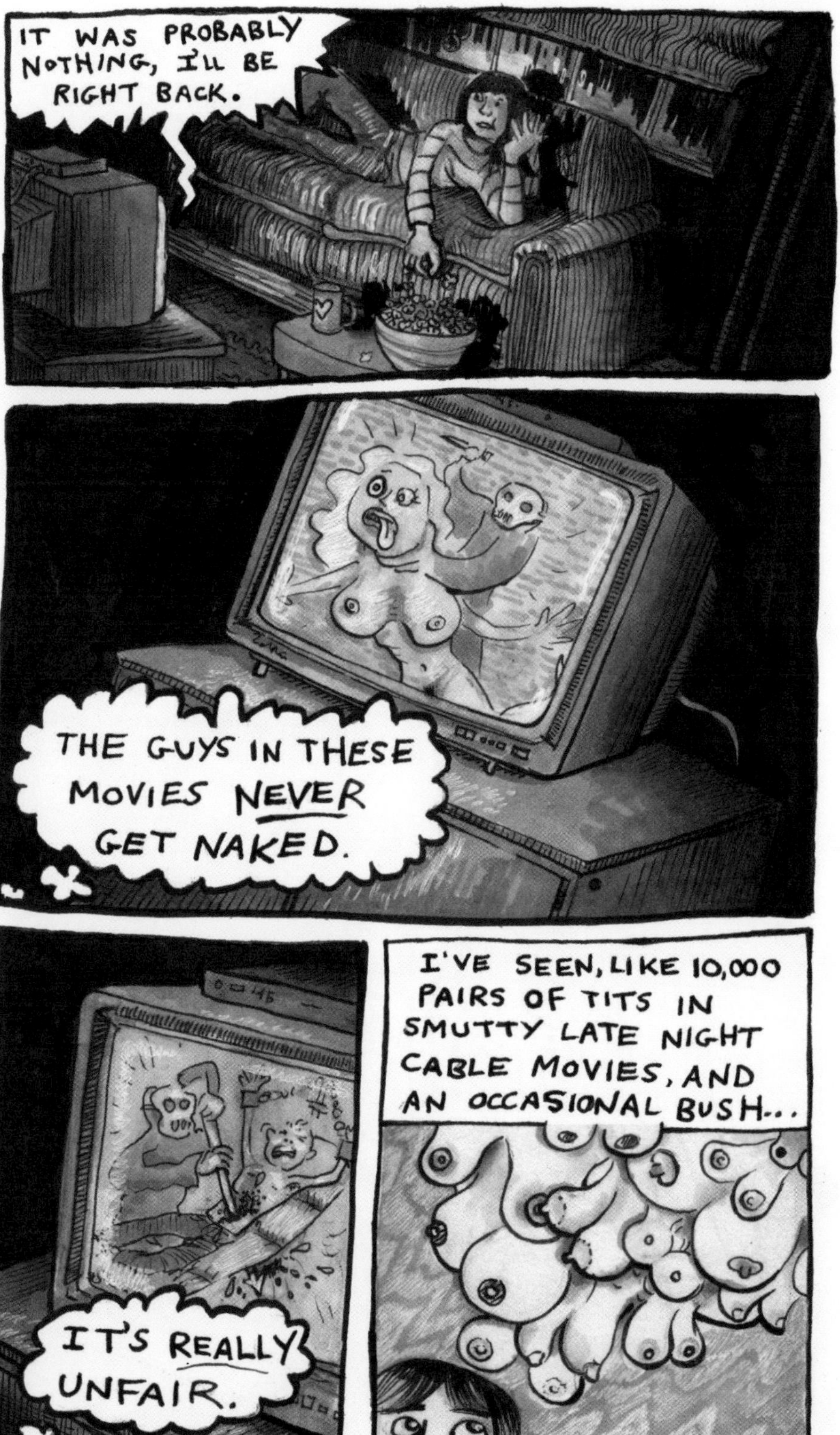
IT WAS PROBABLY NOTHING, I'LL BE RIGHT BACK.
THE GUYS IN THESE MOVIES NEVER GET NAKED.
IT'S REALLY UNFAIR.
I'VE SEEN, LIKE 10,000 PAIRS OF TITS IN SMUTTY LATE NIGHT CABLE MOVIES, AND AN OCCASIONAL BUSH...

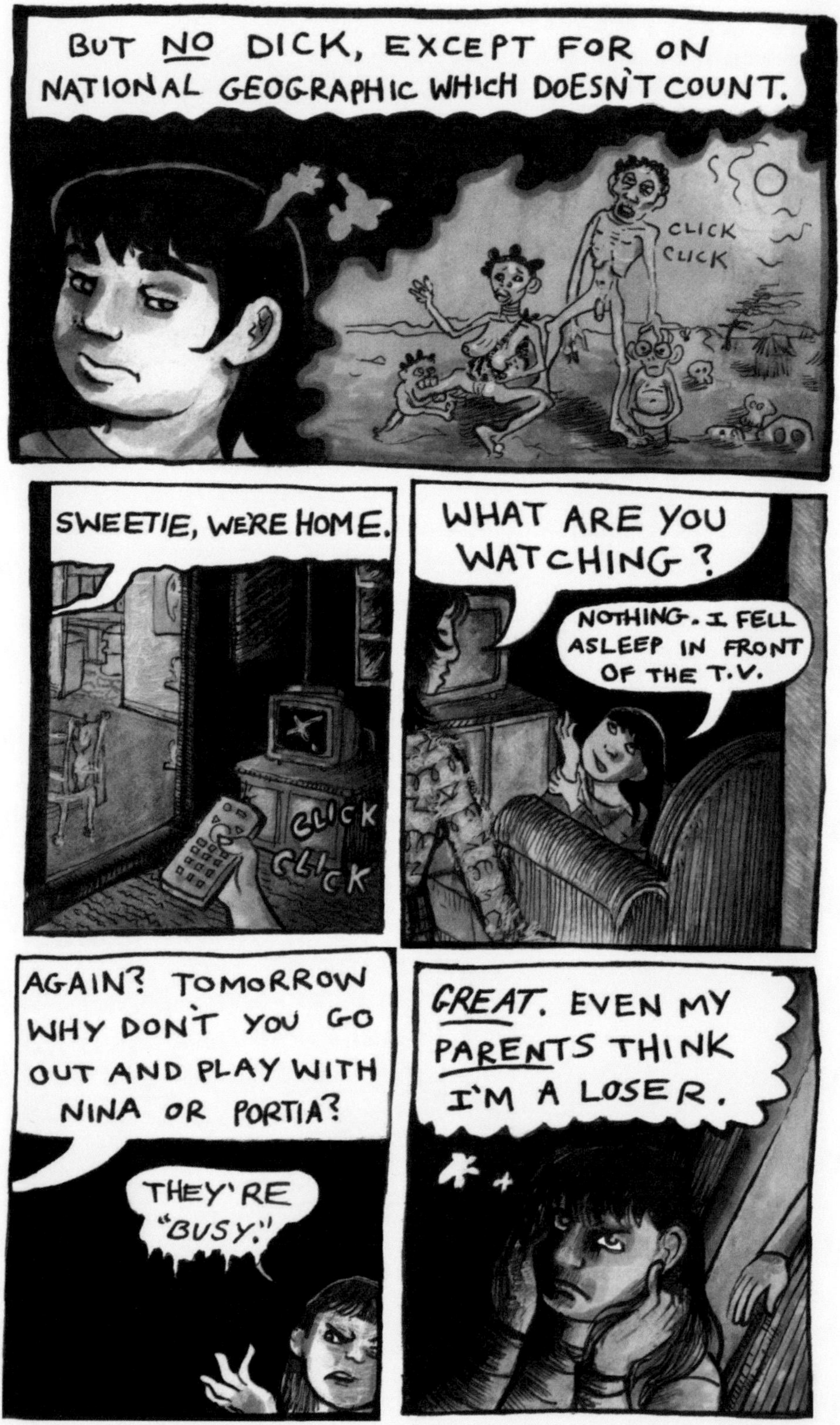
BUT NO DICK, EXCEPT FOR ON NATIONAL GEOGRAPHIC WHICH DOESN'T COUNT.
CLICK CLICK
SWEETIE, WE'RE HOME.
CLICK CLICK
WHAT ARE YOU WATCHING?
NOTHING. I FELL ASLEEP IN FRONT OF THE T.V.
AGAIN? TOMORROW WHY DON'T YOU GO OUT AND PLAY WITH NINA OR PORTIA?
THEY'RE "BUSY."
GREAT. EVEN MY PARENTS THINK I'M A LOSER.

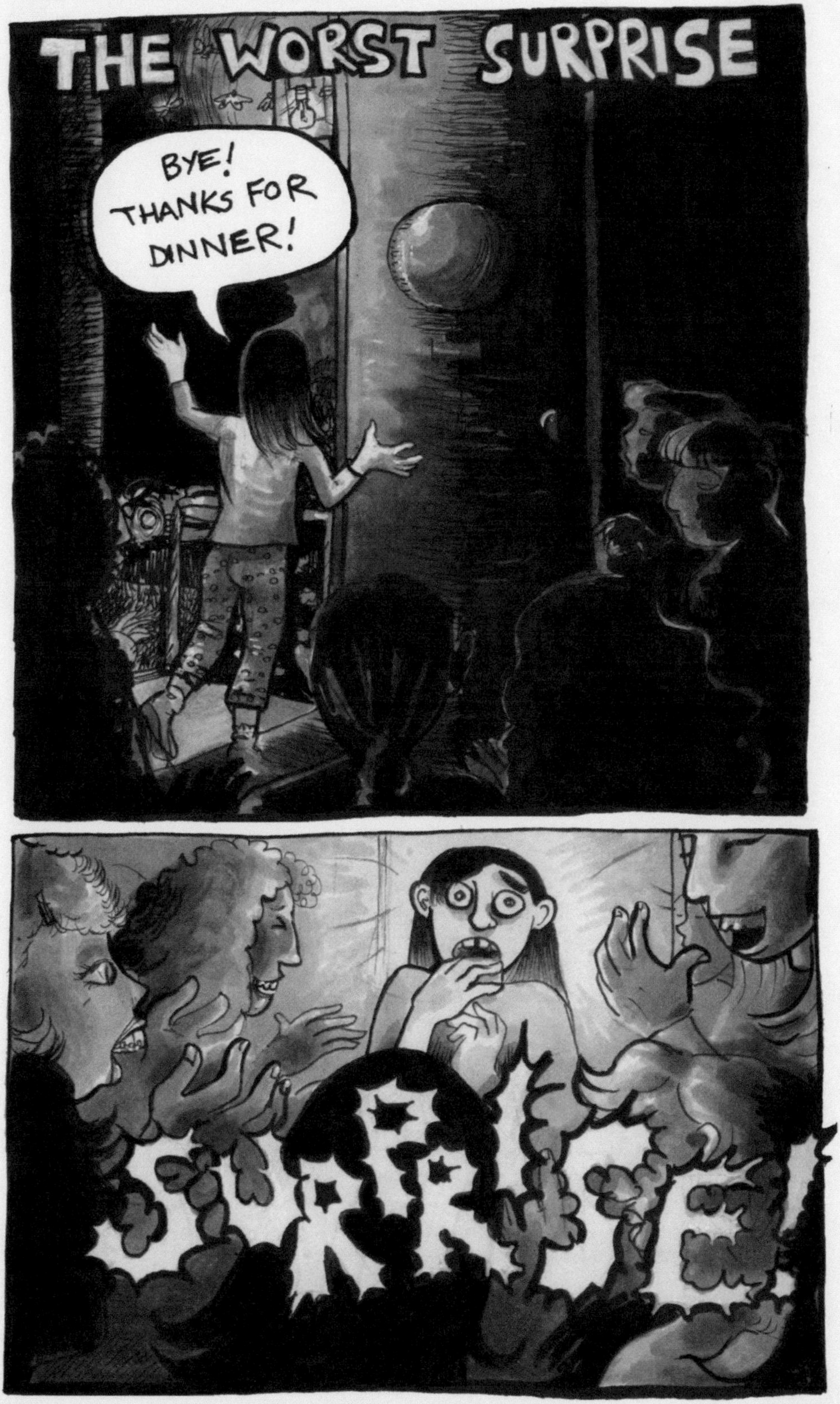
THE WORST SURPRISE
BYE! THANKS FOR DINNER!

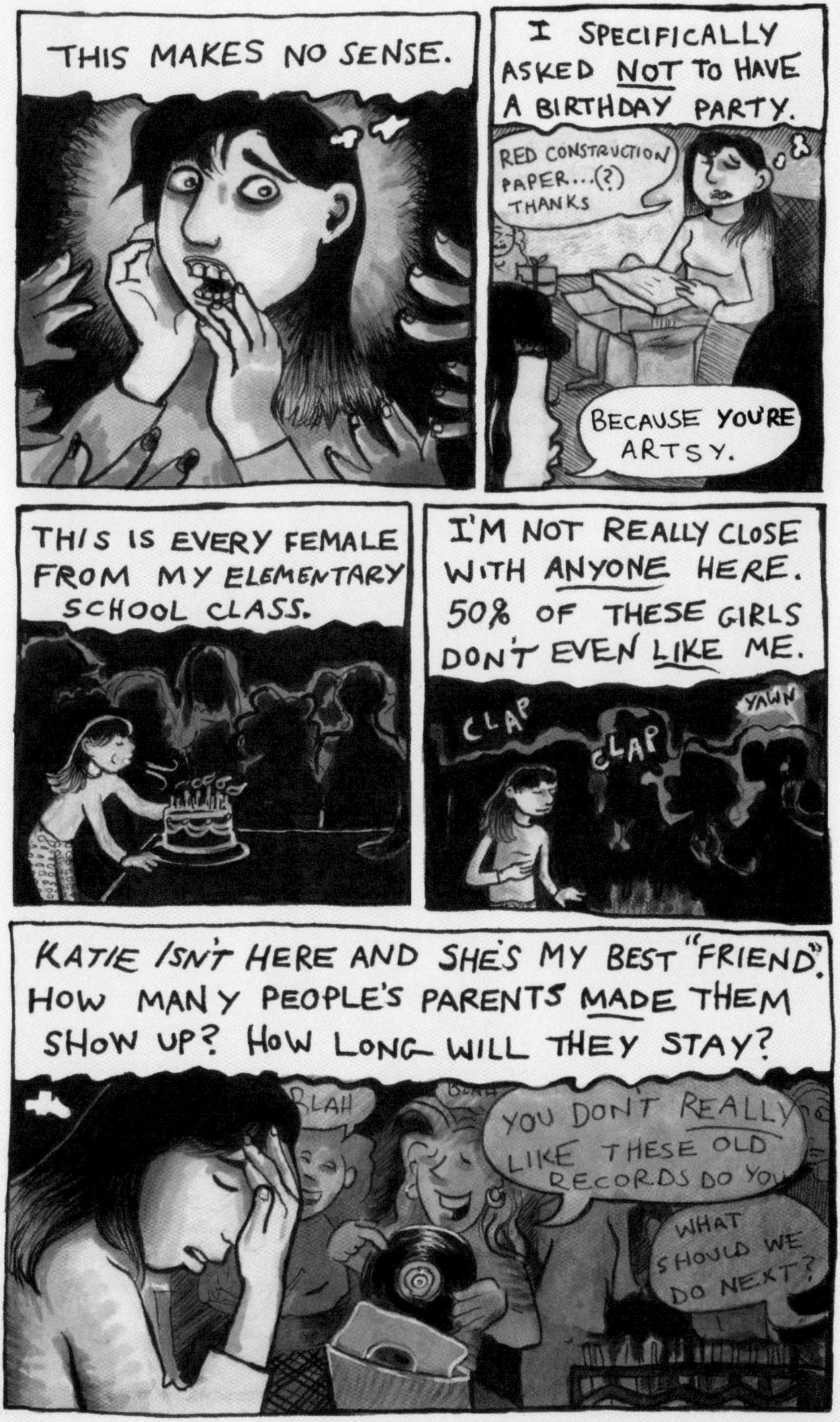
THIS MAKES NO SENSE.
I SPECIFICALLY ASKED NOT TO HAVE A BIRTHDAY PARTY.
RED CONSTRUCTION PAPER...(?) THANKS
BECAUSE YOU'RE ARTSY.
THIS IS EVERY FEMALE FROM MY ELEMENTARY SCHOOL CLASS.
I'M NOT REALLY CLOSE WITH ANYONE HERE. 50% OF THESE GIRLS DON'T EVEN LIKE ME.
CLAP
CLAP
YAWN
KATIE ISN'T HERE AND SHE'S MY BEST "FRIEND". HOW MANY PEOPLE'S PARENTS MADE THEM SHOW UP? HOW LONG WILL THEY STAY?
BLAH
YOU DON'T REALLY LIKE THESE OLD RECORDS DO YOU
WHAT SHOULD WE DO NEXT?

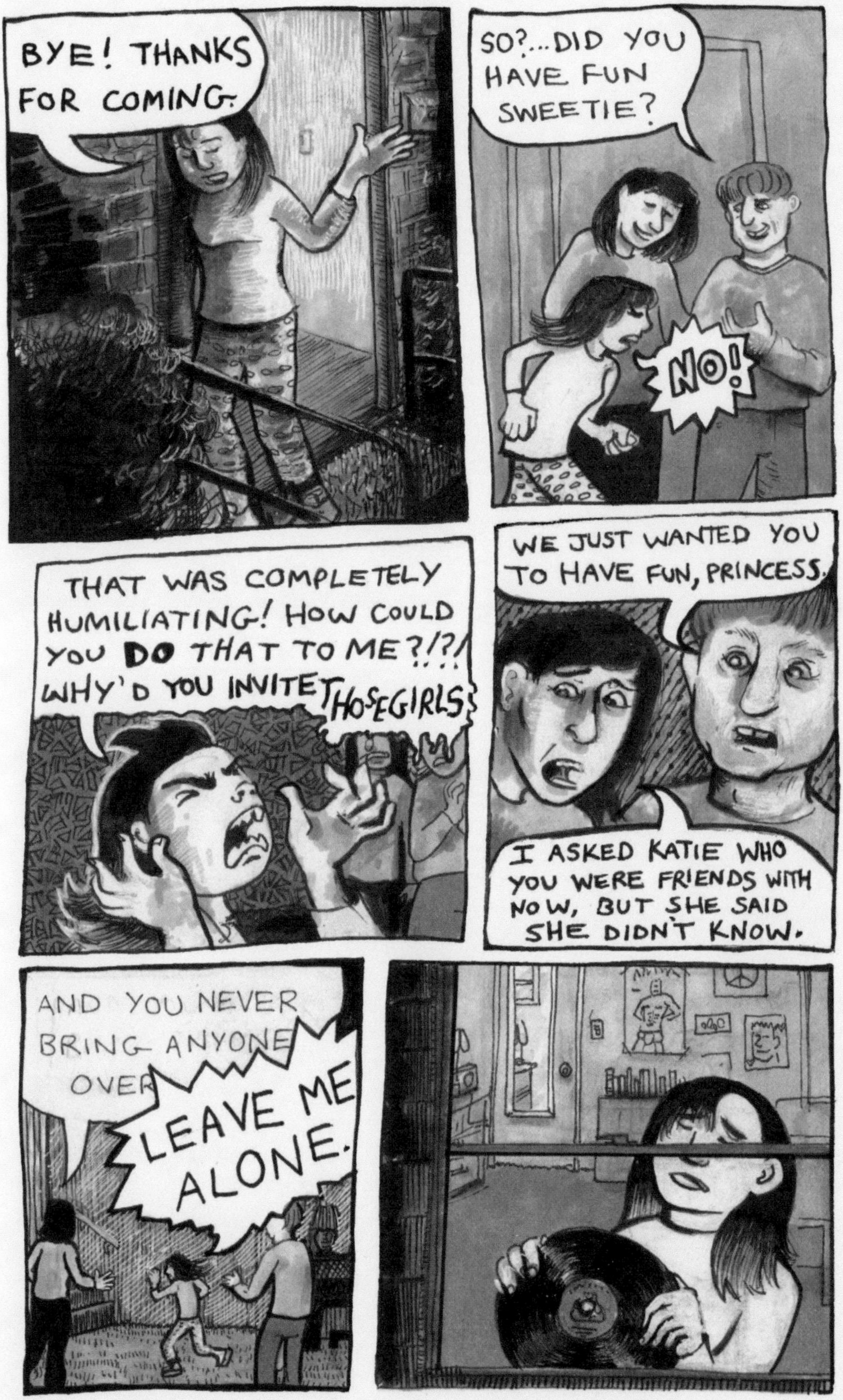
BYE! THANKS FOR COMING.
SO?...DID YOU HAVE FUN SWEETIE?
NO!
THAT WAS COMPLETELY HUMILIATING! HOW COULD YOU DO THAT TO ME?!?! WHY'D YOU INVITE THOSE GIRLS
WE JUST WANTED YOU TO HAVE FUN, PRINCESS.
I ASKED KATIE WHO YOU WERE FRIENDS WITH NOW, BUT SHE SAID SHE DIDN'T KNOW.
AND YOU NEVER BRING ANYONE OVER
LEAVE ME ALONE.

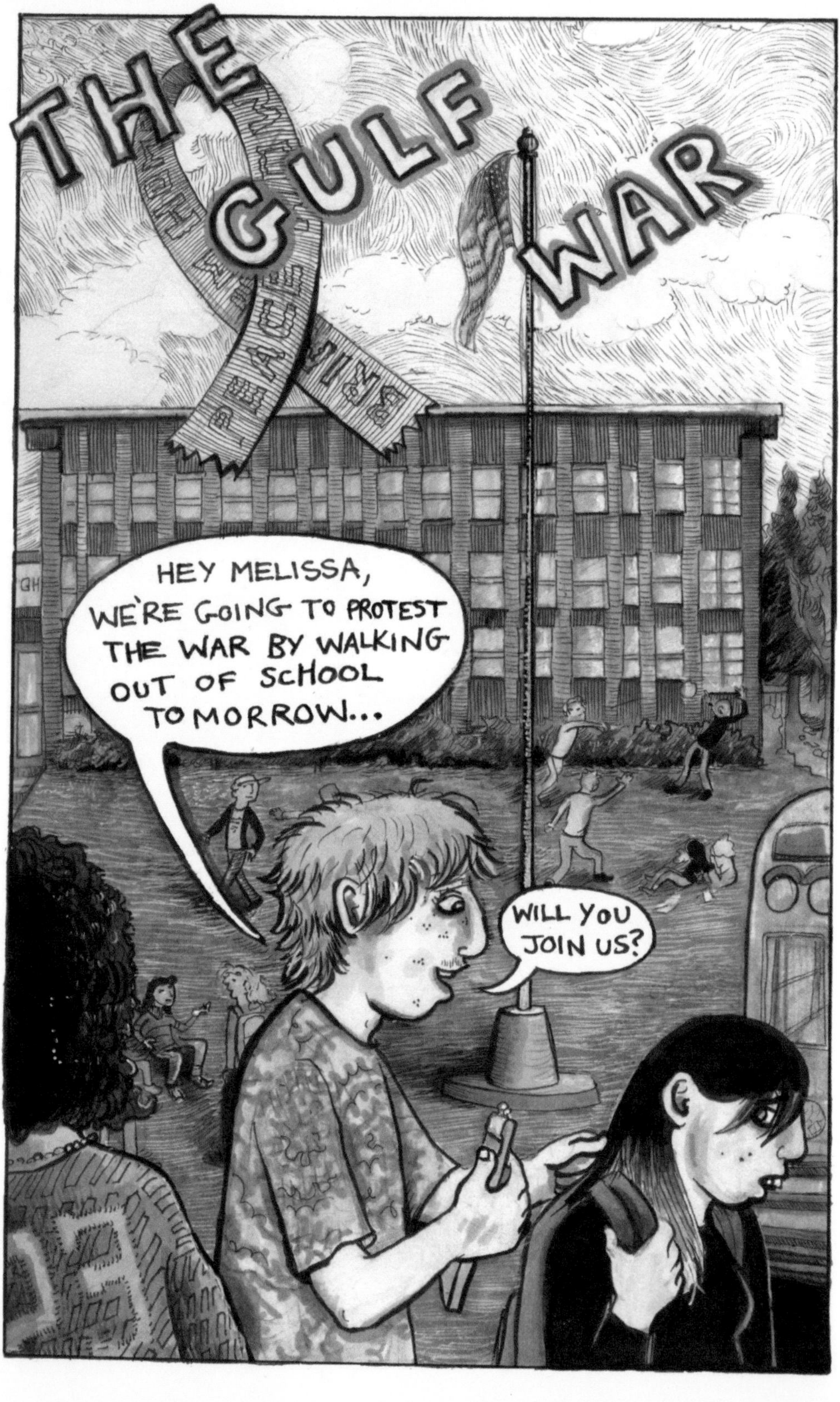
THE GULF WAR
HEY MELISSA, WE'RE GOING TO PROTEST THE WAR BY WALKING OUT OF SCHOOL TOMORROW...
WILL YOU JOIN US?

uh...WELL, I'M AGAINST THE WAR _OF COURSE_ BUT WHEN I WAS A KID I DID TONS OF POLITICAL THINGS WITH MY PARENTS.

I DID ANTI-NUCLEAR PROLIFERATION RALLIES, "WALKED FOR HUNGER," "WALKED FOR PEACE," "SANG TO END THE COLD WAR..."

AND FOR WHAT?! THE GOVERNMENT DOES **WHATEVER** IT WANTS. WE'D HAVE TO LITERALLY OVERTHROW WASHINGTON TO SEE ANY REAL CHANGE. So...uh, NO I WON'T JOIN YOU.

OK

I LOVE THAT YOU ARE SO INTELLIGENT AND OPPINIONATED. WANNA SEE MY PENIS?

IF WE'RE GOING TO PROTEST...

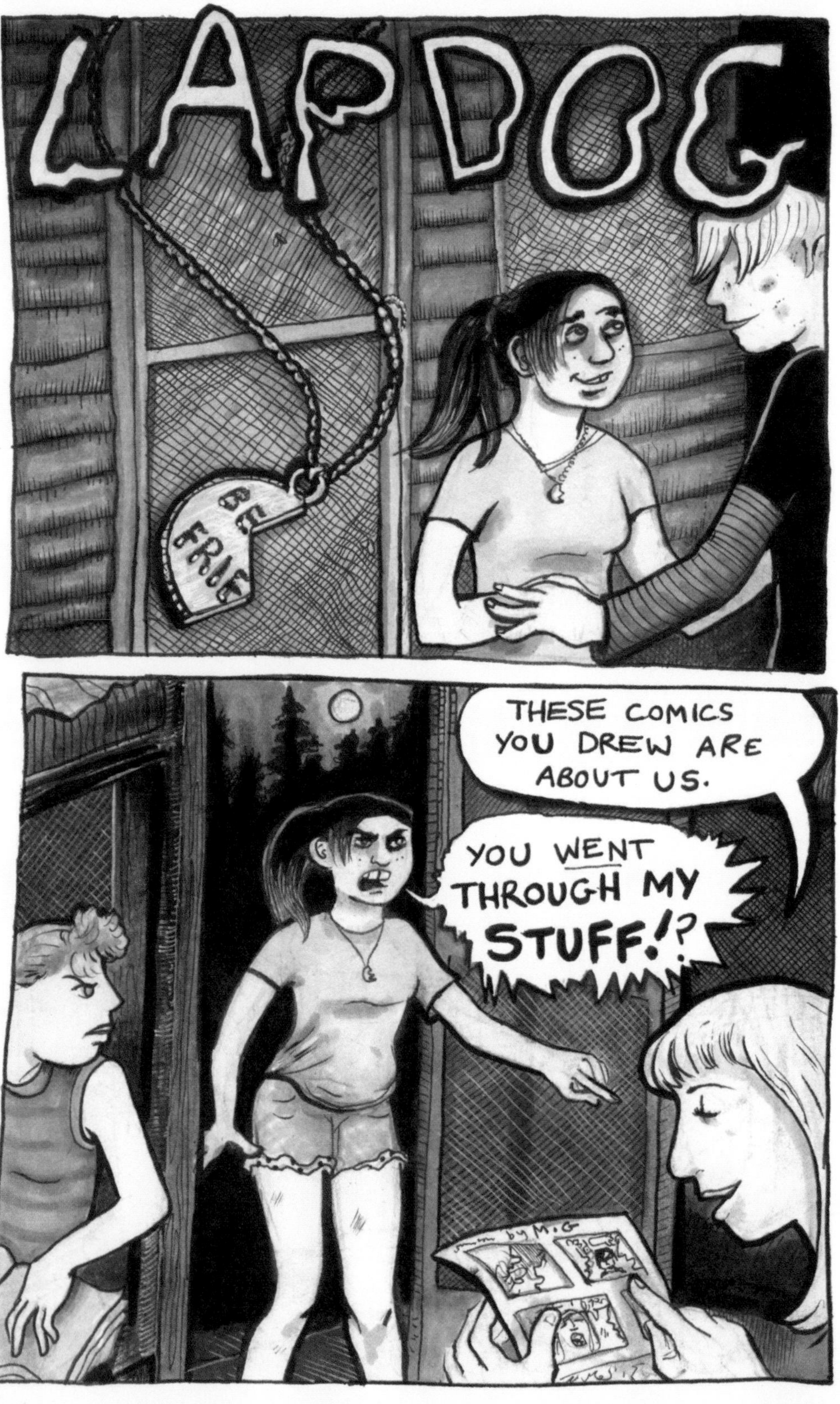
LAPDOG
BE FRIE
THESE COMICS YOU DREW ARE ABOUT US.
YOU WENT THROUGH MY STUFF!?
by M.G

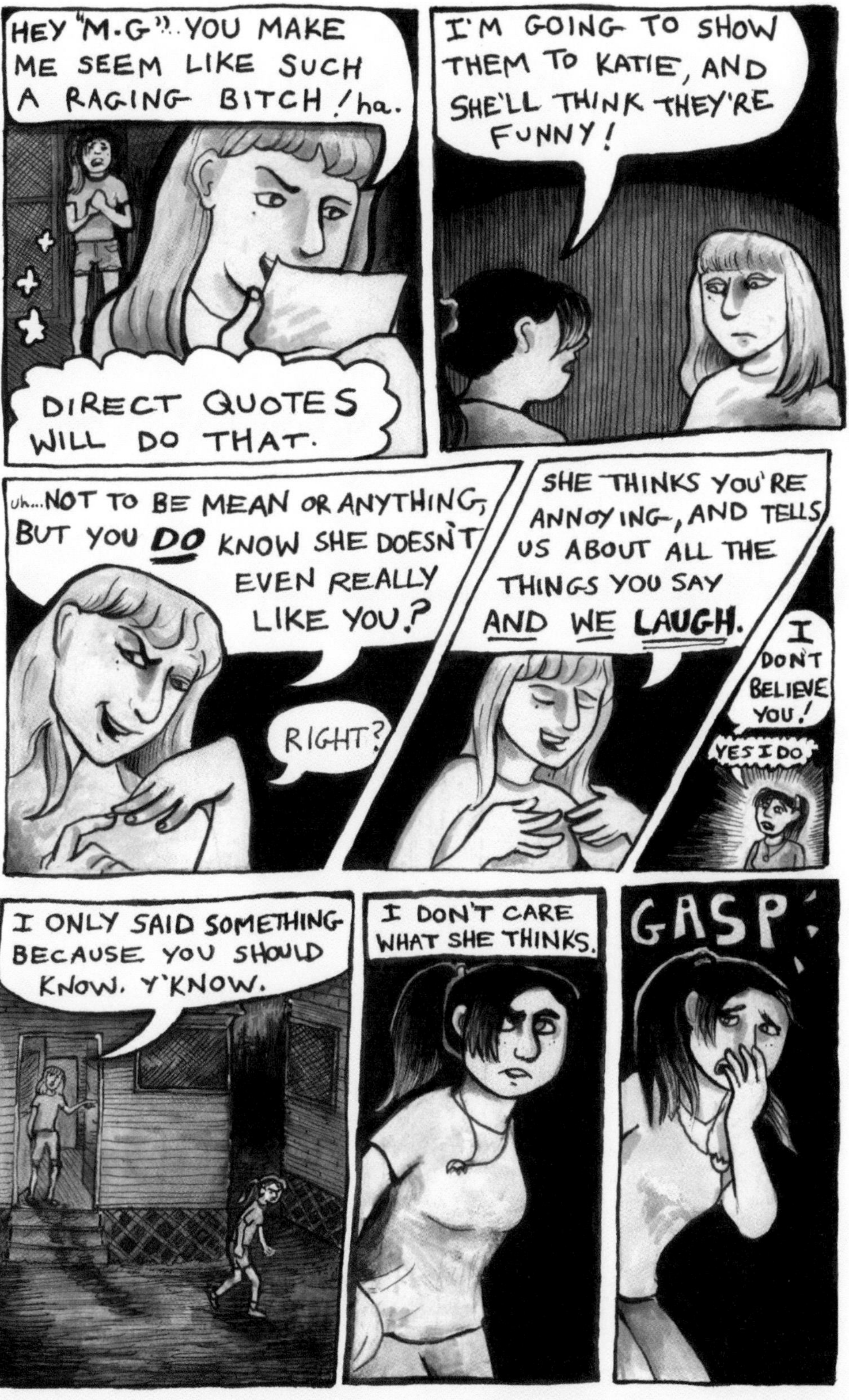
HEY "M.G"... YOU MAKE ME SEEM LIKE SUCH A RAGING BITCH! ha.
DIRECT QUOTES WILL DO THAT.
I'M GOING TO SHOW THEM TO KATIE, AND SHE'LL THINK THEY'RE FUNNY!
uh...NOT TO BE MEAN OR ANYTHING, BUT YOU DO KNOW SHE DOESN'T EVEN REALLY LIKE YOU?
RIGHT?
SHE THINKS YOU'RE ANNOYING, AND TELLS US ABOUT ALL THE THINGS YOU SAY AND WE LAUGH.
I DON'T BELIEVE YOU!
YES I DO
I ONLY SAID SOMETHING BECAUSE YOU SHOULD KNOW. Y'KNOW.
I DON'T CARE WHAT SHE THINKS.
GASP

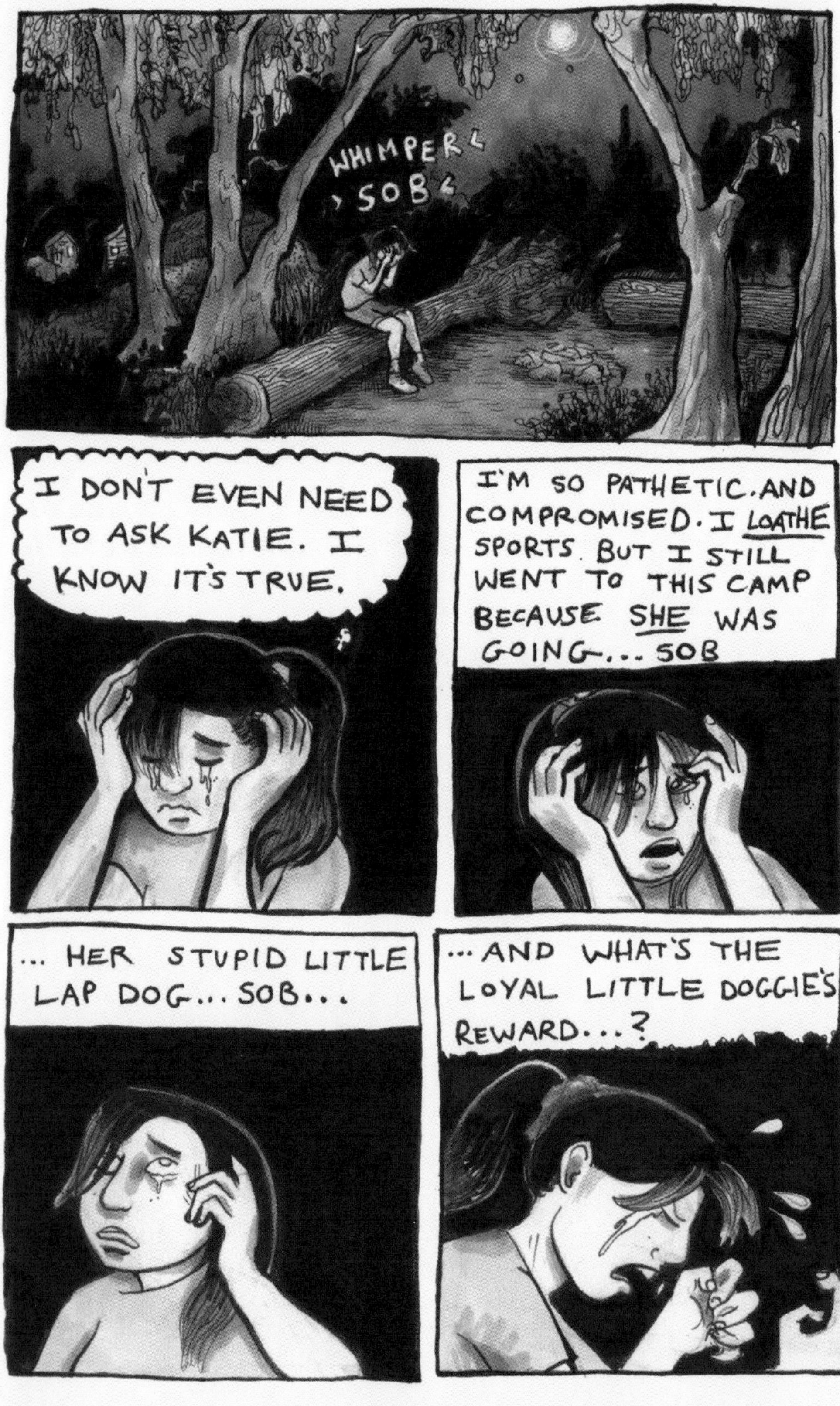
WHIMPER
SOB
I DON'T EVEN NEED TO ASK KATIE. I KNOW IT'S TRUE.
I'M SO PATHETIC. AND COMPROMISED. I LOATHE SPORTS. BUT I STILL WENT TO THIS CAMP BECAUSE SHE WAS GOING... SOB
... HER STUPID LITTLE LAP DOG... SOB...
... AND WHAT'S THE LOYAL LITTLE DOGGIE'S REWARD...?

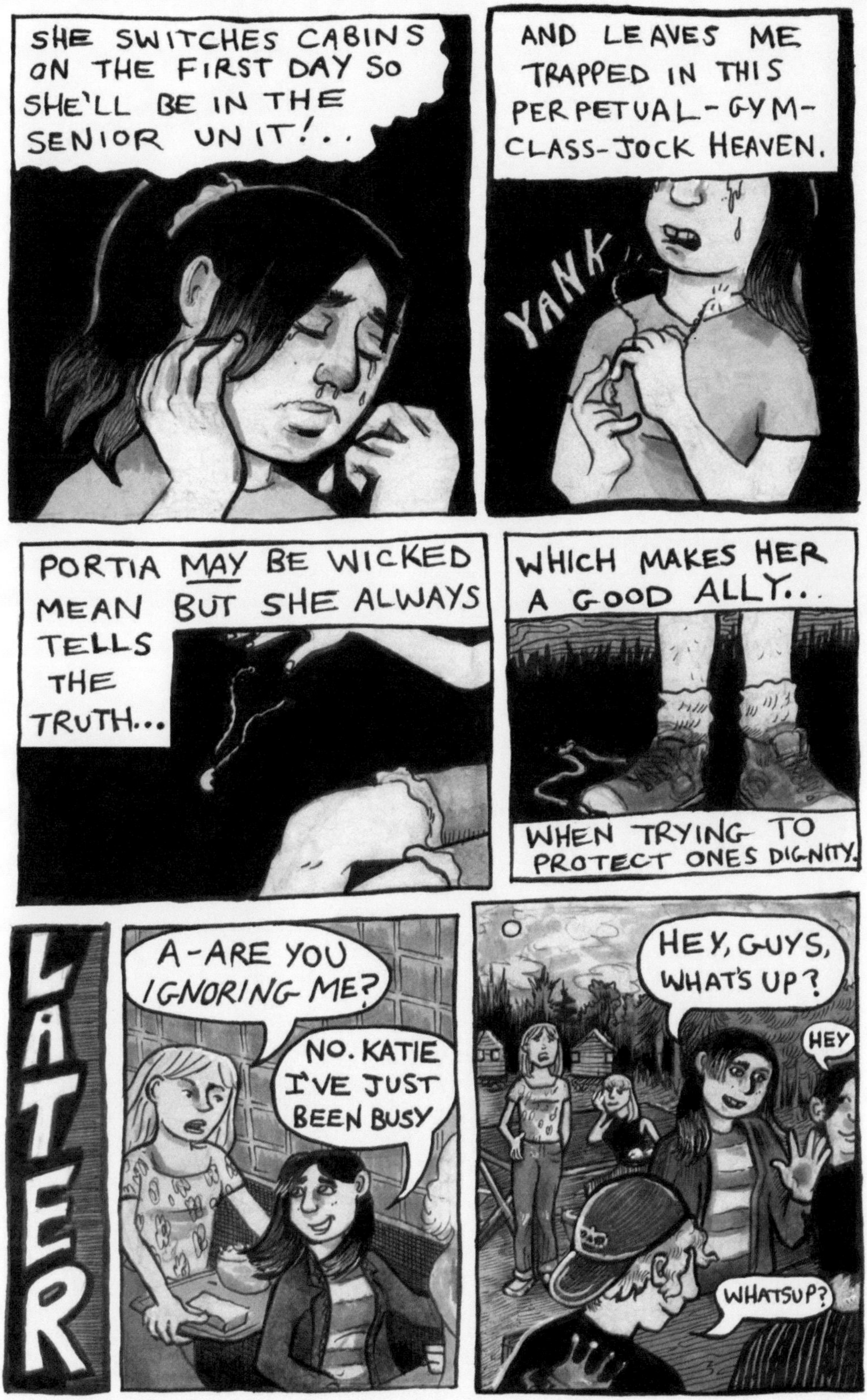
SHE SWITCHES CABINS ON THE FIRST DAY SO SHE'LL BE IN THE SENIOR UNIT!..
AND LEAVES ME TRAPPED IN THIS PERPETUAL-GYM-CLASS-JOCK HEAVEN.
YANK
PORTIA MAY BE WICKED MEAN BUT SHE ALWAYS TELLS THE TRUTH...
WHICH MAKES HER A GOOD ALLY...
WHEN TRYING TO PROTECT ONES DIGNITY.
LATER
A-ARE YOU IGNORING ME?
NO. KATIE I'VE JUST BEEN BUSY
HEY, GUYS, WHAT'S UP?
HEY
WHATSUP?

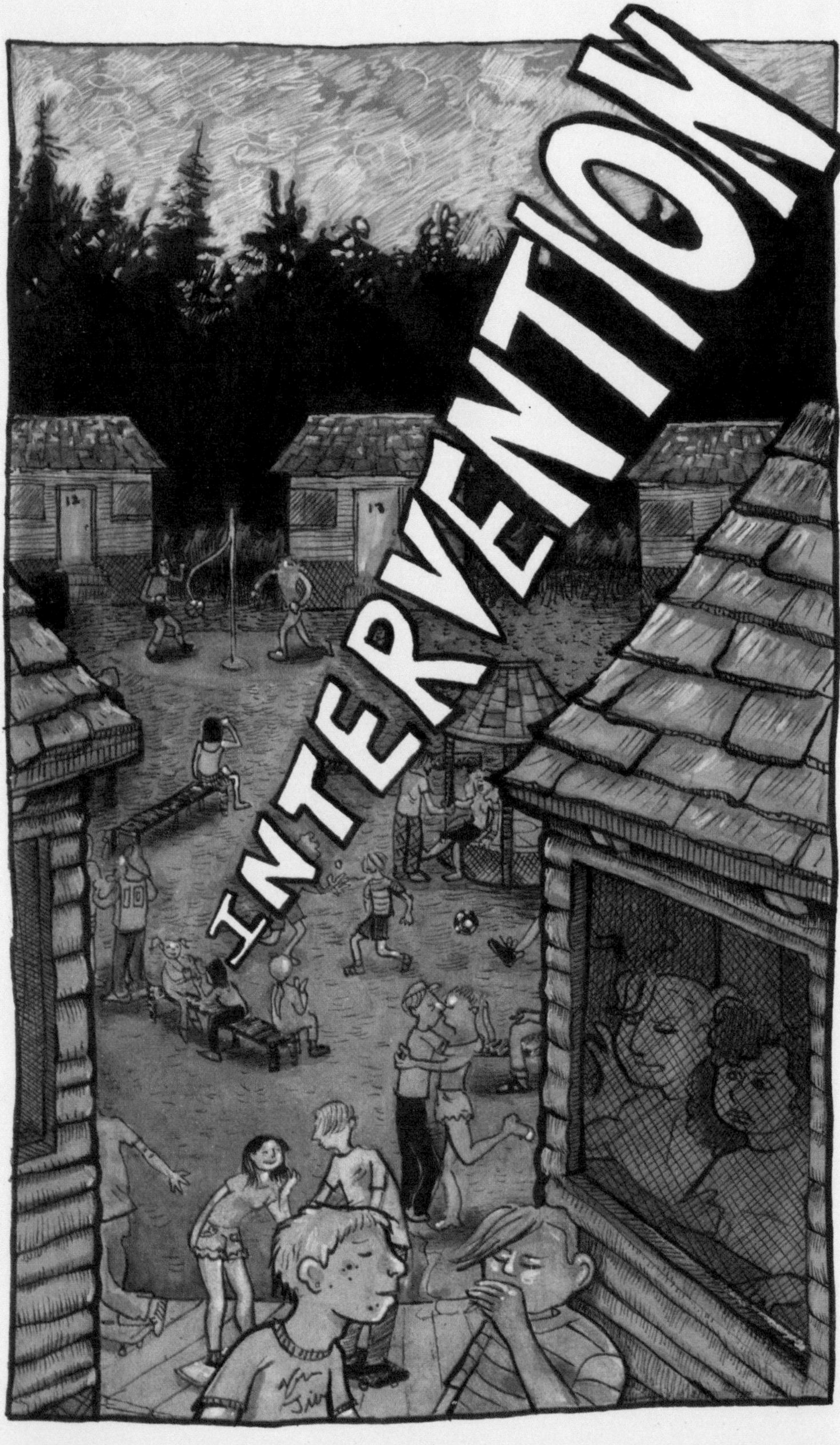
INTERVENTION

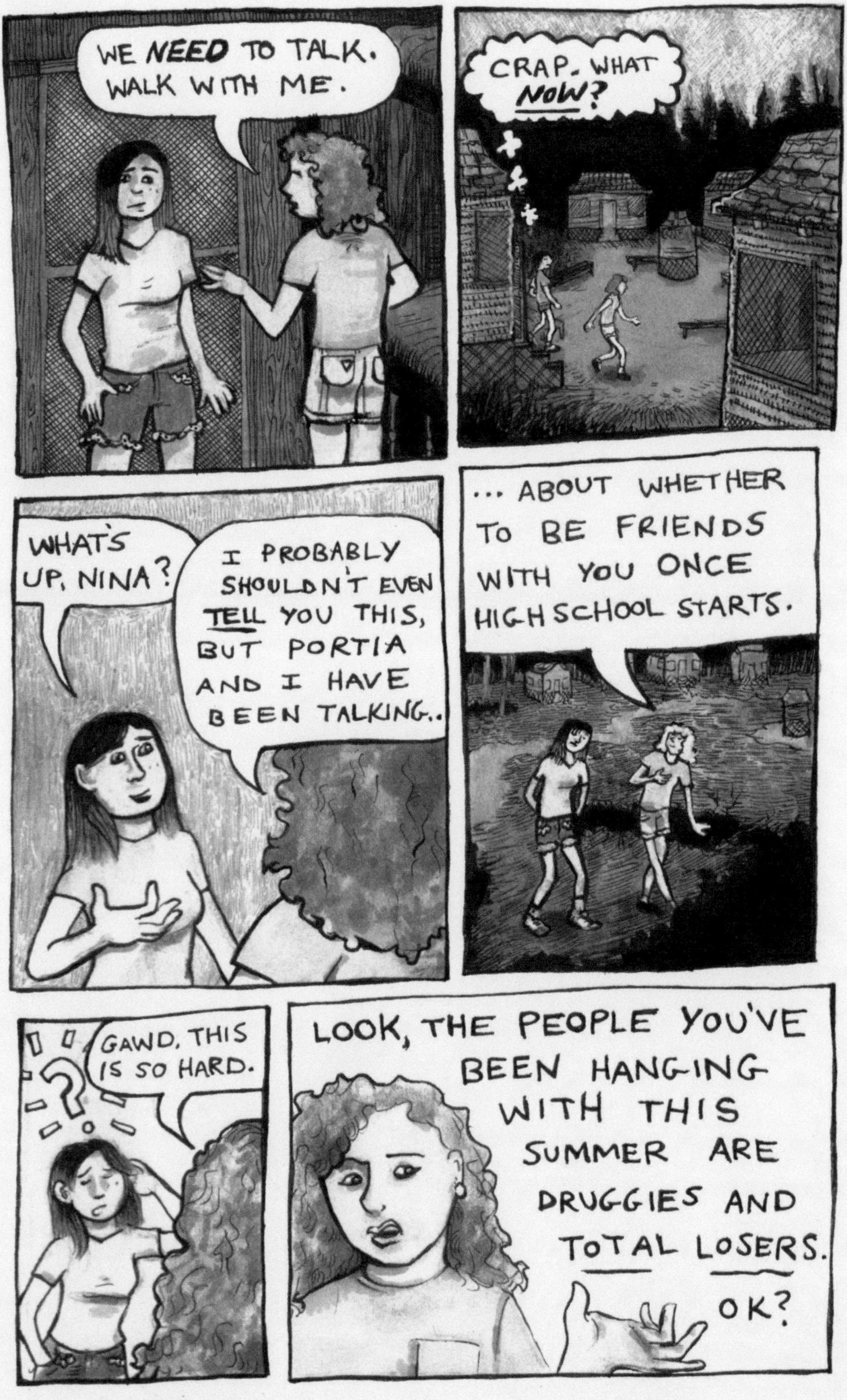
WE NEED TO TALK. WALK WITH ME.
CRAP. WHAT NOW?
WHAT'S UP, NINA?
I PROBABLY SHOULDN'T EVEN TELL YOU THIS, BUT PORTIA AND I HAVE BEEN TALKING..
... ABOUT WHETHER TO BE FRIENDS WITH YOU ONCE HIGH SCHOOL STARTS.
GAWD, THIS IS SO HARD.
LOOK, THE PEOPLE YOU'VE BEEN HANGING WITH THIS SUMMER ARE DRUGGIES AND TOTAL LOSERS.
OK?

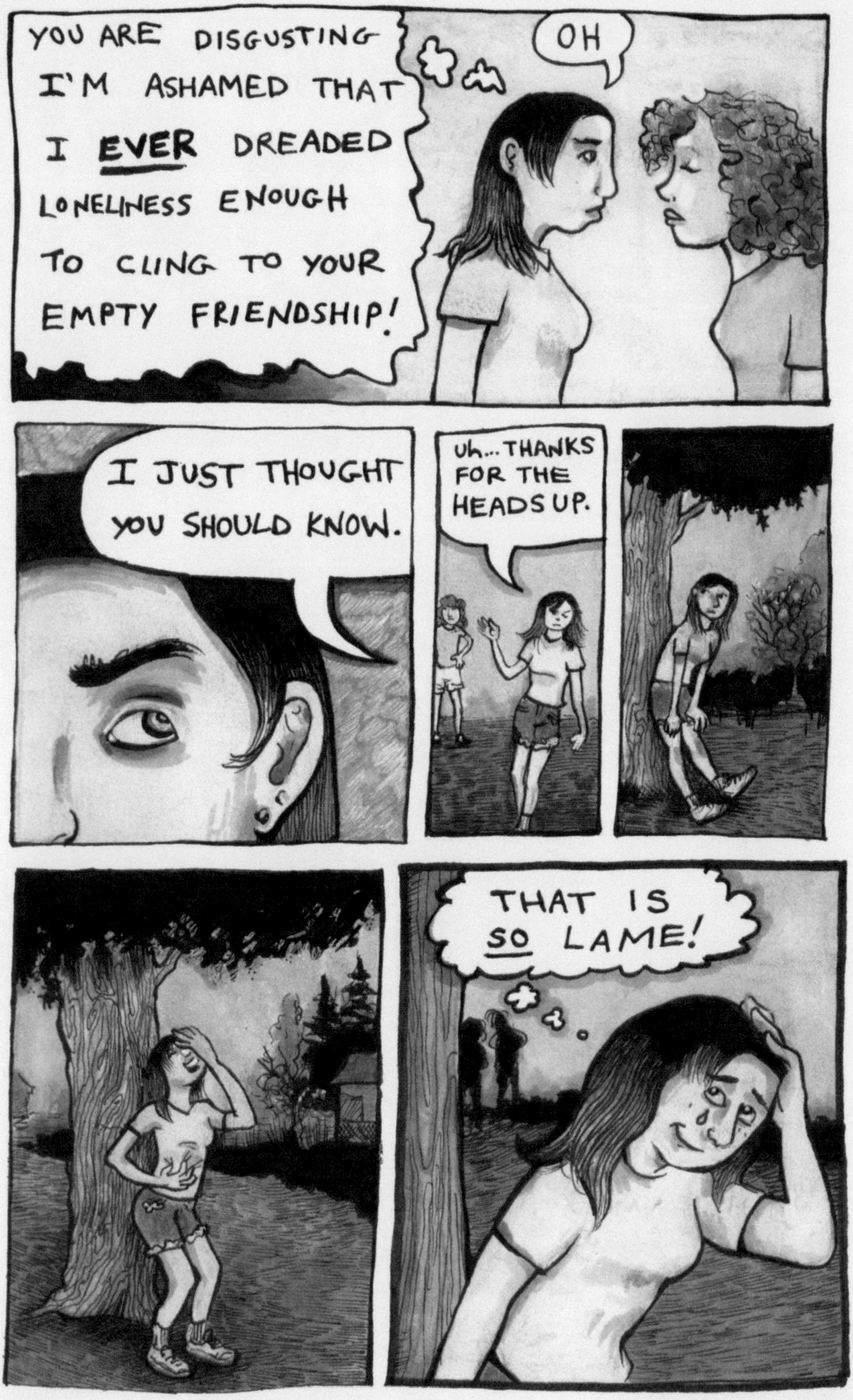
YOU ARE DISGUSTING I'M ASHAMED THAT I EVER DREADED LONELINESS ENOUGH TO CLING TO YOUR EMPTY FRIENDSHIP!
OH
I JUST THOUGHT YOU SHOULD KNOW.
Uh... THANKS FOR THE HEADS UP.
THAT IS SO LAME!

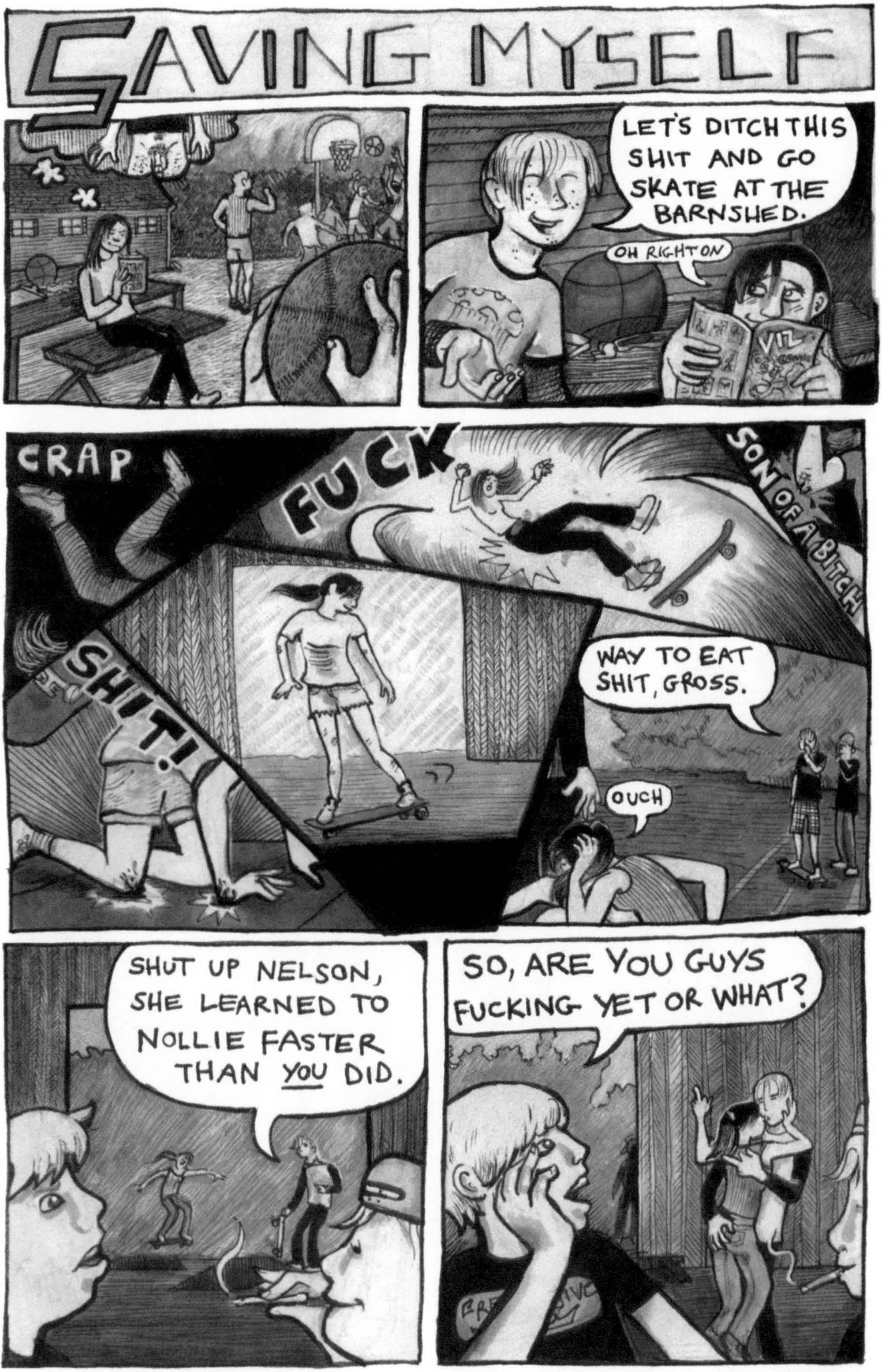
SAVING MYSELF
LET'S DITCH THIS SHIT AND GO SKATE AT THE BARNSHED.
OH RIGHT ON
CRAP
FUCK
SON OF A BITCH
SHIT!
WAY TO EAT SHIT, GROSS.
OUCH
SHUT UP NELSON, SHE LEARNED TO NOLLIE FASTER THAN YOU DID.
SO, ARE YOU GUYS FUCKING YET OR WHAT?

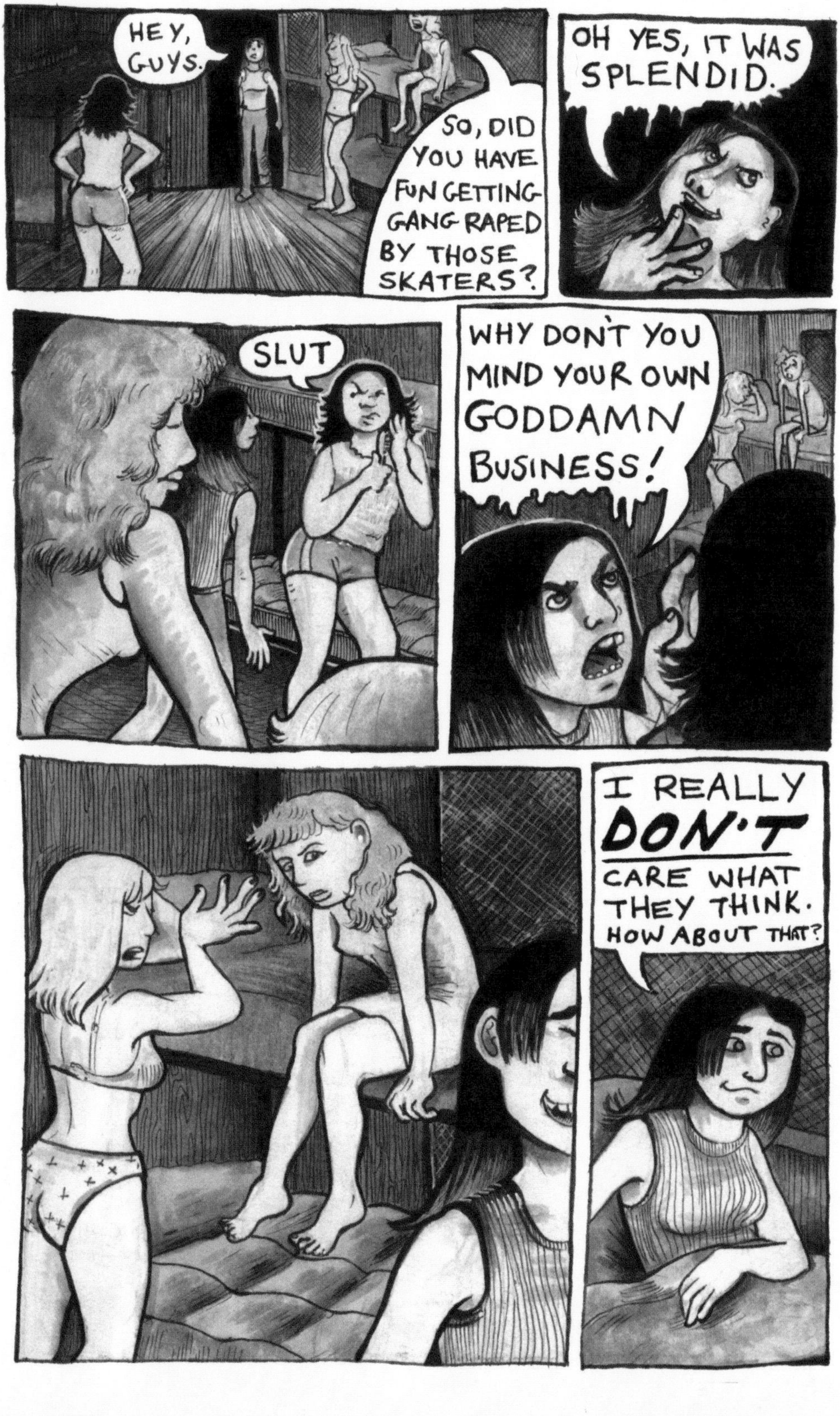
HEY, GUYS.
SO, DID YOU HAVE FUN GETTING GANG RAPED BY THOSE SKATERS?
OH YES, IT WAS SPLENDID.
SLUT
WHY DON'T YOU MIND YOUR OWN GODDAMN BUSINESS!
I REALLY DON'T CARE WHAT THEY THINK. HOW ABOUT THAT?

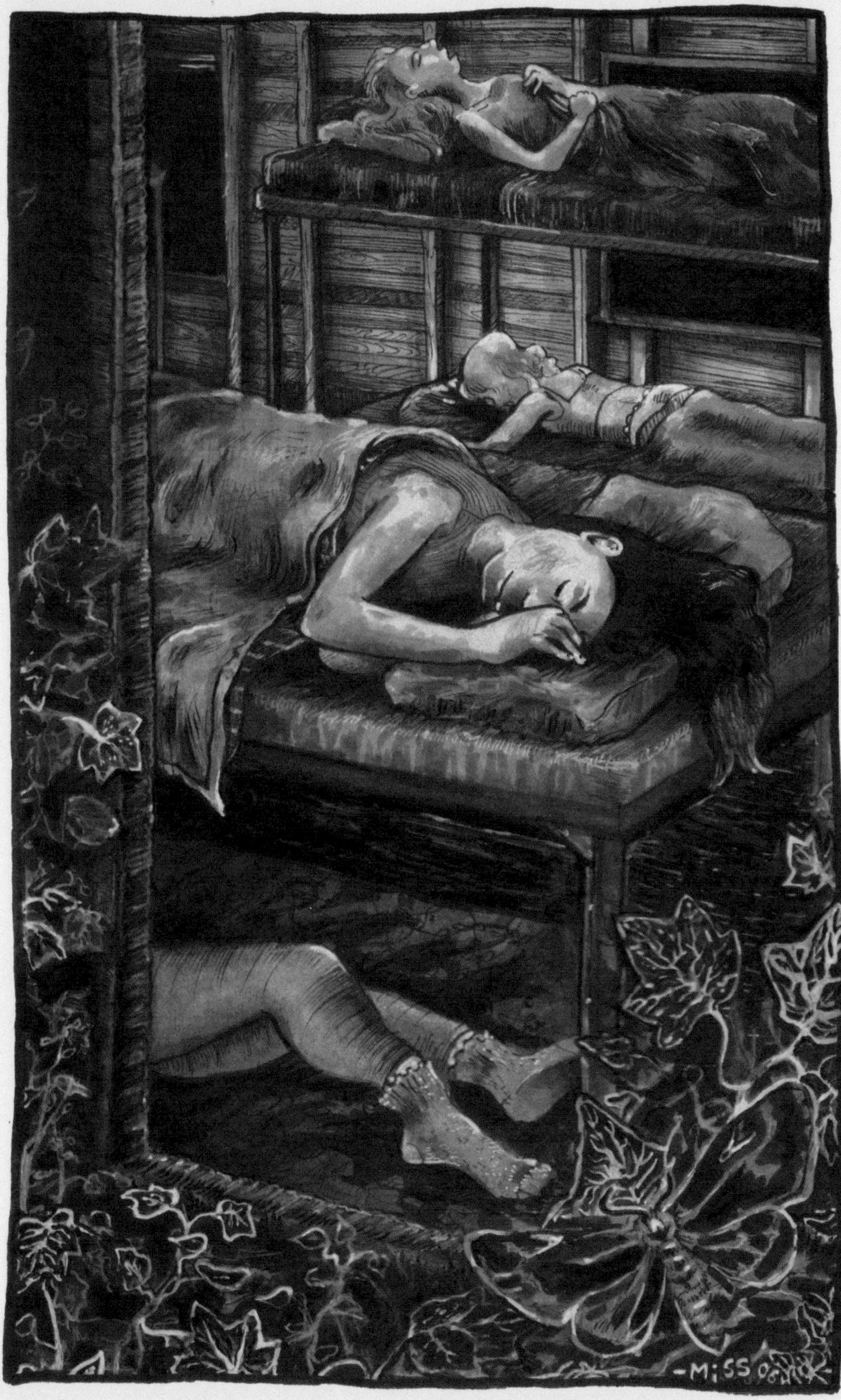